DEPARTMENT OF CORRUPTION

RESEARCH EDITION

I wrote this book to expose corruption in the Florida Department of Corrections. I hope it will spur others to undertake investigations, studies, and actions directed at improving the welfare of imprisoned persons, particularly those who suffer from disabilities and mental health issues.

In the other edition the material was largely presented according to the time lines in my journals and notes. In this research edition, I have reorganized the material by grouping it by topic, and have provided an index to the interview so readers can quickly find topics of interest to them.

Harold Hempstead

March 2019

DEPARTMENT OF CORRUPTION
DARREN RAINEY
THE UNTOLD STORY

RESEARCH EDITION

HAROLD W.J. HEMPSTEAD

For information about bulk purchases, please contact
Hempstead Publications at
HEMPSTEADPUBLICATIONS8@GMAIL.COM

Cover by Judith Lessler and Jay Niver

iv

DEDICATIONS

Josandre Hempstead

When people are being hurt, they need someone with a caring heart to be their voice in their time of need. God blessed me with my beloved mom, who has always been there for me and who has taught me to believe in God and what strength is.

Windy Hempstead

As far back as I can remember, my sister Windy has always been my best friend, and she has always been by my side. She is the smartest, strongest, and most loving woman I know. God blessed me when He gave me Windy as my sister.

Casey Frank and Julie K. Brown

Casey and Julie have shown by action and words that they have beautiful souls with big hearts. It's impossible to state how many lives in the Florida Department of Corrections (FDC) have been saved because of them. Mere words cannot express how much I appreciate all they and *The Miami Herald* have done on the Darren Rainey case. They have been a voice for the voiceless in FDC and Florida. God blessed me in allowing me to meet them and communicate with them over these years.

SPECIAL THANKS

I want to thank the **American Civil Liberties Union** of Florida, Stop Prison Abuse Now, Florida Legal Services, the Florida Justice Institute and the other civil rights groups in Florida for their diligence in fighting for the civil rights of those incarcerated in the FDC.

Thank you **Jeremy Schanche and Susan Chandler**. You both have been persistent voices for the voiceless, and a great help to me for several years.

Thank you **Pastors Myles and Dorothy Shaw** for all that you both have done for me. You both have helped me in ways that no one else has and have always shown great kindness and love. Words cannot express my thankfulness for all that you both have done.

Thank you **Judith Lessler** for your kindness in helping me get my journal and books copyrighted and your assistance in preparing this research edition.

Table of Contents

Introduction

On April 2014, I met with a *Miami Herald* newspaper representative at Dade Correctional Institution. The purpose of our conversation was to discuss a mentally disabled inmate named Darren Rainey who prison staff placed in a shower that reached temperatures more than 160° Fahrenheit. When he was taken out of the shower, he was dead, and his skin was falling off. Rainey wasn't the first mentally disabled inmate subjected to the *Hot-Water-Shower Treatment*; there were several others. I also discussed with the *Miami Herald* representative other forms of abuse and torture that mentally disabled inmates were being subjected to in the mental health facility where Rainey died.

After the *Miami Herald* published their first article on Rainey's death and the *Hot-Water-Shower Treatment* of mentally disabled inmates at Dade CI, they started their investigation into the unconstitutional conditions of the Florida Department of Corrections (FDC).

Over the years to follow, dozens of investigations by federal, legislative, and civil rights groups, and by the media have been and are still being conducted into all types of matters in the FDC.

My sister Windy previously recommended that I write a book on the Darren Rainey case and the events that happened in the Florida Department of Corrections over the last several years. She expressed her belief that the book would be of interest to many people because I was a witness to everything that happened to Rainey and because I was responsible for bringing about tens of millions of dollars in changes and lawsuit settlements in the FDC.

I agreed with Windy's suggestion. I also felt that writing this book would allow me to tell everything (that I can tell at this time) that has not been told. Additionally, I felt that I could address other problems in the FDC that still need to be corrected.

Windy chose the name for this book. I liked it and agreed to use it because it truly describes its contents. This book provides a lot of information on the Florida Department of Corrections which a lot of people call the Department of Corruption. This book also provides a lot of information on the Darren Rainey case and the FDC that people are not aware of.

1

For the last several years, the events and circumstances I describe in this book have been of interest to the Department of Justice, the FBI, more than a dozen civil rights groups, and the media. Media attention to the FDC has led to the citizens of Florida and of America having a public interest in knowing about the conditions in the FDC and events that I've written about. Accordingly, this book meets the criteria of a historical book that documents events which are of current, legitimate interest to a large number of people.

This book also meets the criteria of a civil rights book in that it addresses dozens of civil rights violations in the FDC.

As I wrote this book, I had to look back at all that happened since I was born again on June 11, 2009. To relive the events as I wrote them, caused me to remember all the sadness, fears, and worries I experienced as I did all that I could to advocate for justice for Darren Rainey and for the rights of the voiceless in the FDC. As I wrote this book, each page brought more tears. Several times, I had to stop writing while I waited for the tears to cease. I also wanted to note that as I wrote about several situations over the years where my life was in danger, I thanked God that He always rescued me from harm. I am so grateful that God is sovereign and that He has shown Himself to be my protector every time I have needed one.

Finally, this book meets the criteria of a Christian book in that I am a Christian, and this book is testimonial. There are also several references to the Bible and Christian doctrines in this book.

I wrote this book in a question and answer format for two reasons: Frist, many people will read my book because they want to investigate or learn about the crimes and civil rights violations that are documented herein. The questions will help such a reader to quickly find the particular material he or she desires.

Second, the question and answer format is similar to a formal testimony of all I have witnessed, and, as I discussed with, my sister Windy in 2014, this book is our attempt to do all we can to try to help as many inmates as possible

Except for five people, I've used the real names of the people involved with the events and circumstances in this book. I've done my best to spell the real names correctly. I apologize if I have made any mistakes. I used fake names with two prison staff who helped me in different ways at Dade CI. I don't know if they are still employed with the FDC. If they are, they could lose their jobs, and possibly be placed in danger if I used their real names.

For reasons I cannot state, I used pseudonyms (Randy Evans and Jim Knowels) when talking about two people who I've spoken with several times since 2013.

I used the real first name and the first letter of the last name of some of the inmates at Dade CI. I did this to protect their identities.

Even though the Department of Justice and the FBI are still investigating Darren Rainey's death, and several of the other incidents mentioned herein, presently none of the people named in this book have been arrested or convicted of any crimes. Our U.S. and Florida Constitutions state that they have a right to be presumed innocent until proven guilty

Chapter 1: My History, My Faith

I was seven years old when my dad passed away. Before he died, my family consisted of my mom, dad, older brother and sister, and me. My dad's death deeply affected us all, especially my mom. Over the following years, I watched her as she was crushed under an ocean of sadness. She tried her best to fight against it, but she wasn't successful.

When I was in third grade, my mom started suffering from mental health problems. My siblings and I saw that her mental health problem could cause her to get physically hurt, so the three of us and one of my brother's friends started taking turns watching her. My brother and his friend did a shift, and my sister and I did another shift. We rotated shifts. None of us wanted to see our mom get hurt.

As my mom went in and out of mental hospitals for short periods, she never got better. Eventually, they kept her in one of the hospitals for close to a year.

During that year-long stay, my siblings and I stayed with our Uncle Morris and Aunt Carole. While we stayed with them, I went to a school called S.A. Hall. Most of the students at that school were from crime-infested neighborhoods where they constantly fought.

My second day in school, I saw three kids beating up another kid in the boy's bathroom. I felt bad for the kid they were beating. When I yelled at the kids who were hitting him to stop, they turned their wrath toward me and attacked me.

Fighting was fun and common sport for the kids in that school. They constantly fought. A lot of that school year, I was their punching and kicking bag. I certainly didn't enjoy being jumped and attacked, but I also didn't like watching other kids in pain. When I saw other kids being abused, it was like a natural response for me to yell and try to stop the aggressors. Even though I knew that every time I yelled, the violent kids would turn their wrath toward me, I couldn't just sit there and watch kids get hurt. Several kids called me stupid because of all the times I was beat-up for speaking out. That didn't stop me from

4

trying to stop other kids from being jumped. Kids used to also say I enjoyed getting beat-up. I wondered what would cause them to think that anybody would enjoy such a thing. I didn't enjoy going to school at S.A. Hall.

I wasn't always beat-up for trying to stop another kid from getting hurt. Many times, it was for other reasons.

My older brother and my sister didn't attend the same school as me. They went to another one, so I didn't have any help at my school. The teachers would merely break the fights up without disciplining the troublemakers.

I was very happy when my siblings and I were returned to my mom's custody after her health got better. Several months after our return to St. Petersburg, Florida to live with her, I was arrested. I was caught with some stolen goods that a kid I went to school with stole from a store. When a St. Petersburg Police detective asked why I had the stolen merchandise, I told him that my family was poor, and I was going to sell it to help pay for bills and food for my family. I told him that my dad had died and I didn't know how else I could help my mom. I was arrested for possessing the stolen merchandise, but I was not processed into the Juvenile Detention Center.

I was only about 13 years old when I met the detective who arrested me. At first, I thought that he was a good man. He didn't process me into the Juvenile Detention Center. Additionally, he seemed like a nice adult who liked helping people. Over the following years, I found out that wasn't true.

When I was 17 years old, I spoke out about that detective engaging in sexual misconduct with kids. Since he worked for the St. Petersburg Police Department, I erred in bringing my accusations to that same agency. Within a short time of reporting that he was sexually abusing kids, I was set-up for two first degree felonies. After being in the county jail less than two months, the state attorney's office dismissed the charges. The state attorney's report as to why they were dismissing the charges supported that I was set-up by the St. Petersburg Police Department. The detective I reported on stayed employed with the police department for more than a decade before something was done about his misconduct. I was told that he was forced to resign. Not long ago, I was talking with a Christian woman about the detective. She told me that he attempted to sexually molest her daughter more than two decades ago.

I got married when I was 17 years old. My wife and I had a son (Joseph) and daughter (Kaitlin).

Not long after I got married, I started a lawn service to supplement my income and worked in fundraising for non-profit organizations. Not long after I started my lawn service, I started cutting the lawn of a man I will call Jerry.

I eventually found out that Jerry wasn't a good man. He had been involved with a lot of violence throughout his life, and many people were hurt and killed because of him. I didn't find out about his past until after he had learned several things about my family and me. The things I found out about him gave me cause to worry. I was a married man, working two jobs, and trying to raise a son and daughter.

I felt I had to do something to protect my family and me, so I reached out to a man named Philipi in Tampa, Florida. Philipi was not a criminal. He was considered an intelligent man of high integrity. Instead of helping me, he placed me in a position where I was eventually set-up and arrested on several burglary charges.

While I was housed in the Pinellas County, Florida Jail, I was offered dismissal of all my charges, and witness relocation if I helped the government on matters they verified that I knew. When the government said they couldn't assure the protection of my kids, I refused the offer. I wasn't going to take a chance with my kid's safety. After being convicted, I was transferred to the FDC.

Over my first year of incarceration, I witnessed a lot of staff on inmate abuse and inmate on inmate physical and sexual abuse. Every time I saw inmates being hurt, it made me sad.

I felt I had to do something to try to stop the violence. Over the following years, I engaged in all types of activities to try to put a stop to the violence and unconstitutional conditions in the FDC. I submitted thousands of grievances; I filed two 42 U.S.C. § 1983 Civil Rights Complaint federal lawsuits against prison staff; and I communicated with people in society who had jobs which caused them to be interested in the conditions in the Florida prison system, and the list goes on.

As a result of my activism and attempts to bring reform, I was subjected to all types of retaliation. Security staff physically battered me several times. On one occasion, the staff broke one of my ribs. Several times they attempted to have me hurt by inmates, and twice staff conspired with inmates to have me killed. Additionally, I was set-up with frivolous disciplinary reports, the majority of which I beat. I was placed on close management twice and under frivolous investigations several times. The staff disposed of hundreds of dollars of my property; I was denied my meals and subjected to retaliatory transfers, and I was denied medical care on numerous occasions.

When I arrived at Wakulla CI Annex on April 14, 2009, I was stressed, full of anxiety, and restless. My mom, children, wife, sister, family, and life were taken from me. I had been in the Florida prison system for close to nine years. During that time, I had been incarcerated at close to two dozen institutions in the FDC.

After being at Wakulla CI Annex for a couple of weeks, something happened that changed my life forever.

One night, as I lay in my bed, God by grace, caused me to think about my life. As my thoughts about my past weighed heavily on my mind, I saw that my actions showed that I thought I had it all together and was in control of my life. I had thought this my whole life, but, actually, my life showed otherwise. My life before and even after my incarceration was a life of sin and failures. I lived in rebellion against God, and I was in prison separated from all that was dear to me. As all my sins flashed through my mind, God showed me that as He pursued me throughout my life, I spent my life running from Him.

As I thought about my life, I remembered being taught as a child that the Trinitarian God of the Christian Bible is the only real God and that heaven and hell exist. When I was 15 years old, I left the teaching of the Roman Catholic Church and became a Protestant Christian.

My first two Protestant Bible teachers were officers in the Pinellas County, Florida Jail. One was a Baptist; the other was a Charismatic Mennonite. After meeting them, I read the Bible four or five times before I turned 16 years old. Between the ages 15 to 23, I had several conversations with the Mennonite pastor.

Department of Corruption

God showed me something that night at Wakulla CI Annex that I had never seen before. God revealed to me that I was living the life of a religious person, but I wasn't a child of God. I wasn't born again.

I was using religion to try to obtain self-justification, but I always failed. My life was a life of depending upon myself and not upon God, although I thought I was.

The replaying of my life that night led me to tears that wouldn't stop. As I lay with my head under my sheet crying, God didn't stop there. The fruit of a man's actions can show how smart he is. On that night, I knew that the fruit of my actions showed that I had to be one of the dumbest men alive.

My losses did not cause my sadness and tears; rather, I grieved because I had offended God. Additionally, I saw that God would've been just if He struck me dead on the spot and threw me in hell forever. Four things were very clear to me that night. (1) God was perfectly holy. (2) I was a worthless sinner. (3) I deserved whatever type of judgment God rendered me. (4) I needed God's mercy. It seemed like God had intensified my thoughts that night. The intensified fear of God about my rebellion against Him was crushing. All I could do was cry out to God to forgive me and to have mercy on me. That night seemed like it would never end. At one point, I started pleading with God to please let me fall asleep so I would not have to bear my sorrows and fear all night. God by grace, allowed me to fall asleep around 3:00 am.

When I woke up the next morning, I learned that God didn't take away the sorrow and fear from me. My heart was not a normal heart of stone; it was a stone heart with steel in it. God had ordained that He'd use the intensified sorrow and fear to take away my heart of stone and steel, and give me a heart of flesh. God by grace, ordained that I would live with the intensified sorrow and fear not for days, but for weeks. The weight of my sorrow and the fear of God that I had was devastating.

For the next several weeks, I repeatedly prayed, "God, please forgive me; please have mercy on me." For a person to know he needs the Savior, he must know he is a sinner and that he can't be declared justified in the eyes of God based on any righteousness other than the righteousness of Jesus Christ.

8

The Bible tells us "by the law is the knowledge of sin"[1] "that "whoever sins also commits lawlessness, and sin is lawlessness."[2] Additionally, the Bible says, "The law is our tutor to bring us to Christ that we may be justified by faith."[3]

The fear of God that He gave me was a blessing because "The fear of the Lord is the beginning of wisdom."[4] Additionally, we are commanded to fear God for Jesus said, "... Do not fear those who kill the body but cannot kill the soul. But rather fear Him who is able to destroy both soul and body in hell."[5]

Weeks later, I was placed in administrative confinement. While there, I read the Bible, worked on my Bible correspondence courses and law work, and wrote letters.

The Bible says, "If you then, being evil, know how to give good gifts to your children, how much more will your Heavenly Father give the Holy Spirit to those who ask Him!"[6] In 2006, this verse started meaning a lot to me. I wanted the Holy Spirit in my life. I took this verse to mean exactly what it says. During that year, I started asking God one or more times a day in prayer, "Please give me the Holy Spirit." Three years later, I was still praying daily for the Holy Spirit.

On June 9, 2009, I was transferred from Wakulla CI Annex to Columbia Correctional Institution Annex.

When I boarded the bus at Wakulla CI Annex, an inmate from Wakulla CI Main Unit sat next to me. As we sat there, I took out a pack of loose tobacco and rolled a cigarette. I had started smoking cigarettes my first day in prison. The stress and anxiety of prison, combined with all that I had been through, led me to try to seek peace in nicotine. When the inmate next to me saw I had tobacco, he asked if he could have a cigarette. After I gave him one, we started talking about our lives and prison. I found out that he had just completed the faith-based program at Wakulla CI Main Unit. Based on that information, I assumed he was Christian.

For this reason, I started discussing God and the Bible with him. After about 20 minutes of talking with him, he said, "Hey, no disrespect, but I'm not a Christian. I completed the faith-based program so I could get the "good adjustment" transfer I've been trying to get for a long time." I was shocked at his words. I also felt I had to do what I could to share Jesus with him in hopes of saving his soul.

Since I wasn't born again, I was not thinking biblically when I assumed that I understood the gospel. Additionally, I wasn't thinking biblically when I thought that I could do something to contribute to the inmate's salvation. Salvation is by faith alone, in Christ alone, for the glory of God alone.

For the next 30 minutes, I tried to evangelize the inmate even though I wasn't saved. Eventually, he said he didn't want anything to do with Christ or the Christian faith, and asked me if I would please stop talking about them. I did what the inmate requested and switched the subject.

When we arrived at Columbia CI Annex, I was placed in administrative confinement. Since I was in administrative confinement at Wakulla CI Annex, by policy, I had to be placed in administrative confinement at Columbia CI Annex.

I wasn't in confinement for doing anything wrong. I was in confinement because the FDC Inspector General's office believed that I'd be hurt (or possibly killed) in general population at Wakulla CI Annex. They thought my safety was at risk due to my actions in trying to address some of the problems at Wakulla CI Annex.

While at Columbia CI Annex, God by grace, caused me to have a strong desire to attempt again to evangelize the inmate on the bus if, by any chance, I saw him again. Every day, several buses full of inmates transferred to and from Columbia CI, and it was my opinion that the chances were slim that I would ever see him again.

On June 11, 2009, when I was transferred from Columbia CI, I was one of the first 10 or so inmates to get on the bus. While I was on the bus, I wasn't watching the other inmates who got on after me. As I sat there rolling a cigarette, I was shocked when the same inmate I previously tried to evangelize sat down next to me on the bus. I took him sitting next to me as a sure sign from God that I was to do my best to try to evangelize him. I planned to evangelize him and not stop until either he moved away from me or I got off the bus. I waited until all of the seats on the bus were filled and the door of the bus was locked. With no vacant seats for him to move to, he was stuck next to me, at least until we got to Central Florida Reception Center.

Once we were on the road leaving Columbia CI Annex, I switched the subject from small talk to what I, at the time, thought God wanted me to tell the inmate. I told the inmate that when we talked after leaving Wakulla CI, I felt a desire to talk with him about God and the Christian faith. When he wasn't receptive to what I was telling him, I stopped talking with him about those things. I then told him how I felt bad when I was at Columbia CI Annex about not continuing with my evangelizing of him on the bus when we left Wakulla CI. I explained how I thought God placed on my heart a strong desire to try again to evangelize him (the inmate) if by any chance I saw him again. I told him that the odds were highly unlikely we would ever end up on a bus again next to each other because of the number of inmates getting on buses daily to transfer. After I said these things to him, he seemed somewhat receptive to allowing me to talk to him about God and the Christian faith.

After talking with the inmate for about an hour, the inmate on the other side of him said, "Excuse me, may I interject?"

I responded, "Yes, please do."

That inmate then talked about how the Lord is our Shepherd and how He seeks His sheep until He gets them. The inmate explained how we don't pursue Christ, but He pursues us. He then talked about how the Father sometimes allows His elect to pursue the pleasures of the world, knowing that the temporary pleasures of the world will cause them heartache, anxiety, stress, worries, etc., and that these things lead the elect to His son Jesus. The inmate also spoke about how God chastises those whom He loves, and His chastisement comes in many ways. He explained how God's chastisement isn't to hurt or kill. It is done in love to correct and bring His elect to Jesus. Finally, the inmate spoke about Godly sorrow producing repentance, and he explained several things that God does in the lives of his elect to bring about Godly sorrow.

As he was talking, I realized God was speaking to me through that inmate. God was clarifying things that I had been thinking about for a long time and that I couldn't understand. I thought about how the Lord had pursued me as a lost sheep throughout my life and how I spent my life running from Him. I had been exposed to religion throughout my life, but I wasn't born again, so I didn't have the Lord. I had spent my life chasing the temporary pleasures of this world, which never gave me peace. I had been an offense to God my whole life. I had been laboring under severe fear and sorrow for several weeks ever since that night at Wakulla CI Annex.

It's difficult to explain what was going on with me subjectively that morning on the bus. The best way for me to describe it is that I had an intense fear of God and, at the same time, an intense feeling of Godly sorrow for my life of sin and running from God. I wanted God's love and not His justice and chastisement.

When I was experiencing the above event, I had an all-consuming desire to stop running from God. I knew that I had to stop my life of rebellion. I had to give my life to God. I was a broken man, and I had to be fixed.

The feelings and thoughts I was having were so clear and compelling, I told the inmate who was talking to me that I believed God sent him to talk to me and that I was going to give my life to God.

God by decree gave me the desire to talk to the inmate on the bus, so that, as I was obeying Him, the inmate on the other side of the inmate I was talking to would hear me talking and would speak the words of life to me.

That morning on the bus, I knew it was impossible to resist the grace of God. More than anything, I wanted God's mercy and love. I wanted all He could give me. During this Damascus Road experience, I felt the fear and sorrow I had been laboring under lifted from me.

At that time, I immediately noticed a change in my thinking and desires. I had an intense desire to stop swearing and smoking cigarettes and to stop doing everything else that violated the Commandments of God. Additionally, I had a strong desire to learn as much as I could about God, the Bible, and all that God required of me. I had been studying the Bible since I was 15 years old, but I knew that I didn't understand it.

The inmate I tried to evangelize and the inmate that evangelized me both got off the bus at Central Florida Reception Center. I switched to another bus that was going to South Florida Reception Center.

I thought I would be placed in administrative confinement when I got there because I was in said status at the last two institutions I had been incarcerated at.

I told God on the way to South Florida Reception Center that I would quit smoking upon my arrival there. I thought going to administrative confinement at South Florida Reception Center would help me quit smoking since inmates couldn't smoke in confinement. I was told when we arrived that I would not be placed in confinement. Right away, I knew I couldn't start my walk with God by lying to Him. Even though I was going to the general population where I could smoke, I had to keep my promise to God that I would quit smoking. Just before I stepped off the bus, I gave away my last pack of tobacco, and I haven't smoked since.

I started smoking cigarettes on June 1, 2000, and by the grace of God, I quit on June 11, 2009. By the grace of God, I haven't had any desire to smoke since that day. When I smell people smoking tobacco, it doesn't tempt me. Instead, it's extremely irritating to my lungs. I also stopped swearing that same day.

I've learned there are many ways my Lord brings people from the kingdom of darkness to the kingdom of light. To bring me into the kingdom of light, God ordained that I be raised knowing and desiring to do what He required of me; however, He did not ordain that I be given the grace to do what He requires. This made my life restless. My life was a life of trying to please God by my own strength and ability. By God ordaining this way for me, I sought God in religion, and I sought to please Him with my works (good deeds). I wanted all God had to offer, so I tried to earn it with religion throughout my life, but I didn't want God (although I thought I did).

Before that morning on the bus, I to some degree thought I was saved. I thought I knew God, I thought I could justify myself in the eyes of God, and I thought I had sufficient righteousness to please Him. I was wrong about all these things.

What I had was a prideful and presumptuous heart. I didn't understand my spiritual condition outside of Christ. I didn't understand that I had to be in Christ to be saved. Prior to being born again that morning on the bus, I looked but I did not see, and I listened but I did not hear, [7] because I wasn't spiritual, [8] and that is why I didn't understand the things of the Spirit of God. [9] I had to die to self in order to live for Christ. [10] The Bible states, "For Godly sorrow produces repentance leading to salvation, not to be regretted; but the sorrow of the world produces death." [11] I had been living with the extreme fear of God and with Godly sorrow for my sins for weeks, and that morning I was finally free in Christ.

In Christianity, the phrase "mountaintop experience" is based on passages in the Bible where God meets with people on a mountaintop. The prime example is the transfiguration of Jesus, which occurred during Jesus's ministry and before his crucifixion. Jesus took Peter, James, and John to the top of a mountain. When they were there, Jesus's face and clothes took on a bright, white light revealing his divinity. They also met Elijah and Moses and heard the voice of God declaring that Jesus was his son with whom he was well-pleased.

Christianity uses the phrase, "mountaintop experience" to denote when a person has an influx of grace into his life as the result of an event between God and that person. God provides the influx of grace for various reasons. One of the most common reasons is for the person's spiritual growth. I believe the reason God by grace allowed me to have a mountaintop experience was for my spiritual growth and that, during this experience, He filled me with an influx of grace.

The mountaintop experience I had caused me to be head over heels in love with God. After the experience on the bus that morning, I was supposed to come down off the mountain. Instead, I remained somewhat stuck in the clouds consumed by the love of God. I constantly thought about Him. I spent every available second studying the Bible, praying, evangelizing, and doing all I could to learn about Him. I wanted to learn everything I could about Him. I thought what manner of love is this that the Father would send the Son to die for me! I didn't deserve anything but hell. However, God chose to show me mercy, grace, and love by electing me to eternal life.

What added to the beauty of this period in my life, was that on June 12, 2009, I was transferred from South Florida Reception Center to Everglades CI, which was a faith-based prison with hundreds of Christians and constant Christian activity all day long, every day.

I was serving 165 years in prison, but to me, I was in heaven. I loved God so much I wanted only Him and did not want anything in my life to take away from my time with Him. It would take me some time to realize that I wasn't given faith to believe in Jesus[12] so I could be a non-working part of the Body of Christ.[13] Since I was born again[14] that meant I was "… His workmanship, created in Christ Jesus for good works, which God prepared beforehand that we should walk in them."[15]

I remained in Everglades CI until I was transferred to Dade CI in January 2010. I entered Dade CI for the first time approximately six months after my conversion.

The information I have presented in this chapter is important for understanding the events documented in the interview part of this book.

INTERVIEW

Chapter 2: The Nature of Prison

1) Please state your name, date of birth, and current place of incarceration?

Harold William Joseph Hempstead, March 5, 1976, presently incarcerated at Tennessee Department of Corrections, Northeast Correctional Complex.

2) Why are you in the Tennessee Department of Correction?

On March 17, 2017, I was involuntarily interstate compacted from the Florida Department of Corrections (FDC) to here. I believe I was interstate compacted for three reasons. First, the FDC and the Dade County, Florida State Attorney's Office wanted to hinder my communications with the media and the Department of Justice on the Darren Rainey case. Second, because of my numerous challenges to the unconstitutional conditions in the FDC. Third, because at the end of 2016 and beginning of 2017, I attempted to expose that FDC staff were allowing convicted sexual predators to go to prison visitation parks where children congregate.

3) Please describe your education.

I have a GED, a Doctor of Biblical Studies Degree from Calvary Christian College and Seminary, and a Paralegal Certification from Blackstone Career Institute, all of which I obtained while incarcerated.

4) Why are you in prison?

In June 2000, at the age of 24, I was sentenced to 165 years for 34 counts of burglary and one count of dealing in stolen property. The residences were unoccupied during the alleged burglaries, and no one was physically harmed.

5) How many years were you incarcerated in the FDC?

Seventeen, June 2000 through March 17, 2017. I have been in incarcerated in Tennessee for nearly 2 years.

6) Please explain mental health services in the FDC?

By law, FDC is mandated to provide mental health services to all inmates in their custody who need them. Inmates enter the FDC from county jails. County staff provides prison staff with information on the inmate's mental health status. County staff lists the inmate's mental health diagnoses and prescribed medicines if any. Also, mental health staff employed by FDC reception centers interview all newly arrived inmates to determine if they have mental health issues.

Every inmate who enters the FDC is issued an S-Grade, commonly referred to as a psych-grade. Each inmate is given a grade between S-1 and S-6. Grade S-1, the lowest level, is reserved for inmates with no significant impairment and who require no mental health treatment. S-6 is reserved for severely mentally disabled inmates who require full-time, inpatient mental health care. During incarceration, mental health staff may raise or lower an inmate's S-grade as deemed necessary.

Inmates designated as S-1 don't require medicine or counseling; those designated as S-2 also do not require medicines for mental health issues but must be interviewed by a mental health counselor every 60-days. S-1 and S-2 inmates may be housed at any institution in Florida.

Inmates designated as S-3 receive both therapy and medicine for their mental-health issues; however, they can refuse one or both. Grades S-4 through S-6 have more serious disabilities and require more intensive care.

FDC institutions vary in their ability to provide different levels of care, and are, thus, classified accordingly. All FDC institutions can house inmates in grades S-1 and S-2. Some are also qualified house inmates in grade S-3. They are called Psych-3-Institutions, and an inmate graded as S-3 must be housed in an S-3 institution.

Some Psych-3-Institutions also contain special units for more seriously ill inmates. These include those with a:

Department of Corruption

- **Transitional Care Unit** (TCU) are for inmates graded S-4 and who have " chronic or residual symptomology who don't require crisis stabilization care or placement in a corrections mental health care facility, but whose impairment in functioning nevertheless renders him or her incapable of adaptive functioning within the incarceration environment" (FAC. 33-404.103 (8)).
- **Crisis Stabilization Unit** (CSU) are "intended for inmates who are experiencing debilitating symptoms of acute mental impairment and who cannot be adequately evaluated and treated in a TCU or Infirmary Mental Health Care unit." Inmates classified as S-5 must be housed in CSUs within Psych-3 facilities. The only way an inmate may be placed in Corrections Mental Health Units is by order of a judge. (FAC. 33-404.103 (G) and FAC. 33-404.101 (S)).

The following are FDC, Psych-3 institutions. Those with a TCU or a CSU are noted.

Apalachee CI East Unit
Central Florida Reception Center
Charlotte CI. *TCU and CSU*
Columbia CI Main Unit and Annex
Dade CI. *TCU and CSU*
Everglades CI
Florida State Prison
Jefferson CI
Lake CI *TCU and CSU*
Martin CI
Northwest Florida Reception Center (Main Unit and Annex)
Regional Medical Center. *TCU and CSU*
Santa Rosa Annex. *TCU and CSU*
Suwanee CI Main Unit. *TCU and CSU*
South Bay Correctional Facility
South Florida Reception Center; *TCU and CSU*
Tomoka CI
Union CI. *TCU and CSU*
Wakulla CI Annex
Zephyrhills CI *TCU and CSU*

Most people enter the field of psychology because they believe they can help others. In my opinion, when mental health professionals are first employed by the Florida prison system, they are not prepared to deal with the manipulation they will receive from inmates. As it relates to prison life, inmates have found ways to solve almost all of their incarcerated related problems. When an inmate finds a way to solve a problem with what inmates call "The System," he shares his findings with other inmates, who share them with other inmates, and so on. The longer an inmate is incarcerated, the more knowledge he has at solving problems in his prison life.

The sayings, "going-psych" and the "psych-game" are two commonly used sayings in the FDC. When an inmate is said to be "going-psych," it means the inmate is planning to do something to try to convince staff that he is having a serious psychological problem. This is called the *psych-game*, because, most inmates are manipulators who are pretending to have psychological problems. This makes prison life much harder for inmates who need help.

Examples of psych-games an inmate may use with the hope of being transferred to a CSU or a TCU include: 1) cutting one's wrist or another part of her his or her body, 2) telling staff he plans to kill himself or another person, 3) consuming a large quantity of medication, swallow batteries or paperclips. Or an inmate will 4) wipe feces on himself, on the walls, etc., 5) drink his urine, 6) strip and refuse to get dressed, 7) fake crying and act as if he can't stop, or 8) refuse to talk.

A psychiatrist in the FDC has authority to have any disciplinary report an inmate receives dismissed. If an inmate convinces a psychiatrist that a psychological problem caused him to commit a disciplinary infraction or caused him not to understand the difference between right and wrong at the time of the infraction, the psychiatrist has the authority to dismiss the disciplinary infraction. Inmates in the Florida prison system know they can *go-psych* and have a good chance of having a serious disciplinary report dismissed.

Inmates commonly *go-psych* to try to beat a disciplinary report. As soon as an inmate learns he's going to confinement, the inmate will institute one of the psych-games. Most of the time, this results in the inmate being placed in a self-harm observation status cell. He cannot be served with a disciplinary report while he's housed in that cell. The inmate will continue to play the psych-game and remain in the self-harm observation status cell until a psychiatrist dismisses the disciplinary report, or recommends the inmate be transferred to a Crisis Stabilization Unit or TCU. If the inmate is transferred, he'll continue to play like he's having serious psychological problems until the psychiatrist at the Crisis Stabilization Unit or TCU dismisses the disciplinary report.

Inmates at Psych 1 and Psych 2 institutions, who don't like the institution they are at, *go-psych* to get their psych grade enhanced. As soon as the inmate is enhanced to S-3 status or higher, he has to be transferred from the Psych 1 and Psych 2 institution.

Inmates *go-psych* to get prescribed certain psychological medicines that get them high, when they owe money or canteen to other inmates, or when they have protection problems with staff or inmates. Finally, inmates *go-psych* in order to enter TCUs to engage in hustling activities or for a summer vacation, i.e., take a break in the air-conditioning for the summer.

In contrast, most inmates in a corrections Mental Health Infirmary Unit status belong there. It is very hard for an inmate to be placed in that status.

The following types of inmates commonly end up in TCUs, Crisis Stabilization Units, and Corrections Mental Health Infirmary Unit status.

CUTTER: A cutter is an inmate who cuts his wrist, arms, or other parts of his body. Most cut their arms. There are many cutters in the FDC, and these large numbers is one of the two reasons shaving razors were banned from the FDC.

A major cutter is an inmate who tries to bleed out when he cuts. I've known several such inmates over the years. They say they like the high they get while on the verge of death. A major cutter usually cuts while in a locked cell. Commonly, he barricades his cell door making it hard for staff to open it. Some cutters are also "painters" who paint walls and other surfaces with their blood. They may also move close to a wall and squeeze the wound to shoot their blood onto the wall. Some painters use their blood to write on the walls or the ceiling. They write about the staff and melancholic topics.

STABBERS: A stabber is an inmate who stabs himself with a sharp object, usually with a chow hall spoon or toothbrush that he sharpened to a point. One interesting thing about stabbers is that they know where to stab themselves without causing major damage.

HANGERS: Hangers are inmates who hang themselves. Some are expert at looking like they are hanging when they are not.

POPPERS: A popper is an inmate who likes to overdose on pills. Most poppers have serious drug addictions. If staff catch an inmate not too long after he overdoses, they'll try to get him to eat charcoal. If the inmate refuses or the charcoal doesn't work, staff will take him to the emergency department of a local hospital to have his stomach pumped. The majority of inmates who overdose don't fake it.

Inmates who fake overdoses remove the contents from a large number of capsules and then swallow this large quantity of empty capsules in front of staff. Some accumulate several packs of non-aspirin medicine and consume them in front of staff. Taking eight to twelve 250-milligram-non-aspirin pills will not kill a person. Most staff can't identify that they are non-aspirin pills, so the inmates can say the pills were anything.

If an inmate attempts one of these ways of overdosing and agrees to swallow the charcoal, the staff place the inmate on self-harm observation status. Most of the time the inmate is then transferred to a Crisis Stabilization Unit.

STARVERS: Starvers go on hunger strikes. A large percentage of those who go on hunger strikes practice by going without food for long periods of time. The practice conditions their body. Before beginning a seven day fast, an inmate starts with one day. He fasts several times for one day and then moves up to two or three-day fasts. He continues this gradual increase until he gets to seven days. Some starvers don't condition their bodies to go without food. They're just really motivated to obtain their goals.

Department of Corruption

DO-DO MAN: A do-do man is an inmate who plays with his feces. He wipes it on himself, or on Florida prison property. There are scores of do-do men in the Florida prison system.

STREAKERS: Streakers are inmates who go on the recreation yards or to a location where there are a lot of inmates. Then they remove their clothes and run around naked. Many streakers are also jumpers. If they can find a suitable building, they climb up and threaten to jump. For this reason, most institutions in FDC have razor wire going around all four corners of the roofs on their buildings.

EATERS: Eaters are inmates who swallow batteries, razors, paperclips, or other items. They usually swallow used batteries, so that, if the battery bursts in their stomach, there is less of a chance of harm or death. Quite a few inmates swallow old razor blades. While FDC no longer allows shaving razors in their facilities, many inmates have them. Inmates dull blades and place tape around them prior to swallowing. This prevents the razor from cutting their throats, etc. The acid in their stomachs eats the tape off the razor.

Medical staff x-ray an inmate's stomach to verify they swallowed the item, and, if so, place the inmate on a liquid diet, which, I am told, makes it easier for the items to travel through the digestive system.

PEE-PEE MAN: A pee-pee man sticks things down the head of his penis. This is not common, although I have met several who do this. The only item I have heard mentioned as being used is an empty ink cartridge.

CRY BABIES: A cry baby can cry on command. They pretend something bad and very sad has happened, and then cry as evidence of the trauma.

Transitional Care Units and Crisis Stabilization Units are full of inmates who manipulate staff. When I say inmates are manipulating staff, I mean they commit the act with the goal of obtaining the benefit they desire. I've talked with several mental health staff who say they are only con men who do not have mental health problems but are just manipulating the system.

I disagree with their position. A mentally stable person wouldn't do any of the above things.

7) Have you been incarcerated in many FDC institutions?

Yes, 23.

8) What is "special housing status?"

Special housing status is any status other than general population status. To be specific these statuses include: Death Row, Close Management, Disciplinary Confinement, Administrative Confinement, Corrections Mental Health Infirmary Unit, Crisis Stabilization Unit, Transitional Care Unit, Self-Harm Observation Status, and Infirmary Status.

Chapter 3: Dade CI (January – May 2010)

9) How many times have you been incarcerated at Dade CI?

I have been incarcerated there three times at the Dade Correctional Institute three times. The first time was for about four months (January 2010 – May 2010); the second time was from April 29, 2011 till January 17, 2013; and the third time was from June 2013 till May 19, 2014.

10) Where is Dade CI located?

It's located at: 19000 Southwest, 377th Street, Florida City, Florida.

11) Were you ever housed in the Dade CI Transitional Care Unit (TCU)?

Yes. I was housed in the Dade CI TCU my first and second incarcerations at Dade CI.

12) Why were you placed in the TCU in 2010?

I was representing myself in a 42 U.S.C. § 1983 Civil Right Complaint lawsuit (Case number 4:07-CV-00513 RH/AK) filed in the Tallahassee, Florida Federal District Court and in post-conviction proceedings on my criminal case. These legal matters, Christian studies, and the evangelism I had been involved at Everglades CI caused me to feel that I had too much going on at one time. I wanted to take a break; therefore, I had myself placed in a TCU so I could focus on my Christian studies and law work. In TCU status, inmates are not required to participate in the majority of activities the general population inmates are involved with. Thus, inmates in TCU status have more time for themselves.

13) Please describe the Dade CI and its TCU.

Dade CI has two sections, Sections One and Two. Section One contains a security building, visitation park, library, law library, chapel, education department, chow hall, medical department, classification, a partially constructed building, and the TCU.

Section Two is the main compound where general population inmates are housed. The gate separating the two sections is called Center Gate. A small officers' shack is located on the Section Two side of Center Gate.

Section Two contains five open bay dorms (Dorms A-E) on the "Southside." On the "Northside" there are three T-Buildings, buildings with dorms containing two-man cells (Dorms F-H). Section Two has four inmate canteens, two inmate barbershops, a property room, a captain's office, caustics room, and the inmate recreation yard. The recreation yard has a small building containing two or three small offices, an outside TV area for inmates, and a section that was used for the weight pile. The recreation yard is fairly large. The female inmates at Homestead CI washed the laundry for the male inmates housed at Dade CI. The laundry office at Dade CI was just for sewing, picking up laundry, and laundry complaints.

Dade CI is known as a corrupt institution. When I was first incarcerated in 2000, Dade CI was known as the drug capitol of the FDC. Florida inmates claim one can get any drug one wants there. If the drug exists in society, it can be obtained at Dade CI. Drugs at Dade CI have always cost less than at the other institutions in Florida. Similarly, when the smuggling of cell phones began, Dade CI quickly obtained the title of "Cell Phone Capitol" of the Florida prison system. Prices were half what they were in other prisons.

The federal government has a long history of investigating Dade CI. To read an example, google "Operation Bird Cage."

In the following, I describe the layout of Dade CI TCU.

At the end of the road that went through the front gate at Dade CI there was a two-story building with "Transitional Care

Unit" written on the front. This building was the section of the TCU called, "Central." Just outside the front door of Central were the stairs and an elevator that staff and inmates used to go the second floor.

"Outpatient Mental Health" was located on the second floor. It contained offices for secretaries, clerks, nurses, counselors, psychologists, psychiatrists, etc. It also had an inmate waiting room, several conference rooms, an inmate bathroom, and an officers' station. Outpatient Mental Health staff provided mental health services to inmates housed in general population.

As soon as you entered the first floor of Central, there was an officers' station. Central also had offices for psychiatrists, psychologists, counselors, lieutenants, and the major and his secretary. It had a medical records room, laundry room, property room, two staff bathrooms, a staff dining room, and staff barbershop, which was also used as an intake room for inmates arriving at the TCU.

If you walked about 20 feet into the front door of Central and turned right, you would be walking toward what was called the "Eastside". Turn left and you would be walking toward "Westside". Eastside and Westside sections are both connected to Central by breezeways about 15 feet long.

The Eastside consisted of wings J-4 and J-5, a recreation yard, an officers' station, a nurses' station, and several offices. Similarly, the Westside consisted or wings J-1, J-2, and J-3, a recreation yard, and officers' station, a nurses' station, and offices.

There were many problems with the facilities in Westside.

- The Westside was supposed to be air-conditioned, but the air-conditioning was constantly broken.
- The plumbing was constantly backing up, causing the toilets in the cells to clog. This caused feces and urine to back up out of the toilets and out of the drains on to the floors.
- Water constantly leaked through the roofs of the offices in Wings J-1 and J-3. This created mildew problems. Water leaking from pipes also ruined sections of the roof on the Westside.

The heat and the almost constant odor of feces and urine was oppressive and made life in the Westside TCU unpleasant for most staff and inmates.

14) Were staff at Dade CI ever interviewed about the conditions in the TCU?

Yes. The *Miami Herald* interviewed Dade CI Warden Jerry Cummings at the end of 2014 or the beginning of 2015. Coach (and Counselor) Harriet Kryscowski was interviewed by *The New Yorker* magazine for their 2016 article *Madness*. Both of these staff mentioned some of the conditions that I have mentioned. Also, TCU Counselor George Mallinckrodt published a book, *Getting Away with Murder* that discussed the conditions inside the Dade CI TCU. These articles and this book show that staff who worked in the TCU agreed with me about a lot of the conditions in the TCU.

15) Did you ever work as an orderly in the Dade CI TCU?

Yes. During my first incarceration at Dade CI (January through May of 2010) I began work as an orderly approximately two weeks after I was placed in the Dade TCU. Altogether, I worked as an orderly three times, in 2010, 2011, and 2012.

16) Before Dade CI, did you work as an orderly?

Yes, Before that, I was a Special Housing orderly on close management status at Columbia CI, in confinement status at Washington CI, and in TCU and Crisis Stabilization Unit statuses at Lake CI and Zephyrhills CI.

17) What were your duties as an orderly?

In the Dade CI Westside TCU, I had more duties in 2011 than I did in 2010 and even more in 2012 than I did in either 2010 or 2011. In 2010, my duties were to prepare the food trays and juice for serving on the shifts I worked, serve the meals, and keep the Westside clean. I passed out cleaning supplies to inmates who could clean their own cells and cleaned the cells of inmates who could not. I picked up trays, cleaned the recreation yards, helped pass-out laundry and passed-out toilet paper, toothpaste, toothbrushes, and soap. I also cleaned up biohazardous substances. In 2011, I performed all of those duties, plus I helped pass out canteen, and I monitored who was on diet trays. In 2012,

I did everything I did in 2010 and 2011, plus I told staff on each shift how many diet trays and sandwiches they needed to order, helped the coaches with passing-out magazines, books, puzzles, etc., and passed-out the laundry on the Westside.

18) Did you want a job as an orderly?

No. My original plan was to not leave my cell and spend every day in Bible study, listening to Christian music, working on my law work, and writing to my family. Agreeing to do orderly work was the opposite of what I wanted to do.

19) If you did not want work as an orderly, why did you?

When I first started working as an orderly, I was shocked to see the things I saw. Every time we served a meal, numerous inmates were denied their food. The majority of the time it was for no reason. It was normal for staff not to feed 15 to 25 inmates per meal. Most of the time, staff laughed at the inmates as we passed their cells without giving them a tray. It was spiritually draining to witness this. Prior to 2010, I had worked as an orderly in the TCUs at Lake CI once, and Zephyrhills CI twice. I never witnessed staff mistreat mentally disabled inmates at those institutions.

I wanted so desperately to quit working as an orderly and stay in my cell. I went to the Dade CI TCU to relax, not to constantly work and constantly witness evil. I didn't quit in the beginning of my orderly work in 2010, because I thought if I continued working, I could stop the non-feeding of inmates and fix the other problems. I felt bad for the inmates who were not being fed. I wasn't fed several meals when I was incarcerated at Santa Rosa CI, so I knew how it felt to be denied my meals and to be hungry. The inmates at Dade CI were being denied a lot more food than I had been, and they were mentally disabled. Although I didn't quit in the beginning, I did eventually quit the midnight shift, then the 8:00 am to 4:00 pm shift, and finally I asked to be discharged from the TCU.

I tried to fix the problems while I was there. I wasn't successful, and I gave up. In 2010, I put myself first over those who needed my help and I quit. I not only quit, but I asked to leave Dade CI after I quit. After I discharged from the Dade CI TCU in 2010, I had so much conviction for quitting and leaving

Dade CI, I knew I had to go back and try to fix what was going on there.

20) How many shifts did you work as an orderly in 2010?

I worked all three shifts for about two months. I eventually quit the 12:00 am to 8:00 am shift, and then I quit the 8:00 am to 4:00 pm shift

21) Please tell me more about the non-feeding of inmate patients in 2010.

When a meal was being served in the TCU, an officer or sergeant would be in the front of the food line opening the food flaps of the inmates who were going to be given a tray. After him there would be another officer and then me. I passed trays info the cells with open flaps. A closed food flap was security staff's way of telling not give food to the inmate in that cell.

Security staff would also remove all of the food or some of the food from the trays of inmates they didn't want to feed.

22) In 2010, did you ever say anything to staff about withholding food?

I didn't say anything to staff that would cause them to think I was a threat to them. They would've fired me if I did. If they looked upon me as a threat, they wouldn't have been receptive to me. I thought I had a better chance of getting staff to feed the inmates by trying to get them to fear getting caught for not feeding the inmates.

I did everything I could to express concern for the staff and show that I cared about them. I went above and beyond my duties as an orderly and did all I could to make their jobs physically easier. When staff did something wrong, I expressed my concerns to them about them being caught. I warned them about the mounted security cameras and about how other staff and inmates were witnessing these illegal acts. I also reminded staff about the mentally stable inmates housed in the TCU who were running from disciplinary reports or problems at the institutions they came from.

I told the staff about different state and federal laws that prohibited the abuse of the mentally disabled. I explained how those laws gave state and federal agencies authority to conduct all types of investigations into activities in the TCU. I did all these things in a nice and humble way, which caused them to look upon me as non-threatening.

23) Why did you think you would be if reported or criticized the non-feeding of inmates?

Experience and common sense dictated my actions. Prior to June 2009, when I witnessed staff doing something wrong, I objected to their actions right away. I also filed thousands of grievances prior to June 2009 on FDC prison staff. I knew from experience that prison staff would do what they could to avoid an inmate they did not trust. Staff will not be receptive to an inmate whom they deem to be a threat or whom they think will report their actions.

Prison staff are taught all the basic state and federal rights of inmates. Most of the time, it is intentional when prison staff violate the well-established rights of inmates. If staff repetitively violate a specific right of an inmate, they are obviously doing it intentionally. Staff who intentionally violate the rights of a prisoner, engage in an intentional course of action that they deem is in their best interest. They believe it is in their best interest to do, because they believe the benefit from doing so outweighs the right of the prisoner. When an inmate tells a staff member that their actions are wrong or that the staff shouldn't be doing what they are doing, the staff will think that inmate is attempting to stop the staff from obtaining the benefit the staff desires from his actions. Staff deems inmates who do this as a threat to the staff's authority. Prison staff, like most people, don't want to be told they're doing wrong.

24) Do you have any evidence that you've filed thousands of grievances during your incarceration?

Yes. My FDC inmate files show that I have filed more than 4,000 grievances since my June 1, 2000 incarceration.

25) What is chemical warfare?

Inmate patients often didn't like coming out of their cells when the staff told them to. Inmates on two-point status could only leave their cells after being handcuffed. An inmate on zero-point status could leave his cell without being handcuffed. If an inmate on two-point status refused to be handcuffed so staff could take him out of his cell, staff would place pure bleach and/or ammonia in the inmate's cell. These strong chemicals irritated the inmate's eyes and his respiratory system. The inmate would usually agree to be handcuffed within five minutes of the chemicals being placed in his cell.

The staff brought the bleach and/or ammonia in from society. The Major would allow staff to bring chemicals into work, because of the lack of chemicals at Dade CI.

26) Were you ever present when staff used chemical warfare on an inmate?

Yes, I was present every time it was done on an inmate patient in 2010 while I was an orderly in the TCU.

The staff who brought chemicals in from society had me hide any we didn't use, so the chemicals were there when staff needed them. Every time the staff used chemical warfare, I was told to get the bleach or ammonia. I would go to my hiding place, get the chemical, and bring it to the staff at the cell where an inmate was refusing to leave. I placed the bleach or ammonia in a spray bottle before bringing it to the cell, so it looked normal for the mounted cameras, which would only show me walking to the cell with a spray bottle and giving it to an officer. I loosened the spray bottle top before handing it to the officer. After the officer took possession of the bottle, he used his body to block the view of the mounted cameras and removed the bottle top. He would then open the food flap, place the bottle in, and pour about half of the chemical on the floor in the cell. The officer would then shut the food flap, and he and I would walk away from the cell. In about five minutes, the inmate in the cell wouldn't be able to deal with the strength of the chemical anymore, and he would agree to come out of his cell.

27) Did staff ever say anything to the inmates after they dropped the chemical in their cells?

Yes. Different staff would say different things. They would usually say, "enjoy," "let's see how tough you are now," or "you'll be begging me to take you out of your cell in five minutes." What added to this abuse, was most of the inmates they did this to were severely mentally disabled. The inmates didn't have the thinking ability to realize that all they had to do was use toilet paper and water to clean up the chemical.

28) Did a mental health staff question you about chemical warfare in 2010?

Yes, Ms. Arencibia told me that an inmate patient told her I was at a cell door with Officer Gibson when he poured bleach or ammonia in Cell J-1101. Ms. Arencibia asked me what happened. I told her that she was a mental health staff, and I didn't feel comfortable talking with her about what security staff did or did not do.

29) Why did you tell her that?

Ms. Arencibia had been working in the TCU for several years. She knew what security staff did. It was my position that since she didn't take any action to stop them prior to me arriving there, she wouldn't take any action after my arrival there. I felt it would be better, if I kept the things I was witnessing to myself until I could find a way to try to fix the problems myself.

30) What did you do to stop chemical warfare in 2010?

I told several of the security staff who didn't bring chemicals in from society where the chemicals that other staff brought in were hidden. This resulted in staff using chemicals that belonged to other staff. I also started pouring the bleach and ammonia down sinks without staff knowing it. When the staff asked me to get them bleach or ammonia, I acted shocked to find the bottles empty. I knew they would blame the other staff. This led to chemical warfare stopping for the last month I was in the TCU.

31) What did Officer Gibson tell you to do with the feces of the inmate who defecated in a shower?

I was told to place the feces in an empty Styrofoam tray that I got from one of the trash cans and to place it in the closet upstairs in Wing J-3. When staff finished showering the inmates, Officer Gibson went with me to get the tray from the closet. We then walked to the cell of the inmate who left the feces in the shower. The officer opened the food flap, dropped the tray through the food flap, shut the food flap, and said, "You forgot that in the shower."

32) What happened when another inmate pushed feces under his cell door out into the wing?

I was in Wing J-1 talking with Officer Piggot when Officer Gums came in and said he needed help with returning some property to an inmate. He told us that the inmate in Cell J-2112 pushed several "turds" up under his door. Gums, trying to be funny, said he didn't have a property slip to give the inmate for the feces, so he had to give the turds back to the inmate. He told me to get a mop and a mop-bucket of water and go to Wing J-2 with him to help give the inmate back his property/feces. He said he wanted me to place the mop bucket in front of the inmate's door, to act as though I was mopping up the mess, and then intentionally knock the mop bucket over so that the water would push the feces back into the inmate's cell. Gums wanted me to make it look like it was an accident. He then wanted me to barricade the bottom of the inmate's cell door, where the inmate wouldn't be able to use water from his toilet to push the feces back out of his cell.

On the way to Wing J-2, I told Officer Gums I was concerned about the mounted cameras, and that I would be fired if I was caught doing what he wanted me to do. He said, "OK, I'll knock the bucket over. Just put the bucket in front of the cell and barricade the door after I get the feces back in the cell." When we got to Wing J-2, everything happened as Gums directed. He knocked the bucket over, the water from the bucket pushed the feces back into the cell, and I barricaded the bottom of the cell door so the inmate couldn't push his feces back out of his cell.

33) Will you explain what a loaf is and how "loafing" was carried out in 2010?

If an inmate in a special housing unit throws his food, tray, cup, or spork, or refuses to give any of these back to staff after a meal, security staff can get approval from a captain to place the inmate on a loaf. A loaf is all the food from one meal stuck together in a loaf. For instance, all the food from breakfast, from lunch, or from dinner stuck together in a loaf. Inmates placed on loaf rarely eat them. They taste so nasty most inmates would rather starve than eat them.

In 2010, security staff use to lie and say that inmates were throwing their trays and then have the inmates placed on loafs. When staff did this, it was called "loafing an inmate." Staff were falsely loafing inmates a lot in 2010.

Mental health medication is not supposed to be taken on an empty stomach. Inmate patients who were being loafed weren't eating and were taking their medications on an empty stomach. This caused other medical and mental health problems with the inmate patients.

The senior psychiatrist (Doctor Basaga) in the TCU eventually asked me privately what was going on with the loafing on the Westside. I told him, that if some of the inmate patients took medicine that would injure them if taken on an empty stomach, then he should order that loafs not be allowed in the TCU. He knew he had a duty to do his best to make sure the medications he was prescribing helped the inmates instead of harming them. For this reason, he issued a memo discontinuing the use of loaves in the TCU during my last month in the TCU.

34) Will you tell me about the inmate patients breaking sprinklers in 2010?

A few of the inmates who staff kept denying food to broke sprinklers in their cells. They did this because the inmates knew staff would press criminal charges against the inmates and send them to a Dade County, Florida Jail for prosecution. While in the jail, the inmates would be given food to eat. I'm not sure, but it's reasonable to say that the inmates who went to Dade County, Florida Jail from Dade CI in 2010 for breaking sprinklers, would've told their lawyers, the state attorney, or the court that staff at Dade CI weren't feeding them.

35) In 2010, did security staff ever use chemicals to bathe an inmate who was refusing to shower?

Yes. When that happened, I was told to fill up two five-gallon buckets with one-quarter of chemicals and three-quarters water. Security staff would place the inmate in the shower next to Cell J-1110 and then tell the inmate to takeoff his clothes and shower. If the inmate refused to shower, staff would tell him to stay in the shower and to not try to get out or they would hurt him. Staff would then open the shower door and stand to the side as a third staff threw a bucket of chemicals and water on the inmate. I would be sent to fill that bucket up with just water. Staff would then try again to get the inmate to turn on the water and shower. Usually the chemicals were strong enough to cause the inmate to shower in order get the chemicals off his body. But, if the inmate didn't turn the shower water on after a few minutes, staff would throw the second bucket of chemicals and water on the inmate. I would then fill that bucket up with just water.

Generally staff would then try for about five minutes to get the inmate to shower. If the inmate continued to refuse to shower, staff would throw both buckets of water on the inmate, take him out of the shower, give him a change of clothes, and place him back into his cell.

36) Was that considered a legal way to shower inmates?

No. There was nothing legal about it.

37) Please tell me about the classification officer who was assigned to the TCU.

Ms. Koel was responsible for all the classification matters relating to the inmates housed in the TCU. She was also responsible for picking up and processing the grievances filed by the inmate. Several of the inmates accused her of throwing away grievances and not processing them.

My relationship with Ms. Koel was good in 2010. In 2011 and 2012, my relationship with her changed when she learned more about my past and my federal lawsuit against prison officials filed in the Tallahassee Federal District Court.

38) Did you discuss the Bible with any TCU staff in 2010?

Yes. I discussed it a lot with Officer Eli, Eli's brother Officer Saneck, and Officers Jenkins and Piggot. Officer Piggot didn't really like discussing the Bible in 2010. In my opinion, he put up with me talking about it, because I was his orderly and I lived in the wing he was posted to work in. I remember constantly saying the following things to him, "If you were to die today, would you go to heaven or hell?", "I hope you don't die today, in the condition you're in", or "How many people do you think know the day they're going to die?" My goal with Piggot in 2010 was to try to get him to realize that he had to take his eternal salvation serious, because he could die any day. I wanted him to know that he didn't want to die and meet God in His wrath.

39) Why did you quit working with Lieutenant McCrae in 2010?

Lieutenant McCrae worked on the 4:00 pm to 12:00 am shift when I first got to the TCU in 2010. About three months later, he became the lieutenant on the 8:00 am to 4:00 pm shift. He said he was going to the 8 till 4 shift because the troublemaking staff were on that shift, and he was going to "get them straight." Yes, there were some rough staff on that shift, but they weren't as bad as the staff on the 4 till 12 shift that he was on. McCrae was one of the most violent, not by the book lieutenants I ever met in South Florida. To say he was going to stop troublemaking staff was unreal.

On his first day on the 8 to 4 shift, McCrae told me I couldn't keep a change of clothes in my cell. He knew that I worked about 12 hours a day and cleaned up feces, urine, and blood on a regular basis. Not having a set of clean clothes in my cell would mean I would have to go to bed in my work clothes and wear them when I was not working. I told him this, even though I knew he already knew it. When he continued to contend that I could only have my work clothes, I told him that I was quitting.

What McCrae didn't know was that none of the other stable inmates on the Westside wanted to work as an orderly. They didn't feel safe doing orderly work. They felt that the abuses of the security staff would eventually cause one or more inmate patients to try to hurt the orderlies who worked with security staff. He also didn't know that, every morning, Officer Piggot and I were going cell to cell trying to get one of the stable inmates in the TCU to help me do the orderly work.

When I quit, security staff weren't able to get any of the other inmates on the Westside to work. Thus, McCrae had to allow inmates housed in Wing J-5 on the Eastside to come to the Westside to do orderly work. That opened up tobacco and drug smuggling activities between Wing J-5 and the Westside. This caused more problems in the TCU.

McCrae tried to get the lieutenants on the other shifts to not work me, but they didn't listen to him. They agreed that McCrae was wrong in not letting to have a clean set of clothes to change into when I wasn't working.

I didn't work on McCrae's shift the rest of the time I was housed in the TCU in 2010.

40) Did inmates housed on the Westside get to change their clothes and receive toiletries as mandated by FDC rules?

No, Florida Administrative Code 33 stated that the inmate patients were supposed to have clothing exchange three times a week. The inmate patients were lucky if they got to change their clothes once a week.

FDC policy also stated that the inmate patients were supposed to receive a bar of soap and a roll of toilet paper once a week, a tube of toothpaste every month, and a toothbrush every 90 days.

Most of the time staff didn't have soap to give the inmates to shower and wash their hands. Toilet paper was passed-out about every 10 days, but most of the time there wasn't enough to give every inmate patient a roll. The toothpaste was always late, but there was enough to give every inmate a tube apiece. While I was in the TCU in 2010, no toothbrushes were distributed.

Lack of necessary toiletries and clean clothes upset the inmate patients and created a lot of stress on the Westside. Some inmate patients even developed scabies.

41) Please tell me about your relationship with Officer Gibson in 2010.

Officer Gibson went by the nickname "Big Gib." He was about 6'4", 340 pounds. In 2010, several inmates contended that he was violent with them, engaged in chemical warfare, and did not feed them. A few of the inmates told staff that I was always around when Officer Gibson was engaging in those activities. Because of these reports, some of the lieutenants and Ms. Arencibia questioned me about Officer Gibson. It was my position that the lieutenants and Ms. Arencibia knew about Officer Gibson's activities, and they were just wanting to see if I would tell on him.

I never told any Dade CI staff about Gibson's activities in 2010.

42) Were there any mounted security cameras on the Westside in 2010?

Yes, I believe there were four in Wing J-1, three in Wing J-2, and three in Wing J-3.

However, the mounted cameras didn't always work. Additionally, the lieutenants and major over the TCU knew what the security staff were doing, and they didn't care. They believed that Westside staff had to do abusive things in order to manage the Westside. For these reasons, the mounted cameras were of no real help even when they did work.

Security staff at Dade CI all stuck together. This is one of the reasons why none of the TCU staff lost their job when Darren Rainey was found dead with his skin falling off him in a TCU shower.

43) What were the names of the mental health staff, security staff, and nurses who worked on the Westside in 2010?

MENTAL HEALTH STAFF: Dr. Basaga was the senior psychiatrist, Dr. Perez was the senior psychologist, and George Mallinckrodt and Ms. Arencibia were both mental health counselors. I don't know if Ms. Cortada worked on the Westside in 2010. Nichole Ocanna started working as a coach in the TCU about a month before I discharged from there in 2010.

SECURITY STAFF: Major Marlow; Lieutenants McCrae, Donaldson, Olds, Pinkney; Sergeants Johnathan, Tarver, Anderson, Pierri, Seals, Lopez, Lewis, and Officers Piggot, Eli, Gruben, Perez, Weary, Saneck, Wood, David, Jenkins, Gibson, Clarke, Alverez, Collado, Pena, Patterson, Gums, Jenkins (female), Jackson, and Harrison.

MEDICAL STAFF (NURSES): The only nurses that I can remember are nurses Jensen, Astre, Edgehill, Robinson, Hidrobo, and Nickolis.

I discuss issues and events related to some of these staff later in the book

44) Why did you ask to discharge from the TCU in 2010?

I gave up. In the beginning of 2010, I thought I could help the inmates. However, I found out I wasn't able to. I did some minor things that were helpful, but overall I couldn't stop the abuse and non-feeding. It was grieving my spirit to constantly be around such activity. I didn't want to keep dealing with it, so I put myself in front of others and asked to discharge back to general population.

I suggest combining these last two questions

45) What happen after you were discharged back to general population?

Immediately after I was discharged, in fact, on the very day I was discharged, I started receiving conviction about not staying in the TCU to help the inmates. Godly conviction is when God brings a person to realization of his own guilt for failure to do what God commands. I felt that I had sinned in not doing more to help them. The Bible commanded me to put others first, and I didn't do that.

About a week after I left the Dade CI TCU, I was transferred back to Everglade Correction Institution, where I was immediately prior to transferring to Dade CI.

Chapter 4: Everglades CI/Pinellas County Jail (May-October, 2010)

46) Did you see an old friend upon your return to Everglades CI?

Yes, my Christian brother and friend Michael Blatch. We both attended many of the same Bible studies and chapel services during my prior incarceration at Everglades CI.

Blatch was housed in the same wing I was housed in this incarceration at Everglades CI. Several other Christians were also housed in the same wing with us.

Within an hour of my return there, Blatch told me that he wanted to introduce me to a new Christian that had just transferred there whose name was Russel Rogers.

I was told that Rogers transferred there from Okeechobee CI, because medical staff wanted him to be close to a Miami, Florida hospital where he was going for therapy on his hand. Rogers said he broke his hand punching an inmate. When he told me it happened after he was allegedly born again, I knew I had to be watchful of him.

Rogers was about 6'2" and 215 pounds of muscle. He was also an amateur boxer prior to his incarceration. He had been housed on close management twice while incarcerated in the Florida Department of Corrections (FDC).

47) How is Russel Rogers connected to the Darren Rainey case?

When I first met Rogers he took a liking to me. Blatch and others told him that I took Bible study serious, and that I was known by the Christian community at Everglades CI for being a strong student of the Bible, and defender of the Christian faith.

Rogers expressed his desire to get into preaching. I encouraged him to do such and told him I would go with him to the recreation yards, and guide and support him in open air preaching. In prison, we call open air preaching, "Sodom Preaching."

About 10 days after my return to Everglades CI, Batch, Rogers, an older Christian we called "Blind Man" and I all agreed to engage in Christian services on the recreation yards three times a week. Blind Man was missing both of his eyes. He was very good at singing Christian gospel music. Every time he sang on one of the recreation yards, everybody in both yards could hear him. Many inmates and staff came to listen to him sing.

Blind Man opened each service with two gospel songs. After the second song, Rogers or Batch would ask the crowd to stay for 15 minutes to listen to a short message from the Lord. In the beginning, I was only overseeing the dynamics of the service and reviewing the gospel message that was preached.

Rogers did very well in the beginning and I was proud of him. After he had preached for about two weeks, he started making statements that concerned me. He said things like, "Did you hear me?", "Did you hear my voice?", and "Did you see how I presented the message?" Blatch, other inmates, and I were concerned because Rogers was taking all the credit, and not giving any glory to God.

I didn't want to say anything to Rogers because I knew he would run from me if I did. However, I knew I had to for the glory of God. I came to this conclusion after praying about it and discussing it with Blatch, who agreed I should say something to

Rogers. The next time a service was held and Rogers brought up how well he preached, I said, "Was that you, or Jesus in you?"

He responded, "You know what I mean."

I responded, "I only know what you said, but if you didn't mean it the way you said it, I understand."

He responded by saying that he didn't want to talk about it. From that day on, Rogers started pulling away from me. He attended services that claimed to be Christian but didn't teach Biblical Christianity. However, every now and then he came to me to get my position on Bible doctrine.

About two weeks later, the services we were having on the recreation yards broke up. Rogers didn't want to have the service with Blatch and me anymore. Blind Man didn't like the service splitting, and he didn't want to go out alone with Rogers to conduct services. He also didn't want Rogers to get mad at him, if Blind Man did services with Blatch and me, so he decided to not go with any of us. Blatch and I ended up doing a service by ourselves, and Rogers went out by himself and preached.

How is Rogers connected to the Darren Rainy case? I returned to the Dade CI Transitional Care Unit (TCU) at the end of April 2011. On June 23, 2012, I witnessed Darren Rainey die in the Dade CI TCU. In January 2013, I transferred from Dade CI back to Everglades CI. A couple weeks after my return, a sergeant and I were discussing inmates I knew. When I brought up Rogers, the sergeant told me about a lot of things that happened with Rogers while I was away. The sergeant told me Rogers severely beat his cellmate. This cellmate went psych and was transferred to the Dade CI TCU. I eventually learned the name of the person. It Darren Rainey.

I will discuss this in more detail when we get to that point in this interview.

48) How long were you at Everglades CI this incarceration?

Approximately three months, while I was waiting to be transferred back to the Pinellas County, Florida Jail to start post-conviction proceedings on the case I'm incarcerated on.

In 2008, the Second District Court of Appeal of Florida, issued a written opinion on my criminal case for which I am incarcerated. This resulted in a second evidentiary hearing on the

40

case. I represented myself without the assistance of an attorney on the appeal that led to this second evidentiary hearing.

Everglades CI staff didn't allow me to bring any of my law work or property to the Pinellas County jail. Since I needed my law work for the evidentiary hearing, the circuit court judge issued an order for me to be transferred to Everglades CI in order to get my law work and property. Then I was to be transferred back to the Pinellas County Jail again.

I stayed in Everglades CI with my property and law work for about another month before returning to the Pinellas County Jail.

Chapter 5: Pinellas County Jail (October 2019 – January 2011)

49) Tell me about your stay in the Pinellas County Jail.

My first two days in the jail I noticed an inmate reading his Bible for hours every day. When he prayed, he prayed on his knees. On my second day, I asked him what he was reading. I did this as a way of starting a conversation with him. In my first conversation with him, he agreed to study the Bible with me every day. The third day in the jail, I held my first Bible study in that wing, and only one inmate attended. As the days passed, more and more inmates attended. It got to where four to 12 inmates attended the study daily. The wing held about 30 inmates. About three weeks after being in the wing, God moved me to start a nightly prayer service. More inmates attended the prayer service than the Bible study.

Since my conversion, I always had a desire to do some type of evangelism in society even though I'm incarcerated.

The Bible teaches that Christ and all believers make up the Body of Christ[1]. The Bible also teaches that the believers union with Christ is organic[2], vital[3], mediated by the Holy Spirit[4]; it implies reciprocal action[5]; it's personal[6] and it's transforming[7]. For these reasons, I believed God was moving me to start a Christian newsletter called, "One Body." I wrote this newsletter monthly for five or six months and mailed copies of it to 15 to 20 people in society.

Around December 2010, an inmate started telling me how bad society had become since my incarceration. He went into a lot of detail about the quantity of homeless people in society. He also explained how a lot of people in society were addicted to pain pills and other types of drugs. He explained how the family structure was deteriorating and large numbers of children were homeless. While he was telling me these things, he brought to my attention how the majority of the inmates in the jail were between 18 and 26 years of age.

What he told me made me feel sad for what people in society were experiencing. I wasn't aware of the conditions that he told me about until he informed me of them. I stopped watching the news years prior to this conversation because I felt sad about the things I was watching on the news.

After finding out about the conditions in society, I realized that if I was ever set free, I no longer wanted to teach Systematic Theology in a seminary. It was very clear to me, that if I was ever set free, I would devote my life to preaching Jesus Christ and his crucifixion.[8] It was my position that the world was in more need of Jesus than seminary students were in need of learning Systematic Theology.

I did my best to follow the Biblical command to pray without ceasing[9] while in the jail. It was difficult with the constant talking, noise, and movement going on in the wing I lived in. The only place I could find time alone with God in prayer was in the shower. I use to pray for the inmates who attended my Bible study and prayer group. I prayed for God to give them saving faith if they didn't have it.

Prior to going to the jail, I was aware of the different types of "faith" that are not saving faith. I didn't know if the men in the Bible study and prayer group had saving faith. As I prayed in the shower for God to give them saving faith if they didn't have it, I also thought, "what if I didn't have saving faith?" The Bible has several verses that tell Christians to examine themselves as to whether they are of the faith[10]. The Bible talks about people who live their whole lives and even die thinking they're saved just to find out that they were never saved[11]. I conducted several examinations of myself since I was born again, and I was being led by God at that time to conduct another one[12]. What caused me to have some concern about my faith was the thought of losing the evidentiary hearing that I had pending on my criminal case. I was confused and worried, and I didn't know how I would respond if I lost the evidentiary hearing. I didn't want to fall back into sin.

Many prison inmates seemed like they only wanted what Jesus could offer and not Jesus. I had many conversations with them about if they wanted Jesus or Santa Claus. The majority of the inmates only talked about how Jesus was going to set them free from prison. Many didn't like it when I told them it appeared they wanted Santa Claus and not Jesus. It wasn't Biblical to think God was going to set all Christian inmates free from prison.

Despite telling this to other inmates, I always thought that God was going to set me free if I ever received an evidentiary hearing. I thought if I wasn't set free and I lost the hearing, Satan might attack my faith. This caused me great concern.

I believe God wanted me to seek the guidance of another Christian on this issue. I continued my regular activities, as I prayed for spiritual help and guidance. Soon, I began attending a Bible study by a preacher from society. He was an older man in his sixties who had a fire and brimstone preaching style. He said he had been saved for over 30 years and he was dying of cancer. He was Biblical and had a lot of life experience. God led me to this preacher for help. After a month, I submitted an inmate request form to him asking if he would call me out and talk with me. He did.

Several days later, when he called me out to talk with him, I brought the certificates I had obtained from the Bible Studies and Christian programs I had completed. I wanted to show the preacher I had been diligently studying the Bible, but for some reason, I was confused on a personal spiritual issue.

When I met with the preacher, I said, "Chaplain, I brought my certificates with me because I want you to know that I've been diligently studying the Bible for a while, and I have an issue that's somewhat different than others."

"I was incarcerated on March 23, 1999, I went to prison on June 1, 2000, and I started doing Bible studies in prison in 2007. I was born again in June 11, 2009. Since then, I've diligently studied the Bible, evangelized, and taught the Bible on a daily basis for eight to 15 hours a day. Even though I'm serving a 165 year sentence; since I was born again, I've had so much peace and happiness I don't want to ever lose it. Jesus gave me the peace and happiness. However, I have a concern. For many years, I've thought if I ever received a hearing on a specific legal error that happened in my criminal case, I would be set free. I'm now back here in the jail from prison for a hearing on that legal error. My concern is what's going to happen if I lose the evidentiary hearing."

He responded, "What do you mean, you're concerned?"

I said, "When I was in prison a lot of the inmates who professed to be Christian would always talk about how Jesus was going to set them free. I used to ask them if they wanted Jesus or Santa Claus. In other words, did they want what Jesus could offer or did they want Jesus! A lot of inmates in prison incorrectly believe that Jesus is obligated to set all Christians free to society from jails and prisons. Chaplain, just because I've thought I would be set free doesn't mean it's God's will that I'll be set free. The Bible doesn't teach that God will release every inmate back to society after he becomes a Christian. If God released every Christian inmate back to society, there would be no Christian inmates in prison to evangelize the lost. What if it is God's will that I'm one of the inmates He wants to stay in prison to evangelize the lost? What if I lose the hearing and Satan uses the loss to attack my faith? What happens if I have to go back to prison for the rest of my life?"

He responded, "Do you love Jesus?"

I said, "Yes, of course."

He responded, "Who are you?"

"What do you mean?" I asked.

He responded "Are you one of Jesus' sheep?"

I said, "Yes, I'm one of his sheep."

He responded, "Then follow the Shepherd."

I knew what the preacher was saying, but I still asked him, "What do you mean?"

He responded, "The duty of the sheep, is to follow the Shepherd wherever He leads you. The Shepherd will never leave you or forsake you."

I said, "Even if He leads me back into prison for life?"

He responded, "The Shepherd loves us and knows what is best for your eternal salvation. He'll always be there for you, even when you can't understand the troubles of life. When you're in the valley loaded down with sorrows, fears, and concerns, the Shepherd is with you always loving, protecting, and providing for you. The life of the sheep is to place all your faith, hope and trust in Jesus knowing that He will get you through your pilgrimage to the promise land. Do you love Jesus?"

I said, "Yes."

He responded, "Then follow Him wherever He leads you and keep your eyes focused on the eternal award that waits for you."

I replied, "I know what you're saying is right. It's just that I need His grace to deal with the possibility of losing this hearing. I don't want to come under the chastisement of God. I know Christianity is based on facts and not feelings. However, the Christian does have feelings that are important to his relationship with God and others. I would rather die in prison with Christ than die in society without Him. I believe God has allowed me to see this potential spiritual issue now so I could start praying in advance for grace to deal with losing the hearing, if it's God's will that I lose it."

He responded, "Study, pray, and meditate on the scriptures that deal with Jesus being your Shepherd and you being His sheep,[13] and I'll come back and see you next week. Now let me pray for you."

For the rest of the time I was in the jail, I went to this preacher's weekly chapel service. We also met together weekly to talk. A lot of our discussions were on what the Bible says about Jesus being our Shepherd and Christians being His sheep. By God's grace, this preacher taught me and helped me get into my heart one of the most important duties of a child of God. That is for the Christian to follow the Shepherd wherever the Shepherd leads him.

I never knew while I was in the jail that within months of talking with the preacher, my Shepherd would lead me back to the Dade CI Transitional Care Unit (TCU) where I would witness more abuse and non-feeding of inmates than I did during my first stay. I did not know I would witness mentally disabled inmates tortured in a hot shower, the death of Darren Rainey, and the deaths of two other inmates whom, I believe, died of starvation. I did not know six of my relatives would die in the following two years. Finally, I never had any idea I would become the most disliked inmate by Florida Department of Corrections (FDC) staff for following the Shepherd of my soul.

50) Did you continue to have conviction about your discharged from the TCU?

Yes, I had conviction for asking to be discharged from the Dade CI TCU from the time I was discharged, while I was waiting to transfer from Dade CI back to Everglades CI, while at Everglades CI, during both stays in the jail, and upon returning to Everglades CI.

The last few weeks I was in jail, the conviction got so strong, I felt that God wanted me to take action to return to the TCU immediately upon my return to Everglades CI.

51) What was the result of the second evidentiary?

I remained in the Pinellas County jail waiting to hear the results of my second evidentiary hearing. At the end of January 2011, I learned I lost the hearing.

Chapter 6: Everglades CI (January - April 2011)

52) Who did you see upon your return to Everglades CI?

Within 30 minutes of arriving back at Everglades CI, the senior psychiatrist Dr. Rita made arrangements to see me. Her signature on a referral was all I needed to go back to the Transitional Care Unit (TCU). God arranged for Dr. Rita to contact me upon my return and to ask me if I wanted to return to the Dade CI TCU. Dr. Rita asked if I lost the evidentiary hearing. When I told her that I did, she said, "Harold, you have a very long sentence, and things like that can be stressful. If you want, I can refer you to TCU status, so you can take a break. If you want me to do that, I'll do that for you." I found it amazing that God had her meet me upon my return to Everglades CI. I knew God wanted me to go back to the TCU and try to help the inmates there, but I wanted so bad to not go back there. For this reason, I told Dr. Rita I wanted to stay at Everglades CI and not return to the TCU.

I felt very bad about leaving my last time at the Dade CI TCU. I knew the Bible said I should have stayed and tried to help the inmates. The peace and happiness I had from being born again in June 2009 made me feel like I was in heaven while on earth in prison. I seemed all I witnessed when I was in the TCU in 2010 were trying to steal my peace and happiness. I knew the Bible commanded me to help the inmates the best I could, and I tried, but it was too much. I just wanted my peace and happiness. I asked God several times in 2010 why He led me to the TCU to witness such evils, and why couldn't I just enjoy my peace and happiness!

Prior to my conversion, I spent several years trying to make changes in the Florida Department of Corrections (FDC) and help others who needed it. I filed thousands of grievances and engaged in all types of other activities. I really didn't want to do that anymore. I wanted to spend all my time studying the Bible, praying, worshipping, evangelizing and enjoying this peace and happiness that God gave me.

In 2010 and the beginning of 2011, I had a serious inner struggle going on. I was commanded by God in the Bible to put others first, but, to me, my peace and happiness were more important. I sinned in putting myself first. What also added to the seriousness of my sin was that I clearly knew that I was sinning. That's what gave me so much conviction. I was refusing to do what God, who gave me so much, commanded me to do and clearly wanted me to do. I made up every excuse to justify my actions. I dreaded a return to the Dade CI TCU. As I continued to do my best to justify my actions and run from doing what God clearly wanted me to do, God continued to enhance my conviction more and more. He also created conditions that aided me returning to the TCU. As I look back, I realize that I was being like Jonah in my running from what God wanted me to do.

53) Will you tell me about Colonel Clemmons?

My first day back at Everglade CI from court, I found out that Mr. Clemmons was the new colonel. I knew Mr. Clemmons when he was a captain at Apalachee Correctional Institution East Unit in the end of 2007 and beginning of 2008. Mr. Clemmons was known as one of the meanest captains. He worked for Warden Samuel Culpepper. The last time I saw Mr. Clemmons in 2008, he threaten to set me up with several disciplinary reports, if I didn't give him some information he was trying to get. A confidentiality agreement I had signed prevented me from giving him the information he wanted. I was transferred from Apalachee CI East Unit before he could set me up. Mr. Clemmons knew me prior to my conversion, as an inmate who filed lawsuits and grievances against prison staff, and as one who associated with people who investigated the conditions, etc. in prisons. He was not fond of me.

Additionally, while I was in the Dade CI TCU in 2010, a new major took over at Everglades CI. He was considered to be the worst major in South Florida. A lot of staff also thought that. He was still working at Everglades CI, when I returned there from the jail in 2011.

54) What did you think when you saw Colonel Clemmons and Major Morris at Everglades CI?

That God had created conditions that would eventually lead me to returning to the Dade CI TCU.

I liked Everglades CI a lot and didn't want to leave for any reason. Therefore I decided to do my best to stay out of sight and hide from the colonel and the major.

55) Was hiding from the colonel and major stressful?

Yes, I felt like God was saying, "you can stay at Everglades CI with staff who will cause you trouble, or return to Dade CI where staff like you." I also felt like God was saying, "I'll make it where you have to help yourself, if you don't return to Dade CI and help the inmates there who need help."

I understood what God was saying, but I sinned in trying to resist what I knew God wanted me to do.

56) Did you do engage in any evangelism?

Yes, I held a nightly Bible study in my housing wing, and I did open air preaching with Michael Blatch two to three days a week on the recreation yards. I also attended several chapel services a week, and engaged in dozens of apologetics discussions.

57) Did you talk with an assistant attorney general?

Yes. Pinellas County jail records will show that I had two legal calls with an assistant attorney general and that she came and saw me for a legal visit. I also spoke with her on two legal calls while at Everglades CI. I cannot discuss what we spoke about.

58) Does the Bible teach that God chastises those he loves?

Yes, the Bible says:

"For consider Him who endured such hostility from sinners against Himself. Lest you become weary and discouraged in your souls. You have not resisted to bloodshed, striving against sin. And you have forgotten the extortion which speaks to you as sons: My son do not despise the chastening of the Lord, nor be discouraged when you are rebuked by Him; for whom the Lord loves He chastens, and scourges every son whom He receives?

"If you endure chastening, God deals with you as with sons; for what son is there whom a father does not chasten? But if you are without chastening, of which all have become partakers, then you are illegitimate and not sons. Furthermore, we have had human fathers who corrected us, and we paid them respect. Shall we not much more readily be in subjection to the Father of spirits and live? For they indeed for a few days chastened us as seemed best to them, but He for our profit, that we may be partakers of His holiness. Now, no chastening seems to be joyful for the present, but painful; nevertheless, after it yields the peaceable fruit of righteousness to those who have been trained by it[1]."

There's also several other verses in Bible that deal with the chastening of the Lord[2].

59) Please tell me about your prayers to God.

During this period, I prayed to God for help with understanding, in my soul, God's love for His children, and how

49

Christians are called to love others. Christians commonly call a person who hasn't been born again but has religion in his life a "religious person." Prior to being born again, I was a religious person. I was raised to believe in the Trinitarian God of the Bible, that Jesus Christ died for my sins, and that the Bible is the Word of God without any errors. I also attended church, and I read the complete Bible several times. I knew the Bible taught the unconditional love of God and that we are to love one another as Jesus loved us, but I didn't fully understand in my soul the love of God and how the Children of God[3] are to love others. After my conversion I started understanding these things intimately.

I spent a lot of time studying what the Bible and what Christian teachers taught on love. In all my prayers, I also asked God to help me fully understand in my soul His love and how I was to love others. I wanted to love passionately and how God wanted me to love.

60) Did you tell anyone at Everglades about your conviction?

Yes. Prior to going back to the jail, I discussed the things I had witnessed at the Dade CI and the religious conviction I had had since leaving there with my preaching partner Michael Blatch. After returning to Everglades CI from the jail, I told him how my conviction increased while in the jail and how I believed God wanted me to return to the Dade CI TCU. I also told Blatch about my past issues with Colonel Clemmons when Clemmons was a captain.

Blatch said, "I don't want to see you go, but have you ever thought about what happened with Jonah when he tried to run from doing what God wanted him to do?"

Trying to make humor out of the matter, I stated, "Yes, but there's no boats, oceans or whales, so I shouldn't have that problem."

He said, "No, seriously speaking."

I responded, "You're right, but I don't want to go back. Have you ever been in a location that constantly smells like feces and urine, where inmates are constantly asking for food, and the reason why they're so hungry, is because staff won't open the food flaps and let you give them a tray? Have you ever spent hours a day around people who laugh and make jokes out of hurting mentally disabled inmates who can't help themselves? The staff at Dade CI don't victimize the stable inmates. They only victimize the unstable inmates.

"When I was 12 years old, my sister, brother, brother's friend, and I had to take turns babysitting my mom to make sure she wouldn't run away or hurt herself. My mom had a mental breakdown. When my siblings and I fell asleep one time, our mom disappeared. We went looking for her and found her miles away. We knew she wasn't mentally stable, and we didn't want her to get hurt so we decided to do shifts watching her. My brother and his friend would do a 12 hour shift and my sister and I would do another 12 hour shift.

"I learned as a kid, you have to do all you can to help the mentally disabled. A lot of times they don't know what they're doing. I can't be where the mentally disabled are being victimized. It's not right and if I'm around, I'm going to do something about it."

He said, "Maybe God wants you to do something about it."

I responded, "I don't know. That's why I've been discussing it with Him. A lot of me tells me that He does, but I would rather not deal with it."

He said, "Sometimes God wants us to do things that we don't want to do."

I responded, "I know. I also know that if it's God's will that I return to Dade CI, I'll be going back there one way or another."

He said, "Hopefully you don't go like Jonah."

I responded, "I hope not."

61) What happened when Colonel Clemmons identified you?

A few weeks after I returned to Everglades CI from the jail, medical staff issued me a pass to receive two extra rolls of toilet paper a week. I had a stomach problem that caused me to use the bathroom more than most inmates. Back then, inmates were only issued a roll apiece every week.

There were about 10 inmates at Everglades CI who had medical passes for extra toilet paper. Inmates with medical passes for extra toilet paper had to go to the supply room once a week to receive their extra rolls. One morning, I went to the supply room earlier than normal.

When I was leaving there walking toward Center Gate, I noticed Colonel Clemmons and Major Morris talking at Center Gate. I was going to turn and walk toward the chow hall, but I figured that would make me look suspicious. Since I had a hat on, I thought I would be able to walk past the colonel and he wouldn't recognize me. As I walked past him and the major, the major yelled, "Inmate, where did you get those two rolls of toilet paper?"

I said, "Medical staff issued me a pass for extra toilet paper."

He responded, "I didn't ask you that. I asked you where you got the toilet paper from."

I said, "The supply officer."

He responded, "Why did he give you that toilet paper?"

I said, "Because medical staff issued me a pass for two extra rolls of toilet paper a week." After I showed him my medical pass, he took it and my two rolls of toilet paper and walked away from me toward the colonel. The colonel and he then went to the medical department. I thought they would return to Center Gate and give me my pass and toilet paper back, so I asked the Center Gate officer if I could wait there.

About 10 minutes later, I noticed a captain walking toward Center Gate. I thought the captain could help me find out if the colonel and major were coming back, and the captain might help get my pass and toilet paper back.

This captain started working at Everglades CI while I was in the jail. Prior to this situation, I never got close to him, so I didn't know that I knew him. As I walked closer to him, I thought that he looked familiar, but I couldn't remember from where. As I started talking with him about what just happened with the colonel, and major; the captain said, "Weren't you at Apalachee CI East Unit?" When he said that, I knew that was not good. That meant Colonel Clemmons had brought the captain to Everglades CI with him. As soon as the captain mentioned Apalachee CI East Unit, I remembered having several conversations with him when he was a sergeant there.

I responded to the captain's question, "Yes. I knew you looked familiar."

The captain said, "I'm not going to be able to help you. I'm also sure you know that the colonel and major are not going to give you back your pass and toilet paper, and that it probably wouldn't be good for you to wait for them to return, or say anything to them. What do you think?"

I responded, "You know what, you're right. It would be best for me to go to my dorm."

As I walked away, I realized that if the colonel didn't recognize my face when he saw me at Center Gate, he would definitely remember my name when he saw it on my medical pass. The colonel would also definitely remember who I was when he spoke with the captain who remembered me from Apalachee CI.

The rest of that day and afterwards, I thought about how God more than likely caused those events to happen to encourage me to return to Dade CI.

About a week later, all of the inmates with medical passes for extra toilet paper had their passes taken by medical staff. I looked into the matter and learned the colonel ordered medical to void all the medical passes. He did this even though prison procedure stated that security staff were not to hinder the orders of medical staff. The medical passes were authorized by medical staff, so the colonel's actions violated prison procedure. The colonel's actions also violated our Eighth Amendment Right to Adequate Medical Attention, because the medical passes were issued as part of our medical care.

As I thought about how the other inmates lost their passes because of me, it made me feel bad. I wanted to file grievances on the matter and institute other forms of legal actions to get our medical passes back.

Over the next couple weeks, I was subjected to harassment that I believed was brought about by the colonel. I believed that God was creating conditions to encourage me to return to Dade CI. The conditions at Everglades CI were so bad that I started filing paperwork to protect myself from potentially serious retaliation. After I started filing the paperwork, I began weighing the circumstances. If I stayed at Everglades CI, I would probably be subjected to more serious forms of retaliation by Colonel Clemmons. The retaliation could result in me being transferred from there for a long time. If I went back to Dade CI, I could control how long I stayed there simply by asking to be discharged from the TCU whenever I wanted to.

The call to return to the Dade CI TCU was so overwhelming that I finally realized I couldn't continue to run. One night as I lay in my bed thinking about returning, I felt a burden of confusion and sorrow. I was confused because I knew God wanted me to go back to the TCU and try to help the inmates, but I didn't know how to help them. I had sorrow because I didn't really want to return to the TCU, but I knew that God wanted me to and I had to. Despite these feelings, I knew I had to give up what I wanted and try to help others.

When I went to sleep that night I had a dream that I still remember vividly. In my dream, I was back in the county jail talking with the preacher about following the Shepherd (Jesus) wherever He leads me. In my dream, the preacher was stressing the importance of following the Shepherd. In the dream, neither of us mentioned Dade CI, but I knew we were talking about me returning to the Dade CI TCU. When I woke, I knew I had to take action to return to Dade CI as soon as possible. That was where the Shepherd wanted me to go.

That morning, I went to see Ms. Boute. I told her that "When I came back to Everglades CI from the jail, Doctor Rita asked me if I wanted to go back to the TCU. I told her that I didn't want to go. Since then, I've changed my mind. Now, I want to go back to Dade CI as soon as possible. Can we go see Doctor Rita?"

Ms. Boute was surprised to have me in her office without any notice or a call-out pass. She said, "Hempstead, what's going on? You've showed no desire to go back to the TCU. Now you want to go. Is everything OK?"

I responded, "It would be better if you could take me to see Doctor Rita today. If you can't, I understand. I can send her a few dozen requests explaining my reasons for wanting to go back."

Ms. Boute said, "Let me call her and see if she'll see you today." Dr. Rita agreed to talk with me that day, and Ms. Boute walked with me over to her office.

When we got there, Dr. Rita said, "Hempstead, Ms. Boute tells me that you changed your mind and you want to go back to the TCU. I have to have a reason to refer you to a TCU. I can't just refer you without a reason. What reason can I place on the referral?"

I responded, "You can write down that I lost my evidentiary hearing in January, and I'm having a lot of anxiety and stress."

Dr. Rita said, "You haven't shown any signs that losing the hearing has bothered you. Nor have you shown any signs of anxiety or stress."

I responded, "If you're saying you need a record, I understand."

Dr. Rita said, "Yes, I need a record to protect me. I can't just refer you out of nowhere. In January, I had just cause for an immediate referral because you had just lost the hearing. It's now months later. Let's build a record, and I'll do the referral for you. OK?"

I responded, "OK."

I knew what she meant when she said she wanted to build a record. She wanted me to have several meetings with her over a four to six week period and use that record to do the referral. I knew she didn't want me to send her a whole bunch of inmate request forms that were written in such a way that she could use them to support my referral to the TCU. However, I decided to send her the request forms anyway. Over the next week, I sent her about 35 request forms. She didn't want me to do this, because she had to respond to all of them. Dr. Rita also knew that my prison files showed that I had the ability to file hundreds of requests and grievances per month.

About two weeks later, she did the referral to send me back to the TCU.

62) Tell me about conversation with Michael Blatch concerning your return to the Dade CI TCU.

Acts 16:6-10 talks about when Paul received the Macedonian call. *Acts 16:9* mentions how a man appeared to Paul in a vision and pleaded with him saying, "Come over to Macedonia and help us." This vision is what caused Paul to go to Macedonia. In my conversation with Blatch, I mentioned I believed God was giving me a Macedonian call to return to the Dade CI TCU. I told Blatch that I obviously didn't have any visions, but the conviction, call, and urging to go was so strong, I took it as a clear call that I had to go back to Dade CI.

Blatch didn't know much about how the FDC was managed; thus, he was surprised I was actually able to actually obtain a transfer so quickly.

I transferred back to Dade CI about a week or two after this conversation. I never saw Blatch, Rogers or any of the Christian brothers at Everglade CI again. And, I never imagined I would witness things that would change my life and the history of the FDC.

Chapter 7: Dade CI (April 2011 - January 17, 2013)

63) Please tell me about your first day back at the Dade CI TCU.

I believe I arrived on April 28, 2011. When I arrived at Dade CI, Officers Eli and Townsend escorted me from the bus to the TCU. While they were inventorying my property, Dr. Basasa and Ms. Koel stopped by and told the officers and me that I was zero-point status and approved to work as an orderly. I was somewhat surprised that the Treatment Team did that so quickly. They usually take two or more days to place and inmate on zero-point status.

Point status refers to whether or not an inmate is put in restraints prior to leaving their cells. Zero-point status is no restraints. Inmates with two-point status are to wear both handcuffs and shackles when exiting their cells. Sometimes security staff only put handcuffs on two-point status inmates.

Security staff said they were happy to see me back. This was probably because they deemed me to be a fast and effective orderly. In other words, I made their jobs easier.

I remember the following security staff as working on the Westside my first day back: Lieutenant McCrae; Sergeants Lewis and Johnathan; and Officers Eli, Gruben, Weary, Perez, Gibson, Cobas, and Clarke.

The 8:00 am to 4:00 pm shift already had orderlies working when I arrived on the Westside TCU. Officer Gruben told me security staff would have me out to work the next day.

That night, on the 4:00 pm to 12:00 am shift, medical staff were taking the vitals of the inmates housed on the Westside. Officer Gibson came to my cell to escort me to have my vitals taken. While at my cell, he told me that Lieutenant McCrae was back on that shift, and he was in the room where the nurses were taken vitals. Officer Gibson also said that he and Sergeant Johnathan had spoken with Lieutenant McCrae, and he said they could use me as an orderly. Finally, Officer Gibson said it would be best if I didn't say anything to McCrae unless he said something to me. Officer Gibson said this because he didn't know if McCrae remembered the issue he had with me in 2010. When I went in the room, Lieutenant McCrae said, "Yeah, I remember him. You can use him as an orderly. He was a good worker." I looked upon this as God wanting me to start orderly work on all the shifts as soon as possible.

64) How did you feel upon your return to the TCU?

Prior to my return, I found it hard to believe I was actually going back. I discussed my return with God in my prayers. I wanted to do what God wanted me to do which was return to the TCU and help the inmate patients, but several things weighed on my mind. I had to give up a lot of my privileges, everything that I could do in population, and all of my friends at Everglades CI. Additionally, I would be confined to one building for months, constantly witness starving and abuse, and constantly hear inmates saying they were hungry and wanted food; I had to constantly smell feces and urine and deal with the heat on the Westside, and numerous other things. It was hard to accept all these factors. My motivation was that God had shown me since I left the TCU in 2010 that He wanted me to do my best to help the inmates in the TCU.

Even though there were many negatives to being housed in the TCU, I tried to focus on the positives. One of the positives was that I no longer had the conviction I had from running from God's will. A second positive was that I was happy that I was doing what God wanted me to do. A third positive was that I was around a lot of staff who liked me. A fourth positive was that I had several benefits from being an orderly.

65) Did you have a plan to try to stop the starving and abuse?

From the time I was discharged from the TCU in 2010 until I was placed back in that unit in 2011, I had close to a year of conversations with God about what I could have done to help the inmates in 2010, and what I could do if I returned there. As a result of all of my prayers and giving it a lot of thought, I decided (1) I would pray without ceasing for God's guidance, for Him to convert the staff in the TCU, and for Him to soften their hearts so they stopped hurting the inmate patients. (2) I would engage in as much evangelism as possible with the staff. (3) I would try to raise their awareness of the legal consequences they would face if they were caught starving and abusing the mentally disabled inmates. (4) I would help the staff as much as possible, be as much as a friend to them as I could be, and show as much concern as I could for them.

66) How did you make staff aware of the legal consequences?

I told them stable inmates in the TCU who witnessed abusive staff actions could report those actions to the Department of Justice, Federal Bureau of Investigations, Florida Department of Health, and other agencies. I also explained to the staff how the mounted security cameras were a threat to them. Finally, I told the staff how all it would take was for one bad incident to occur to an inmate, and everything could come crumbling down.

67) What type of inmates were being starved and abused?

It was always the severely mentally disabled inmates. They were the inmates who really needed mental health care.

68) Were all the security staff in the Westside TCU starving and abusing inmates?

No, but they all knew about it.

69) What privileges did the inmates have who were housed on the Westside?

Most of them were allowed out of their cells for one or two hours of recreation or day room activities per week. They didn't have access to a television. If they owned a radio, they could have it in their cells under certain conditions. They could make one or two collect phone calls a week, if staff were in the mood to allow them to do such. They could send and receive mail. Once a week, a coach would pass-out books and magazines. The inmates could also have certain types of personal property in their cells if they weren't on certain statuses. They could also order a limited number of items from the canteen once a week if they had money in their inmate account and they weren't on certain statuses.

70) What types of abuse were inmates experiencing when you arrived to the Westside TCU in 2011?

- Inmates were still being denied food.
- Inmates were still being physically abused.
- Inmates were still being subjected to chemical warfare with bleach and ammonia.
- Inmates were still being forced to shower by staff who used buckets of chemicals and water.
- Inmates were still being denied clean clothes, toilet paper, soap, toothpaste, and toothbrushes.

Staff had stopped loafing inmates prior to my 2010 discharge from the Westside TCU

71) Were there any benefits to being an orderly?

Yes. Staff ordered extra food for the orderlies to eat, sell, or give away. Orderlies were allowed out of their cells for hours a day moving all around the TCU, and they had access to more toilet paper, soap, toothpaste, books, magazines, and changes of clothes than the other inmates. Finally, staff would bring the orderlies food from society.

72) How was your relationship with security staff in the TCU?

It was good in 2010, and it continued to improve as the years passed.

73) Did you sign up for any college courses in 2011 while in the TCU?

Yes. I signed up for a college course in Biblical studies to obtain a Doctor of Biblical Studies Degree. It was a six year course that I completed in less than three years. I had to write 4,000 to 6,000 words in essays on each book of the Bible. I scored an "A" on every essay. I obtained my Doctor of Biblical Studies Degree in 2013.

I also signed up to do a college course in Paralegal Studies with Blackstone Career Institute. I completed this course in 2013 and obtained a Paralegal Certification. I scored an overall grade of 96% in Paralegal Studies.

I worked on both of these college courses while I was housed in the TCU in 2011 and 2012.

74) Did the college courses and your grades cause staff to see you as knowledgeable in the Bible and law?

Yes. Along with my ability to effectively answer the questions they asked me about the Bible, religions, and the law.

Chapter 8: Dade CI (April 2011 - July 5, 2011)

75) How many shifts did security staff work in 2011 and 2012?

They worked three shifts (12:00 am to 8:00 am, 8:00 am to 4:00 pm, and 4:00 pm to 12:00 am) until August 2012. Around August 2012, the majority of the security staff in the Florida Department of Correction (FDC) went to 12-hour shifts. Some of the security staff worked swing shifts which were eight-hour shifts.

76) How many shifts did you work in the TCU?

Until July 5, 2011, I worked all three shifts, which totaled about 14 hours a day.

77) Tell me more about the non-feeding of inmates.

The non-feeding of inmates was just like it was in 2010. Security staff were not feeding one or more inmates during almost every meal. Sometimes up to about 20 inmates would be skipped per meal. Some inmates were consistently denied one or more meals per day for days and sometimes for several weeks straight. Security staff only did this to the severely mentally disabled. Several who were being denied food continually asked staff and other inmates for food.

78) Please tell me about Oscar Davis.

I was told that Oscar Davis was missing both of his eyes because he pulled them both out. I was also told that he was in prison for raping an elderly lady. He was very mentally unstable, very loud, and much disliked by security staff. He was one of the inmates who was denied the most food by staff on the Westside. I remember him being denied one to three meals a day almost every day. Davis died at the end of 2011, while I was housed in the TCU. I'll explain more about him later on in this book.

79) What about Darryl Richardson?

I was told that Darryl Richardson was in prison for three counts of murder. When I first met him, he was around 185 to 195 pounds of muscle. He was very mentally unstable and would continuously talk and argue with himself. During his first few days on the Westside, he refused to return the food trays when we were picking them up after meals were served. Thus, the staff assigned him to receive Styrofoam trays for all his meals. Then Richardson refused to give those trays back and began flushing the Styrofoam down his toilet. Several times the flushed trays clogged the main sewage pipe on the wing were Richardson was housed. After this, staff only fed Richardson when they had time to deal with him or when people security staff wanted to hide the abuse from were in the wing.

Richardson eventually died. I explain more about him later on in this book.

80) Tell me the issue with inmates breaking sprinklers in their cells on the Westside.

Between 2010 and the end of December 2012, several of the inmates, who were disciplinary problems and who had not been fed, broke sprinklers that were in their cells. They did this because they knew the staff would charge them with felony destruction of state property and send them to a Dade County, Florida Jail. During 2011 and 2012, I told many of the inmates who broke sprinkles to tell law enforcement, their attorney, the state attorney, and the court that the inmates broke the sprinkler because the staff was not feeding them and other inmates in the TCU. The first inmate I told to do this was a Spanish inmate who broke a sprinkler in his Wing J-2 cell in May 2011.

I told them to do this because I hoped one of the people the inmates talked to would do something to help put a stop to the non-feeding of the inmates. I also wanted a paper trail that I could use later on as evidence.

81) Did you tell the federal government and media in 2014 and 2015 about the above sprinkler issue?

Yes. If you purchase the police and fire marshal reports, and court papers on the inmates who broke sprinklers in 2011 and 2012 in the Dade CI TCU, they should show that several of the inmates told the police, fire marshals, attorneys, and the court that they broke the sprinklers because security staff weren't feeding them.

82) Why did staff remove food from inmate food trays?

There were lots of situations when security staff couldn't just deny an inmate a food tray at meal times. Under those conditions, security staff removed one or more items from their trays before the tray was distributed. Usually, they removed the main course or dessert.

The food was removed from the trays in the hallway that ran from Central to the Westside. By removing the food in the hallway, staff avoided any inmates witnessing the food being removed, other than orderlies who staff trusted. Staff would then put the trays that had the food missing on them on top of the food cart and tell the orderly who was passing-out the trays what cells those trays were to be given to. When we were serving meals and inmates got the trays with food missing, they would tell the staff that their trays were missing food. Staff would then act like it was just a mistake that was made by chow hall workers. Most of the time staff acted like they were going to do their best to get the chow hall to send the food that was missing, or staff would say they were going to replace it with leftover food. However, they never replaced it. The majority of stable inmates on the Westside knew that staff was responsible for the food being removed from the trays. This abuse occurred both of the times I was housed in the Westside TCU.

83) Did you ever witness security staff place medicine in an inmate's food?

Yes. In May or June 2011 inmate Cecil Livingston was acting out as a result of his mental health disability. He was yelling, kicking his cell door, and throwing feces and urine under it. Sergeant Lewis told me to go to the inmates on the Westside and offer each inmate two extra trays of food for a pill that would make a person sleep. He wanted me to tell the inmates I needed the medicine because I was tired and I couldn't sleep. While Sergeant Lewis was instructing me to do this, his officers were laughing with each other, and joking about killing Livingston. Sergeant Lewis responded to their jokes by saying, "We're not going to kill anybody. We're just going to help him go to sleep."

I went to the cell door on the Westside and acted like I was doing what the staff told me to do. However, I didn't ask any inmates for any medicine. When I was finished, I went back to the officer station and told staff "I couldn't find any medicine."

They continued to joke with each other about Sergeant Lewis wanting to spike Livingston's food. They also joked about me not looking good enough for the medicine because I was scared. Since staff wasn't able to find any medicine to make Livingston go to sleep, they decided to go into his cell and physically try to make him calm down.

Around 2:30 pm, Sergeant Lewis told me to get the cleaning supplies together and go to Livingston's cell. Sergeant Lewis, and Officers Gruben, Weary, Sakay, and Piggot met me in front of Livingston's cell. Staff knew Livingston was out of feces and urine to throw under his cell door because he had been throwing it for two to three hours. However, Livingston was still yelling and kicking his cell door, and the inside of his cell had to be cleaned.

After the cell door was opened, the sergeant and officers entered Livingston's cell. They then forced Livingston to lay face down on one part of his mattress and folded the other part of Livingston's mattress on top of him. Once the mattress was over him, staff took turns punching his legs which weren't protected by the mattress and in his upper body, which was under the mattress. This was done while Officer Gruben used his body weight to keep Livingston under the mattress. As this was going on, and the staff was laughing about the situation, Officer Piggot directed me to clean up the area of Livingston's cell next to his cell door.

Even though staff tried to make humor out of the situation, I could tell afterward that Livingston was physically hurt. The rest of the day, he was quiet. That same night, Livingston complained a great deal about pain. Staff on that shift allowed him to see a nurse. I don't know if the nurse who saw Livingston made any notations in Livingston's medical files about his pain. It is possible she recorded something in his file.

About a week or two after this incident when we were doing cell clean up, Officer Weary found some medicine in an inmate's cell that the inmate wasn't supposed to have. When the officer showed the medicine to Sergeant Lewis, he joked about wishing they had the medicine when they had the issue with Livingston. Sergeant Lewis said, "I wonder what type of medicine it is." He then went and asked a nurse what type of medicine it was. The nurse identified the medication as the type of medicine that would make a person tired. Sergeant Lewis then hid the medication so he'd have it when he needed it.

The next time Sergeant Lewis worked on the Westside, and an inmate in Wing J-2 refused to give his food tray back, Sergeant Lewis ordered a Styrofoam tray of food from the chow hall. He crushed one of these pills into powder form and sprinkled the crushed pill on the icing of the cake being served. He then told Officer Gruben to go tell the inmate that he would give him the Styrofoam tray of food in exchange for the hard tray with no food on it that was in the inmate's cell.

Officer Gruben laughed and responded, "I'm not going to be seen on camera giving the inmate that tray. If he dies, I'll be blamed. I'm already in too much trouble." Sergeant Lewis then tried to convince his other officers to do such. As everybody joked and laughed, they told Sergeant Lewis they weren't going to give the inmate the tray that had the crushed pill in the desert. Eventually, the sergeant said he'd do it.

Sergeant Lewis was able to use the Styrofoam tray of food to convince the mentally disabled inmate to give him the empty hard tray. He came back and told us that the first thing the inmate ate was the cake. For the next hour or so, the staff joked with each other about matters relating to the inmate dying. When the staff saw the inmate laying down and not moving, some of them continued to joke, saying the inmate was dead.

Sergeant Lewis wasn't joking. I could tell he was worried because he told Officer Piggot to escort me to my cell and lock me in. About 10 minutes later, Officer Piggot came to my cell to get me and told me the inmate was not dead. He also said that Sergeant Lewis wanted me to clean the inmate's cell.

When we got to Wing J-2, the inmate was handcuffed, and Sergeant Lewis was slapping the inmate and saying "You think you're crazy. I'm crazier than you. The next time I tell you to give me my tray back, you better listen to me. Do you understand?"

The officers were laughing because Sergeant Lewis was making a lot of faces trying to play crazy.

Later on, I was told the staff opened the inmate's cell door, went in together, and quickly handcuffed him, in case he was sleeping and woke up. After handcuffing him, the felt his pulse and found out he was still alive. After numerous unsuccessful attempts to wake him up, Sergeant Lewis used the inmate's drinking cup to obtain water from the toilet and poured it on the inmate's face. When the water hit the inmate's face, he woke up.

About a month after this incident, this tactic was being used by several staff members on the 8:00 am to 4:00 pm, and 4:00 pm to 12:00 am shifts. Throughout 2011 and 2012, this tactic was probably used 30 or more times. Mainly, staff used mental health medicines, but they also used blood pressure medicines.

A few of the security staff became very good at identifying pills just by looking at them. After a nurse told the staff about the book called ***Physicians' Desk Reference***, staff learned how to identify pills. Security staff eventually started adding other substances, etc. to the food of inmates.

In 2011 and 2012, I made several unsuccessful attempts to find the locations where security staff hid the pills they had taken from inmates.

The staff who spiked the food of inmates were Sergeants Lewis and Seals; and Officers Gruben, Weary, Gibson, Clarke, Cobas, and Sakay. Staff added medicines to the food of the following inmates on the Westside: William Wallace, Michael Alfonso, Daniel Geiger, Oscar Davis, Halden Casey, Ricky Schieb, Brian Hernandez, Marion Odom, Wendel Sanders, and several others.

84) Will you tell me about the Joseph Swilling incident?

In May or June 2011, when I was housed in Cell J-1104, Joseph Swilling lived in Cell J-1102 or J-1103. One day, Coach Ocanna took about 20 inmates out of their cells for day room activities in Wing J-1. Sergeant Tarver had Officers Gruben and Weary supervising the day room activities with Coach Ocanna.

Officers Lyn Ping, Perez, Eli, and Day were also assigned to the Westside that day. While day room activities were going on, I was in the Wing J-1 day room with all the inmates. I was cleaning up a minor flood of feces and sewage in front of Cell J-1111. About five minutes after Officer Day entered Wing J-1, I heard Inmate Swilling tell her "You're not supposed to be working in Wing J-1 because you're a lady."

Officer Day responded, "Go to your cell and lock in Swilling." When Swilling didn't comply, she directed him a second time to go back to his cell.

When Officers Gruben and Weary stood up from the tables they were sitting at, Swilling stood up and said, "Fine, I'll go back to my cell."

Swilling walked about 20 feet toward his cell before Officer Weary got in front of Swilling and said, "Swilling, stop bucking and go back to your cell."

Swilling responded, "I was going back to my cell, and you jumped in my way."

When Swilling attempted to walk around Officer Weary to continue walking back to his cell, Officer Weary grabbed Swilling. Officer Gruben then grabbed Swilling from behind. Both officers then started moving Swilling in the direction of the front door of Wing J-1, which was in the opposite direction of Swilling's cell. As the officers did this, Swilling kept yelling, "Let me go, I'm trying to go back to my cell."

When the officers got Swilling to the front door of Wing J-1, the booth officer pushed the button to open the front door. When the front door was open, Sergeant Tarver grabbed Swilling and slammed him to the ground in the hallway. Within seconds, Sergeant Tarver and Officers Weary, Gruben, Eli, and Jenkins were kicking and stomping Swilling. While this was happening, Counselor Ms. Arencibia came out from the back office in Wing J-1 yelling, "Stop kicking him! Stop kicking him now!"

Officers Day and Lyn Ping then began escorting the inmates who were in the Wing J-1 day room back into their cells and locking them in. Staff then passed-out witness statement forms to the mentally disabled inmates in Wing J-1. They didn't offer any witness statement forms to any of the stable inmates who witnessed what happened. The reason the officers pushed Swilling into the hallway beyond the front door was that there were no security cameras in the hallway.

The next day, when I was cleaning in Wing J-3, Officer Weary opened the fire exit door for that wing. After he and Officer Piggot went outside, Officer Weary yelled, "Hempstead, come out here and check this out." I didn't feel comfortable going outside with them, but I had to go. When I got outside, Officers Weary and Piggot were joking about the Swilling incident. In the middle of their joking, Officer Weary said, "What happened yesterday, Hempstead?"

I knew he wanted me to answer "nothing," so I responded, "I didn't see anything. I was cleaning the mess in front of Cell 111." I said this because I thought it was best for my safety at that time.

In 2012, I brought this incident up to Officer Eli inquiring how they were able to get Ms. Arencibia not to say anything that would get security staff in trouble for the Swilling incident. Officer Eli responded, "We had a talk with her."

Swilling received a disciplinary report for this incident. It's my position that the disciplinary report was false because he was set up to be physically battered. I also believe that Swilling filed some grievances on this incident.

I believe fear of security staff is what kept Ms. Arencibia from taking any action in 2011 to help Swilling. George Mallinckrodt mentioned this incident in his book, ***Getting Away with Murder***. I also believe this incident is briefly mentioned in one or more ***Miami Herald*** newspaper articles

85) Tell me about Officer Gibson's actions on the 4:00 pm to12:00 am shift.

Officer Gibson's nickname was "Big Gib." Most of the inmates in the TCU considered him to be Sergeant Johnathan's muscle. He was about 6'4" tall and weighed 340 pounds. I can't remember how many cells I saw Officer Gibson enter and use physical force to batter inmates. Officer Gibson pushed inmates in their cells and into walls, grabbed them by their throats, and slapped their faces. When he slapped an inmate, he never used all his strength. A few inmates accused Officer Gibson of using serious force on them on the Eastside section of the TCU, but I never witnessed any of those incidents.

86) Which nurses were helping cover up abuses in the TCU?

It's my position that nurses Nickolis, Robinson, Mayweather, Jensen, and Astre were aiding in covering up abuses. Nurse Nickolis was the longtime girlfriend of Sergeant Lewis. I was told that Nurse Robinson had dated a sergeant on the midnight shift and Officers Piggot and Thompson. Nurse Mayweather was an ex-correctional officer (possibly sergeant) from South Florida Reception Center. Nurse Jensen was Officer Eli's girlfriend. Nurse Astre was allegedly Nurse Edgehill's husband, and he was also personal friends with several security staff.

87) What did an inmate do to Officer Perez in Wing J-2 in May or June 2011?

There was an inmate on the Westside with a big cut across his throat. I was told he killed his girlfriend and sliced his own throat. Somehow he didn't die and ended up in prison for killing his girlfriend. He was in the TCU because he wasn't stable.

Officer Perez was well known for harassing inmates for no reason. I believe he liked to upset inmates as a form of a sport. In May or June 2011, Officer Perez upset the inmate with the scar across his throat. The inmate punched Officer Perez in the face and broke his nose and, possibly, his jaw. The inmate was transferred a short time later. I believe the inmate was issued a disciplinary report for punching Officer Perez.

88) What happened with Inmate Dics in spring 2011?

Dics slept in or around Cell J-1218. He constantly lay in his bed and barely moved. When we served the meals, he never got up to get his trays or drinks. When staff slid his mail under his cell door, he never got up to read it and left it on his cell floor. He also never showered, never ordered canteen, never wrote letters or read the mail he received, never talked, and never made any noise. He was always given a Styrofoam tray of food for each meal. Most of the time, staff told me to leave Dics Styrofoam tray of food on his sink.

One of my many jobs was to clean the cells of the inmates who were too mentally disabled to clean them. Every time I cleaned Dics' cell, staff physically removed him from the bed so I could clean it. His bed was covered with dry skin and more large flakes fell to the floor when the staff removed him from the bed. He had a serious issue that caused his skin to be dehydrated and to flake off. I had to clean his bed and the floor of his cell.

Once while we were cleaning his cell, Officers Sakay and Piggot couldn't get Dics to get out of bed. A lot of security staff didn't like touching Dics because of how bad his skin looked. As these Officers joked with each other, Officer Sakay said, "I know how to get Dics out of bed. Hempstead, give me the bio-hazard mop." I gave him the mop not knowing what he was going to do with it. Officer Sakay then said, "Dics, you get out of that bed and get against the wall, or I'm going to rub this crap, blood, and urine mop all over you." When Dics didn't move, Officer Sakay said, "This is your last chance."

When Dics still did not move, Officer Sakay rubbed the mop all over Dics' body from his neck to his feet. Despite the sickness (and evilness) of this act, Dics' still didn't move. They gave up on trying to get him out of bed that day.

All the staff knew I used the bio-hazard mop to clean up feces, blood, and urine.

89) Was inmate Dics ever given a Forced Hygiene Compliance Shower?

Yes. In May of June 2011, the Mental Health Treatment Team ordered that Dics be showered, and if he refused to shower, he was to receive a Forced Hygiene Compliance Shower. The staff made several attempts to get Dics to shower that day. When Dics continued to refuse to respond to staff, the duty warden was contacted and told that the Mental Health Treatment Team ordered that Dics receive a Forced Hygiene Compliance Shower. After the warden authorized such, the cell extraction team was activated.

A cell extraction team consists of five security staff, usually all men who are big and in good shape. Members of this team wear padded clothing (called turtle suits), helmets, and gloves.

I was placed on standby to clean Dics' cell when the cell extraction team removed him to Wing J-2 to shower. An assistant warden, captain, major, the senior psychiatrist, a counselor, and two or three nurses all convened in Wing J-1 and in the officers' station to supervise the cell extraction and Forced Hygiene Compliance Shower. The cell extraction team and an officer holding a camera entered Wing J-1. As the team did the extraction, the officer with the camera recorded it. The team took Dics to Wing J-2 and stripped him behind a half-body shield. The team then went in the shower with Dics and showered him. A half-body shield was placed in front of the shower so the camera officer could record the Forced Hygiene Compliance Shower, but not record below Dics' waist. When the team was done showering Dics, they escorted him to a cell in Wing J-2. Dics never returned to his cell in Wing J-1. The camera officer recorded Dics and the team until Dics was secured in a cell in Wing J-2. Sergeant Donaldson and Officer Gruben were two of the staff on the extraction team.

90) Will you tell me about your food smuggling operations?

In 2010, I smuggled a lot of food to the inmates who were being denied such. In 2011 and 2012, I smuggled even more food to hungry inmates. Security staff ordered extra trays each meal to give to the orderlies. Additionally, the orderlies would get the trays of food that weren't given to the inmates. The extra trays were divided between the orderlies. From each meal, I put all the food I could in baggies, potato chip bags, etc. When I cleaned the wings, I slid the bags of food under the doors of inmates who weren't being fed. I hid the bags of food in my pockets and socks, and down my shirt, which I kept tucked in. I never had enough food to give some to all the inmates being denied food, so I tried to focus on the ones who were being denied the most food. A few times, staff caught me doing this, and most of the time staff believed my excuses. A few inmates told staff what I was doing. Sometimes when I was caught or told on, staff kept a closer eye on me and made it harder for me to get extra food.

91) How did security staff treat the stable inmates?

They would give an average of one to five extra trays away per meal to stable inmates housed on the Westside. They also wouldn't harass the stable inmates and would commonly engage them in small talk on sports, movies, music, etc. This was done to keep the stable inmates as "cool" as possible with security staff, and less likely to tell on security staff for mistreating inmates.

The majority of security staff tried to make humor out of everything, including the evil things they did.

92) Why do you keep a journal?

Over my first several years in prison, I was involved with a lot of things that caused me to think I might one day be killed by Florida prison staff in retaliation for asserting my First Amendment rights. I wanted to make sure if I was, there would be numerous paper trails that showed my activities in the days, weeks, months, etc. prior to my death. The paper trails could be followed to find out what happened to me.

I kept a journal both times I was in the Dade CI TCU. Following Darren Rainey's death, the Miami-Dade Police Department and federal government found out that I kept a journal. They asked me for a copy of my journal entries I made while I was housed in the TCU. I provided them and the media with copies. The ***Miami Herald*** newspaper and other media representative mentioned my journal in several articles. In 2016, I copyrighted my journal to make sure it's not used for any reasons

I did not approve of. My journal mentions a lot of things I witnessed while housed in the TCU.

93) What type of evangelism did you engage in on the Westside before July 5, 2011?

I used several different evangelism styles on the staff, and at that time, I was only able to use one style on the inmates. I asked the Pentecostal staff and Jehovah Witness staff, a lot of questions about the controversial doctrines of these two religions. For instance, with the Pentecostals, I asked questions about their beliefs concerning the gospel, tongues, miracles, healings, prophets, apostles, and worship. With the staff who were Jehovah Witnesses, I asked questions about their beliefs concerning the being of God, the deities of Jesus and the Holy Spirit, and the Jehovah Witness translation of the Bible. I always asked questions I knew they couldn't answer. This caused them to research, and come back to tell me what they found. By doing this, it allowed me to discuss the Bible with them.

Additionally, I constantly discussed with them how God is a just God who commands us to be obedient to His commandments[1]; and how we are commanded to fear God[2]. Finally, I constantly discussed hell and how nobody knows when they're going to die. With the staff who weren't Christian, I used apologetics to explain the reasonableness of the existence of God and the historicity and authority of the Bible. I constantly discussed with them how God has made it where there is no peace for the wicked[3], how God could give them up to the uncleanness in the lusts of their hearts and their vile passions, and give them over to a reprobated mind[4], and how God could give them Godly sorrow to lead them to repentance[5]. Finally, I constantly discussed the gospel[6], with the staff, during the times I was housed in the TCU. I also had a lot of Christian books that I was able to use in my evangelism.

As it concerned the inmates, I slid Christian tracts under their cell doors every chance I could get.

94) Tell me about your conversations with Classification Officer Ms. Koel.

I previously mentioned I had a civil rights complaint lawsuit pending in the Tallahassee, Florida Federal District Court since

December 2007. Following my conversion, I greatly desired to dismiss the lawsuit. Upon my return to Dade CI, I told Ms. Koel how I was in settlement discussions on my lawsuit, and I wanted to dismiss it.

Back then, I thought that I wanted to be interstate compacted to another state prison system because of the things that had happened to me during my first several years in prison. I told Ms. Koel I wanted to be interstate compacted, and that I would dismiss the lawsuit if the Florida Department of Correction (FDC) agreed to such. After about a month of discussions, Ms. Koel said that this was agreeable to the FDC. She also said it could take years for me to be interstate compacted unless I agreed to be placed on protective management status first. She said if I agreed to be placed on protective management, to give her a request to do so and would be approved. Being on protective management status would cause me to be placed higher on the list for an interstate compact. I agreed and gave Ms. Koel the request.

I really didn't think prison officials would approve my request because the reason I stated I needed protection was also the primary reason behind my federal lawsuit. Ms. Koel processed my request around the beginning of June 2011, and the Institutional Classification Team recommended I be placed on protective management status.

95) How was your prayer life during this period?

I constantly prayed about everything that was going on. I was under tremendous stress, and I always felt physically and spiritually drained. A lot of my prayers resulted in tears because I was doing my best to fix the problems I saw, but I continually felt it was more than I could handle. I spent hours either on my knees praying or pacing the floor of my cell in prayer, praying to God for strength, wisdom, and guidance.

96) Please summarize the TCU in April - July 5, 2011?

Security staff was engaging in chemical warfare pouring ammonia and bleach in inmates' cells, placing mental health and blood pressure medicines in inmates' food, constantly denying inmates their food and physically abusing them, throwing buckets of chemicals and water on inmates like they were animals, and denying inmates clean clothes and hygiene items.

Every day and on every shift, I heard inmates yelling, constantly asking for food and saying how hungry they were, and I constantly had to listen to staff making humorous remarks about all the evils they did.

I was constantly bagging food and trying to find ways to get the food to inmates without getting caught. I had to look for the pills that were being placed in the food inmates ate. I was always thinking of ways to get staff to stop what they were doing without them deeming me a threat. I had to think of evangelism tactics that could be helpful. Finally, I had to do all my normal duties as an orderly, in addition to working on my law work and college courses, studying the Bible, praying, writing my family, and the list keeps going.

Chapter 9: Dade CI (July 5, 2011 - January 1, 2012)

97) What happened on July 5, 2011?

Classification and security staff recognized that I was approved for placement on protective management status. Thus, I was moved from Wing J-1 to Wing J-3, Cell 101. Security staff were supposed to stop working me as an orderly weeks prior to July 5, 2011, but they didn't. I continued working all three shifts for several more days.

98) Why couldn't you work as an orderly while on protective management status?

There's no prison rule or procedure that said I couldn't. It was just that prior to 2011, security staff never allowed an inmate on protective management status to work as an orderly. Security staff knew that inmates on protective management status were supposed to be given the highest degree of protection in the Florida Department of Corrections (FDC). Security staff thought the best way to provide protection was to not allow protective management inmates to work as orderlies. FDC rules specify as long as staff kept inmates on general population status from having physical contact with protective management inmates, then protective management inmates could work as orderlies. Also, by rule, my protective management status could have been suspended while I was in the Transitional Care Unit (TCU).

99) Who were the officers assigned to Wings J-1 and J-3 between 8:00 am and 12:00 am?

In Wing J-1, Officer Piggot was assigned on the 8:00 am to 4:00 pm shift, and Officer Sakay was on the 4:00 pm to 12:00 am shift. In Wing J-3, Officer Lyn Ping was assigned to the 8:00 am to 4:00 pm shift, and Officer Clarke was on the 4:00 pm to 12:00 am shift.

100) Who got security to stop working you as an orderly?

At the beginning of July 2011, classification officer Ms. Koel got security staff to stop working me as an orderly. I was told that Ms. Koel told security staff I had a long history of speaking out against things I deemed to be wrong. She also told them that if anything happened to me, I would, more than likely, sue staff. Additionally, if I saw something I disagreed with, I would speak-out against it. Ms. Koel came to her conclusions from my prison files and the federal lawsuit I had pending.

I didn't think it was right that she said these things to security staff because it could have created serious problems for me. What I still can't understand is that, even though Ms. Koel had documents that proved everything she said, for some reason security staff didn't take her advice. I know Ms. Koel ended up showing the documents that proved what she was saying about me to Major McCarter in December 2011 or January 2012, but I don't think she ever showed them to any other security staff.

101) When did you first speak out against a state official who did wrong?

The first time was with Roosevelt Copeland when I was a teenager. He was a guard at the Pinellas County, Florida Juvenile Detention Center. As a result of me speaking out against his improper conduct, he lost his job. The second time I spoke out was against St. Petersburg Police Officer Mike Brown. He was committing sexual misconduct with kids at the Police Athletic League. The police set me up with two frivolous felony charges for it. The state attorney knew I was set-up, so they dismissed the charges.

102) You had a history of speaking out. Why did you wait until inmates died to speak out against staff in the TCU?

A lot of times when a person speaks out against something that's wrong, it doesn't stop the improper conduct and sometimes it'll stop it temporarily, but not permanently. For instance, when I spoke out against St. Petersburg Police Officer Mike Brown, his friends aided in covering up his abuse for almost a decade.

When I first spoke out about the Dade CI TCU staff, they continued to engage in misconduct for more than a year and a half. When the *Miami Herald* newspaper started publishing articles on the Dade CI TCU staff, and multiple federal, state, etc. investigations were initiated against staff in the TCU, the Dade CI staff misconduct stopped for several months. Close to a year later, I was told by reliable sources that TCU staff were back to denying inmates their food and physically abusing them.

Back then I felt that God wanted me to try and reform the staff. I thought that if I could do this, it would cause permanent change in the TCU. I tried my best to bring about this change, but unfortunately it didn't work.

103) Why did security staff house you in Wing J-3, Cell 101?

It was the closest cell to the front door of Wing J-3. The food carts were stationed in front of Cell 101 when they came into Wing J-3 for each meal. Additionally, Cell J3-101 was situated off from the rest of the cells with a table located outside of the cell that staff could sit on while they talked with me. Moreover, inmates who like to masturbate while looking at female staff are Called "Gunners." The staff didn't want any "Gunners" in that cell.

Finally, by placing me in that cell, it was easier for staff to give me extra trays at each meal. They could also sit down and talk with me without worrying about inmates interrupting or eavesdropping on our conversations.

104) What happed with Sergeant Bruny Pierri?

Sergeant Pierri was the most known professing Christian staff at Dade CI. I met him for the first time in 2010, when I was housed at Dade CI. He said he was a Pentecostal preacher in society. In 2011, he worked on the 4:00 pm to 12:00 am shift.

Around the end of July 2011, he came to my cell round 9:30 pm with a boom box radio. He opened my cell door and said, "God said I must worship with you. Come with me." After we went to the back office in Wing J-3, he said, "We're going to pray for 20 to 30 minutes, and then we're going to worship."

He then pushed play on the boom box and started a CD of gospel music. He set the volume low, so I could hear him praying. About 20 to 30 minutes later, we both stood up from our chairs and started worshiping God. We stopped around midnight. As soon as we were done, his shift was over, so he had to go home. The next five to seven nights he worked, we spent from around 9:30 pm to 12:00 am every night praying and worshipping in the back office in Wing J-3. Every staff (including the lieutenants) who worked in Central and on the Westside saw Sergeant Pierri and me engaged in one or more of these prayer and worship services.

About a month or two after we had these worship sessions, Sergeant Pierri told me he put in to become a lieutenant around the time we were doing the worship services, and that he was denied the promotion. He said the "higher-ups" didn't like that he was so friendly with inmates, and that they called him an, "Inmate Lover." The name, "Inmate Lover" is considered a put down by FDC staff.

Sergeant Pierri believed he could cast out demons. Several times he took mentally disabled inmates who he thought were possessed with demons and attempted to cast the demons out of the inmates. The inmates were worse mentally after Sergeant Pierri got done with them.

Throughout the years I was at Dade CI, Sergeant Pierri and I had hundreds of conversations about the Bible, evangelism, and our personal lives.

105) What Christian denomination are you, and what area of Christian study do you believe God has gifted you in?

I'm Presbyterian in America, I'm Protestant, and I'm Reformed. I believe God has gifted me in the Christian Studies of Systematic Theology and Apologetics.

106) Tell me about your journal entries that reference Sergeant Pierri.

I wrote everything in my journal as I saw and perceived everything during real time. I didn't make my journal entries in light of what the Bible says. I made them in light of what my feelings said, and my perception of the events. I knew then and I know now that as a Christian, I must look at all things in light of what the Bible says. In other words, the Bible is supposed to be my sole authority. Even though I knew this then and I know it now, I do sometimes sin.

107) Will you tell me about mental health Counselor George Mallinckrodt?

Upon my April 28, 2011 return to the Dade CI TCU, Mallinckrodt was assigned to me as my counselor. Part of his job was to meet with the inmates assigned to him every two weeks and ask them questions that were on a form he had to fill out. As long as the questions weren't answered the wrong way, the meetings would end in five minutes or less. None of the items were relevant to me, so I was usually in and out of his office in less than five minutes.

After Coach Nichole Ocanna convinced me to start attending her groups, I decided to also attend Mallinckrodt's groups. I liked him as a person, and I didn't want him to think I wasn't attending his groups because I didn't like him.

During his groups, he mentioned his moral standard. He contended that certain things were morally wrong. In groups, he talked about how he didn't like that Officer Gruben and other security staff mistreated inmate patients in the TCU.

Over a few week period, Mallinckrodt told the group that he was preparing to speak with Warden Jerry Cummings about security staff mistreating the inmates. Mallinckrodt said that, if we had any incidents we wanted to report, we could describe them to him and he would then complete incident reports and give them to the warden. I liked that Mallinckrodt wanted to help the inmates who were mistreated. I just disagreed with him telling prison staff that other prison staff were doing wrong. From my more than 11 years of incarceration at that time, I knew that FDC staff didn't like hearing that they or their co-workers were doing wrong.

After Mallinckrodt started talking about going to Warden Cummings with incident reports on the evil acts security staff were doing, I believed I could no longer attend Mallinckrodt's groups. If security staff found out, I knew Mr. Mallinckrodt planned to report them to the warden and that if I didn't tell them, they would deem me an enemy and a traitor. I had worked too hard to get security staff to view me as a friend, and as somebody, they could trust. I couldn't jeopardize all that I had worked for to aid Mallinckrodt when I knew what he was doing wouldn't work. I knew from what he was saying that he had never done any research on Warden Jerry Cummings. Additionally, I believed that Mallinckrodt didn't understand that FDC staff didn't like being told about their wrongs.

Within days of deciding I wouldn't attend any more of Mallinckrodt's groups, he called me to his office for what was supposed to be my bi-weekly meeting. When I sat down in Mr. Mallinckrodt's office, he said, "With your experiences as an orderly for security, you know a lot that I could report to the warden. The information you have could help out a lot. If you want to tell me anything, I'll put it on an incident report and deliver it to the warden."

I responded, "Mr. Mallinckrodt, what makes you think that the warden cares?"

He responded, "He's the warden. Why wouldn't he care?"

I responded, "Those who go against FDC never become a warden. I don't think that you should go to FDC staff and tell them they're doing wrong. If you go to the warden with anything, the staff will retaliate against you."

He said, "What makes you say that, and what can they do to me?"

I responded, "My prison files and lawsuits show I have years of experience at trying to stop corruption and trying to get prison officials to follow the law and their own rules. I talk from experience. If you go to the warden regarding security staff, they will probably slice your car tires or key your car. They could make it difficult for you to get in and out of the Westside, they could leave you alone with very violent inmates, or lie about you and fire you. They could do all types of things. I'm not trying to scare you. I'm telling you this because I like you. I like that you're trying to help inmates. I just disagree with the way you're trying to do it. I believe it would be better if you contacted the Department of Justice, Department of Health, or the Department of Children and Families and tell them what's going on here. Because you work here as staff, they would investigate what you told them. Those agencies have the legal authority to investigate the types of problems going on here."

He said, "So you don't want to give me any information to give to the warden?"

I responded, "I can't do that because he's not going to help. Warden Cummings is not stupid. He knows what's going on."

He said, "OK. Then let me ask you these questions so that you can be on your way." Mallinckrodt then asked me the same questions that he asked me every two weeks.

I didn't go to Mallinckrodt's next group. A few days after that group meeting, Officer Gruben came to my cell door looking mad and said, "I need to ask you something. Did you tell Mallinckrodt that I kicked your flap or any flap closed?"

I responded, "What are you talking about? Of course not. Why would I tell Mr. Mallinckrodt anything like that?"

He said, "Mallinckrodt has been filing incident reports on me. I just left the lieutenant's office from being questioned. He said Mallinckrodt told the warden that you told him that I kicked your flap or some other flap closed."

I responded, "Gruben, kicking a flap closed is very petty considering everything else I know. You know darn well if I was trying to get you in trouble, I know a lot more stuff than you kicking a flap. I don't know what Mallinckrodt did, but if he said I told him anything negative about you, then he lied. If need be, I'll tell that to the lieutenant, and if Mallinckrodt said I told him anything negative about any staff, then he's trying to get you guys mad at me so you'll turn against me."

He said, "I think I know what's going on. He probably thinks that if he can get us mad at you, you'll help him."

I responded, "I don't know. I just know that, if he told anybody I said anything negative about the staff here, he lied. I don't like this whole thing, and if it's OK with you, I'd like to say something to him."

He said, "You can say anything you want to him. You're your own man".

The whole situation was upsetting. I felt I needed to pray to God for guidance. I didn't know if Officer Gruben was telling me the truth, or if he was lying to see if I knew anything about what Mallinckrodt was doing. I also didn't want to take any chance of causing any trouble for Mallinckrodt. After praying and thinking about the situation, I thought that Officer Gruben had to be lying to me. Mr. Mallinckrodt didn't seem like the type to place an inmate in potential danger. I previously said I wasn't going to go to any more of his groups. After the situation with Officer Gruben, I thought that the best time to question Mr. Mallinckrodt would be during one of his groups.

When he had his next session, I attended. After all the inmates got in the room and the door was shut, Mr. Mallinckrodt started the group by saying, "Let me catch you guys up to date. I provided the warden with some information before my formal meeting with him. When I met with him, I gave him some more information. He said he's going to check into it and see what he can find out. That means that so far everything is going good."

The other inmates in the room then started asking him questions. About 10 minutes into the group, I asked him, "Was my name on any of the information you gave to the warden?"

Mr. Mallinckrodt seemed somewhat lost for words before responding, "Yes, why?"

I said, "Because Gruben came to my cell saying you said that I told you stuff that I didn't tell you. Did you tell the warden that I told you that Officer Gruben kicked a flap closed?"

He responded, "Yes, I did Hempstead."

I was lost for words when I heard his response. I was dumbfounded. I'd thought that Gruben was lying to me and that if Mallinckrodt told the warden anything involving me, he wouldn't admit it to me.

When he admitted to it, my shock caused me only to respond by saying, "OK. I just wanted to see if Gruben was lying to me."

The rest of the inmates stayed silent. I was in an unusual situation. Gruben and other security staff had previously mistreated several of the inmates who were in the room with me. If I showed that I was upset about what Mr. Mallinckrodt did, it would cause the other inmates to think that I was trying to stop him from helping them. I decided I would say something to Mr. Mallinckrodt at our next bi-weekly meeting.

During this group meeting, I had another issue I had to think about. Gruben was working, and as soon as I got out of the group, he was going to ask me what Mallinckrodt had said. I had to decide if I was going to tell Officer Gruben or not tell him. After thinking about the matter, I realized I had to tell Gruben what Mr. Mallinckrodt said. I told Gruben I was going to question Mr. Mallinckrodt about what he said to the warden. If I didn't do this, it would make me look fishy to Officer Gruben.

After informing Officer Gruben that Mr. Mallinckrodt had admitted to telling the warden stuff I did not say, Officer Gruben said, "Mallinckrodt is trying to turn us against each other. I also think Lowe is involved with it. Lowe's been snitching on me to Mallinckrodt, but that's OK. I got something for Lowe." Gruben was talking about Inmate Bobby Lowe, who slept a few cells from me. Gruben had been harassing Lowe for a while.

I went to the next group with Mr. Mallinckrodt so I could listen and see if Mr. Mallinckrodt said anything that could lead to more trouble involving me. He started the group by saying, "I want to start by letting you guys know that this is my last day. I can't continue to deal with the things that are going on here, so I'm quitting." When Mr. Mallinckrodt said he was quitting, I thought security staff had engaged in some type of retaliation to make him quit. I felt bad for Mr. Mallinckrodt. If he had followed my advice, the inmates might have received real help from outside agencies, and Mr. Mallinckrodt possibly wouldn't have lost his job in vain.

In 2014, Mr. Mallinckrodt wrote his book, ***Getting Away with Murder***. In his book he says he didn't quit but that he was fired. I was confused. In his book, he said he reported to work and wasn't let into Dade CI because he was fired for taking late lunches. Possibly, Mr. Mallinckrodt had planned to quit and was fired before he could quit.

After Mr. Mallinckrodt stopped working in the TCU, I wanted to talk with him and ask why he did what he did. Mr. Mallinckrodt has done a lot to help Florida prisoners since he published his book in 2014.

I know several people who have talked with him regularly since 2014. I've asked those people to tell him that I would like to speak with him. Additionally, I've written him several letters at his post office box. Mr. Mallinckrodt has never responded to my letters and never arranged for us to talk. People who have talked with M. Mallinckrodt told me he received my messages and letters.

108) Did George Mallinckrodt witness any physical abuse in the TCU?

Mr. Mallinckrodt's office was in Wing J-3 which is on the Westside. Additionally, the inmates he was assigned to as a counselor for the years he worked there were all housed on the Westside. Thus, for years, Mr. Mallinckrodt spent the majority of his 40 hour work week in the Westside where the abuse, starving, and torture were almost constant. It's reasonable to think he witnessed a lot of physical abuse.

109) Who moved into George Mallinckrodt's office?

Coach Nichole Ocanna who was Officer Gruben's girlfriend.

110) Who replaced George Mallinckrodt as the counselor?

Dr. Cesar who previously filled in for TCU counselors who were on vacation or sick leave. She also used to work at Homestead Correctional Institution for women.

I believe she had completed the requirements for a doctor's degree in psychology, which was why everybody referred to her as Dr. Cesar. At Dade CI she worked as a counselor and not as a psychologist. As far as I understood, while she worked in the TCU, she attended a Pentecostal church in Dade County. Since Dr. Cesar replaced Mr. Mallinckrodt, she became my assigned counselor. As with Mr. Mallinckrodt, I met with her every two weeks. In the weeks following Darren Rainey's death, I met with her every week. After a few meetings, I saw she had the heart to try to help people. I say much more her later in this book

111) Were there other staffing changes around August 2011?

Yes. Sergeant Tarver was promoted to lieutenant; Sergeant Mizeal replaced Tarver as Westside sergeant on the 8:00 am to 4:00 pm shift; Lieutenant McCrae was promoted to captain and posted to work in general population; and Major Royce Marlow was promoted to colonel. Ms. Martin took over as a major in the TCU.

112) Will you tell me about Sergeant Mizeal?

I was told that Mizeal used to work as the sergeant in the Control Room at Dade CI. About a week after he started working in the TCU, Officer Eli came to my cell and said, "The new sergeant is into the Bible. I told him about you. He said he's going to come and check you out."

"I'm sure I'll enjoy talking with him," I responded.

About an hour later, Sergeant Mizeal stopped at my cell and said, "Eli said you know the Bible."

"By God's grace, I study to show myself approved," I replied. "Are you Christian?" He confirmed he was. We then discussed Bible Doctrine for about 30 minutes. From that day on, we discussed the Bible one to three hours a day during every shift he worked.

At the end of September 2011, Sergeant Mizeal asked me if I'd like to teach a weekly Bible study in the large office in Wing J-3.

I told him "Yes."

Only staff and protective management inmates attended the Bible study. Security staff in the TCU participated in every service. Some security staff who worked in general population also attended my study sessions. Even Dr. Cesar and Coach Ocanna attended a couple of times. I taught the Bible study every Sunday between September 2011 until the end of May 2012 when I was taken out of protective management status.

By God's grace, the Bible study led to more than eight months of constant Bible discussions, debates, and Christian activity on the Westside. It was through the Bible study and the continuous Christian activity on the Westside that I first met Officer Terry and several other staff who worked in the general population.

The almost constant Bible discussions on the Westside caused some of the medical and mental health staff to get a little upset. They felt they were not getting the help they needed because the security staff spent so much time discussing and debating the Bible.

113) Did you document your conversations with staff about the Bible and other interactions?

Yes. In my October 3, 2011 journal entry, I name sergeants Mizeal and Pierri, Officers Clarke, Jenkins, Eli, Piggot, Gruben, Saneck, Coach Ocanna, Dr. Cesar, and Nurse Astre as people I had conversations with. Other entries document the instances of staff bringing me food or books from society.

114) Did Sergeant Mizeal and you disagree on the Bible?

Yes. He didn't believe in the deities of Jesus or the Holy Spirit, the Trinity, Limited Atonement, or in fire and brimstone preaching. I believe in all of these doctrines.

115) Tell me about your attempts to get off protective management status at the end of 2011.

After being on protective management for about a month, God started giving me conviction for getting myself placed on that status without first going to Him in the Word (Bible) and prayer to see if He wanted me to do such. I acted on my own understanding and desires and didn't seek God's guidance to direct my path[1]. God caused me to see that protective management had many negatives. If I stayed on it, I wouldn't be able to return to Everglades CI, when I discharged from the TCU. I wouldn't be able to evangelize a whole compound and do the Christian things I enjoyed doing on a compound. God caused me to realize that my mom was old, and if I were transferred to another state by interstate compact, I would never get to see her or spend time with her before she died. Finally, He caused me to realize, that protective management status prohibited me from helping the inmates in the TCU like God wanted me to. I should have thought about all these things before pushing to be placed on protective management. I decided not to dwell on the past.

Department of Corruption

I realized I had to take action to correct my mistakes and get off protective management so I told Classification Officer, Ms. Koel, I made a mistake and I wanted off Protective Management status. She said I should've thought harder before I requested to be placed on it.

For about two weeks, she and I discussed my wish to be removed from protective management status. Then I realized talking with her wasn't going to work. I decided to file grievances asking to be removed from protective management status. Mysteriously, within a week of submitting some of these grievances, chow hall staff and security staff stopped honoring my need for a low residue diet.

They took me off my diet and only gave me food I had problems digesting. After I developed medical problems as a result of being taken off my low residue diet, I stopped filing requests to leave protective management. I had to focus on getting placed back on my diet and ending to the retaliation.

116) Why do you need a low residue diet?

In the past, my mom and brother were both diagnosed with problems that make it difficult to digest certain foods. Around 2008, I also developed problems digesting certain foods, which worsened over the years. I needed to be on a low residue diet because my digestive system was not processing much of the food on the regular diet.

Inmates on a low residue diet should not eat processed meat, beans, cold vegetables, oatmeal and other types of food that are high in fiber.

After security and chow hall staff stopped honoring my low residue diet pass, I had to eat food that I could not digest. I got stomach pains and defecated several times a day. Within two weeks, these issues got so bad that I had to go to the medical department for help. The doctor ordered that I be placed back on my low residue diet immediately. Security and chow hall staff still didn't honor my low residue diet for about three more weeks, at which time, I finally received a low-residue diet tray but only at breakfast meals. I thought that within a day or two I would start receiving my diet for all three meals. I was wrong. Instead, on

86

October 11, 2011, staff stopped giving me my low-residue diet at breakfast.

Officer Wood denied me my diet tray for breakfast on October 11, 2011. I had been incarcerated with Wood's father inmate, Michael Ferguson, at Washington CI. In 2010, Michael Ferguson told Officer Wood that he knew me from when we were both incarcerated at Washington CI.

On the same day that Officer Wood didn't give me the correct breakfast tray, I filed a grievance of reprisal and two informal grievances on him. That night, my grievance of reprisal came back approved by the assistant warden.

The next morning, I asked Officer Saneck not to get involved with what was happening with Officer Wood. I showed Officers Wood, Saneck, David, and Sergeant Anderson the approved grievance from the assistant warden. I asked Officer Saneck to ask Major Martin to come and talk with me. When she came to my cell, I showed her the approved grievance and said, "Major, my medical file which is less than a hundred feet from my cell shows I have a valid low residue diet pass. Wood and these staff are making up excuses as to why they are not giving me my diet tray. I used to be their orderly. I know all their tricks. They are saying they have to go by a diet list that chow hall staff has. I believe chow hall staff are intentionally not putting my name on that list, because of all the grievances I filed on the chow hall supervisor.

As long as this diet pass can be verified with the documentation in my medical file as being legitimate, staff are supposed to give me my diet tray. I'm being denied my Eighth Amendment right to Adequate Medical Attention in that the doctor ordered that I receive a low residue diet as part of my medical care for my stomach."

Major Martin responded, "Hempstead, you're right." She then told security to make sure I received my diet tray.

That same day, I was taken to see Advanced Registered Nurse Practitioner Dwares. She ordered that I again start receiving my low residue diet. She also prescribed medicine to try to slow my bowel movements.

When the medical staff weighed me that day, they found I had lost approximately 16 pounds in the prior month during which I was denied my low residue diet.

117) Did Sergeant Mizeal use you as an orderly while you were on protective management status?

Yes. Sergeant Mizeal started using me as an orderly in Wing J-3, and, in the middle of September 2011, he began using me as an orderly in Wing J-2. He didn't like having to stand in front of my cell to discuss the Bible. By using me as an orderly, he could do security work while I completed the orderly work. Then, we had time to sit in offices in Wings J-2 and J-3 and discuss the Bible.

Most of the time Sergeant Mizeal didn't allow me to work in Wing J-1. He was not concerned that TCU staff had never used protective management inmates as orderlies in the past. He knew that as long as he kept general population inmates away from me, he wasn't violating any rules.

He used me as an orderly for several months between September 2011 and May 2012. For the most part, Sergeant Mizeal didn't allow me near general population inmates. When he did, security staff were always present.

118) What happened with inmate Dwight Rochester at the end of 2011?

I knew Rochester from my 2010 incarceration in the Westside TCU. As far as I know, he was the last inmate who security staff tried to place on a loaf in 2010. Rochester had lost a lot of weight, and he was more mentally unstable than he was in 2010. In 2010, I wasn't aware of Rochester having medical problems.

In 2011, security and nursing staff frequently went to Rochester's cell and asked to see his penis. One of Rochester's testicles was nearly as large as two softballs. The staff made fun of Rochester's private area when he showed it to them. Some staff said Rochester had Elephantiasis. One or two others said it was something else.

Rochester was completing his prison sentence at the end of 2011, and the senior psychiatrist didn't think Rochester was stable enough to be released to society and planned to request a judge to involuntarily commit him to a mental hospital (Baker Act) before his release date. For Rochester to be moved to a mental hospital, his severity rating must be raised from TCU status to Crisis Stabilization Unit status. Once he was on Crisis Stabilization Unit status, Doctor Basaga could ask a county circuit court judge to "Baker Act Rochester." Baker Acting Rochester at the time of his release meant he would be admitted into a mental hospital in society.

The Mental Health Treatment Team ordered Rochester be moved from Wing J-1 to Wing J-2 and placed in the Crisis Stabilization Unit. Security were supposed to move Rochester to Wing J-2 on a Friday. However, Sergeant Lewis didn't want to move Rochester to Wing J-2 on Friday because more staff are present on Friday than on Saturday, it was more likely someone would witness any use of excessive force when they moved Rochester.

When Saturday came, Sergeant Lewis and Officers McGriff, Jenkins, Eli, Jackson, and Harrison were working. As always, Sergeant Lewis ended up using excessive force on Rochester. A witness reported Sergeant Lewis and his officers to people outside of the Dade CI. The following Monday, an investigation was initiated into security staff physically battering Rochester. All of the above officers were placed on leave for several days and Sergeant Lewis and Officer Jenkins ended up being reassigned to work in the general population. The remaining officers came back to the TCU a week or two after the incident. If I remember correctly, Sergeant Lewis was told that he couldn't work in the TCU for a year.

119) What was Sergeant Lewis' nickname?

Teflon. I heard he got this nickname because no matter what he did, he never got in any serious trouble.

120) What did Sergeant Lewis do to Oscar Davis?

At the end of 2011, Oscar Davis was moved into Wing J-3. Throughout the entire time Davis was housed in Wing J-3, if Sergeant Lewis was working, Lewis denied Davis every meal. Regularly, he would go into Davis's cell, push Davis to the ground, get on top of him, and then slap him numerous times. Davis couldn't do anything. Several of the inmates who slept in

Wing J-3 witnessed Sergeant Lewis physically abusing Davis every time he entered Davis' cell.

121) Did you talk with Dr. Cesar about Oscar Davis?

Yes, once when Dr. Cesar and I were talking in an office in Wing J-3, she said, "Hempstead, Oscar Davis was just seen by a doctor from society. The doctor said Davis' blood test showed he was missing a vitamin in his blood that he shouldn't be missing unless he's not eating. Are security staff feeding Davis?"

I was somewhat shocked that Dr. Cesar asked me this. The blood test she referenced should have been enough evidence to show Davis wasn't being fed. I responded to her, "Dr. Cesar, you know I'm in an unusual situation. Can't you just listen to what the doctor said?"

She said, "What is that supposed to mean?"

I responded, "I'm an inmate. He's a doctor. He told you what the blood test showed. Isn't that enough evidence?"

She said, "I understand."

About a month or two after this conversation with Dr. Cesar, Oscar Davis died. I believe the medical problems Davis developed from not being fed killed him. Essentially, he was starved to death.

I also think there is enough evidence to support prosecuting the staff who denied Davis his right to be fed.

122) What happened with Officer Piggot at the end of 2011?

Around August 2011, Officer Piggot went on leave. Upon returning to work, he came to my cell, and said, "How have you been, while I've been gone?"

I responded, "Good. How was your vacation?"

He said, "A lot happened. My girl had our daughter, I got married, and I've been born again."

I responded, "To make sure I heard you right. Did you say you are now a married, born-again dad of a baby girl?"

He said, "Yes."

I responded, "Congratulations three times. If it's OK, may I ask why you believe you were born again?"

Chapter 9: Dade CI (July 5, 2011 - January 1, 2012)

He said, "Over these last few years, God has been working on me. He has placed a lot of people in my life who have been constantly coming at me with the Bible. You know my wife's Pentecostal, and her father is a preacher. When I wasn't at work, they were always getting on me about changing and coming to Jesus. I've had Officer Eli talking with me about God at work for the last few years. Also since 2010, you have constantly been telling me I didn't know when I was going to die and asking if I die would I go to hell for eternity. All this finally made me feel that enough was enough. I had to quit playing games with God.

"Now I don't desire a lot of the things I used to crave. I don't want to party or have sex with every woman I can get. I want God, and I want to learn everything I can about Him. I know what He did for me, and I want to know more about Him. I want to be able to share Him with others. My wife, stepdad, and Eli always said things to me about Jesus, but you're the only person who ever explained God and hell to me. What do I need to do to learn more about God?"

I responded, "I wasn't expecting this, but it's a beautiful thing." The study of God is the coolest and deepest subject to study. You have to get good books by respectable teachers of our faith. People like John Calvin, Martin Luther, Johnathan Edwards, Charles H. Spurgeon, Francis Schaffer, R.C. Sproul, and John MacArthur. Another good thing to do is find a Presbyterian in America Church."

He said, "Who are all those people, and what denomination are you?"

I responded, "The people I named are Protestant Reformers, and I'm Presbyterian in America."

He asked, "Do you have any books by the guys you named? Show me the books you have. I want to get the same books you have. If they helped you learn the Bible, they could help me."

For the next 20 to 30 minutes as I showed Officer Piggot my books, he wrote down the names of the authors and titles of the books while we discussed them. During this conversation, he also asked me to explain the Presbyterian in America Christian denomination and what Protestant and Reformed meant.

After this conversation, Officer Piggot and I spent one to four hours a day discussing the Bible every day he worked. The amount of time we spent led to several unofficial investigations into whether we had a personal relationship.

Officer Piggot purchased copies of all the Christian books I had. Over the next year, he also carried a pocket Bible with him every day to work. He told me that he and his wife joined a Reformed Baptist church.

123) Please summarize your last five months of 2011.

I participated in a lot of evangelism and Bible discussions during that time, as many as, four to eight hours a day, seven days a week with several staff members. When Sergeant Mizeal first took over as the sergeant on the 8:00 am to 4:00 pm shift, he cut back the non-feeding of inmates a considerable amount. However, around April 2011, he started allowing security staff more leeway in depriving inmates of food. Mostly it was the staff on the 4:00 pm to 12:00 am and 12:00 am to 8:00 am shifts who physically abused and denied food to Westside inmates. I worked as an orderly on the 12:00 am to 8:00 am and 8:00 am to 4:00 pm shifts for several months at the end of 2011. I did my best to smuggle food to the inmates who weren't fed. As far as I know, during that period, the staff on the shifts I worked didn't place any medicine in any inmate's food.

I was under a lot of stress. The issues with George Mallinckrodt and with my low residue diet caused me some anxiety; however, the most stressful situation during this period was witnessing the non-feeding and abuse of Oscar Davis. When I heard he died, I remembered how many times I saw staff who were passing out the meals refuse to open Davis' food flap so I could give him a tray. After Davis's death, I thought about how Bobby Lowe, Walter Fyler, Lawrence Smith, and other inmates gave Davis their food the last few months before his death.

I was sad. I felt that I should have done more to prevent Davis' death, such as, convince staff to treat him better, smuggle more food to him, and so on.

124) Were you able to pray and worship during those 5 months?

My prayer and worship life during that time period was very good. In 2013, I looked back and saw that God by grace led me to devote a lot more time to Him in prayer and worship. God was preparing me for all that would happen in 2012.

Looking back, I realized that by allowing me to experience those events, God was not only strengthening my love and my relationship with Him but also my love for others.

Chapter 10: `Dade CI (January 1, 2012 - July 25, 2012)

125) What is important about the first six months of 2012?

During this time staff started using a shower upstairs in Wing J-3 to punish mentally disabled inmates. Darryl Richardson and Darren Rainey died. I will cover their deaths later and, first, cover other issues.

126) Did Dr. Cesar help obtain mattresses for inmates?

Yes. Around February 2012, an inmate in one of her groups told Dr. Cesar that several of the severely mentally disabled inmates were sleeping on the cement floor without mattresses, pillows, linen, and blankets.

A few days after that group meeting, I was speaking with Dr. Cesar her in an office when she asked, "Hempstead, why are inmates sleeping on the cement floor without mattresses?"

I responded, "Security staff refuses to give those inmates mattresses because the inmates are using the red sporks that come with each meal to destroy their mattresses, blankets, and sheets. I asked security staff to give those inmates the flimsy sporks because they were not strong enough destroy anything. I also told security they could give those inmates Styrofoam trays which do not come with any sporks. By following those recommendations, staff would then be able to give the inmates mattresses and linen and also feed them. It's cold outside, and with the air-conditioning working, it's really cold in here.

I don't know if you noticed, but a few of the inmates without mattresses crawl up under their bunks and ball up like babies. If you can get them their mattresses and linen back, I'll do everything I can to have those inmates' meals placed on Styrofoam trays, or at least I will try to get staff to give them the flimsy white sporks when they serve the meals.

She said, "I don't know if I can get them mattresses, but I'm going to try."

I responded, "I forgot to mention that those inmates are here in the TCU to receive treatment from the Mental Health Treatment Team. I know security took the mattresses from them, but the Mental Health Treatment Team is responsible for the treatment of those inmates while they're housed here. If the Department of Health came in here, I'm sure they would the blame mental health staff and not the security staff for those inmates not having mattresses."

She said, "Hempstead, I brought this issue up because I want those inmates to have mattresses. I'm going to try to help them obtain mattresses. They shouldn't be sleeping on the cement floor!"

About a week later, I found out that Dr. Cesar was successful in getting mattresses for the inmates who didn't have any. Throughout the rest of 2012, all of the inmates on the Westside had mattresses.

127)   Will you tell me about Major McCarter?

Around January 2012, Major Martin left the TCU, and Major McCarter took over as Security Chief in the TCU. Major McCarter acted like he opposed things that he didn't oppose.

A short time after he started working in the TCU, Classification Officer, Ms. Koel, told him about my past and showed him several documents that proved I had a long history of speaking out against things I disagreed with. Ms. Koel also showed him information from my files that proved I would sue Dade CI staff if I was ever physically harmed by any of them. She also showed him documents that proved I had a history of communicating with people who investigated staff misconduct in the FDC. As soon as Ms. Koel shared all of this information with the major, he told security staff to stop using me as an orderly. He also told Lieutenants Tarver and Bush what Ms. Koel shared with him. The lieutenants and the security staff didn't believe what the major or Ms. Koel said about me. They had known me since

2010, and they knew that I saw them do all types of evil things, and I never repeated what I witnessed. They believed that I showed them by my actions and words that they could trust me.

I was always amazed that God caused the security staff not to believe anything Ms. Koel said about me. I think Ms. Koel stopped being friendly toward me after she looked through my prison files and learned about me speaking out in the past against things I disagreed with, something I had done since I was a teenager.

Security staff on the Westside thought she stopped being friendly toward me because I started filing grievances against her and because I threatened court action against her unless I was taken off protective management. Security thought these things caused her to make false allegations against me, and, thus, did not trust anything Ms. Koel said about me. Since Major McCarter was new to the TCU and believed what Ms. Koel said about me, security staff felt they could not believe anything the major said about me. Security staff felt Ms. Koel got the major to side with her and to dislike me.

128) How did you get off protective management status in 2012?

Around the end of February, I started filing dozens of grievances asking to be removed from protective management status. In the middle of March, I found out that Ms. Koel was going on vacation in April for a few weeks, so I stopped filing grievances and began planning what I would present to get off protective management when she went on vacation.

During the court proceeding on my Tallahassee, Florida Federal District Court lawsuit, the Assistant Bureau Chief for Classification Records at the central office for the FDC filed an affidavit with the court stating I never qualified for placement in a Protective Management Unit throughout my incarceration. When Ms. Koel recommended placing me on protective management she used the same reason to claim I needed protective management as the Assistant Bureau Chief used to claim I never qualified for protective management.

A few days prior to Ms. Koel going on vacation in April 2012, I mailed several envelopes full of grievances to the main office for the FDC. In my grievances, I stated that Ms. Koel recommended I be placed on protective management for the same reason the Assistant Bureau Chief told a federal judge I didn't qualify for placement on protective management. I also stated that placing me on protective management was either a mistake or that the Assistant Bureau Chief lied to a federal judge. I further stated that I wanted prison officials to say it was a mistake and to release me from protective management status. I explained that if they did so, I would be satisfied to drop the issue. Moreover, I explained that if prison officials didn't want to look upon it as a mistake and release me from protective management status, I would seek federal perjury proceedings against the Assistant Bureau Chief for lying to a federal judge. I contended that I would use my protective management paperwork that stated the reason I was placed on protective management status, as evidence to prove the Assistant Bureau Chief lied to the federal judge. Finally, I explained that I would use what Ms. Koel documented to put me on protective management status to reinstate my Tallahassee, Florida Federal District Court lawsuit. In addition to sending grievances and letters to the main office for the FDC stating these things, I told the Institutional Classification Team at Dade CI that since they agreed with Ms. Koel's reason for placing me on protective management, I would be calling them as witnesses in a federal perjury proceeding against the second highest classification staff member in the Florida Department of Corrections. About two weeks after mailing that paperwork, I was told that I would be meeting with a state classification officer.

On May 11, 2012, I met with State Classification Officer Lawyer Thorton and Dade CI Classification Supervisor Ms. Jackson. After that meeting, Lawyer Thorton took me off protective management status.

On May 14, 2012, Dr. Cesar told me that Classification Officer Mr. Mendez talked about retaliating against me in a recent Mental Health Treatment Team meeting. Dr. Cesar said the "Higher Ups" that worked outside the TCU were mad because of what I did to be removed from protective management status and that they were trying to get the Treatment Team to discharge me. She also mentioned that the Treatment Team had nothing to do with my protective management status. I told Dr. Cesar that I had a First Amendment right to Redress of Grievances. After listening to her, I asked if I could go in front of the Treatment Team to talk with them.

On May 15, 2012, I went in front of the TCU Mental Health Treatment Team which consisted of Officer Jenkins (this was not the same Officer Jenkins assigned to work on the compound), Sergeants Mizeal and Seals, Lieutenant Bush, Nurse Pierri, Coach Ocanna, Ms. Cortada, Mr. Mendez, and Doctors Basaga, Franco, Perez, Sanchez, and Cesar. When I stood up to address them, Dr. Basaga said, "Mr. Hempstead, you asked to speak with us."

I responded, "Yes, I know some people are angry because of the paperwork I filed to be removed from protective management status. My TCU status has nothing to do with my protective management status. I have a constitutional right to file grievances. Whoever's trying to get you all to discharge me, is, in essence, trying to get you all to retaliate against me."

Mr. Mendez said, "Hempstead, there's nothing wrong with you. You don't need to be in TCU status."

I responded, "You're just filling in for Ms. Koel. You don't know anything about me, and you don't know anything about my files. If you did, you would know that I'm not here for being retarded, hearing voices, or being delusional. No rule or law says I can't file grievances if I'm housed in a TCU. If you discharge me or take any retaliatory action against me for my filing of grievances and paperwork to be removed from protective management that would violate my First Amendment Right to Redress of Grievances. I also believe that I have a fairly good understanding of my right to file grievances, considering I've previously filed two federal lawsuits against prison officials for retaliating against me for filing grievances."

Dr. Basaga then said, "Hempstead, you will not be discharged or retaliated against. You'll remain housed on the Westside until you feel that you would like to be discharged, OK?"

I responded, "Ok. Thank you, Doctor." I then left the Treatment Team meeting. I was happy with the answer Dr. Basaga gave me.

129) What happened with Darryl Richardson?

One sometime near the beginning of 2012 when I was performing my orderly duties, Sergeant Mizeal, Officers Piggot, Eli, Gruben and I all went to Wing J-2. When we got there and went to Cell J-2112, Officer Piggot said to me, "Do you remember him?" He then pointed to the inmate inside the cell. I didn't recognize the inmate at first because of how skinny he was.

I responded, "No. Who is that?"

Piggot said, "Look at his name."

When I saw the inmate's name, I was shocked to see it was Darryl Richardson. It looked as if he had lost 60 to 80 pounds since I last saw him. I couldn't help but say, "Oh my gosh, what happened to him?"

Piggot responded, "He hasn't been eating." When Officer Piggot said that, I knew immediately what that meant. It meant staff hadn't been feeding Richardson.

If an inmate was truthfully refusing to eat, staff would have told the Mental Health Treatment Team, and they would have taken some type of action with the inmate who was refusing to eat. When security staff didn't feed an inmate for a long period of time and somebody asked why the inmate was losing so much weight, security staff always responded, "He hasn't been eating," thus blaming the inmate for his loss of weight. Security staff always told the Treatment Team right away when an inmate was truthfully refusing to eat (if security didn't have any problems with the inmate) because security didn't want to be blamed for not feeding an inmate who was himself refusing to eat.

Richardson held a Bible in his hand all the time we were at his cell. When Sergeant Mizeal had Richardson's cell door opened, Mizeal told Officer Gruben to take Richardson's Bible from him because he couldn't bring it with him where he was going. I was told that Richardson was going somewhere for medical help. Gruben, while laughing, said, "I can't take the Bible from him. I've already done too much bad in my life. I can't have God say 'Do you remember that Bible you took from Richardson?'"

Sergeant Mizeal ended up taking the Bible from Richardson. Security staff then helped Richardson get in a wheelchair and they then pushed him out of the wing and down the Westside hallway.

A couple weeks later, I was told that Darryl Richardson had died. I thought about all the food the staff had denied Richardson while he was housed on the Westside. They had to have denied him a large quantity for him to have reached the sad state he was in when I last saw him. This was almost identical to what happened to Oscar Davis.

130) How many of your relatives died during this six months?

Four uncles and two aunts. My uncles, Art and Joe, with whom I was in regular communications died. Sometime around March 2012, I also learned from my sister Windy that Uncle Billy, Uncle Franky, and my aunts Midge and Ida had died.

131) Tell me about Officer Day.

A lot of staff said Officer Day was the "Real Police" because she would tell her supervisors if the staff she didn't like did anything they weren't supposed to do. On several occasions at the end of 2014 and the beginning of 2015, she told Majors Martin and McCarter that Sergeant Mizeal had used me as an orderly after he had been told not to use me. Also, more than once, she told Martin and McCarter about Officers Piggot and Eli spending hours talking with me about the Bible when they were supposed to be working. She also reported numerous other infractions by staff to Major McCarter Thus, Officer Day was disliked by all the security staff on the shift she worked.

132) Tell about Ms. Arencibia during this period.

At the end of 2011, Ms. Arencibia from the mental health staff started showing a serious dislike for Officer Gruben and me. She disliked Officer Gruben because he targeted inmates and subjected them to all types of evil. He wouldn't feed them; if he was put in a situation where he had to feed them, he would add chemicals or medicine to their food; he subjected them to psychological warfare; ransacked their cells and took their property: physically abused them if he could get away with it. He did these things to any inmate who got on his bad side. However, most of the time, he targeted inmates who were incarcerated for sex crimes.

I previously mentioned that I ranked Officers Sakay and Gibson as the evilest officers in the TCU. I think Officers Weary and Gruben were the third and fourth evilest officers in the TCU.

I believe Ms. Arencibia started disliking me because Classification Officer Ms. Koel told her about my prior employment as a confidential informant and because of my frequent conversations with Officer Gruben and other security staff. She knew from my past and my Christian beliefs that I had an objective standard of right and wrong.

Ms. Arencibia said she was raised by strict parents who taught her that it was OK to tell on people who committed wrongful acts as long as the speaking out did not get the person arrested or incarcerated. I think she said it was her dad who taught her this principle. This caused me to think that her father, or possibly both of her parents, were criminals.

In my opinion, Ms. Arencibia followed that standard during the years she worked in TCU. Obviously, she must have witnessed security staff engage in all types of criminal abuse, torture, etc. of inmates. I believe inmates assigned to her would have told her about the physical abuse, etc. they were subjected to. As far as I know, Ms. Arencibia never reported any of the abuse, torture, etc. that was deemed criminal to the proper people. She only spoke out against the things that happened in the TCU that wouldn't get the security staff arrested or incarcerated.

At the end of 2011, Ms. Koel told Ms. Arencibia about my long history of speaking out against anybody who harmed children and people that couldn't help themselves. I believe they both thought that if I ever spoke out against the matters going on in the TCU, they would get in trouble. They both knew about the abuse for years, and neither took any action to stop it.

In 2011 and 2012, Ms. Arencibia made numerous attempts to get staff to stop using me as an orderly.

133) What were the names of some of the inmates targeted by Officer Gruben?

Lawrence Smith, Gregory Shevlin, Bobby Lowe, an inmate with the last name Kitchen, and an inmate with the nickname "Red Neck" who lived in Cell J-1226. There were others, but I can't remember their names.

134) What happened with Lawrence Smith and Officer Gruben?

When Lawrence Smith first came to the Westside, he was housed in Wing J-2. He was running from disciplinary reports he received while at the institution he came from. Throughout his stay in Wing J-2 and during his first two weeks or so in Cell J-3102, I gave him extra food when I could. We both got along fairly well. After he left Wing J-2, he was placed in the cell next to mine.

One night in 2012, the 4:00 pm to 12:00 am shift needed an extra orderly to work. Sergeant Jonathan decided to see how Smith would work as an orderly. Smith ended up doing a good job, so Sergeant Jonathan continued to use him as an orderly.

A few days after Smith started working as an orderly, Officer Gruben had to work overtime on the 4:00 pm to 12:00 am shift. Gruben saw that two of the three orderlies were in prison for sex crimes against kid and he called them child molesters. Smith was in prison for masturbating in a public location while looking at a child. This is a sex-crime against children, but Smith did not want to be called-out as a child molester because both staff and other inmates consider this to be a particularly heinous crime.

I wasn't working that night, so I didn't witness the interaction between Smith and Gruben. I heard about it from Smith.

When Smith went back to his cell, he yelled over and told me what happened. I told him that Gruben had a long history of doing that and to not take it personally. I also told Smith that Gruben was more than likely talking to the two other inmates and that I didn't think Gruben even knew what Smith was in prison for because if he did, he would have mentioned it to me. Smith had not hidden his reason for being in prison and had told me about his charges weeks earlier. I thought I calmed Smith down and convinced him to leave the matter with Officer Gruben alone. I was wrong.

The next night, Officer Gruben again worked overtime on the 4:00 pm to 12:00 am shift. That night he got inmate Timothy Siders out of his cell so they could play cards in the office upstairs between Wings J-2 and J-3. When Smith saw Lieutenant Pinkney walking around on the Westside, Smith stopped her and told her that Gruben was playing cards with Siders in the office. When the lieutenant started walking toward the office to see if what Smith said was true, Gruben sent Siders out an office door which went into Wing J-2 and that the lieutenant couldn't see. Siders went back to his cell and locked in. The lieutenant told Gruben what Smith said.

The next day when Officer Gruben was working on his regular shift, he went to Smith's cell door and called him a "child molesting snitch." He also told Smith that he would "teach him about messing with kids and snitching." From then on, when Gruben worked a meal, he would remove an item from Smith's tray and would, also, say things to Smith like, "I hope you enjoy what I put in it for you," or "It might be a little salty," or "I hope you don't die from eating this."

Gruben was well known for using this psychological warfare to frighten inmates. Smith became paranoid and stopped eating every meal that Gruben served him.

Within two or three days of Officer Gruben starting to abuse Smith, Smith asked me to tell him specific rules in Florida Administrative Code 33 that could get Officer Gruben in trouble. I knew from experience what Smith wanted to do. If I gave him the rules he was asking for, he would have told Gruben on me. This would have caused Gruben and other security staff to turn on me and would have put me on Smith's side in a war with Gruben. In addition, this would have hindered and possibly stopped all my efforts to bring change inside the TCU.

I told Smith that he chose to war with Officer Gruben by telling the lieutenant on him and that I wasn't going to join the war Smith started. I also told Smith that I had informed the security staff many times the problems they had with inmates had nothing to do with me, and that I didn't want to be involved with any wars between staff and inmates.

Smith got mad at me for not siding with him in his war with Officer Gruben. I told Smith that I highly recommended he apologize to Officer Gruben and tell him he didn't want any trouble. I then explained that Gruben was undefeated in his wars with inmates. Finally, I told Smith that Gruben would either set him up with disciplinary reports, get him to sign out of the TCU, or get him placed on close management. I told Smith these things because I had personal knowledge of Grubens' tactics.

Smith didn't take my advice. In addition to the games that Gruben played involving Smith's food, he searched Smith's cell several times when Smith wasn't in his cell. Each time Gruben stole some of Smith's personal property and ransacked his cell. Smith was successful in getting Gruben reposted for a few days from the Westside, but overall Gruben won their war. Gruben was successful in getting Smith set up with a few disciplinary reports, placed on close management two, and transferred from the Dade CI.

Additionally, Smith filed several grievances on Timothy Siders and me. In some of Smith's grievances, he contended that the mounted security cameras showed that I had a personal relationship with staff.

Chapter 11: Hot-Water-Shower Treatment of Mentally Disabled Inmates

135) When were inmates showered on the Westside?

Inmates were showered on Monday, Wednesday, and Friday. In the two years I was housed on the Westside only orderlies were showered on Sundays, Tuesdays, Thursdays, or Saturdays.

136) How were the inmates who were housed in Wings J-2 and J-3 showered?

The inmates housed on J-3 were on TCU status, protective management status, disciplinary confinement status, and two-point status. Those on disciplinary confinement status or two-point status were supposed to be handcuffed when they were escorted to or from a shower. Inmates not on any of these statuses could go to and from a shower without wearing handcuffs. In addition, security staff were supposed to escort all the inmates housed on the Westside to and from the showers on shower nights. Staff never did this except with the inmates on either disciplinary or two-point confinement statuses.

On shower nights, the officer working in Wing J-3 always started showers with the protective management inmates. Most of the time, none of these inmates had to be handcuffed or escorted to a shower. There were always three working showers in Wing J-3, and two working showers in Wing J-2. About five minutes before shower time, the officer working Wing J-3 turned on the shower next to Cell J-3201 (AKA the *Hot-Water-Shower*). There was a closet between the *Hot-Water-Shower* and Cell J-3201. The officer turned on the water in the *Hot-Water-Shower* by going into that closet and only turning on the hot water for the *Hot-Water-Shower*. Inmates using that shower adjusted the cold water to mix it with the hot water before he started to shower.

Five inmates were showered at a time. An officer called over his radio and told a booth officer to open the cell doors of five inmates. When those five zero point status inmates were let out of their cells, the officer told each of them which of the five working showers in Wings J-2 and J-3 they should use to shower. Inmates were told to not lock themselves in the shower stalls and to go back to their cells when they were done. When all the zero point protective management status inmates were finished showering, the officer would then proceed to shower the zero point status inmates who were not on protective management status.

While the zero point status inmates housed in Wing J-3 were showering, the officer would usually sit in a chair located downstairs, or stand or sit at the table in front of Cell J-3101. When the officer was done showering the zero point status inmates in Wing J-3, he would then shower the zero point inmates in Wing J-2 using the same procedures as was used for inmates in Wing J-3. When they were nearly done showering the zero point status inmates, another officer arrived to assist with showering the two point status inmates. Officers from Wings J-1, J-2, and J-3 helped each other as needed.

To shower the two point status inmates in Wings J-2 and J-3, two officers went to the cell, opened the flap, handcuffed the inmate through the flap, and escorted him to a shower. They locked the inmate in the shower and removed his handcuffs through a hole in the shower door. When the inmate was done, he was again handcuffed, and the two officers escorted him back to his cell. This process would be repeated until all the two point status inmates were done showering.

Chapter 11: Hot-Water-Shower Treatment of Mentally Disabled Inmates

137) How many showers worked on the Westside?

There were 12 showers on the Westside. During the entire time I was housed in the TCU, the one, which was located upstairs on wing J-2 next to cell 201, never worked. Eleven others did, and, in ten of these, inmates were able to control the water while they were using them by simply pushing a button on the back wall of the shower. None of these ten were in a blind spot, which is a spot or area not monitored by a mounted security camera. However, the water in the shower next to Cell J-3201 (wing J-3, cell 201) was not controlled by the inmate who took the shower. It had been rigged.

138) Please describe the upstairs shower next to Cell 201?

If you were looking toward the door of Cell 201, there would be a closet on your right. Next to that closet was a shower with a door that locked. There was a square hole in the door. Inmates who were in the shower put their hands through the hole, so staff could put them in handcuffs or remove handcuffs. The shower door didn't go from the floor to the ceiling.

The shower was approximately three feet wide by 10 to 12 feet long. There was a fluorescent light fixture hanging on the ceiling in the shower. There was a button, showerhead, and a soap holder on the back wall in the shower. Similar to the other showers, when an inmate pushed the button on the back wall, water came out of the shower head positioned over the button.

However, this shower had another source of water. The left wall of the shower was adjacent to the closet that was next to Cell J-3201. In this side wall and about two feet from the back wall and six feet off the floor, there was a hole with a small PVC pipe in it, which was, in turn, attached to a commercial sink which was in the closet. The PVC pipe did not protrude from the wall and could not be seen by someone looking through the door into the shower.

In the closet, the PVC pipe ran down the wall of the closet and was attached to a hose which was, in turn, attached to the faucet of the sink. The sink had two handles that were clearly color coded, blue for cold water and red for hot water. Water travelled from this faucet to the hose, up the PVC pipe, and into the shower.

Department of Corruption

See figure on next page,

Shower Where Rainey Died and Adjacent Room with Water Controls

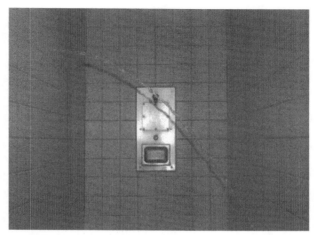

Stream of water in shower coming from adjacent room.

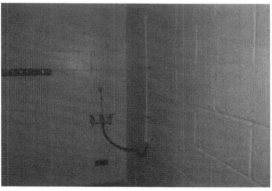

Adjacent room, water controls, and pipe carrying water to shower

139) Tell me about your history with Officer Roland Clarke.

Officer Clarke was hired in 2010 and soon began working in the TCU on the Westside where I was an orderly on the Westside. Other officers who worked there looked upon me as a good inmate and worker whom they could trust. Officers Sakay and Gibson, who trained Clarke, were the two officers who trusted me the most.

In 2011, when I returned to the TCU, Officer Clarke told me he was raised as a Baptist. When I went over several doctrines with him and asked him if he believed them, he said he did. This showed me he was possibly raised in a Reformed Baptist family. Officer Clarke had more intellectual knowledge of the Bible than most of the other staff in the TCU.

He believed he was one of God's elect who was predestined to eternal life. He liked the story of Samson in the Bible and said he could really relate to Samson. He felt that he was like Samson because, like Samson, he was both big and strong and had issues with becoming violent and chasing after women. Officer Clarke said he played football in college and lost his football career due to an injury. He also claimed to have tried to pursue a career in boxing but stopped because of an eye injury. He said he was warned by a doctor that, if he continued boxing, one good punch to his damaged eye would blind that eye. I believe he said he obtained a Bachelors' Degree in Criminal Justice. When I moved to Wing J-3, he was the wing officer on the 4:00 pm to 12:00 am shift. He used to stand in front of my cell and talk with me when he was showering the zero point status inmates. We talked a lot.

140) Will you describe Officer Clarke?

He was approximately 6'5." During the time I knew him, he maintained a bodyweight of between 270 and 310 pounds. The majority of it was muscle. He was very soft spoken and calm, even when he was angry and violent. Usually, people lose their calmness when they get mad. Officer Clarke never did.

141) Will you tell me about Inmate Shaun McKinley?

The majority of the time McKinley was housed in the TCU, he was housed Wing J-3111.

McKinley was in the TCU running from disciplinary reports he received while at Columbia CI. Most officers took a liking to him within days of his arrival because he knew a lot about sports, the hip-hop world, and rap music. Within days of McKinley arriving, Officer Clarke started talking with him.

McKinley and I worked together as orderlies on the 8:00 am to 4:00 pm shift for a short period of time. He received a disciplinary report for breaking an elderly white inmate's thumb. I was told he was placed on close management for that incident. The victim said McKinley punched him in the face and knocked him out. The elderly inmate said he woke up to McKinley bending his thumb back to his wrist until it broke. The doctor who examined the inmate's thumb said he could tell that McKinley intentionally broke it. After this incident, McKinley was on two point status the rest of the time he was in the TCU. McKinley was very racist. He referred to all white people as "Crackers" and "Devils."

Shaun McKinley, Officer Clarke, and the majority of the security staff employed at Dade CI were black. During all the time I was housed at Dade CI, fewer than 10 white security staff were employed there.

142) Why did staff move Daniel Geiger into Wing J-3?

In my opinion, Daniel Geiger was the most severely mentally disabled inmate housed in the TCU. He yelled and made noise almost constantly day and night. Geiger was so impaired that you couldn't converse with him, and he had no knowledge of anything going on around him. He wouldn't shower, and, when he defecated and urinated, he did it on the floor in his cell.

I first heard about Geiger from inmate Billy Joe Ziesmer. He and Geiger were both housed in Wing J-1. Trying to deprive Ziesmer of sleep, security staff moved Geiger into the adjacent cell. Ziesmer found it very difficult and sometimes impossible to sleep because the noise Geiger made. Ziesmer filed a Federal Civil Rights complaint in the Dade County, Florida Federal District Court against Sergeant Mizeal, Officer Williams, and others for physically abusing Ziesmer.

Ziesmer told me that, as a form of retaliation, security staff moved Geiger next to inmates who filed grievances and whom they did not like. It was the staff's way of saying, "If you file grievances on us or get on our bad side, we will move Daniel

Geiger next to you so that you can't sleep." When Geiger was moved into Wing J-3, staff placed him one or two cells away from Daniel Medberry who was filing a lot of grievances on staff. Similarly when inmate Lawrence Smith started filing grievances on Officer Gruben, the security staff moved Geiger into the cell next to Smith.

143) What happened with Geiger, McKinley, and Officer Clarke?

Clarke was the Wing J-3 officer five days a week on the 4:00 pm to 12:00 am shift, and it was his duty to keep his wing as quiet and as peaceful as possible. Wing J-3 was a small wing. It was only about half the size of Wing J-1. Officer Clarke didn't appreciate Geiger being moved into his wing, which had been fairly quiet until then. Geiger's presence also upset many of the inmates housed in Wing J-3, especially McKinley.

McKinley started telling Officer Clarke, "You should take that fucking cracker, put him in that shower upstairs, and turn it on full hot. I bet you, he'll stop all that yelling if you put him in that shower." At first, Officer Clarke just smiled at McKinley when he said that. However, McKinley didn't give up. He continued to coerce Officer Clarke for two or three days to place Geiger in the shower next to Cell J-3201 and turn that shower on full hot.

After two or three days of this and of dealing with Geiger's constant yelling, Clarke followed McKinley's recommendation, placed Geiger in the shower next to Cell J-3201, went into the closet, and turned the hot water on full blast with no cold water. The hot water went through the rubber hose and PVC pipe, then into the shower Geiger was in.

144) What happened after inmate Daniel Geiger was placed in the *Hot-Water-Shower*?

After about five or 10 minutes, Geiger started yelling like crazy and kicking the shower door. It sounded like he was repeatedly saying, "Let me out".

After about 10 or 15 minutes of Geiger being in the shower, Officer Clarke went to the shower and told Geiger, "I'll let you out when you stop yelling and kicking the door and show me that you're going to be quiet." About five minutes after this, Geiger stopped yelling and making noise and was quite for the next hour and 45 minutes. Altogether, inmate Geiger was in the shower for about two hours before Clarke took him out.

145) What happened when Daniel Geiger put back in his cell?

He didn't yell or make any noise for the rest of the night. This caused Inmate Shaun McKinley to say to Officer Clarke, "I told you it would work, and that Cracker would shut up."

It also caused a lot of inmates in the wing to say to Clarke, "You got Geiger to stop yelling."

Several of the inmates were so frustrated by Geiger's constant yelling and noise that they were actually happy that Clarke got him to stop yelling.

146) How do you know the shower was hot?

It was on a non-shower night. Geiger was in his cell yelling and making noise. McKinley had been working on convincing Clarke to place Geiger in that shower and turn it on only hot. Several times that night McKinley yelled to Clarke (when Clarke wasn't near McKinley's cell) to place Geiger in the shower and turn it on only hot. Eventually, Clarke took Geiger out of his cell and placed him in the shower next to Cell J-3201.

1) Everything happened in a chronological order consistent with Officer Clarke following McKinley's advice.

2) About 5 or 10 minutes after Clarke put Geiger was in the shower, Geiger began yelling and kicking the shower door. It was as if he was trying to say, "Let me out."

After about 10 or 15 more minutes, Officer Clarke went to the shower and told Geiger, "I'll let you out when you stop yelling and kicking the door and show me that you're going to stay quiet." Geiger wouldn't have wanted to get out of that shower so badly if the water temperature was tolerable.

3) When Officer Clarke took inmate Geiger out of the shower, Officer Clarke told Geiger that if he started yelling when he was returned to his cell, Officer Clarke would again put him into the shower. The shower

wouldn't be looked upon as a punishment if the shower water was tolerable.

4) After Clarke found out that "*Hot-Water-Shower*" worked on Geiger, he told me he "found something to shut Geiger up." I knew what Officer Clarke meant, but I asked him, to see what he would say, "What do you mean?" He responded, "Putting him in the shower upstairs and turning only the hot water on." After this incident, Officer Clarke continued to place inmates in that shower and turn only the hot water on.

This led to months of conversations between Officer Clarke and me about him using that shower to punish inmates who didn't follow his orders.

147) Were inmates in the wing supportive of what Officer Clarke did to Daniel Geiger?

Yes. Several of them were only concerned about their own peace and comfort. They didn't care that Geiger didn't know what he was doing, or that he shouldn't be tortured as a result of his mental disability.

I know that some of the inmates were scared. They were moved by fear to pretend they were supportive of Officer Clarke's actions because they didn't want to become his next victim.

148) Why did you use the word "torture?"

The shower was big enough for inmate Geiger to avoid the hot water getting on his body. All Geiger had to do was stand in any of the four sections of the shower where the hot water would not fall on his body.

I used the word "torture" to describe the extreme heat and steam generated from the hot water. After Darren Rainey died in that shower, the water temperature was tested and found to have been in excess of 160° Fahrenheit. This was the temperature after the hot water in the shower was on for about five minutes. Geiger was in the shower for approximately two hours with only the hot water on. The heat and steam made breathing very difficult. The shower was worse than a sweatbox.

Chapter 11: Hot-Water-Shower Treatment of Mentally Disabled Inmates

149) Do you have personal knowledge of the heat and steam?

Yes. My October 1, 2011 journal entry shows that around August 2011, I moved from Cell J-3101 to Cell J-3204 which was upstairs in Wing J-3. Earlier I explained how the Wing J-3 officer would usually turn only the hot water on in the shower next to Cell J-3201 about five minutes prior to starting the showering process. On several occasions, the security staff let the hot water run for more than five minutes before an officer began showering the inmates. When this happened, I could feel the temperature in my cell rising from the steam coming from the shower. The steam was so thick, it engulfed about half of the upper tier and remained there even after a lot of the steam sank down the stairway from the upper tier to the lower tier.

Also, I was able to personally investigate. As I mentioned earlier, orderlies can were allowed to shower on any shift they worked. On two occasions, after Officer Clarke started using the *Hot-Water-Shower* on mentally disabled inmates; I went to that shower, turned on the hot water, shut the shower door without locking it, and then went to my cell to grab things I needed to shower. On both occasions, I timed myself and made sure it took about 10 minutes for me to return to the shower from my cell. When I opened the shower door, I was shocked to feel the extreme heat. At that time, I didn't know the temperature of the water and wanted to experience what inmates experienced when they were put in the *Hot-Water-Shower*. Both times, I thought it had to be over 150° Fahrenheit in that shower.

150) What cell were you housed in when Daniel Geiger was placed in the *Hot-Water-Shower*?

I was in Cell J-3101 on the lower tier and under Cell J-3201. Facing my cell, the shower was upstairs and about 10 feet to the right. Around August 2011, I moved from Cell J-3101 to Cell J-3204. Between either December 2011 or the beginning of January 2012, I moved back into Cell J-3101.

I was in Cell J-3101 during the times that the shower was being used as a torturing device to punish mentally disabled inmates.

151) What was going through your mind when Officer Clarke placed Daniel Geiger in the *Hot-Water-Shower*?

I never expected security officers would began to use the *Hot-Water-Shower* shower the way Officer Clarke did that first night. Even when Shaun McKinley started telling Officer Clarke to use that shower to get Geiger to stop yelling and making noise, I didn't think Clarke would do it. I was caught off guard when Clarke first placed Geiger in the *Hot-Water-Shower*. So many things went through my mind; I couldn't thoroughly analyze all of them. When Geiger became quiet and, also, didn't yell or make any noise when Clarke put him back in his cell, I found some peace in thinking that Clarke got what he wanted. I didn't think he would place Geiger back in the *Hot-Water-Shower* again.

As I found out later, I was wrong.

152) Will you tell me about inmate Halden Casey?

When Halden Casey came to Dade CI, he was housed on Crisis Stabilization Unit status in Wing J-2. Casey looked like he weighed about 165 to 175 pounds. I met Casey when Officer Weary came to me and said, "Hempstead we have a bad a*s in Wing J-2. Come and meet him." When we got to Wing J-2, Sergeant Mizeal and Officers Gruben and Eli were in front of Casey's cell messing with him. Casey was cursing at them and being verbally aggressive with them. The security staff was laughing and making humor out of the situation. When I looked in Casey's cell, I saw that he still had a tray in his cell from breakfast.

After being at the cell for about a minute with the staff, Officer Gruben said, "Hempstead, tell this tough guy what he's getting himself into by talking trash, destroying his mattress, and not giving us that tray!"

I looked at Casey and said, I'm saying this because you're a fellow prisoner. I've been an orderly here a long time. They're going to starve you to death, and do all types of things you would never imagine if you keep harassing them and don't give them the tray back."

Casey responded, "Oh, you all want this tray. Here I'll give you the tray." Casey then picked up the tray and started hitting the cell door with it. The security staff laughed.

Chapter 11: Hot-Water-Shower Treatment of Mentally Disabled Inmates

When he stopped hitting the door with the tray, Officer Weary said, "That's all you got?" Casey then went back to beating the cell door again with the tray.

This time when Casey stopped hitting the cell door, Officer Gruben said, "You can keep that tray because you're not going to get another one until you give it back."

At lunch time Sergeant Mizeal went to Inmate Casey's cell with a Styrofoam tray and told Casey, "When you give me the tray in your cell, you can have this one." Sergeant Mizeal then placed the Styrofoam tray on the table where Casey could see it. About two hours later, Casey agreed to give Officer Eli the hard tray in his cell in exchange for the Styrofoam tray of food.

Staff on the 8:00 am to 4:00 pm shift told staff on the 4:00 pm to 12:00 am shift about this incident with Casey. This led to Officers Gibson and Cobas harassing Casey. Gibson and Cobas told staff on the 12:00 am to 8:00 am shift about Casey and this led to Officers David and Wood harassing Casey. Within three or four days of being on the Westside, Casey was being denied one to three trays of food a day almost every day of the week.

When Casey received a tray on Sergeant Mizeal's shift, Officer Gruben drastically reduced the portion sizes without informing Mizeal. On every shift, Casey would kick the cell door, yell, and talk trash to the officers.

Other than these things, Casey acted like a normal person. He had numerous intelligent conversations with staff and inmates. Therefore, security staff thought Casey didn't have any mental health problems and was, merely, a disciplinary problem.

Casey had issues with security staff on every shift, but he never had any issues with Officer Clarke until Casey was moved to Clarke's wing. As soon as Casey moved to Wing J-3, he started calling Clarke, "Big Dummy" and talking trash to him. Within days of being placed in Wing J-3, Casey was constantly making noise trying to upset the other inmates in that wing. When Officer Clarke saw that the *Hot-Water-Shower* caused Daniel Geiger to stop yelling and making noise, Clarke decided to use the same technique on Halden Casey. There was no advanced notice. One night, Clarke was standing in front of Casey's cell, listening to him talk trash and hit the cell door. Clarke then called over his radio and asked the booth officer to open Casey's cell door. After Clarke stepped inside Casey's cell and told him to submit to handcuffing, Casey did what he was told to do and didn't say anything disrespectful.

Casey was about 5'10" and weighed about 165 to 175 pounds. Officer Clarke was about 6'5", weighed between 270 and 300 pounds, was all muscle, and was an ex-boxer and college football player. Casey had enough sense to realize what the consequences would have been if he didn't listen to Officer Clarke.

153) Did Officer Clarke put Halden Casey in the *Hot-Water-Shower*?

Yes. About five or 10 minutes after Casey was placed in the shower, he started yelling and kicking the door. He yelled louder and kicked the shower door harder than Daniel Geiger. Casey yelled for several minutes, "Get me out of here. It's hot." He also yelled to the inmates in the wing, saying, "Hey, tell staff to take me out of here. It's hot." After yelling for about 15 or 20 minutes, Casey stopped. He was in the shower for around two hours.

154) What was going through your mind when Halden Casey was in the *Hot-Water-Shower*?

I was thinking about when Officer Clarke placed Daniel Geiger in the shower. I never thought he would place another inmate in that shower. I thought how it was only days later, and Clarke had another inmate in the same shower. The whole situation was crazy to me. I didn't know what to think about it. Clarke, who told me he was one of God's elect who God had predestined to eternal life, was torturing mentally disabled inmates in the shower over my cell.

I had returned to the TCU to try and help the inmates and make the place safer for them. For a while, I thought I was on the right track with the Bible study, constant evangelism, Officer Piggott's conversion, and other things. After Halden Casey was placed in the shower, I started seeing things in a different light. I thought about the things that happened in 2010 when I was in the TCU, and the things that happened since my return to the TCU in 2011. It appeared that things had gotten worse since I returned to the TCU in 2011. I had to do something to try to stop Clarke from placing any more inmates in that shower.

I decided I would talk with Clarke the first chance I got. At that time, I thought Major McCarter was opposed to the mistreatment of inmates. I figured I would try and get Officer Clarke to stop his abuse by trying to get him to fear Major McCarter catching Clarke using the shower to punish mentally disabled inmates. Within a day or two of Halden Casey being placed in the shower, I had a chance to speak with Officer Clarke alone. I asked him, "Do you know anything about the new major?"

Officer Clarke responded, "No. Why?"

I said, "I know a lot about him from staff on day shift. It appears that the major is opposed to a lot of stuff. If any of the inmates in this wing told the major about Daniel Geiger or Halden Casey being placed in that shower, you could get in trouble, especially if the cameras show what you have been doing. I don't want to see you get in trouble."

Clarke responded, "The only thing the cameras show, is me putting an inmate in a shower. I'm not worried about the major."

That attempt with Clarke was unsuccessful. I made several more attempts in the months to follow.

155) Please summarize Officer Clarke's use of the *Hot-Water-Shower* with Geiger and Casey.

- Daniel Geiger was placed in the *Hot-Water-Shower* several times.
- Officer Roland Clarke put him there each time.
- Each time Daniel Geiger was put in the shower, he yelled and kicked the shower door, wanting to get out.
- He eventually stopped yelling and kicking the door, and focused on fighting to breathe until he was taken out the shower.
- Halden Casey was placed in the *Hot-Water-Shower* several times.
- Officer Roland Clarke put him there each time.
- Every time he was in the *Hot-Water-Shower*, Halden Casey yelled for several minutes about how hot the water

was and about wanting to get out of the shower. Sometimes he yelled that it was hard to breathe, he and always kicked the shower door for several minutes.

- Eventually, he stopped yelling and kicking the shower door and started focusing on breathing until he was taken out of the shower.

Officer Roland Clarke kept these inmates in the shower for between 45 minutes and three hours.

156) Will you tell me about Michael Alfonso?

When Michael Alfonso was first placed on the Westside, he was housed in Wing J-1 on the upper tier around Cell 208. Not long after he was placed in that cell, all of the inmates who were housed in the cells around him asked security staff to move him. They wanted him moved because Alfonso liked to sing very loud while clapping his hands and dancing. He didn't just sing and clap his hands for one or two songs. He did it for hours straight. Eventually, security staff moved him from Wing J-1 to Wing J-3.

While he was housed in Wing J-3, he continued his singing, clapping, and dancing. Alfonso didn't have any issues with Officer Clarke until Clarke learned that the *Hot-Water-Shower* got Geiger and Casey to stop yelling and making noise.

One night, Clarke told Alfonso to stop singing so loud and clapping his hands. After telling Alfonso numerous times to stop, Clarke opened Alfonso's cell door, escorted him to the *Hot-Water-Shower*, placed him in it, and turned the water on full hot. Alfonso started yelling loudly and kicking the door after being in the shower about five to 10 minutes. Alfonso yelled numerous times, "Get me out of here." He also stated numerous times, "It's hot", which was always followed by cursing. Eventually, Alfonso stopped yelling and making noise, and was quiet the rest of the time he was in the shower.

- Michael Alfonso placed in the *Hot-Water-Shower* two or three times.
- Officer Roland Clarke Michael Alfonso in the *Hot-Water-Shower* every time?
- Every time Michael Alfonso was in the *Hot-Water-Shower*, he yelled to try to get out. He would kick the shower door and

curse for a short period of time and eventually, he stopped yelling and kicking the door and focused on breathing.

157) Will you tell me about William Wallace?

I knew William Wallace from when I was housed in the TCU in 2010. Wallace used to sit in his cell and talk to himself for hours straight, and sometimes the whole day. He talked very quickly and fairly loud. He didn't like to leave his cell for any reason, especially to shower. Sometime around the beginning of February 2011, Officer Clarke escorted Wallace from Wing J-1 where he was housed to Wing J-3, placed him in the *Hot-Water-Shower*, and turned it on only hot. Wallace yelled about wanting out of the shower and said the shower was hot, but he didn't yell for very long. While Wallace was in the shower, he talked fairly low and very quickly, when he was talking.

Wallace was in the shower for about two hours. All of the time that he was in the shower, Officer Clarke stood in front of my cell door and talked with me. That night we spoke about the Bible and his past college football and boxing days.

158) How many times was William Wallace placed in the *Hot-Water-Shower*?

Once. Officer Clarke tried to place him in the *Hot-Water-Shower* a second time. However, when Clarke brought Wallace into Wing J-3 and they started walking past my cell toward the stairs that led to the *Hot-Water-Shower*, Wallace dropped to the ground and made his body go deadweight. Wallace did this attempting to not be placed in the *Hot-Water-Shower*. This caused Clarke to have to stand there with Wallace for about a minute threatening him and attempting to get him to stand. Sergeant Johnathan saw what was happening and entered Wing J-3 saying, "No, no, no. Not that shower." Sergeant Johnathan then took Wallace back to Wing J-1. I don't know what happened after Wallace left Wing J-3.

159) Tell me about your journal entries on *Hot-Water-Shower* treatment in January-June 6, 2012.

I'm going to list what my journal states about inmates being placed in the *Hot-Water-Shower*, and nothing else.

January 21, 2021 journal entry: *"Daniel Geiger was placed in the Hot-Water-Shower again. This was the second time. I told Officer Clarke after he put Casey in the Hot-Water-Shower that he could get in trouble if Major McCarter found out and that the Major was opposed to a lot of stuff."*

February 6, 2012 journal entry: *"I forgot to mention William Wallace being placed in the Hot-Water-Shower the other day. He didn't yell very long. He sure talked a lot. Clarke spent the time in front of my cell talking about his college football days and boxing days."*

March 1, 2012 journal entry: *"Officer Clarke had Michael Alfonso in the shower the other night. Alfonso was yelling and calling Clarke curse-words. Officer Clarke told Alfonso the next time he wanted to shower, he would put him back in the same shower. Alfonso refused his next shower. It seems like Officer Clarke is just putting every person in there that plays with him or upsets him."*

March 18, 2012 journal entry: *"Officer Clarke just did Geiger and Casey again both in the same night. Geiger wasn't that long this time. Casey was in there about two hours. Geiger was in there for about 45 minutes. Casey could have avoided it. A few nights ago, an inmate from the Eastside was placed in the Hot-Water-Shower. I don't know who he was, but it was all like a joke when the staff brought him in. It seems like Officer Clarke is using it more now than in the beginning."*

April 4, 2012 journal entry: *"Officer Clarke tried to put Wallace in the shower, but Sergeant Johnathan stopped Clarke this time. Wallace dropped to the ground almost in front of my cell when he saw Clarke taking him towards the stairs. The sergeant came in and took inmate Wallace back to Wing J-1, and sort of yelled at Clarke a little."*

June 6, 2012 journal entry: *"Placed Eastside inmate in the Hot-Water-Shower that I forgot to mention."*

160) **Do you remember every inmate who received the *Hot-Water-Shower* treatment and each time an inmate was placed in that shower?**

No. I only remember inmates Daniel Geiger, Halden Casey, Michael Alfonso, William Wallace, and Darren Rainey being

120

placed in the *Hot-Water-Shower* one or more times. My journal entries were made in real time. This makes my journal entries very reliable.

161) Did other staff know Officer Clarke was placing inmates in the *Hot-Water-Shower*?

Yes. Officer Clarke used the *Hot-Water-Shower* to punish inmates for approximately six months. It was always done on the 4:00 pm to 12:00 am shift. The inmates who were placed in that shower always yelled and kicked the shower door.

Other staff had to hear them. Other staff saw Officer Clarke put inmates in the *Hot-Water-Shower* for long periods of time. Staff did security checks while the inmates were in that shower. They felt and saw how hot the shower water was when they looked in the shower during their security checks. Officer Clarke told the staff who worked with him that the *Hot-Water-Shower* treatment got the inmates to calm down.

I discussed Officer Clarke actions with Sergeants Johnathan and Pierri, and Officers Piggot, Eli, Gruben, Gibson, and Thompson. Officer Clarke's fiancée (Officer Jackson) worked on the Westside with him. Surely he didn't hide what he was doing from his fiancée. Also, many nurses were in Wing J-3 while inmates were in the *Hot-Water-Shower* during the six months that it was used.

So many people knew.

162) Will you tell me about Gregory Shevlin and the inmate nicknamed "Redneck"?

Gregory Shevlin and Redneck frequently worked as orderlies on each shift. Throughout most of 2011 and 2012, Shevlin slept in Cell J-1225, and Redneck slept in Cell J-1226. Out of all the orderlies I worked with while housed in the TCU, I worked with Shevlin the most. His nickname was "New York." He had a New York accent and most of the time he was very loud when he talked. I believe he was in the TCU because he was somewhat fearful to live in of general population. He was the neighbor and a friend of Redneck

163) Which regular security worked on the Westside on the 4:00 pm to 12:00 am shift from January to June 23, 2012?

Lieutenant Pinkney was in charge of that shift; Johnathan was the regular sergeant, and Pierri and Fanfan were relief sergeants. The regular officers were Clarke, Gibson, Sakay, Cobas, Millhorn, Pena, Mac, Hood, Thompson, Forbes, and Lemelis. They didn't all work on the same days.

164) How is Officer Clarke ranked in the list of evil officers you previously mentioned?

Officers Sakay, Gibson, Weary, and Gruben did more acts of evil than Officer Clarke. However, in my opinion, Clarke committed the evilest acts I witnessed in the TCU, which was the *Hot-Water-Shower* treatment of mentally disabled inmates.

165) How were you affected by the abuse being inflicted on the inmates during the months inmates were being placed in the *Hot-Water-Shower*?

When I saw that Officer Clarke was continuing to place inmates in the *Hot-Water-Shower*, I knew I had to say something to him about it. In the following months, I spoke with him several times about his use of the *Hot-Water-Shower*. Additionally, I told him what the Bible says about how we are to treat others. I constantly mentioned how I didn't want him to get in trouble, and I did my best to approach him as a loving Christian brother who cared about him and his earthly and eternal destiny.

It makes me sad to say what I'm about to say, but I have to say it. After three or four months of continually hearing inmates yelling from the shower over me, I started thinking it was just another evil thing that I couldn't stop. I had seen so much evil over my time in the TCU, I had somewhat accepted that was the way things were and would always be on the Westside TCU. In other words, violence and torture were the normal life in the TCU. All I ever heard was constant yelling by inmates for some reason or another. Inmate patients were continually denied toilet paper, hygiene items, and clean clothes. They were constantly harassed, physically abused, starved, poisoned with pills, subjected to chemical and psychological warfare, and the list goes on.

Additionally, the staff who committed all the abuse were the staff who I really thought God had moved me to evangelize. I constantly evangelized and prayed for their conversion, really believing that if they were converted, it would lead to the TCU becoming a safe place for the mentally disabled inmates. I reasoned that the conversion of the staff was the best help for the staff and the inmates. Even though I started thinking that the *Hot-Water-Shower* treatment was just another type of abuse I couldn't stop, I didn't give up trying to help the inmates. This was one of the reasons I fought to not be discharged when I went in front of the treatment team after I was successful in getting off protective management status in May 2012.

I was beset by grief. In the last eighteen months, six of my relatives had died as had two inmates I had known on Westside. Now I has witnessed the murder of Darren Rainey.

Chapter 12: Darren Rainey

166) Will you tell me about Darren Rainey?

Around May 2012, Darren Rainey was moved into Cell J-3211. He was not on protective management, which was unusual because the upper tier in Wing J-3 was primarily for inmates who were on both TCU status and protective management status. I was an orderly at that time.

A few days later, Rainey asked me to sell him a lunch tray. I was allowed to sell the extra lunch trays staff ordered but never had any to sell because I used them to smuggle food to the inmates who weren't being fed. Officer Piggot heard Rainey ask for an extra tray, so he directed me to give him one, which I did

A day or two later Officer Piggot said to me, "You said the Quran referred to the Christian Bible and Jesus. I have a Quran. Will you show me in the Quran where it talks about the Bible and Jesus?"

Since Piggot told me he was born again, we spent hours discussing Christianity, apologetics, church history, evangelism, etc. When we talked about evangelism, and I brought up evangelizing Muslims. Piggot wanted me to prove what I said about Jesus and the bible was actually in the Quran. I retrieved a book from my cell to help me find the answer to his question and

123

brought it to the table where he was and asked him, "Where did you get that Quran from?"

He responded, "Inmate Rainey in 11 upstairs." I then told Piggot where to turn to in the Quran. As he turned the pages, he saw that several pages had brown spots on them. When Piggot saw the brown spots, he said, "What is that, crap?"

Piggot was turning the book with his bare hands and, to get a laugh, I decided to say it was crap and then tell him I was just kidding. So I said, "It looks like crap, and you don't have any gloves on." Piggot immediately dropped the Quran and jumped back from it.

I started laughing and said, "I could be wrong. You won't know unless you smell it."

Piggot said, "I'm not smelling it. You're the crap expert. You smell it."

I responded, "I'm just messing with you. It's not crap. It looks like dry coffee."

He said, "Are you sure? The brown spots look too big to be coffee."

I picked up the Quran, looked at the brown spots on the pages, and said again, "It looks like coffee. If you don't think it is coffee, put gloves on."

I was wearing latex gloves from the time the conversation started. Piggot put on a pair of latex gloves, and I then showed him where in the Quran it mentioned the Bible and Jesus. In the middle of our discussion, I was called by the sergeant to do something in another wing.

About an hour later, when Officer Piggot and I got back together to talk, I asked him if he still had the Quran, or if he had given it back to Rainey. I wanted to show him some more Surahs in the Quran that were interesting things to bring out while evangelizing Muslims. Piggot responded, "I threw the Quran in the trash. It was crap, not coffee."

I said, "I believe it was coffee, and Rainey is going to be angry if you don't give him back his Quran."

He responded, "It looked like crap to me, but even if it wasn't, I'm still helping Rainey by not giving it back to him.

Maybe he'll take a Bible to read, now that he doesn't have a Quran. I'm also possibly stopping a potential suicide bomber."

I said, "If you don't give him his Quran back, he's probably going to try to throw crap on you at lunchtime."

He responded, "He's not going to get it on me. I'm too quick."

I said, "I think you should give him the Quran back. If you want, I'll give it to him."

He responded, "He'll be OK. We just have to watch him at lunchtime."

Officer Piggot didn't tell Rainey that he threw away his Quran until after we served lunch. When Piggot told Rainey that he threw away his Quran because it had feces on it, Rainey got really angry and said it wasn't feces. Rainey explained that while his property was being packed by officers in preparation for his transfer to Dade CI, coffee got on his Quran.

A few days after this incident a cell opened in Wing J-1 and Darren Rainey was moved into that cell. I was told that Rainey was only housed on the upper tier in Wing J-3 with the protective management inmates because there weren't any cells for him to move into in Wing J-1. After that day, I didn't see Rainey again until June 23, 2012.

167) What happened with Darren Rainey on June 23, 2012?

In the evening hours, I placed my door sheet over the window in my cell door to engage in prayer and worship. While my sheet was up, I heard the door shut at the front of the small hallway that led to the Wing J-3 front door. I looked out the side of my sheet and saw Officer Clarke escorting an inmate into Wing J-3. When I saw the inmate, I knew him, but I couldn't remember that his name was Darren Rainey. It was around 8:50 pm when I watched Clarke pass my cell door with the inmate. I then looked out the other side of my sheet to see if Clarke was escorting him to Cell J-3110. It was the only empty cell in the wing.

When I saw Clarke and the inmate turn out of my sight towards the stairs that lead to the upper tier, I knew it was another inmate going to the *Hot-Water-Shower*. At that time, I didn't look upon that night different from any of the other nights when inmates were put in the hot shower. I continued what I was doing as if it was just another normal night in the TCU.

About five or 10 minutes after Clarke put Rainey in the shower, Rainey started yelling. "Get me out of here. It's hot!" He also yelled, "I'm sorry. Get me out of here! I won't do it again!" He kept yelling these things and didn't stop. While Rainey was yelling, he was also hitting or kicking the door constantly. As he continued to yell, hit, and kick the door, I thought, "Why isn't he stopping so he can focus on breathing?"

Rainey's yelling and kicking were so loud that Sergeant Fanfan and Officers Clarke, Thompson, and Hood came into Wing J-3. Clarke went upstairs to the shower where Rainey was. Sergeant Fanfan and Officer Hood stayed downstairs. Fanfan yelled up to Clarke, "Did he shower?"

Clarke responded, "No. He doesn't have any soap."

Fanfan said, "I thought he already showered, I didn't know he was standing in there not showering. Keep him in there."

Hood then said, "He can stay in there for six hours. You can take him out. Then put him back in for another six hours."

Officer Clarke then came to my cell and said, "Hempstead, do you have a bar of soap?"

I responded, "Fanfan is not going to fall for that."

Clarke repeated, "Can I have a bar of soap?" I then gave him the bar of soap

In 2012, I thought Sergeant Fanfan was by the book and was opposed to inmates being abused. He was also known for being smart in prison matters. I did not think Fanfan would fall for Clarke's tricks, which was why I told Officer Clarke, "Fanfan is not going to fall for that." The soap trick was one of several tricks that Clarke used in situations where a sergeant or another staff member was attempting to get Clarke to remove an inmate from the *Hot-Water-Shower* before Officer Clarke wanted to remove the inmate. Fanfan ended up falling for Officer Clarke's trick.

After I gave Officer Clarke the bar of soap, he walked away from my cell. I then had a short conversation with Sergeant Fanfan and Officer Hood before the sergeant and officers exited the wing.

Rainey continued to yell and kick or hit the shower door while the security staff was in the wing and after they left. About five to eight minutes after the security staff exited, the yelling and kicking and hitting of the shower door slowed down. Rainey then started repeating the following words for what felt like several minutes: "I'm sorry, I can't take it anymore. I won't do it again." I eventually heard what sounded like a fall, and all the yelling, kicking and banging on the shower door stopped.

When I heard what sounded like a fall and all the noise from the shower stopped, I wondered, "Did he fall or pass-out?" I thought that he couldn't have fallen or passed out. None of the other inmates had who were placed in the hot shower had fallen or passed out. Reason and instinct told me to hit my cell door, flood my cell, break the sprinkler in my cell if need be. I thought, "Just do something!"

That night, I went against what was reasonable and my instincts. So many inmates over the months had been placed in the *Hot-Water-Shower*, and they all came out alive. A big part of me believed that nothing serious was wrong, but, at the same time' I had an overwhelming sense that Rainey died, or would die if I didn't do something. As these thoughts raced through my mind, the whole wing was totally quiet as the *Hot-Water-Shower* ran on and on. Twice I went near the toilet in my cell and waved at the officers' station. I started worrying about what was going to happen if Rainey died. I thought I would be wrapped up in an investigation, and I didn't want to be involved. Those thoughts weighed on my mind for about 10 minutes, but the prevailing feeling was that I should do whatever needed to be done to help Rainey.

About 10 minutes after Rainey fell, Officer Thompson entered Wing J-3. When he walked past my cell, door he had a grin on his face. Thompson walked around the lower tier, went into Wing J-2, and performed the security check. He then returned to Wing J-3 by walking through the big office that separated the upper levels in Wings J-2 and J-3 and continued his security check upstairs in Wing J-3. When he got to the shower, I heard the *Hot-Water-Shower* shut off. A few seconds later, I heard Officer Thompson say, "Rainey. Rainey." Rainey did not respond to Thompson.

I then heard Thompson walking down the stairs from the upper tier. I saw the shock on his face as he walked past my cell. I knew that Rainey was dead. I then thought, "Why isn't he calling over his radio and telling the staff that Rainey is dead?"

Thompson returned to the officers' station. Within a couple of seconds of him being in the officers' station, the other security staff started acting very frantic. When I saw that the security staff were not running out of the officers' station back to the *Hot-Water-Shower*, I sank into my frantic thoughts. I watched them with my eyes, but my mind was trying to deal with a horrible realization. They had to be thinking of how they could cover up Rainey's death. And I was at risk. I would be wrapped up in a murder investigation. I would probably have to talk with the Dade CI Inspector General and law enforcement officials from society that night. What was I was going to say to them? Finally, I asked myself, "Will staff be worried about me being a threat?" In the past, I had witnessed security staff do a lot, but I had never witnessed them kill an inmate.

As I stared at the officers' station with these and other thoughts racing through my mind, I didn't notice Officers Clarke and Thompson leave the officers station. Then I heard Officer Clarke say, "He's not breathing. Get medical." Officer Thompson then ran down the stairs to go to the nurses' station to get a nurse. I was so lost in my thoughts, I didn't see Officers Clarke or Thompson go to the shower.

Nurses Robinson and Hidrobo (Patino) responded to the shower. Within about two minutes, Lieutenant Pinkney and more security staff with a stretcher entered the wing. Officers Clarke and Thompson took Rainey out of the shower, down the stairs, and placed him on the stretcher. Rainey was then pushed past my cell door and out of the wing.

When I saw Rainey's body on the stretcher, I noticed that his skin looked cooked/burned. A very short time later, Officer Gibson showed up at my cell door. We went right into talking about what just happened with Rainey. During that conversation, Gibson said he told Officer Clarke earlier that night to skip Rainey on trays because if Rainey didn't eat, he couldn't defecate.

Also, two or three people who I never saw before went into Wing J-3. Officer Patterson showed up while I was talking with Gibson, and asked Gibson, "Did you see his body and how dry his skin was?"

Officer Gibson responded, "Pat, will you come and talk to me?"

Patterson said, "For sure." They then left Wing J-3, and I didn't see either of them again that night.

168) What does your June 24, 2012 journal entry state?

It states: "*June 24, 2012: Yesterday when they were doing vitals, Officer Perez kicked Geiger (cell J-3103) in the day room. Geiger attempted to kick Officer Perez, and Perez did kick Geiger. Last night around 8:50 pm Officer Clarke brought Rainey to the shower over me. He was in a green shroud. He had been playing with his feces in his cell. Around 9:15 pm, security staff arrived to remove Rainey from the shower. Officer Hood told Sergeant Fanfan, who was standing next to him in the day room, that they could keep Rainey in the shower six hours, take him out, put him in his cell, take him out of his cell, and put him back in the shower for another six hours. Before this conversation, Clarke came to my cell and got a bar of soap to fool Fanfan. After Hood said that, Fanfan said, "I thought Rainey already showered. I didn't know he was standing in there not showering". Sergeant Fanfan then told Officer Clarke to "Keep Rainey in the shower." From 8:50 pm to 9:15 pm Rainey just stood in the shower with the water running while yelling, and hitting or kicking the door. He obviously didn't have any soap. That is why Officer Clarke got some from me when they came back at 9:15 pm. When Sergeant Fanfan told Clarke to keep him in the shower, Officer Clarke turned the water back on and left. Over the next about 20 minutes, Rainey yelled several times, "Please take me out! I can't take it anymore!", and "I promise I won't do it anymore." He also hit the shower door multiple times between 8:50 pm and 9:15 pm, and between 9:15 pm and 9:30 pm. Around 9:40 pm, Officer Thompson performed a security check. He shut off the shower water, called Rainey's name once or twice, and then left the wing by himself. About eight minutes later, Officers Thompson and Clarke, and I believe Hood came to the shower and then left, yelling for medical. Nurses Robinson and Hidrobo*

129

(Patino) came into the wing. At this time Fanfan and Officers Clarke, Thompson, and Hood were in the area. The nurses said Rainey was dead. Then the radio activity started, and Officer Hood went to get the stretcher. Sergeant Fanfan tried to administer CPR by compressing activity. Lieutenant Pinkney was in the wing from the time the stretcher arrived, along with Officer Gibson and a female officer with short hair. About 10 minutes after Rainey was taken away on the stretcher, Officer Patterson came to the wing. He said something to Officer Gibson about how dry Rainey's skin was, and Officer Gibson responded, "Pat you'll come and talk to me." Officer Patterson responded, "For sure."

When inmates play with feces and refuse to take showers, third shift has been using the shower over me as a form of punishment with these inmates. They put inmates in the shower and turn the hot water on full blast with no cold water at all. The steam gets so thick in the shower, the inmate has to stay near the shower door in the hand area, in order to breathe. While he is fighting to breathe, blasting hot water gets on them. Security staff have done this to Lewis (cell J-1121), Geiger (cell J-3103), Casey (cell J-3104), (cell J-1121), (cell J-1115). After Rainey kicked or hit the door two finale times, there wasn't any more noise from the shower stall. Security staff has been doing this for so long, I thought they wouldn't have come, and I didn't actually think the inmate would die. Now I think maybe they would have come and maybe I could have saved Rainey's life. He was dead when Thompson shut off the water, but he left him in there about eight minutes longer. Talked to Officers Clarke and Thompson cell side tonight. Mailed Philippians to PMI and a letter to mom. Officer Gibson also worked tonight. One or two waves was not good enough, and now somebody's dead."

169) Who is Sergeant Fanfan?

He was a relief sergeant who worked on the Westside two or three nights a month. Since Sergeant Fanfan liked to micromanage (complain about small things), most security staff expressed distrust in him.

170) What were some of the tricks used by Officer Clarke to keep inmates in the *Hot-Water-Shower* longer?

During the approximately six months the *Hot-Water-Shower* was used, Officer Clarke was questioned several times about his *Hot-Water-Shower* treatment of inmates. If anyone ever asked Clarke why an inmate was in the shower, he would say that the inmate was dirty and had been refusing to shower.

Officer Clarke told me that if anybody ever asked me why an inmate was in that shower on a night or at a time inmates weren't supposed to be showering, I was to respond, "that the inmate hasn't showered in a while and he needed a shower." If a sergeant, lieutenant, or nurse caught an inmate in the shower with the water extremely hot, Clarke would act like he accidentally incorrectly adjusted the hot and cold water. If a sergeant asked Clarke to take an inmate out of the *Hot-Water-Shower* before Clarke wanted to take the inmate out, Officer Clarke always acted like he was going to do so. He went to the shower, looked in and said something like, "The inmate hasn't got under the water and showered. He needs some soap." Clarke would then come to my cell and ask me to give him a bar of soap.

171) Why did you state in your journal, "While the inmate is fighting to breathe, blasting hot water is getting on him"?

The hot water on the shower floor, and some of the hot water bouncing off the wall that the hot water stream shot at, would splash on the inmate who was in that shower.

172) Your June 24, 2012 journal entry uses plural nouns. Were other staff using the *Hot-Water-Shower* to punish inmates?

Officer Clarke was the only staff member who used the *Hot-Water-Shower* to punish mentally disabled inmates. However, all of the other security staff who worked on the Westside on his shift knew what he was doing. Additionally, some of Clarke's co-workers contributed to his use of the shower treatment in different ways. Therefore, they were all tacitly involved with the *Hot-Water-Shower* treatment in different ways.

173) What happened on June 25, 2012?

I thought that Officer Clarke and the other officers wouldn't come to work the day after Rainey's death. I thought they would have been arrested, fired, or suspended, but I was wrong. When the food carts came into Wing J-3, Officers Clarke and Thompson were there. Their eyes were wider than normal, and they were showing obvious signs of nervousness. When Clarke gave me my dinner tray, I said, "It's just another day at work. Nothing's different."

He responded, "What?"

I said again, "It's just another day at work. Nothing's different." Officers Clarke and Thompson then got smiles on their face and started acting normal.

When they both came back to my cell later that day, Officer Clarke said, "What's going on, Hempstead?"

I responded, "Nothing much."

He said, "Are you good?"

I responded, "Yeah, why wouldn't I be? Everything is normal. I hope you both know you have only one of two choices. Either yesterday was just another day at work, or it wasn't. If it wasn't, then what happened was your fault."

Officer Thompson said, "It was just another day at work. Nothing happened that we could stop."

I responded, "That's why I told you at dinner, it's just another day at work. Nothing different."

Clarke said, "The doctor in the medical department tried to say I beat Rainey up. He said his body looked like I physically beat him."

I responded, "I didn't see you do anything. You're a big dude. If you hit somebody, it would leave damage."

Thompson said, "One of the nurses said Rainey had lung issues. He probably died from the lung issues."

I responded, "With you guys being at work today, it looks like you both don't have any reason to worry."

We then talked about me going back to work as an orderly.

174) Why did say those things to the officers?

Right after Rainey's body was taken out of the wing, Officer Gibson came to my cell door to discuss what happened to Rainey. When Officers Clarke and Thompson returned to work, they also came to my cell door and began talking about Rainey. I was fairly sure the staff wouldn't harm me, but if they deemed me a threat, they were likely to do anything. The staff had shown me they were very evil and could not be trusted. I talked to Officers Clarke and Thompson the way I did so they would not consider me to be a threat.

175) What did you find out on June 24, 2012 concerning Gregory Shevlin?

Security staff told me that Shevlin was one of the orderlies working on June 23, 2012 when Rainey died. I was also told that Rainey defecated in the middle of his cell on the floor and Shevlin refused to clean it up. After security staff removed Rainey from his cell, the staff ordered Shevlin to clean up Rainey's feces, and Shevlin refused. Sergeant Fanfan expected Shevlin to clean it up because he was one of the orderlies working that night.

When Shevlin refused, Sergeant Fanfan locked Shevlin in his cell and told Shevlin he was going to receive a disciplinary report for refusing the verbal order to clean up the feces. Shevlin got mad and cut a deep slice into his own hand. While everything was going on with Rainey, Shevlin was bleeding-out in his cell. Eventually, the staff discovered him. By that time Shevlin lost a large quantity of blood and needed to be taken to a hospital in society to receive a blood transfusion.

176) On June 24, 2012, did Lieutenant Tarver tell anybody to clean the shower where Darren Rainey died?

Yes. He told the sergeant and several officers on the 8:00 am to 4:00 pm shift to have an orderly clean the shower. Security staff did not follow his order that day.

177) Will you tell me about June 25, 2012?

Between 9:00 am and 9:40 am Lieutenant Tarver and Sergeant Dixon entered Wing J-3. Sergeant Dixon then tested the water temperature in all the showers in Wing J-3. After she tested the water temperature in the shower where Rainey died, she told Lieutenant Tarver, "It's over 160° Fahrenheit. You need to have the shower disconnected, or we'll all lose our jobs!"

Lieutenant Tarver responded, "I don't have the authority to do that. It's still a crime scene." Sergeant Dixon then told Lieutenant Tarver that she was leaving and that she would be back. A short time later, a plumber entered Wing J-3 and disconnected the *Hot-Water-Shower*.

When Lieutenant Tarver discovered that the shower still wasn't cleaned, he became angry and demanded it to be cleaned that day. Tarver and other staff had been saying since June 24, 2012 that a lot of Rainey's skin was stuck to the walls in the shower. Officer Eli arranged for Inmate Mark Joiner to clean the shower. Joiner was another orderly who had been used on the Westside in the past. While the shower was being cleaned, Officer Eli stood in front of my cell talking with me. As Joiner cleaned the shower, he yelled down from the upper tier to Officer Eli and me, telling us about all the skin he found in the shower. About 30 to 45 minutes after Joiner started cleaning the shower, he came to my cell and showed Eli and me a canvas shoe full of Rainey's skin that Joiner got off the shower walls and floor, and from other locations between the shower and the lower tier. When Joiner asked Eli what he wanted him to do with the canvas shoe full of skin, Eli said, "Throw it in the trash." That same day, Sergeant Dixon also took several pictures of the *Hot-Water-Shower* and the closet next to it.

Sargent Dixon was not the first person to test the water temperature in the *Hot-Water-Shower*. On the night Rainey died, a man tested the water temperature in that shower and took pictures of it.

178) What does your June 25, 2012 journal entry state?

It states: "*This morning two white men came into Wing J-3 around 7:40 am, went upstairs, ran the shower water for about 10 minutes, then left. Between 9:00 am and 9:40 am Lieutenant Tarver and Sergeant Dixon came in and took photographs of the shower. The plumbing crew came in right behind them and disconnected the shower equipment that was connected to the sink in the closet, and that ran into the shower. The plumbing crew had two white and two black inmates on it with a Spanish staff member. Sergeant Dixon checked the water temperatures in the other showers. Lieutenant Tarver told security staff several times yesterday and today to clean the shower. He also said skin was stuck to the walls in the shower. The man that was killed was named Rainey, Darren (D.C. #060954). His end of sentence was July 21, 2013, as of May 18, 2012. I still have to verify this information. On May 18, 2012, he was in Cell J-3211 and was eventually moved to Cell J-1109. Read "A Simple Way to Pray (For Master Peter the Barber) 1535 by Dr. Martin Luther."*

I wasn't sure about Rainey's D.C. number and his end of sentence release date, so I verified it with staff.

Chapter 13: The Valley of Sorrows (June 26, 2012- January 17, 2013)

179) Why do you call this section of your life the "Valley of Sorrows?"

On June 26, 2012, I entered into a period in my life that I named, the "Valley of Sorrows." It lasted for about a year. It was a time of continuous deep sorrow and tears. It was the only time in my life I had to fight for my own mental stability against an overwhelming sadness that was crushing. The one resounding statement I repeated hundreds of time during that year of sadness was, "I could have done more."

180) How did you enter into the, "Valley of Sorrows"?

On June 26, 2012, Officer Piggot and Coach Ocanna came into Wing J-3 to take zero point inmates out to the recreation yard. It was Piggot's first day back from his weekly two days off. When he entered Wing J-3, he came up to my cell door and said, "I heard they're cooking inmates on the night shift."

I responded, "Let's talk outside on the recreation yard."

I was concerned about talking with Piggot about Rainey while Lawrence Smith slept in the cell next to me. Smith had already filed several grievances stating I had a personal relationship with staff.

When Officer Piggot and I got out on the recreation yard, we started talking about how, over the past six months, Officer

Department of Corruption

Clarke had used the *Hot-Water-Shower* to punish mentally disabled inmates. We also discussed the night that Piggot worked overtime and an inmate was in the *Hot-Water-Shower*. After I explained everything that happened on the night of Rainey's death, I said, "I did all that I could do."

As soon as I said, "I did all that I could do, it felt like a million pounds of sadness fell on me,   and God opened my eyes to see that I didn't do enough to stop Rainey's death. As soon as these things happened, I switched my statement to, "I didn't do enough."

When I said, "I didn't do enough," Sergeant Seals opened the door that led to the recreation yard and said, "Hempstead, I need you to come in and move your property. You're moving to Wing J-1, Cell 117."

The best way I can describe the million pounds of sadness is to say it was all-consuming and crushing. I felt like I had entered another world. A world of severe sorrow. I left the recreation yard and moved my property from Cell J-3101 to Cell J-1117. When I got all of my property moved into Cell J-1117, I didn't go back out to the recreation yard. I locked myself in my cell. I had to cry. I did all that I could to hold my sadness and tears in, but it had to come out.

After I put the sheet up in my cell door window, I started crying. The sadness brought me to my knees. I was crushed by sadness and regret, thinking, over and over, how I should have kicked the cell door, flooded my cell, or broke the sprinkler when I heard Rainey stop yelling and fall. I thought about how my stupidity caused somebody to die. I thought about how I devoted so much time to trying to make the TCU a safer place, and it only became worse. I thought about how Oscar Davis and Darryl Richardson had died. I'm not a medical expert, but I really believed they died from being denied a lot of food. When I say I cried during this Valley of Sorrows, I don't mean a little bit. My tears were always gushing like a waterfall. Throughout the Valley of Sorrows, I prayed constantly trying to figure out everything that had happened in light of God's word, and asking God for strength and help.

When I was in my cell, crying and praying, Officer Piggot knocked on my cell door and said, "I'll stop by when I do my next round." With my sheet folded and covering my cell door window, Piggot couldn't see in my cell. He likely thought that I was on the toilet. I knew I had 20 to 30 minutes to get myself ready to talk to him. I couldn't let him know I had been crying. If any of the security staff thought I was sad or shedding tears about anything they had done, they would have deemed me a threat to them. It didn't matter that I had a little trust for Piggot. I knew that he had worked with the other staff for years. It was reasonable to say he was very loyal to them. My crying ended about 15 minutes prior to Officer Piggot coming back to my cell, so my eyes were no longer red.

When Officer Piggot returned to my cell, he said, "Why didn't you come back out to the recreation yard? We were in the middle of talking."

I responded, "I'm sorry. I had to clean this cell and reorganize my property."

He said, "Right before you left you said you could have done more. What did you mean?"

I responded, "I would rather not talk about it. I would rather talk about doctrine."

He said, "OK." We then spent about 30 minutes discussing the Bible. I didn't want to talk to him about the Rainey situation. If I did, I wouldn't have been able to hold my tears in.

When Piggot left my cell, I double folded my sheet again, hung it back over my cell window, and immediately started crying. The rest of that day I cried. I took the sheet down from my cell door for meals and to talk with Officers Piggot and Eli. I always made sure that my eyes didn't look like I had been crying.

181) Where was Cell J-1117 located in Wing J-1, and did you have any concerns about being moved to that cell?

Cell J-1117 was in the corner by the door leading to the recreation yard behind Wing J-1. It was in a blind spot not viewable by any mounted security cameras. In front of Cell J-117, was the door leading to the recreation yard. An inmate housed in that cell could have easily been taken from the cell, out to the recreation yard, and physically abused without any cameras recording it.

Yes, I had concerns about being moved into that cell. After witnessing what had been done to Rainey and witnessing everything that staff had done in my presence, I knew they were capable of doing anything, if they believed I was a threat to them.

I was too consumed with sorrow to be fearful. Although in my sorrow, I was aware of the potential threats to my safety.

182) Please tell me about your conversation with Dr. Cesar on June 26, 2012.

After lunch, I was told that Dr. Cesar would be calling me out of my cell to talk with her. The sadness I felt was so overwhelming, I had to talk to somebody. I thought I could trust her, and, even if I couldn't, I had to take the chance. I didn't want to hold in my sadness. I knew that I had to say something to her about what happened to Rainey. I just didn't know what to say. I was so sad, I could not focus. I also knew I had to be very careful to not cry when I was talking with her. Since I was going to be talking with her in one of the Wing J-1 offices, security staff would be able to watch Dr. Cesar and me talking.

I was eventually told to go and talk with Dr. Cesar in the front office in Wing J-1. When I arrived in the office, shut the door, and sat down, Dr. Cesar said, "How are you doing Hempstead?"

I responded, "I was just moved over here. Did you hear what happened on Saturday night?"

She said, "Yes. I heard. It's awful."

I responded, "I don't want to get in trouble or cause any trouble, but can I say something about it?" As I talked, my voice was breaking up.

She said, "Yes, of course."

I responded, "I saw what happened. I heard his last words and heard him fall. I should have done more." I was fighting to keep the tears back, but I couldn't. My eyes got glassy and a few tears came out. As soon as the tears came out, I said, "If we talk about it, I'm going to cry. I can't let security see me crying. If they do, they're going to know there's a problem. Can we go to Central and talk in an office privately?"

She responded, "I don't know. I would have to ask."

Chapter 13: The Valley of Sorrows (June 26, 2012- January 17, 2013)

I said, "Who do you have to ask?"

She responded, "Dr. Perez."

I said, "No, don't ask her. She'll tell security staff. Anything you say to her, will get back to security staff. I only have two options. Talk with you, or suppress my sadness. I don't want to get you in trouble or wrapped up in this matter. It might be good, if we don't talk in detail. Additionally, you can't write in your notes what I'm saying to you. My file is reviewed by too many people. If you have notes in my files, they could cause trouble for us both."

Dr. Cesar responded, "How could notes get me in trouble?"

I said, "You're required by state and federal law to report abuse of the mentally disabled."

She responded, "Hempstead, I'm not going to state in my notes what we specifically discuss. You said option two is suppressing."

I said, "I need to keep my mind busy to fight against the sadness. I've fought against sadness before. It's like a physical wound. It will go away in time. I just have to do my best to fight against it for now."

She responded, "Why don't you write your thoughts down on paper, and flush them down the toilet or rip them up when you're done?"

I said, "I can't do something like that. It doesn't make sense to spend my time writing just to destroy what I wrote."

She responded, "Then what do you think will help?"

I said, "I don't know. I just know I need to talk to somebody, or try to suppress."

She responded, "Why haven't you been working?"

I said, "Ms. Koel got mad after I filed all the paperwork and grievances to get off protective management status, so she had the major tell security staff to not work me."

Dr. Cesar responded, "I think you should be working. Being in your cell is not good for you right now. I'm going to see what I can do. I don't know if I can do anything, but I'm going to try."

I said, "I'm somewhat mad about everything that happened. I don't want to do what I think I should have done from the beginning. I spent more than a year trying to evangelize the staff to bring them to Christ. I really don't want to now start focusing on trying to put them in prison."

She responded, "I think cleaning will keep your mind off that. I'm going to see what I can do. I'll talk with you in a couple of days. Will you promise me something?"

I said, "Yes, what is it?"

She responded, "Don't talk with anybody else about what we've discussed. If you need to talk to somebody, tell one of the staff to call me and I'll come and talk with you. OK?"

I agreed. The glassiness in my eyes, the tears that would every now and then escape, and the constant breaking up in my voice, caused Dr. Cesar to know I was sincere about my state. When this conversation was over, I went back to my cell.

The sadness was so crushing, for most of that day I was on the floor, crying. I remember praying a long time that day for God to help me to maintain my stability. I have always considered myself to be very mentally strong. The only time I ever had concerns about losing my mental stability was in the beginning of the Valley of Sorrows.

That night, I had a nightmare that caused me to wake up crying. In my nightmare, it was the night of Rainey's death. After hearing Rainey stop yelling and fall, I started kicking my cell door trying to get the officers to come. I woke up in the middle of kicking my cell door. My nightmare was about what I failed to do.

183) Why didn't you ask to discharge from the TCU?

I didn't ask to discharge between June 23 and 26, 2012, because my plan was to still try to bring reform to the TCU. I didn't ask for a transfer to another institution after June 26, 2012, because if I was in general population, I wouldn't have had a place to cry in private. In other words, it would have been very difficult for me to live in population with the crushing sadness that I felt.

184) What do you think occurred when Ms. Koel and Major McCarter found out that you witnessed what happened to Darren Rainey?

My prison files showed I had a long history of speaking out against things, a history of filing lawsuits, and that I knew people in society who had the ability to cause legal problems to those who violated federal laws. Ms. Koel had informed staff about me. I believe my past caused Ms. Koel and Major McCarter to talk with Dr. Basaga about starting an investigation to find out if I intended to take any type of legal action against staff for what they did to Darren Rainey.

Think about it. Rainey died on Saturday June 23, 2012. On Monday June 25, everybody came back to work. After they found out that I witnessed what happened to Rainey, I was moved from Wing J-3 to Wing J-1. I also believe I was moved to a different wing to prevent me from talking with any people from society who would possibly go into Wing J-3 to investigate Rainey's death. Finally, I believe I was moved so I didn't have to live in the wing where I had witnessed such evil. I believe I was moved to Cell J1-117 because it was in a blind spot.

Major McCarter knew I wasn't ignorant. That was probably his way of saying, "Staff can do anything they want to you in Cell J-1117 if you say or do something we don't like." I believe Dr. Basaga arranged for Dr. Cesar to come and talk with me on June 26, 2012 to see if she could find out how I was responding to what happened with Rainey. I also believe that, after my conversation with Dr. Cesar, she told Dr. Basaga, Major McCarter, and Ms. Koel about my condition and recommended I be allowed to resume working as an orderly. I believe that on June 26, Major McCarter and Ms. Koel told security staff that I could be used as an orderly as a way to try and buy me to keep my mouth shut.

They thought that I enjoyed doing orderly work, which doesn't make sense to me. There were all types of negatives to being an orderly.

- One: Who would want to work with people who constantly did the types of evil things to inmates that security staff did?

- Two: Some of the inmates in the TCU deemed me an enemy because I worked for the staff who were doing all types of evil to inmates.
- Three: Every day I was cleaning up urine, feces, or blood.
- Four: I worked 12 to 17 hours a day, and the list goes on.

185) Did you pray for help?

Yes. I prayed and asked God for help with keeping my mind busy so I did not focus on the things that were making me sad. I knew from past experience that the sadness would go away in time. Sadness is like a physical wound. Time will heal it. For this reason, I prayed and asked God for help with keeping my mind busy. It was one of the last things I prayed for, prior to going to sleep on June 26, 2012.

186) What happened in the morning hours on June 27, 2012?

I was awakened by Officer David telling me to get ready to work serving the breakfast meal. I had not worked as an orderly since the end of May 2012. I thought God had answered my prayers.

Prior to 10:55 am, Officer Patterson came to my cell and told me that Major McCarter was coming to the Westside to talk with me. Patterson asked me to let him handcuff me prior to being taken out of my cell. I asked him why he wanted to put handcuffs on me when I was a zero point status inmate. Zero point status inmates didn't have to wear handcuffs when outside of their cells. He said, "Hempstead, I'm only asking you to submit to handcuffs because the major wants to talk to you. I don't know what it's about, and I don't know if he wants you in handcuffs."

I responded, "I'm going to submit to the handcuffs, but I want you to know that I think you're trying to intimidate me." Patterson denied that he was trying to intimidate me. After submitting to the handcuffs, I was escorted from my cell to the tables in Wing J-1.

When the major came into Wing J-1, he had Lieutenant Tarver, Sergeant Seals and Officer Townsend with him. Officers Patterson, Piggot, and Eli were already in the wing. Since I couldn't see the watch I was wearing, I looked at Tarver's watch. It showed that the time was 10:55 am when I entered the office.

Once we were in the office, the major asked, "How are you doing Hempstead?"

I responded, "Fine. What is this about, and why am I in handcuffs?"

He said, "I don't know why you're in handcuffs. I just wanted to ask you a few questions. Did you ever use the shower next to Cell J-3201?"

I responded, "Yes, I used that shower several times. However, I've never been placed in it for punishment."

The major asked, "What types of inmates were put in that shower?"

I responded, "Every type of inmate has been placed in that shower." I gave this answer, because on shower nights all the inmates used that shower.

He said, "Did Rainey cry, and if so, what was he crying?"

I responded, "He didn't cry. He yelled."

Major McCarter then asked, "Did you see his dead body, and if so how did it look?"

I responded, "Yes. It looked burned." I answered this question the way that I did, because a mounted security camera recorded me watching Rainey's body pass my cell door.

I didn't trust the major. He had already subjected me to retaliation for filing grievances and paperwork to get off protective management. Additionally, Major McCarter was the supervisor of the TCU security staff. This made him responsible for everything that was happening in the TCU and for what had happened to Darren Rainey. For these reasons, I felt I would be in danger if I told him anything concerning the *Hot-Water-Shower* treatment or about Darren Rainey.

187) What does your June 27, 2012 journal entry state?

It states; "*On June 26, 2012 security staff moved me from Cell J3-101 to Cell J1-117. I'm now in the corner by the recreation yard with no cameras on my cell. Sergeant Seals is the staff member who told me to move. Officer Gibson worked on dinner shift. I didn't see any lieutenants on third shift on June 26, 2012. Officer Hood came into the wing later in the night. Today at 10:55 am, the major had me taken out of my cell to talk to me in the front office in Wing J-1. We spoke for three minutes. He asked me the following questions about what happened on Saturday night. (1) Did you hear him cry and if so what was he crying? (2) Have I ever used that shower? (3) What type of people are put in that shower? (4) Did I see his dead body, and if so how did it look? This is the same major who had me removed from doing orderly job work because of the grievances I filed to get off protective management. The following staff were present during my meeting with the major: Lieutenant Tarver, Sergeant Seals, and Officers Piggot, Eli, Patterson, and Townsend. Officer Patterson took me out of my cell to see him. Coach Ocanna was also briefly present to retrieve her papers from the office. Yesterday, I gave Mrs. Koel two medical grievances concerning my Low Residue Diet that needs to be renewed. Additionally, I gave her another grievance about wanting to go to a faith base institution upon my discharge from the TCU. I can't believe all this is happening."*

188) What did Gregory Shevlin tell you on June 27, 2012?

Shevlin showed me the self-inflicted cut on his hand from the night Rainey died. While showing me his wound, Shevlin said, "Hempstead, Fanfan fired me and said he was going to write me a disciplinary report for not cleaning up the feces in the middle of Rainey's floor. Can he do that? I'm not certified to clean up feces."

I responded, "If Fanfan actually writes you the disciplinary report, you should be able to beat it. Since you're not certified to clean up feces, Fanfan can't make you place yourself in danger by cleaning it up. What exactly happened that night?"

Shevlin said, "When Fanfan started his shift he noticed Rainey defecated in the middle of his cell floor. Security staff tried to get Rainey to clean it up, but he kept refusing. Eventually they got sick of dealing with Rainey and took him out of his cell to the shower over in Wing J-3 and cooked him. They killed him over a turd."

I asked, "How much feces was in the cell?"

Shevlin said, "It was as big as a horse pile right in the middle of the floor. They should have gotten you to clean it up. You would have cleaned it."

I responded, "If you get a disciplinary report, will you show it to me?"

He said, "Of course I'm going to show it to you. I will need your help with fighting it."

I responded, "Why did you cut your hand?"

He said, "When I told Fanfan I wasn't going to clean up the feces, he fired me, locked me in my cell, and told me I was going to get a disciplinary report. I got mad and cut my hand. While they were cooking Rainey, I was bleeding out in my cell. Eventually security came and escorted me to the medical department. Medical staff said I lost a lot of blood, so I had to go to the outside hospital."

I asked, "Did you tell any medical or mental health staff that night or since then, why you cut your hand?"

He said, "Yes, of course I did. I told everybody. It's crazy how Fanfan threatened to write me up because I wouldn't clean up feces."

I responded, "I agree. Let me know if you get the disciplinary report."

189) What happened when the 4:00 pm to 12:00 am shift came on duty on June 27, 2012?

Many of the security staff witnessed my morning conversation with the major. I knew one or more of them would tell Officers Clarke and Thompson that I talked to the major. That is why I made sure I answered the major's questions quickly so I could get out of his office. If I was in the office a long time with the major, staff would have thought I said something to him about Rainey's death. The other security staff also might have assumed that I said something about them. As my June 27, 2012 journal entry shows, I timed the visit and was in the office with Major McCarter for about three minutes.

When the 4:00 pm to 12:00 am shift started, Officer Clarke was walking very quickly while conducting the count to begin the shift. When I tried to stop him, he kept walking. A minute or two later, Officer Thompson came by counting. When I tried to stop him, he stopped. When he stopped I said, "Major McCarter came to talk to me this morning about what happened to Rainey."

Thompson asked, "What did he say?" I told him the questions that the major asked and my answers to them. I did not tell him why I answered the major's questions the way that I did. Thompson then asked, "Is that all that was said?"

I responded, "No. As I was walking out of the office, I asked the major, "All that matters is that security performed did their security checks. Right!"

He responded, "Did they do their security checks?"

I said, "Yes. They all left the wing at about 9:15 pm or 9:20 pm, and Officer Thompson did a security check around 9:40 and found Rainey dead."

Officer Thompson said, "You told the major that I found Rainey dead?"

I responded, "Of course I did. That is what the security cameras show. You can't lie if the cameras show that you did. When you went to the shower and yelled Rainey's name, he didn't respond. You then left and told the sergeant and other officers and all of you came back a short time later. None of you would have had a reasonable excuse for doing a security check about 10 minutes after you just performed one."

As I was saying this, Thompson had his hand on his forehead. Right around the time I finished, Officer Clarke came through the front door of Wing J-1. Officer Thompson called Clarke over to join us. When Clarke got to my cell, Thompson said, "Hempstead, tell Clarke everything you just told me." When I finished repeating everything to Clarke, Thompson said, "We put on the reports that Clarke found Rainey dead."

I responded, "Why did you do that? What's going to be your excuse for returning to the shower about 10 minutes after Officer Thompson did a security check? Additionally, you both know that the security camera on the other side of this wing, records the officer station. I'm sure that camera picked up the actions of everybody in the officer station when you returned to the station and told the other staff that Rainey was dead."

Thompson said, "Hempstead, if the major or anyone else asks, tell them that Clarke found Rainey dead, not me. OK?"

Clarke then said, "Just tell anybody who asks that I found Rainey."

Chapter 13: The Valley of Sorrows (June 26, 2012-January 17, 2013)

I responded, "I'll tell them whatever you want me to tell them. I didn't mean to say anything to get you guys in trouble. I just thought you would have come up with something that was consistent with what the cameras showed. Nobody with a brain is going to believe you did a security check approximately 10 minutes after Thompson did one. Additionally, if the cameras captured the shock on your face, Officer Thompson, as you walked away from the shower after seeing Rainey's dead body, then you're going to also have a problem explaining that. I didn't mean to say anything wrong to the major. If I'm asked again, I'll say that Clarke found Rainey dead."

Clarke said, "We know you didn't mean to say anything wrong. You're cool. So don't sweat what happened. Just tell anybody else who asks that I found Rainey."

I responded, "OK." As they walked off to get the food carts, they both said they would come and talk with me later on that night.

Not only was I dealing with severe sorrow, but I was also having to deal with an interrogation by a retaliatory major, and with Officers Clarke and Thompson telling me to lie to anyone who questioned me about who found Darren Rainey's dead body?

190) Please tell me about your return to work as an orderly.

Within a few days of July 26, 2012, I was working as an orderly on all three shifts. In other words, I was working from 5:00 am to 8:00 pm seven days a week. I was also on call from 8:00 pm to 5:00 am. My work schedule did not change for months.

I believe staff were attempting to keep me very busy and tired, so I didn't have the time or energy to think about or take any action on the Rainey case. I was very tired, so tired that I fell asleep several times while standing and almost fell to the ground. To some degree, I thought this was an answer to my prayer for God's help with keeping my mind busy.

191) In the end of June 2012, did you write any agencies about what happened to Darren Rainey?

Yes. I wanted to find out which law enforcement agency had jurisdiction over the Rainey case. For this reason I mailed public

Department of Corruption

record requests to the Miami-Dade Police Department and the Florida City, Florida Police Department. I asked both agencies if they had jurisdiction over crimes that happened at Dade CI. They both replied that the Miami-Dade Police Department had jurisdiction.

Around the end of July 2012, I mailed another public records request to the Miami-Dade Police Department. In that request, I mentioned that a dead inmate named Darren Rainey was found in a shower at Dade CI. I asked for the case number on the Darren Rainey murder investigation, and the name of the detective investigating that case. A few weeks later, I received a response indicating that the Miami-Dade Police Department Case number was: 120623238979MDPD, and Wilbert Sanchez was the homicide detective investigating the case.

192) Why did you think a law enforcement agency was assigned to investigate what happened to Darren Rainey?

I didn't think there was any way the staff could cover-up what happened to Rainey, because of the condition of his body

193) What did Officer Clarke tell you about how Darren Rainey's body got in the condition it was in?

He said that Rainey fell back after passing out or dying. When this happened, his body fell over the drain in the shower, which blocked the water from going down the drain. Water in excess of 160 degrees Fahrenheit then rose and covered most of Rainey's body. For approximately 18 minutes, Rainey's body lay in scalding hot water. The water level rose so high, it started coming out of the shower and into the hallway in front of the shower.

194) In July of 2012, did you mail a public records request to the Dade County, Florida Medical Examiner's office concerning what happened to Darren Rainey?

Yes. The request was for the case number that the medical examiner's office assigned to the Rainey case. I also requested the name of the medical examiner assigned to examine Rainey's body. They responded by stating that the medical examiner's case number was 2012-1481 and advised me that Dr. Emma Lew was the assigned medical examiner. I was also advised that Brittany

148

McLaurin was the medical examiner investigator assigned to the case.

195) Why did you want to obtain the names of people case numbers associated with the investigation?

I was conflicted about what I should do. A lot of me wanted to continue the course of action I had been on since I returned to the TCU in 2011, that is, to do my best to evangelize the staff and bring reform inside the TCU.

However, another desire was building inside me. I thought this new desire would eventually prevail and cause me to change my course of action. I felt that God wanted me to inform state and federal officials of all the things I had witnessed with respect to Darren Rainey, the security staff, and the inmates in the TCU. When I first began to feel God was leading me in this direction, it was difficult to accept and understand. I had spent more than a year trying to lead the staff to Jesus. If I informed state and federal officials about the abuses I witnessed, I would be taking actions that could put these very same people in prison.

Despite this conflict, I felt that God was directing me to take steps towards this end.

196) Did Gregory Shevlin ever receive the disciplinary report from Sergeant Fanfan?

Yes. Shevlin received it and showed it to me. The disciplinary report referenced feces being on Rainey's cell floor and Shevlin refusing to clean it up. It was dismissed, because Shevlin wasn't certified to clean up feces and because he was not supposed to be cleaning up feces while he was a patient in the TCU.

197) What does your July 4, 2012 journal entry state?

It states: *"Yesterday, I spoke to Dr. Cesar again. She said she didn't ask Ms. Koel or Dr. Basaga to e-mail anyone. To be more specific, she said she didn't know anything about the alleged e-mails by them to the lieutenant saying I can do orderly work. Officer Patterson watched as Dr. Cesar and I conversed. She said security staff also retaliates against mental health staff. I think she misinterpreted what I was saying about Ms. Arencibia witnessing violence and not reporting it. I didn't say Ms.*

Arencibia's name to Dr. Cesar, but I believe she knew that I was talking about Ms. Arencibia. Lieutenant Miller and the major were on the wing last night when the inmates in Cells J-1114, J-1121, and J-1122 were being showered. I went to Dr. Cesar's group yesterday. Cesar alleged she would talk to the major about allowing me to work. Sergeant Pierri stopped by my cell last night and we spoke for about an hour, and so far Officer Piggot is the only staff to talk with me to day. We also talked for about an hour."

198) What happened around August 2012?

The security staff in the FDC went to 12 hour shifts. Instead of daily three shifts of eight hours each, they changed to four shifts of 12 hours each, shifts A through D. Thus, instead of six shifts over 48 hours, there were only four.

- A-shift worked from 6:00 am to 6:00 pm on Monday and Tuesday. C-shift worked from 6:00 pm to 6:00 am on those days.
- B-shift worked from 6:00 am to 6:00 pm on Wednesday and Thursday. D-shift worked from 6:00 pm to 6:00 am on those days. C shift worked
- Similarly, A-shift and C-shift covered Friday, Saturday, and Sunday.

The following Monday, this rotation was repeated with B-shift and D-shift in the Monday-Tuesday time slot.

Several staff quit at Dade CI and statewide when the FDC went to 12 hour shifts.

199) Who was working in your area when the change to 12 hour shifts was made?

SERGEANTS: Seals, Jonathan, Pierri, Collado and Miller.

OFFICERS: Piggot, Gruben, Cobas, Patterson, Eli, Rantin, McGriff, Perez, Wood, David, Jenkins, Collado, Clarke, Lemelis, Forbes, Mac, Saneck, and Weary.

I can't remember the other names.

200) Which lieutenants worked in the TCU during the three times you were there?

2010: Lieutenants Olds, Donaldson, Murray, and McCrae.

Chapter 13: The Valley of Sorrows (June 26, 2012-January 17, 2013)

2011: Lieutenants Pinkney, Murray, Donaldson, and McCrae. End of 2011-end of 2012: Lieutenants Pinkney, Tarver, Bush, Towns, and Hall. Sergeants Miller and Lopez were also acting lieutenants for a while.

201) Why didn't you file any grievances in the end of 2012 concerning Darren Rainey?

If I filed any grievances, I would have immediately been deemed an enemy and untrustworthy. Filing grievances would have also ruined all my efforts to bring reform to the TCU. Additionally, my life would have been in danger. For these reasons, I chose to covertly communicate with agencies in society about Rainey's death and other issues in the Dade CI TCU.

202) In the end of 2012, did TCU inmates discuss what happened to Darren Rainey?

Yes. The inmates and staff talked a lot about what happened to Rainey and about the other inmates who were given the *Hot-Water-Shower* treatment.

203) Please tell me about Sergeant Seals.

The inmates considered Sergeant Seals to be one of the most violent sergeants at Dade CI. When Sergeant Seals took over A-shift, it became the most violent shift on the Westside. By the end of 2012, inmates were being starved and physically abused on a regular basis.

204) Explain Two-Point and Six-Point Conversions and why they were used.

Two-point and six-point conversions are sports terms. Sergeant Seals gave these terms new meanings within the TCU.

When Sergeant Seals gave an inmate a Two-Point-Conversion, the inmate wouldn't receive lunch or dinner for two days straight. A Six-Point Conversion meant the inmate would not receive both lunch and dinner for three days straight.

When Sergeant Seals took over A-shift, an average of three to 20 inmates were on Two and Six-Point Conversions at a time. Inmates who really upset Sergeant Seals were placed on both a Six and Two Point Conversion which is five days of not receiving lunch or dinner on A-shift. Sergeant Seals placed a few inmates on two to three, Six-Point Conversions back to back. If an in inmate was given two Six-Point Conversions, during the A-shift he was denied lunch and dinner for six days. If an inmate was given three Six-Point Conversions, he was denied lunch and dinner for nine A-shift days. Sergeant Seals only worked when the lunch and dinner meals were served, so he wasn't at work when the breakfast meal was served. However, when breakfast was late arriving to the TCU, and A-shift security staff got stuck passing it out, the inmates on Two and Six-Point Conversions were also denied breakfast. What reasons did Seals place an inmate on a Two or Six-Point Conversion?

Seals placed inmates on two or six point conversion for yelling, kicking their cell doors, making a lot of noise in their cells, not returning their food trays, any disrespectful statement or act to staff, disobeying an order given by staff, or any acts of violence on staff.

205) Was there a lot of staff on inmate violence on A-shift in the end of 2012?

Yes. Every time A-shift worked there was violence.

Most of the time staff tried to make humor out of the violence. For instance, there was an inmate who the staff nicknamed "Crack" who slept in Wing J-1. I believe Crack's first or last name was Lewis. They nicknamed him "Crack", because they thought he lost his mental stability from smoking too much crack cocaine. He was a very skinny black man whose eyes were always very wide open. Crack never wore clothes, always played with his feces, never showered willingly, and every time he talked, his whole body would move, especially his arms. He was very well known for writing things on the walls and ceiling in feces, for rubbing feces on his body, and throwing feces out of his food flap. On a few occasions, he was seen eating feces.

Like all the inmates, Crack was supposed to shower. Three of the shifts didn't even attempt to get Crack out of his cell to shower. Thus, Crack was only showered on A-shift. Also, Sergeant Seals only showered Crack on the weekends when fewer staff were working. This limited the number of people who would witness Sergeant Seals' actions. The usual methods of forcing an

Chapter 13: The Valley of Sorrows (June 26, 2012- January 17, 2013)

inmate to leave his cell did not work. He would not submit to handcuffs, even if bleach and ammonia were thrown into his cell.

Physical force was the only way to get Crack to clean himself.

When Sergeant Seals gave the order to shower Crack, I was asked to check his cell and assemble the supplies needed to clean it. After assembling the cleaning supplies, I was sent to the upper tier to watch the show. I was to wait on the upper tier because Crack was known for charging staff and inmates with feces all over his body and in his hands.

The staff used several methods. Initially, Sergeant Seals and Officers Gruben and Cobas (and sometimes Patterson) would sneak up on the sides of Crack's cell door and have the booth officer open Crack's cell door. As soon as the cell door opened, they would rush inside his cell and use physical force to get Crack in handcuffs. Eventually, Crack figured out that on the weekends Sargent Seals worked, if he did not want to be showered, he had best keep feces on his body.

After Crack figured out he needed to smear his body with feces on the weekends, Sergeant Seals needed a new style of getting Crack out of his cell. The new style consisted of Sergeant Seals and two or three officers standing outside of Crack's cell door, about 10 to 15 feet from it. One or two of the officers stood in the front of Crack's cell and one officer stood on each side of the cell door. The officers in front of Crack's cell door then talked trash to Crack, egging him on. Once Crack was worked up, they instructed the booth officer to open Crack's cell door.

When Crack came rushing out toward the officer in front of his cell, the officers on the sides rushed Crack. The first officer who got to Crack either grabbed his legs and pulled them out from under him or used some other move to take Crack to floor. Once crack was on the ground, security staff could usually force him into handcuffs and then forcibly escort him out of Wing J-1. It they were not able to handcuff him, they grabbed his arms and legs and carried him out.

Once Crack was in the hallway outside the wing, the staff put him in an empty office where they had put chemicals, buckets of water, a set of blues, and some rags. The security staff then used physical force to make Crack clean himself. Typically, they sprayed chemicals on him and told him to use the rags and water to scrub off the chemicals. They usually sprayed pure bleach on him, which caused him to feel like his skin was burning. The burning feeling would usually cause Crack to scrub the bleach off his body with the water and rags. After this process was completed, Crack was given a set of blues to change into.

Sergeant Seals was the only one who used this process. This type of forced showering was used on several inmates. It was obviously illegal.

Towards the end of Crack's stay in the TCU, Crack began covering the ceiling of his cell with feces and did not respond to any of Sergeant Seals tactics. Crack knew that as long as the feces was on the ceiling, staff would not go into his cell to get him. After Crack threw feces on Officer Eli, he was recommended for placement on close management and transferred from the Dade CI TCU.

Sergeant Seals also went into inmates' cells to physically abuse them. Below, I explain more about the violence on A-shift.

206) Did Sergeants Seals and Lewis tamper with the cameras?

Yes, they In Wing J-1 there was a door next to Cell J-1201 which led to the attic over the Westside. Behind that door, there was a ladder about eight feet high mounted to a cement wall. That ladder led to the attic area over the Westside. Up in the attic, there was a box over each wing where one could shut off or reset the mounted security cameras in each wing. I was in the attic over the Westside several times in the end of 2012. It was always when Sergeants Seals or Lewis were on duty.

207) Did Sergeant Lewis return to the TCU in the end of 2012?

Yes. However, when he did return to the TCU, he was posted to work on the Eastside. Although, he did act as a relief Sergeant on the Westside a lot. Almost every time he worked on the Westside, there was staff-on-inmate violence or inmates not being fed.

Chapter 13: The Valley of Sorrows (June 26, 2012-January 17, 2013)

208) What does your July 26, 2012 journal entry state?

It states: *"I read Holy, Holy, Holy from Ligonier Ministries. I completed my correspondence studies on Job and Philippians with PMI. I talked with Doctor Cesar weekly for the first three weeks following Darren Rainey's death. I believe it was on July 13, 2012 or July 14, 2012, that I started working on third shift. I'm now working all three shifts. I finally reached mom on the phone last night. The last time I spoke with Dr. Cesar was two weeks ago. I should be talking with her again today, or tomorrow. On July 18, 2012 Inmate David Smith from the Eastside came to the Westside alleging that he was smoking K2 with Bernard Durham, passed-out, and woke up with Inmate Durham's penis in his mouth. He then, allegedly, saw a cell phone camera recording the act. Smith beat up Durham, Sanderfer, and Bartl. Sanderfer and Bartl allegedly tried to help get Smith off Durham. Smith moved to Cell J-1214 today. Doctor Cesar just told me that the death of Darren Rainey was still under investigation, and if I said anything in detail to her about it, she would have to file an incident report."*

209) Tell me more about the incident with David Smith mentioned in your journal.

One morning when we finished serving breakfast, I was told to lockdown in my cell right away. They were bringing a violent inmate down from the Eastside section of the TCU.

When David Smith arrived in Wing J-1, he was handcuffed behind his back and yelling. Officers Ryan and Jenkins were doing all they could to control Smith and to get him in to the shower. After they placed him in the shower and removed the handcuffs, he started yelling, "He raped me! He raped me!" He was very emotional and dealing with all types of emotions at one time.

While he was in the shower, different staff members came in and out of Wing J-1, trying to calm him down. They were unsuccessful. David Smith eventually used a piece of steel from the vent area in the shower to cut his wrist. As soon as he cut his wrist, the staff were forced to get him out of the shower quickly so he didn't bleed out. It was hard for the staff though, because

Smith was slinging his blood from his cut wrist at the staff who were standing about 20 feet from the shower.

This incident happened on a workday, and all of the staff who worked in the TCU were at work. Many of the Westside staff witnessed this incident. The presence of numerous staff meant security staff had to act by the book. After Sergeant Seals and Officer Gruben got dressed in blood prevention clothing, they came to Wing J-1, opened the shower stall that Smith was in, and used force to get Smith to the ground and in handcuffs. After he was handcuffed, they escorted him to the medical department.

A couple hours after Smith went to the medical department, the Miami-Dade Police Department was at Dade CI interviewing Smith on his allegation of being sexually battered by Durham. Just prior to Smith being interviewed by the police, he recanted and said he wasn't sexually battered. He said when he and Durham smoked K2 together, it made him hallucinate that he was sexually battered by Durham.

When Smith said he saw a cell phone recording the incident, it placed the security staff in a position where they had to search the Eastside for that cell phone. Too many high ranking staff at Dade CI heard Smith say he saw a cell phone. Additionally, he was going to be talking with law enforcement. If Smith mentioned the cell phone to the police, they would want the cell phone as evidence. As a result of the security staff searching the Eastside, narcotics and several cell phones were seized. Smith eventually became an orderly and my co-worker in the TCU.

210) Pease tell me about the contraband that was in the TCU.

There were cell phones and unlawful narcotics in the TCU. Inmates consumed the unlawful narcotics and hallucinated as a result. This contraband was brought in by the staff.

For example, Officer Gruben sold aspirin to on the Eastside who was addicted to snorting aspirin. When he came to the Westside in the end of 2012, Officer Gruben gave him two packs of aspirin for an iced honeybun Officer Gruben and all the staff knew that inmate was addicted to snorting aspirin. But, at the time, Officer Gruben wanted an iced honey bun to eat.

Chapter 13: The Valley of Sorrows (June 26, 2012-January 17, 2013)

211) What does your August 6, 2012 journal entry state?

It states: *"On August 3, 2012 Cobas, Seals, and Weary battered Inmate Ashton (Cell J-1104) between 8:30 am and 9:30 am. The other runaround is Joshua Rogers. On August 3, 2012, Ashton attempted to batter Officer Hood during showers. On August 4, 2012, Officers Piggot, Gruben, and Cobas used unlawful force on Ashton to get him back in his cell during vitals. On August 5, 2012, Officer Piggot and Sergeant Seals used unlawful force on Ashton to get him to go and talk to the chaplain. On August 8, 2012, Ashton was discovered to have a swollen black right eye. Sergeant Collado reported the incident. Nobody else did. Between August 6, 2012 and August 14, 2012, Ashton was denied all of his meals by A-Shift staff. Ashton received several kidney punches when he was taken to see the chaplain on August 5, 2012. I talked to Dr. Cesar every week since the June 23, 2012 death of Rainey. When I saw Dr. Cesar the week of July 29, 2012 through August 4, 2012, she said she would have to file an incident report if I said anything in detail to her about what happened to Rainey. On August 8, 2012, I authorized the mailing of two 14 page affidavits. I have spoken with mom and Windy every Wednesday and Saturday for the last two weeks. I've been calling Aunt Jane on Sundays, and I've been working all four shifts."*

212) Why did Dr. Cesar tell Rainey's death was still under investigation and that if you said anything about it to her she would have to file an incident report?

I thought she was trying to get me to stop talking to her about what happened to Darren Rainey.

213) Why do you have dates after August 6, 2012, in your August 6, 2012 entry?

On August 6, 2012, I started the entry to document the things that were happening. I didn't complete the entry. When I went back to write in my journal over the following week, I continued documenting everything in with my August 6, 2012 entry instead of making new entries.

**214) Is there any evidence to support the abuse Inmate
Ashton was subjected to?**

I could be wrong, but I believe he was stable enough to
remember the abuse he was subjected to. His medical and
classification files may also have documentation in them to
support the incidents I mentioned in my journal.

215) Where was Inmate Ashton's cell (Cell J-1104) located?

It was in a blind spot in Wing J-1.

**216) Please explain your references to Inmate Ashton in your
August 6, 2012 journal entry?**

Inmate Ashton was in Cell J-1104, which is a blind spot, that
is, out of view of the security cameras. After Ashton was
physically battered by Sergeant Seals and Officers Cobas and
Weary on August 3, 2012, he attempted to punch Officer Hood in
his face that evening. Officer Hood slammed Ashton to the
ground, handcuffed him, brought him back to his cell, and
slapped him around. On August 4, Officers Piggot, Gruben, and
Cobas physically battered Ashton again, because he refused to go
back to his cell during vitals. On August 5, Seals and Piggot used
unlawful physical force on Ashton to make him go talk to the
chaplain. On August 6, Ashton punched Sergeant Collado during
shower time. Collado hit Ashton in the face with his radio and
gave him a swollen black right eye. Ashton also showed me that
blood was in his urine. He said Seals and Piggot punched him in
his kidneys when they made him go to talk to the chaplain.
Finally, A-Shift denied him all of his meals from August 6
through the 14, 2012. Ashton was another inmate who had mental
difficulty following instructions or complying with procedures.

By the end of 2012, many inmates were complaining about
Sergeant Seals punching them in their kidneys. There were so
many abuses in the second half of 2012 that I could not document
all of the ones I witnessed.

217) Who is Windy Hempstead?

Windy Hempstead is my sister. She and my Aunt Jane were
the first two people in society whom I told about Darren Rainey.
Around the end of June, I told my sister about Rainey's death.
She wanted to take immediate action to have me transferred. I

told her I was physically safe. She trusted my judgment but asked me to call her at least once a week to check in. As the conditions got worse in the TCU, she asked me to call at least twice a week, and I did. I called her every Wednesday and Saturday. These calls were to let her know I was safe.

218) Will you tell me about your telephone calls to Windy in the end of 2012?

Windy has been by my side helping me since we were kids. I wanted her to be aware of everything I witnessed and what was going on with me in the end of 2012. I knew I would need her help tremendously. After what I saw happen to Rainey, I knew the only person I could depend on was my sister Windy.

219) What did you mean in your August 26, 2012 journal entry when you said, "I authorized the mailing of the two 14 page affidavits."?

I made two copies of a 14 page affidavit explaining in detail the *Hot-Water-Shower* treatment of mentally disabled inmates and what happened to Darren Rainey. I mailed those affidavits to the Dade County, Florida Medical Examiner's office and to Detective Wilbert Sanchez of the Miami-Dade Police Department Homicide Bureau. I never received any responses to my affidavits.

220) What does your September 26, 2012 journal entry state?

It states:

"On September 18, 2012 when I went to Sergeant Joiner's office to mail Florida Statute § 119 Public Records Requests to Miami-Dade Police Department Homicide Bureau and to the Dade County, Florida State Attorney's office, the major went to the Westside took a picture of the back office by Cell J-1111, and then he went to my cell and searched it. He took my tape player and tapes, watch, coffee, and salt. Officer Jones stood at my cell door as the major searched my cell. The major questioned me as he was leaving the wing. The Wing J-1 security cameras recorded us talking. He sent Sergeant Joiner and Officer Riley back to talk with me about my tape player, tapes, and watch, which were all returned within 20 minutes, once it was verified that all of the items belonged to me. The major said I was fired as an orderly

that day, but no messages were relayed to the other shifts. On Wednesday, September 19, 2012, Officer Gruben told Sergeant Seals and me that the major said I could work again. I've been working every day since then. I spoke with Dr. Basaga after breakfast on September 19, 2012, and with Dr. Cesar before lunch regarding the issue with the major. On September 20, 2012 and September 24, 2012, I took some of my property from my cell to Officer Riley in the property room. Officer Piggot escorted me there on September 20, 2012, Officer McGriff escorted me there on September 24, 2012. The following staff were present in Wing J-1, when the major searched my cell on September 18, 2012: Sergeant Johnathan, Officers Rantin, Jones, Eli, McGriff, and Ms. Arencibia. Officer Clark told me on September 26, 2012, before 7:00 am, that he was being reassigned to the compound. He supposedly told Joshua Rogers he made sergeant and was going to A-Shift in Foxtrot Dorm."

221) On September 28, 2012, did request public records on the Darren Rainey case?

Yes. I mailed Florida Statute §119 Public Records Requests to the Miami-Dade Police Department Homicide Bureau and to the Dade, Florida County State Attorney's Office on the Darren Rainey case. Additionally, as soon as I arrived at Sergeant Joiner's office to mail them out, Major McCarter went to Wing J-1, and engaged in a retaliatory search of my cell. Sergeant Joiner was the major's secretary.

I believe McCarter subjected me to that retaliatory search of my cell, because that was his way of saying to me, "I will cause you trouble if you write to people in society and cause us trouble".

222) Were you concerned about Major McCarter subjecting you to retaliation?

Yes. However, my concerns did not stop me from continuing to try to covertly communicate with people in society about Darren Rainey's death, and the abuse in the TCU.

223) What did you tell Drs. Basaga and Cesar on September 19, 2012?

I told them I thought that Major McCarter searched my cell and that he took my personal property out of retaliation. I also told them that I felt the retaliation was unjustified considering I had been fighting against the desire to report everything I knew to the U.S. Department of Justice, and the Florida Department of Health. Finally, I mentioned that I was doing everything I could to deal with the overwhelming stress and sadness I had felt, and by the major subjecting me to retaliation, he was just pushing me to go to people in society to get help to stop his retaliation.

224) Why were you so assertive with Drs. Basaga and Cesar?

At that time Windy, my Aunt Jane, the Miami-Dade Police Department, and the Dade County, Florida Medical Examiner all knew that I was a witness to what happened to Darren Rainey. God had allowed me to make others aware of what I had witnessed, so I was no longer standing alone. I knew that if I missed any of my check-in calls to Windy or if I needed her help, she would take whatever action was necessary to have me transferred from Dade CI.

225) In reference to your September, 26, 2012 journal entry, was Officer Clarke promoted to sergeant and reassigned to A-Shift?

Yes.

226) What types of punishment and coercion were being used at the end of 2012?

- Staff were still pouring bleach and ammonia in inmates' cells to persuade them to come out of their cells.
- Staff were still putting medicine in the food of inmates who refused to listen to them.
- Inmates were still being showered by force using chemicals and five gallon buckets of water.

I also witnessed bleach being thrown on the face of Inmate Cecil Livingston. Livingston was yelling through the jamb of his cell door. Officer David got sick of the yelling and told Gregory Shevlin to put some bleach in a Styrofoam cup and to throw it through the side of Livingston's cell door, thereby, getting the bleach in Livingston's face and causing him to stop yelling.

227) Will you tell me about the conversation Officer Piggot and you had concerning Darren Rainey on or around September 2012?

When we were on the recreation yard talking about the Bible and, out of nowhere, Piggot said, "So you're telling me I should feel bad?"

I responded, "What are you talking about?"

He said, "When I went to serve Rainey lunch on the day he died, he showed a lot of anger about his Quran that I threw away. I didn't feel it was safe to open his food flap so I told him that when he calmed down, I would give him a tray. After we served the rest of Wing J-1, I went back to his cell to see if he had calmed down. When I got to his cell, I saw that he had defecated in the middle of his cell floor. I told him when he cleaned it up, I would give him a tray. He was very mad and unreasonable. He was cursing and hitting his cell door, so I gave up trying to talk to him. He continued throughout the day to not clean up the feces. When my shift was over, I went home. That night, they put him in the shower because of the feces on his cell floor."

I responded, "Why didn't you have an orderly clean up the feces? You knew that Officer Clarke was using the *Hot-Water-Shower* to punish mentally disabled inmates who didn't listen to him. How can you not have conviction for what happened? The feces you left in Rainey's cell, is the feces that got him placed in the shower."

He said, "Yeah, but I didn't know Officer Clarke was going to place Rainey in that shower, or that he was going to die. Why should I feel bad?"

I responded, "I don't know how to answer you any other way than how I previously did. If you don't have any conviction, then there's a spiritual problem. You should really pray and ask God for conviction."

While we were going back and forth on this subject, Coach Ocanna interrupted our conversation, which led to the subject being changed. Piggot and I discussed this matter about him not having the feces cleaned in Rainey's cell a few more times in the end of 2012. Piggot never showed remorse for not making sure the feces was cleaned in Rainey's cell on the day Rainey died.

228) Do you believe Officer Piggot's act of throwing Darren Rainey's Quran in the trash led to Rainey's death?

Yes. Rainey showed that he was very angry mad about his Quran being thrown in the trash by Officer Piggot. Piggot told Rainey he wasn't going to receive a lunch tray until he calmed down. Rainey defecated on his cell floor, showing anger about not being fed. Piggot then told Rainey he wouldn't receive a tray of food until he cleaned it up. Rainey's refusal to clean up the feces led to him being placed in the shower. The conditions in the shower led to his death. Accordingly, if Piggot had not thrown away Rainey's Quran, none of the subsequent events would have happened.

229) What happened with Daniel Geiger in the end of 2012?

Geiger was in very poor condition prior to being placed in the *Hot-Water-Shower*. However, his condition worsened after being placed in it. His condition became so bad, the Mental Health Treatment Team had to have him involuntary committed into the Corrections Mental Health Infirmary Unit at Lake CI.

Much later, at the end of 2016, I heard that Geiger died in the Mental Health Unit at Lake CI.

230) What does your October 6, 2012 journal entry state?

It states: *"Angelo Bresile, D.C. #M30807. Last night I received a response in the mail from the Dade County, Florida State Attorney's Office concerning my Public Records Request. They said they didn't have any public records on Darren Rainey. Yesterday, Ms. Koel said I would receive a response to my request about the special reviews I need to have placed on me. Dr. Basaga said yesterday that he spoke with Ms. Koel about this. The inmate in Cell J-1112 has not eaten any meals since last Wednesday breakfast (All Shifts)."*

231) Tell me about your interactions you had with the Dade County, Florida State Attorney at the end of 2012.

During the second half of 2012, I mailed several letters to the Dade County, Florida State Attorney asking for any public records on the Darren Rainey case. The response letter I received from her office on August 5, 2012 said she didn't have any records on the Rainey case.

I did not believe this. I knew that since Rainey's death occurred while he was in custody, it had to be reported as an in-custody death to an on-call assistant state attorney. This was one reason why their office would have had records on the Rainey case. The second reason was because the Miami-Dade Police Department was supposed to be conducting an active homicide investigation into his death.

Then at the end of 2012, I wrote a letter to the Dade County, Florida State Attorney's Office informing them of the details regarding Darren Rainey's death. In this detailed letter, I explained the *Hot-Water-Shower* treatment and what happened to Rainey. I also included diagrams of the *Hot-Water-Shower* and where it was located in Wing J-3.

I never heard anything back from them.

232) Please tell me more about the sentence in your October 6, 2012 journal that states, "The inmate in Cell J-1112 has not eaten any meals since last Wednesday breakfast (All Shifts)".

When the Caucasian inmate first moved into Cell J-1112, he was calling his neighbor in Cell J-1111 racist names. One day at the beginning of Sergeant Seals' shift, the inmate in Cell J-1111 told Sergeant Seals and Officer Patterson that the inmate in Cell J-1112 was racist. These staff went to Cell J-1112, and asked Caucasian inmate if he was racist. Officer Patterson then said, "If you don't like black people, you can let us know. You can call us any racist names you want."

When the inmate didn't respond, Patterson said, "We're going to leave. Hempstead, if you want to stay and tell him about where he's at, you can. If you don't want to, you can leave. It doesn't matter."

As soon as they left, I told the inmate, "You might not believe what I'm about to tell you, but I promise you, I'm not lying. The staff who were just talking to you will starve you to death if you get on their bad sides."

The inmate just responded, "OK." I then walked away from his cell.

The next day when we were serving lunch, the staff and I heard the Caucasian inmate in Cell J-1112 was calling the black inmate in Cell J-1111 racial names. When we got to Cell J-1111 with the trays and juice, the inmate in that cell said, "Pat. The Cracker next door is on that racist s*it again."

We gave the black inmate in cell 111 his food and juice, and moved on to Cell 112. Officer Patterson said, "Are you calling your neighbor racial names?" The inmate admitted that he was calling his neighbor racial names, and he then started calling Patterson racial names and curse words. The inmate was not given a lunch tray.

About 30 minutes after lunch, Sergeant Seals and Officer Patterson went to the white inmate, and Sergeant Seals said, "You'll eat again when you tell your neighbor, Officer Patterson, and me that you're sorry, and when you call each of us 'King Black Man'." The inmate then cursed at Sergeant Seals. After he started cursing, the staff laughed and harassed the inmate for a few more minutes, prior to leaving from in front of his cell.

The next day when A-Shift was not working, I went to the white inmate in cell 112 and said, "I really don't know why you did what you did. I told you what they were going to do. Listen! I'm going to do my best to give you some extra food when the other shifts are on so you're not too hungry when A-Shift works. Just don't tell anybody what I'm doing. OK?"

The inmate responded, "That's OK. You don't have to do that. I'm not going to eat anymore."

I said, "That's easier said than done. I've seen a lot of inmates try to starve themselves and barely anybody makes it past a day or two. You don't have to go through that. It's only A-Shift that won't feed you."

The inmate in Cell J-1112 responded, "Thanks, but you'll see. I'm not going to eat anymore."

For about a week the inmate refused every meal on all of the shifts. I was concerned because none of the security staff reported that he was refusing all of his meals. Usually, when an inmate refused all of his meals, security staff reported it to medical staff and the mental health team. The security staff didn't want to be blamed for denying an inmate food when it was the inmate who was refusing his own food. I decided to go to Sergeants Johnathan and Lopez, who were on the same shift, and tell them that the inmate hadn't eaten anything for about a week. I also explained to them that if something happened to the inmate, that security staff would more than likely be blamed because none of them were reporting it. The sergeants told medical staff and the mental health team that the inmate was refusing to eat.

The mental health team had the inmate moved from Cell J-1112 to Wing J-2, and placed on observation status.

When the inmate was in Wing J-2, Nurse Mayweather took the inmate's vitals and tested his sugar. Nurse Mayweather told Sergeant Lopez that the inmates' vitals and sugar were OK. Nurse Mayweather also said that if the inmate had been a week without eating, his blood sugar would have been very low and, since it wasn't low, it showed he was eating.

Sergeant Lopez told me what Nurse Mayweather said, and I told him I was absolutely positive the inmate hadn't been eating for about a week. I said I believed Nurse Mayweather was lying and that another nurse should retake the inmate's vitals. That night, another nurse took his vitals and checked his blood sugar. After this, the inmate was taken to a hospital in society.

About a week later, the inmate was placed back in Wing J-2. He had been involuntary committed to the Corrections Mental Health Infirmary Unit and was pending a transfer to Lake CI. When the inmate saw me in Wing J-2, he ran to his cell door and said, "Hey, Runaround."

I went to his cell and said, "I haven't seen you in about a week. Where have you been?"

He responded, "The hospital. They said I almost died. Look." He then stuck his tongue out and showed me how white it was. The less liquid a person has in his body, the more white his tongue will be.

When I saw how white his tongue was, I said, "So you haven't been drinking any liquids either?"

He responded, "No. I showed them. I'm crazier than they are. Now I don't have to worry about them anymore. I'm going to Lake CI. They Baker Acted me."

I said, "Well I'm glad you're OK, and that you're leaving. You gave me a lot of stress. I was worried about you dying. Take care of yourself, and don't get into any trouble at Lake CI, OK?"

He responded, "OK." A day or two later, he was transferred from Dade CI.

233) What does your November 5, 2012 journal entry state?

It states: *"On Monday November 1, 2012 just before 5:00 pm Sergeant Lopez disclosed confidential information off the CDC computer system while we were sitting at the tables in Wing J-1. He did this in front of Joshua Roger, David Smith, Sergeant Johnathan, and me.*

Lawrence Smith was referred to close management one in September 2012, for throwing a food tray at Officer Gruben. The Institutional Classification Team recommended close management two. I've been calling mom and Windy every Sunday and Wednesday. I'm currently reading "Old Testament History" by Alfred Edelsheim. Cell J-1112 wasn't fed lunch and dinner on November 3, 2012, and breakfast, lunch, and dinner on November 4, 2012. Cell J-1104 wasn't fed lunch and dinner on November 3, 2012, and on November 4, 2012. I talked to Dr. Cesar on November 2, 2012. Cell J-1105 wasn't fed lunch and dinner on October 28, 29, and 30, 2012. A-Shift worked all of these dates. I heard Officer Clarke became a sergeant on A-Shift in Foxtrot Dorm confinement."

234) What did Sergeant Lopez disclose off the Corrections Data Center computer system?

Only some matters concerning my religious background. What troubled me about Sergeant Lopez having access to the computer was that it meant he had the ability to find out, or might have already known, about my history of speaking out against things I disagreed with.

235) So Officer Gruben was successful in getting Lawrence Smith placed on close management?

Yes. As I previously mentioned, I told Smith that Officer Gruben would be successful in getting Smith discharged or placed on close management, if he didn't back from his conflict with Gruben. Smith didn't take my advice, and Officer Gruben got Smith placed on close management two.

236) Tell me about your conversation with Officer Piggot about inmates dying in the TCU.

Around October 2012, when I was talking with Officer Piggot in Wing J-1 about the Bible, he asked, "How many inmates do you remember dying over the past two years?"

I responded, "Three: Oscar Davis, Darryl Richardson, and Darren Rainey. Why?"

He said, "I remember five. You know, it's strange that every inmate who we skipped on a lot of food trays eventually developed medical problems, left the Westside because of those problems, and died. It's been going on like that since I've been here."

I responded, "Rainey didn't die from not being fed. He died in the *Hot-Water-Shower* that Clarke put him in."

Piggot said, "I know that. I'm not talking about Rainey. I'm talking about the rest of them."

This conversation added to my concerns, because Piggot clearly stated that multiple inmates on the Westside died due to starvation. This caused me to be more determined to find a way to help the TCU inmates.

237) Why did chicken on the bone stop being served to inmates in the TCU?

In the end of 2012, Inmate Gainer started acting up while on the recreation yard. He was yelling and cursing at Officer Williams, who was talking to Coach Ocanna. When Officer Weary came out on the recreation yard, he became angry about Gainer being so loud and disrespectful.

Weary approached Gainer, who was acting manic. When Gainer refused to listen, Weary grabbed Gainer and tried to force him to the ground. Officer Weary was unable to force Gainer to the ground, so Officer Williams went to help Weary. Williams aided in slamming Gainer on to the cement. The officers then got on top of Gainer. When the officers looked up and saw all of the inmates on the recreation yard watching the officers use excessive force on Gainer, they yelled for us to get off the yard and go back into the wing. As all of the inmates were returning to the TCU, more security staff entered the recreation yard.

**Chapter 13: The Valley of Sorrows (June 26, 2012-
January 17, 2013)**

About 10 minutes later, when Gainer was brought off the
yard, he was physically harmed. Weary alleged the reason it took
so long to get Gainer off the recreation yard was because Gainer
pulled a sharpened chicken bone out of his pocket and tried to
stab Weary. He alleged that was why they had to use a lot of
physical force on Gainer after everyone left the yard. As a result
of this alleged incident, Major McCarter ordered that chicken on
the bone no longer would be served to the inmates housed in the
TCU.

What Officer Weary failed to realize was that when all of the
inmates were leaving the recreation yard, Officers Weary and
Williams were on top of Gainer, who was face down on the
cement. Both officers had Gainer controlled, and they were
placing handcuffs on him. It's my position that Weary made up
the story about the chicken bone to justify their physical abuse of
Gainer the inmates.

238) Will you tell me about Coach Harriet Kryscowski?

Everybody called her Coach K. Coach K was an intelligent
lady. She was a professional and very nice. From my
understanding, while she was working as a coach in the TCUs at
South Florida Reception Center and at Dade CI, she was also
working on obtaining her Master's Degree in Psychology. The
security staff didn't like Coach K because she tried to do her job
the way she was supposed to do it. She knew that it was good
therapy for the inmates to get outside of their cells for recreational
and day room activities, and her job was to make sure they
received these things. Coach K wasn't friendly with any of the
evil staff, and she wasn't involved with any of the abusive acts
that were being committed in th

239) Will you tell me about Coach Nichole Ocanna?

In 2012, Coach Ocanna was a 27 year old Peruvian. She was
the main coach on the Westside and the girlfriend of Officer
Gruben. In his book *Getting Away with Murder*, George
Mallinckrodt talked about Coach Ocanna. She was a very nice
lady but she could also be very evil. If an inmate said anything
adverse about security to her, she would tell security staff what
the inmate said. She was given Mallinckrodt's old office in Wing
J-3 when Mallinckrodt stopped working in the TCU.

169

In 2013, Coach Ocanna became pregnant by Officer Gruben. She was very aware of all the unlawful and unprofessional matters occurring in the TCU. She was involved with all types of evil acts.

240) What does your November 27, 2012 journal entry state?

It states:

"Two weeks ago on a Friday or Saturday, Michael Glover came from the Eastside and was placed in Cell J-1209. While in Cell J-1209, he cut his wrist, stabbed himself in the stomach two times and consumed several batteries. He came back to the TCU several days later, on Wednesday or Thursday, and was placed in Cell J-2107 on self-harm observation status. He stabbed himself again twice yesterday. He came from the Eastside during Bravo Shift. The first time he stabbed himself, etc. was also on Bravo Shift. He came back from the hospital both times during Bravo Shift and stabbed himself the second and third time during Delta Shift. Both times Officer Weary kept Glover under observation during Bravo Shift. The second time, Officers Collado or Lester kept him under observation during Delta Shift, and the third time, Officer Ryan watched him during Delta Shift."

241) Was Michael Glover a stabber?

Yes. He had a long history of stabbing himself in the stomach with sharpened hard plastic spoons from the chow hall. On the day mentioned in my journal entry, he cut his wrist, stabbed himself in the stomach twice, and consumed several batteries. I don't know what order he did these thing in.

242) What does your December 1, 2012 journal entry state?

It states: *"I'm working all four shifts and doing all I can to continue covertly providing information concerning Rainey. This is the worst it has been with so many not being fed, constant cutting, constant investigations, etc. I've been working about 14 hours a day, seven days a week for the past several months. Every now and then something will happen that will allow me to take a day or so off. I'm very tired."*

Chapter 13: The Valley of Sorrows (June 26, 2012-January 17, 2013)

243) Who were you covertly providing information to on the Darren Rainey case?

The Miami-Dade Police Department, Dade County, Florida Medical Examiner's Office, and one other person. I cannot name the person at this time. I sent the information by mail.

244) How rough did the Westside TCU become in the end of 2012?

Staff were continually not feeding a large number of inmates. Inmates were frequently cutting their arms and wrists. Staff regularly used caustic chemicals to get inmates out or their cells and to force them to shower. Staff were constantly violent. They threw inmates to the floor. Staff kicked, beat, and slapped inmates after restraining them in handcuffs. Staff abused inmates by adding medicine, chemicals, and other substances to inmates' food.

The list goes on and on.

I was fighting like crazy to suppress the sadness and regret I felt due to my failure to act in the death of Darren Rainey and in the *Hot-Water-Shower* treatment of the other inmates. I was struggling to control and not collapse under the grief and remorse I felt from witnessing a continuous pattern of non-stop violence and evil that was only getting worse.

The Westside became so bad by the end of 2012, Sergeant Seals gave it a new nickname. He started referring to the Westside as Auschwitz, which was a sick joke. Seals' sick humor spread like a cancer and several staff and inmates started referring to the Westside as Auschwitz. Around the end of October, when new arrivals to the Westside came in on A-Shift, if Sergeant Seals was working, he would say, "Welcome to Auschwitz!"

Another sick Auschwitz joke that was going around at that time was the staff saying, "We don't have a gas chamber, but we used to have a *Hot-Water-Shower* Stall."

245) How physically tired were you from constantly working in the end of 2012?

I believe the staff wanted me to be constantly working in order to keep me from taking action against them for what they did to Rainey and the other inmates in the TCU. At that time, I felt I needed to work a lot to keep my mind off my sadness. The constant work was aiding me in that fight. I had to force myself to not cry all day every day when I was working around the staff. When I was in my cell, I couldn't do anything but sleep. When it came to writing letters in my cell, I had to fight to stay awake to complete them.

My main Christian activities during that time were my constant Bible discussions and debates with numerous staff. That Christian activity kept my mind active and strong in the Word during a time in my life when I needed it. Those Bible discussions and debates lasted for hours every day of the week.

246) Who helped you the most personally in the end of 2012?

Three people. First, would be my sister Windy. I knew from past experiences that if anything ever got out of hand, I could be transferred from Dade CI with one phone call or letter to her.

Second, would be Officer Piggot. He engaged me in conversation for hours every day he worked. We talked about systematic theology, apologetics, and church history. He really wanted to learn these subjects. However, what he didn't know was that he was keeping my mind focused on God. God was my only hope to get out of the Valley of Sorrows. Our conversations were keeping my mind thinking about who God is and about His promises in the Bible.

Third was Dr. Cesar. I don't know for sure what her motives were but she aided a lot in keeping my mind busy during that time. If her motives were good, then I'm thankful for what she did. If her motives were bad, then God brought good out of them. The Bible says, "And we know that all things work together for good to those who love God, to those who are called according to his purpose."[1]

247) What does your December 5, 2012 journal entry state?

It states, "*I was fired from Alpha Shift on December 3, 2012. Lieutenant Tarver said I didn't do anything and that it was the staff who did wrong. Inmates Witherspoon (Cell J-1222) and Brooks (Cell J-1221) worked today. On November 25, 2012, Brian Hernandez was battered by Sergeant Seals and Officer Patterson in Wing J-3. I spoke with Dr. Cesar today and told her I was planning to quit all the shifts. I found out that I am under*

172

*another investigation with staff. An inmate that had a problem
with Inmate David Smith was able to persuade the major to
review the cameras and watch Smith, the officers, sergeant, and
me on the floor for several days. Smith has been gambling with A-
Shift staff in card games and getting them to perform dances on
call. The winner of the card game tells the loser what type of
dance to perform and when to perform them. For the last several
weeks, Smith has been winning, and he's been having the staff
perform all kinds of crazy dances. Now, I guess because of my
position and having seniority on the floor, I'm getting pulled in
with this investigation to. This was what I was told, but in a way,
I don't believe it. I believe they found out that I've been writing
the Miami-Dade Police Department, etc., for months now and
that I've been running my mouth. I told Drs. Cesar and Basaga,
and Ms. Arencibia that if they didn't do something to put a stop to
the staff on inmate violence, then I would do all that I could to
stop it. We'll see what happens. At least I have time to catch up
on my sleep and my school studies. So far I've earned straight A's
in my Bible and Paralegal College courses. I prayed and
worshiped."*

248) Is Alpha shift also called A-Team?

Yes. All shifts call themselves Teams. (A-Team, B-Team,
C-Team, and D-Team)

249) Why were you fired from A-Shift?

When Inmate David Smith became my primary co-worker,
he started gambling with A-Shift security staff in cards for on-call
dances. The security staff who were gambling with Smith were
Sergeant Seals and Officers Gruben and Patterson. They won a
lot, but Smith won the most. This went on for about two months.

In November, Smith got an inmate mad at him. That inmate
filed several grievances telling Major McCarter that if he watched
the mounted security camera footage for specific dates and times,
he would see security staff doing all types of crazy dances. The
inmate told the major about Smith gambling in cards with the
staff and that was why the staff were dancing. I had nothing to do
with the cards, gambling, or dancing.

I was told I was fired because I had seniority on the floor. It
was inferred that I was supposed to somehow stop the gambling

and dancing. I believe that was just the major's excuse for firing me. He knew that I had been communicating with outside agencies, and had been telling mental health staff that if the violence didn't stop, or they didn't do anything to stop it, I was going to do my best to stop it.

250) So you told mental health staff that if the violence didn't stop, or they didn't do something to stop it, you were going to do your best to stop it?

Yes. I told that to Drs. Cesar and Basaga and to Ms. Arencibia. I reached the point where I could no longer continue to watch the constant starving and violence. I felt so bad for the inmates. They had no help and no ability to help themselves.

In the end of 2012, I could see that my attempts to bring reform to the TCU were not working. The place had gotten worse, and I had an overwhelming feeling that God wanted me to try a different course of action to get help. I felt like God was leading me to do, what I had been fighting for so long to not do. Additionally, I felt like God was saying that the mentally disabled needed a voice, and He wanted me to be their voice. I had kept everything inside of me for so long, and I could no longer contain the desire to speak out. In the Valley of Sorrows, I was full of sadness but also angry. The staff were abusing the physically and mentally disabled inmates who couldn't defend themselves. I knew I was emotionally weak at the time because of my extreme sadness over all that I had failed to do.

However, I knew that even in my weakness, by God's grace, I was still strong enough to take a stand and to be their voice. In 2012, I looked back and saw that God used the events that happened in 2011 and 2012 to answer my prayers. He helped me to understand His love for us and how I was to love others. A person must truly love in his heart before he can manifest love in action.

251) Did Drs. Basaga and Cesar, and Ms. Arencibia ask you a similar question when you told them you would take action to stop the violence if they didn't?

Yes. They each asked me, "What are you going to do?" I told them that they should check my prison file, because I had a long history of speaking out against things that were wrong.

Chapter 13: The Valley of Sorrows (June 26, 2012-January 17, 2013)

Additionally, I told them I would quit all the shifts and discharge from the TCU. Upon discharging, I would contact the U.S. Department of Justice, Federal Bureau of Investigations, Florida Department of Health, and the Miami-Dade Police Department Homicide Bureau, and tell them everything I witnessed during my incarceration in the TCU. Finally, I told the two doctors and Ms. Arencibia that they were obligated by state and federal laws to report the abuse they had been witnessed for the past several years to the Florida Department of Children and Families and the U.S. Department of Justice, and by them failing to do so, they violated their legal obligation to report the abuse.

252) Were you ever fearful of the staff in the TCU?

I was never afraid of them, but I was always aware that they could be a physical threat to my safety.

253) Tell me about being moved from the Dade TCU to the general population.

When Christmas 2012 came, the majority of the Mental Health Treatment Team staff took off for Christmas vacation. Both Drs. Basaga and Cesar took a Christmas vacation. While they were on vacation, Ms. Arencibia filled in for Dr. Cesar, and Dr. Santaro filled in for Dr. Basaga. Dr. Santaro was a psychiatrist from South Florida Reception Center.

On or about December 29, 2012, Dr. Santaro, Ms. Arencibia, and Ms. Koel completed the paperwork to discharge me from the TCU to the general population.

254) What happened and who did you contact after you were discharged from the TCU?

I was moved to the general population, Golf Dorm, Wing Three. Right away, I telephoned my sister Windy and my Aunt Jane. I told them I thought staff were aware that I had been covertly communicating with agencies, etc. in society about the Rainey case. I also gave Windy the telephone number to the Washington D.C. office of the U.S. Department of Justice and asked her to call them about the Darren Rainey case, and the other inmates who were placed in the *Hot-Water-Shower*.

Windy called the U.S. Department of Justice in January 2013.

175

255) Who is Inmate Alford L.?

He was a 68-year-old Christian who lived in the same wing I lived in. He slept in the cell across from me.

One morning, we started talking about the Bible. During that conversation, he said that he had never seen me before. When I told him what led to me being moved into that wing, he said, "I believe God has called you to take a stand on behalf of those victims in the TCU who need your help." I told him that I thought the same thing and I was taking steps to help them. It was just that I was physically, mentally, and spiritually drained from all that had happened.

He said, "The Shepherd led you here to witness the things you did so that you could be their voice. I believe He will give you the strength you need to stand and be their voice."

When Alford L. said this, I remembered what the preacher told me in the Pinellas County, Florida Jail about following the Shepherd (Jesus) wherever He led me. Everything the preacher in the county jail said was so clear in my mind.

I told Alford L., "For four months in 2010, and the beginning of 2011, I talked with a preacher in the Pinellas County, Jail about following the Shepherd of my soul. I talked with the preacher because I thought that I was going to be set free at a pending court hearing. However, I understood that God was sovereign and it might not have been His will for me to go free. If God didn't set me free, I didn't want Satan to try to use my loss at the hearing for his own ends.

"The Lord led me to that preacher. The Shepherd didn't lead me to society. He chose to lead me to a torture chamber. It's obvious that Jesus led me here because He wants me to help them. It's just that the things that I saw over the last almost two years have personally affected me. I'm confident though that our God, who is a God of grace, will give me the grace I need to do what He wants me to do."

Over the next few weeks, Alford L. and I talked a lot. I could tell he was a humble man every time I spoke with him.

Chapter 13: The Valley of Sorrows (June 26, 2012-January 17, 2013)

256) How did you deal with your sadness while in general population?

I suppressed my tears and sadness when people were around, and I cried myself to sleep at night. I had a lot of tears built up inside, and I knew I wasn't going to make it in population too long. I had to have a place to cry and pray. I needed to spend a lot of time in prayer.

257) Did you oversee a second call to the U.S. Department of Justice by an officer in January 2013?

Yes. An officer from the TCU came to see me in the general population. He said Ms. Koel told him that she convinced the Institutional Classification Team to approve her request to transfer me as a security threat. I was honest with the officer because I looked upon him as somebody I could somewhat trust, so I told him I was going to take action to stop the evil in the TCU. I asked him for help. I told him I wanted him to make a phone call, and that I would be talking with law enforcement about the TCU.

He asked me who I wanted him to call. I told him I wanted to alert the Washington D.C. office of the Department of Justice about what happened to Darren Rainey and the *Hot-Water-Shower* treatment. I explained I wanted him to make the phone call to the telephone number I gave him and leave a message on the answering machine. He did not have to leave his name. Finally, I explained that leaving the message would show me that he had truly changed. Eventually, he agreed.

I wrote out what I wanted him to say. We then went to the sergeant's office. He used the phone in that office to make the phone call and leave the message.

258) What was the officer's name?

I can't answer that. However, I can say that I knew him from the TCU. From here forth, I will call him by the pseudonym of Robert Anderson.

259) Why did you have two calls made to the Washington D.C. office of the U.S. Department of Justice?

That office has the authority under 42 United States Code § 1997 to order Civil Rights of Institutionalized Persons Act

(CRIPA) investigations, and other types of federal investigations. I wanted them to order a CRIPA investigation into the TCU, and a federal investigation into what happened to Darren Rainey.

260) Did you talk to a nurse about your discharge from the TCU?

Yes, she said that Dr. Santaro wrote in my file that he had spoken with me before me being discharged from TCU to the general population. This was a lie.

261) Tell me about your three weeks in the Dade CI general population.

My goals were to make to make contact with the Department of Justice, Florida Department of Law Enforcement, Miami-Dade Police Department Homicide Bureau, and FDC Inspector General's Office about what happened to Darren Rainey and the things I had witnessed in the TCU.

- I wrote letters to agencies in society. Yes. I wrote the Miami-Dade Police Department Homicide Bureau and the Dade County, Florida Medical Examiner's office.
- I filed about a dozen grievances concerning Darren Rainey and my retaliatory discharge from the TCU.
- Windy helped me by calling not only the Department of Justice but also Detective Sanchez of the Miami-Dade Police Department Homicide Bureau and the Dade County, Florida Medical Examiner's Office about what happened to Darren Rainey.

Chapter 14: Interregnum (January – May 2013)

262) Between January and June 2013, were you frequently moved before returning to Dade CI?

Yes. I left Dade CI on January 17, 2013 and returned on June 9, 2013. In the interval, I spent a week at the South Florida Reception Center followed by about five weeks at Everglades CI. From Everglades CI, I was moved to the Regional Medical Center for about two months (March and April 2013). I then passed through the South Florida Reception Center on my way to Martin CI and was housed there in May 2013 and the first week of June. On June 9, 2013, I was returned to Dade CI.

263) Why did Windy call the FDC Inspector General's office for you while you were housed at South Florida Reception Center?

She called and told them that I was a witness to what had happened to Darren Rainey, and that I wanted to talk with them. She informed them that I couldn't be housed at Everglades CI because the new colonel who was there used to work in the Dade CI TCU, and he was close friends with a lot of it's the staff there. I could have stayed at Everglades CI if I kept quiet about what happened to Darren Rainey and the things I witnessed in the TCU. However, I knew I wasn't going to do that. In January 2013, Windy spoke with two assistant inspectors general several times regarding the above matters.

264) Who else did Windy call for you while you were housed at South Florida Reception Center?

She called Miami-Dade Police Department Homicide Detective Sanchez and the Dade County, Florida Medical Examiner. Windy told them that I wanted to speak with them about what happened to Darren Rainey and about the *Hot-Water-Shower* treatment of mentally disabled inmates in the TCU. Additionally, she called the classification department at Everglades CI and told them about me being a witness to what happened to Rainey and to the torturing of mentally disabled inmates at Dade CI. She also let them know I was not safe at Everglades CI because of the colonel and that she wanted me to be transferred from there.

265) Did you call anybody while housed at South Florida Reception Center?

Yes. I called my Aunt Jane and the FDC Inmate TIP line. I called the TIP line four times. My calls were about what happened to Darren Rainey and the abuse I witnessed in the TCU. I explained how and why I couldn't be housed at Everglades CI, and I told them that I wanted to speak with an assistant inspector about what happened to Darren Rainey and the abuse I witnessed at Dade CI. I was assigned TIP mailbox numbers for each of my calls.

266) Did you file any grievances while housed at South Florida Reception Center?

Yes. I filed three or four grievances. I believe they were grievances of a sensitive nature and were emergency grievances. They were also about Darren Rainey, the abuses I witnessed, and my concerns for my safety at Everglades CI.

267) Was Orderly Mark Joiner also discharged from the TCU and transferred from Dade CI?

Yes. He was physically battered by Sergeant Lewis, discharged, and transferred. We were housed in the same wing at South Florida Reception Center. While we were there, we discussed how we were going to try to get justice for Darren Rainey.

268) Did other inmates say they were going to do what they could to get justice for Rainey?

Yes. Immediately following Darren Rainey's death, Inmate Daniel Medberry filed a grievance stating that Darren Rainey had been killed. Medberry also said he was going to do what he could to get justice for Darren Rainey.

269) How long were you at the S. Florida Reception Center?

I arrived at the South Florida Reception Center on January 17, 2013, and I was transferred from there to Everglades CI exactly one week later.

270) Were you interviewed by mental health staff when you arrived at Everglades CI?

Within 30 minutes of my arrival there, I was in an office with Senior Psychiatrist Dr. Rita, another psychiatrist, and Ms. Boute. They said they had heard about what was going on in the Dade CI TCU, and they wanted to talk to me. When I started telling them everything that had happened, I started crying. I had wanted to talk and to cry for so long, and I couldn't continue to suppress my sadness. As I was relaying the events and I mentioned Halden Casey being placed in the *Hot-Water-Shower*, Ms. Boute said, "Oh my God, Halden Casey."

I responded, "How do you know Casey? Is he here?"

She said, "Yes. He told me about that shower."

I talked with the two psychiatrists and Ms. Boute for about an hour. During that discussion, Dr. Rita said, "Harold, you could have Post Traumatic Stress Disorder (PTSD). Are you OK with me doing a referral to have you checked for PTSD?"

The other psychiatrist then said, "You have been through a lot. I agree with Dr. Rita that you should be evaluated for PTSD. If you agree, we would like to place you in administrative confinement on house alone status where you can relax and get some sleep until you transfer. I'll make sure that you keep all of your property while you're in confinement pending a transfer."

I responded, "A referral, means I would be sent to a TCU. If it was approved, I would likely go right back to the Dade CI TCU. I don't want to go back there."

Dr. Rita shook her head. "The referral is going to be for you to be evaluated for PTSD that you possibly have from events that happened at Dade CI. We will state in the referral that you might have PTSD from events you witnessed while at Dade CI, and that will keep you from going back there. They can't send you back there with the PTSD designation in your file."

I responded, "I understand. I'm OK with you doing the referral."

As we continued to talk, a classification officer showed up at Dr. Rita's office. The classification officer said, "Hempstead, your sister Windy called me. She wants me to place you in administrative confinement under protection and have you transferred. Are you OK with that?"

I responded, "Yes. I asked her to call you. I'm already going to confinement."

The classification officer said, 'I'm going to also place you under protection on house alone status. OK?"

I responded, "OK." I was then taken to administrative confinement.

271) Did you file any grievances while at Everglades CI?

Yes. I filed approximately 50 grievances on what happened to Darren Rainey, the *Hot-Water-Shower* treatment, the non-feeding of the inmates, and other matters involving the TCU.

272) What did a sergeant tell you regarding Inmates Russel Rogers and Darren Rainey while you were housed at Everglades CI?

There was a sergeant working in the confinement unit whom I knew from my prior incarcerations there. He and I were discussing things that had happened at Everglades CI since I transferred to Dade CI in 2011. During that conversation, I asked him about different inmates who I knew from my prior incarceration there. I asked him, "Is Russel Rogers still here?"

The sergeant responded, "Wow! Now, Rogers really fell from where he was."

I said, "What do you mean?"

He responded, "Rogers was doing real good for a while. He was preaching on the recreation yards, he got a job as a barber, and he was doing a good job representing Jesus. Then, out of nowhere, he got caught for gunning a female officer. He went to confinement for about two months. After he was released from confinement, he found out that his old cellmate had stolen a lot of his personal property. That made Rogers mad, so he beat-up his old cellmate. The poor guy was scared to return to the compound, so he went to psych, and was sent to Dade CI."

As soon as the sergeant said that, I asked him, "What was the guy's name? If he went psych to Dade CI, I would know who he was."

The sergeant responded, "It was something like Darryl Bainey or Rainey. Something like that."

I said, "Darren Rainey."

He responded, "Yeah, that was it."

The sergeant tried to continue telling me about Rogers, but I said, "You gotta be kidding."

He responded, "No. That was it. Did you know him?"

I said, "Not personally. Please continue."

As he continued telling me about Rogers, I couldn't help but feel sad about what he had just told me. Rogers was my old friend. I helped him get into preaching and evangelism. The fact that he may have been the catalyst which caused Darren Rainey to be transferred to Dade CI where he eventually died made Rainey's death much more personal to me.

273) How did you spend your time while in administrative confinement at Everglades CI?

I wrote letters to the Miami-Dade Police Department Homicide Bureau, Dade County, Florida Medical Examiner, and the Florida Department of Correction's Inspector General's Office about what happened to Darren Rainey. I also told all those agencies that I wanted to talk with them. I wrote mom, Windy, and Aunt Jane, and filed the grievances that I previously mentioned. Primarily though, I got caught up on my sleep, cried, prayed, and studied the Bible.

274) How long were you incarcerated at Everglades CI prior to transferring from there?

I arrived there on or about January 24, 2013. I transferred from there to the Regional Medical Center TCU approximately five weeks later.

275) Will you tell me about Regional Medical Center's bad history?

Regional Medical Center used to be called Lake Butler. It was the first Reception Center in Florida. It was known by inmates as the worst Reception Center in Florida. The security staff who worked there were very violent, and they had a long history of not being held accountable for their violence on inmates. I was told by numerous staff and inmates that a long time ago there was an investigation conducted into staff killing inmates and burying them on the Regional Medical Center recreation yard. Over my 17 years in the FDC, every inmate I spoke with about Regional Medical Center said that the staff there were racist against blacks and discriminatory against inmates raised in big cities. Additionally, since I was imprisoned, I had heard inmates say that Regional Medical Center staff used to kick and beat the gold teeth out of inmates' mouths when they arrived from the county jails.

276) What type of inmates were housed at Regional Medical Center?

Regional Medical Center is one of four Reception Centers that processes inmates from county jails into the FDC. Inmates that are new to the prison system from jails are called "new arrivals." Additionally, it housed inmates with medical and mental health problems. Many of the inmates who have medical problems and are close to death are sent there to die. It only had about 250 inmates permanently housed there. They helped run institution.

I was housed there several times while in transit to other institution

277) Did you file grievances and write letters while you were at the Regional Medical Center TCU?

Yes. I continued the grievance process on all the grievances I had filed at Dade CI and Everglades CI. Toward the end of my stay in the TCU, I filed several grievances concerning why I shouldn't be transferred to a prison in the Panhandle section of Florida when I was discharged from the Regional Medical Center TCU. In 2009, I had been transferred out of the Panhandle area because of the protection problems I had with prison staff in that area.

I mailed two letters to the Dade County, Florida Medical Examiner, two letters to the Miami-Dade Police Department Homicide Bureau, and one letter to the Dade County, Florida State Attorney's office. All of these letters concerned the *Hot-Water-Shower* treatment in the Dade CI TCU and what happened to Darren Rainey. The Dade County, Florida State Attorney's office sent my letter back to me with stamped response, "Send to Pinellas County." I don't know why they did that. Pinellas County, Florida did not have any jurisdiction or involvement with the Rainey case

About two weeks before I discharged from the Regional Medical Center TCU, I wrote a person that I knew had the ability to get me back to Dade CI. I cannot tell you who the person is, or anything about him. I'll use the pseudonym "Randy Evans" to identify him from here forth.

278) Were you able to talk with Windy while you were housed at Regional Medical Center?

Yes. I spoke with her, my mom and Aunt Jane several times. Windy knew that Everglades CI transferred me there because they wanted to see if I had Post Traumatic Stress Disorder. She also knew that Regional Medical Center didn't have a good history, so she called several times to make sure I was OK. It was her way of letting their staff know I had family support and backing. I kept Windy apprised of my actions while I was housed there.

279) Will you tell me about your stay in the Regional Medical Center TCU?

The sadness I felt from my failure to act while at Dade CI TCU weighed tremendously on my conscious. I knew that Regional Medical Center was not known to be a friendly place, but I had to talk to someone.

The day after I arrived there, I met with their mental health team. When I saw an officer sitting on their team, I knew I had to use caution in answering their questions. I stated my name, date of birth, and Department of Corrections (DOC) number. Then a man on the team asked me, "Do you know why you're here?"

I responded, "They said I might have PTSD, because of some things I witnessed."

He asked, "Do you think you have PTSD?"

I responded, "No. I have sadness which will pass with time."

He said, "OK, Ms. McGrutter is your counselor. She'll call you out to speak with you. You may leave."

A few hours later, Ms. McGrutter called me out to speak with her. When I sat down in her office, she said, "Mr. Hempstead, tell me what happened and why you're here." I then told her about the things I witnessed while housed at Dade CI. I cried while I was telling her everything. When I finished, she said, "You're telling me inmates died of starvation and from being cooked in a shower in the Dade CI TCU?"

I responded, "Yes. Do you want their names again?"

She said, "Even if what you said is true, what makes you think you could have done anything to stop Rainey from dying, or stop the staff from doing what they did?"

I responded, "With Rainey, I could have kicked the door, flooded my cell, or broken the sprinkler in my cell. I could have done all types of things I didn't do when I heard him say his last words and fall to the floor. As it concerns the staff, I could have had them placed under all types of investigations. I have a long history of speaking out. My prison files prove that."

She said, "How could you have had them placed under any investigations? That's unreasonable."

I responded, "My prison files show that for four years, I battled the unconstitutional conditions at Washington CI. I was subjected to all types of retaliation and many lies were told against me. After I advised a federal official of my claims regarding Washington CI, he directed the FDC Inspector General's office to investigate my claims. That led to the FDC Inspector General's Office substantiating my claims by special reviewing me from Washington CI. The paperwork in my files also shows why I was transferred from Wakulla CI Annex. I spoke out against the conditions there to people who had the ability to make serious changes. I also filed thousands of grievances since I've been in prison, and I've filed federal lawsuits against prison officials. Trust me, there's a lot I could have done that I failed to do."

She asked, "Do your prison files show the things that you said?"

I responded, "Yes. There's a computer right there. I'm sure you can find a lot about me on that computer."

She said, "OK. Let me do some research, and I'll call you back to talk with me in a few days."

About a week later, Ms. McGrutter called me back to her office. When I arrived there, she said, "Let's discuss what happened at Dade CI. Tell me about it."

I repeated what I told her the first time, and I again cried while doing so. When I was done talking, she said, "Do you know where you're at?"

I responded, "Yes. Regional Medical Center."

She said, "Do you know anything about this place?"

I responded, "What do you mean?"

She said, "Do you know anything about the history of this place?"

Even though I understood her statement as a form of threat, I asked her what she meant. She said, "Who do I work for?"

I responded, "Corizon."

She said, "No, I work for Florida. Who do the people work for that you're accusing of crimes?"

I responded, "The Florida Department of Corrections."

She said, "They work for Florida. We both work for the state. Do you understand me?"

It was clear to me that Ms. McGrutter was threatening me so I responded, "You have no involvement with what happened at Dade CI. What happened there in no way concerns anybody here."

She said, "It does. They are State, and we are State. They transport inmates up here all the time. You need to stop thinking and talking about the things you're saying you witnessed at Dade CI. We're done for now. You may leave."

About a week later, Ms. McGrutter called me to her office for a third discussion. I also cried throughout this discussion with her. She started this discussion by asking, "How have you been doing?"

I responded, "I've been praying and crying and thinking about the things that happened."

She said, "I'm sick of hearing the same thing. You know I can send you back there? Do you want to go back to Dade CI?"

I responded, "You know I have sadness. I'm not delusional."

She said, "What is that supposed to mean?"

I responded, "You can't send me back to Dade CI. In my file, it says I'm a security threat there. I also know the TCU referral says I might have PTSD from the events I witnessed there. I don't know why you're mad. The paperwork you have says that I was sent here to talk about the things I witnessed in the Dade CI TCU. The things I'm talking about don't concern you or this TCU. Why have you been threatening me and trying to intimidate me into not talking about the matters I was sent here to talk about?"

She said, "I'm not threatening you or trying to intimidate you. You just need to stop talking about Dade CI."

I responded, "What do you want me to talk about?"

She said, "I don't care what you talk about as long as it's not about Dade CI."

I responded, "I want to talk about the events that the referral paperwork says I was sent here to talk about. If you don't want to talk to me about those events, then why don't you send me to another TCU?"

She sighed and got a frustrated look on her face. You can leave now. We're done for today."

About a week later, I was called to her office for a fourth discussion. Ms. McGrutter started our discussion by saying, "Hempstead, as it concerns the events you witnessed, what is important is how you interpret those events. You can let them bother you, or not bother you."

I responded, "Are you saying that everything is subjective and not objective?"

She said, "Yes, exactly. When you allow things to affect you, such as the wrongful events you say you witnessed at Dade CI, then you're allowing those events to dictate your emotional stability. In order to stop feeling sorrow, you must tell yourself you didn't have any responsibility to act. You also need to tell yourself that nothing bad happened and you have to believe it. You have to refuse to allow those events to affect you. You mentioned the words subjective and objective. Do you understand those words and how they relate to reality? Everything in your reality is subjective."

I responded, "Are you kidding me?"

She said, "What?"

I responded, "You more than likely have a Bachelor's Degree in Psychology. I have a Doctor's Degree in Biblical Studies. My two primary areas of study are systematic theology and apologetics. I'm very familiar with the differences between objective and subjective truths. I'm also very familiar with the teachings of secular psychology.

"When I was 12 years old, I read secular psychology books, trying to find a way to help my mom. None of the psychologists or psychiatrists wanted to help her. They wanted to tell her that reality was subjective, not objective, and give her all types of drugs to alter her reality. Her mind started needing those drugs to produce the chemicals she needed to stay mentally balanced.

"To tell me that reality is subjective is to say that I control reality and that I can interpret and make it how I want. To me, I would be crazy if I believed such a thing. No person can control or escape reality. If what you're telling me is true, make your reality Disney World, and let me know when it changes from this prison to Disney World."

She said, "If you're so smart and you know everything, why are you here?"

I responded, "I don't think that I'm so smart, and I don't know everything. I didn't know how to change a car tire until I was 19 years old. Furthermore, I'm not trying to get you angry. If I did, then I apologize. Let me see if I can word what I'm saying another way. Are you saying hurting kids and old people is OK, as long as the abuser thinks it's OK?"

She said, "Get out of my office."

As I got up to leave I responded, "I'm supposed to be your patient that you're supposed to be helping. Instead, you're kicking me out of your office. If I offended you, I apologize."

It wasn't my intention to make Ms. McGrutter mad. After she threatened me and told me I could control reality, I felt that I had to explain to her that I wasn't fearful, delusional or mentally weak; I was just sad. I had been through many difficult situations in my life, and God had used those events to shape me into the person I was and that I now am. I had the utmost faith that God was, and is, in absolute sovereign control of all things. This caused me to know that she couldn't have anything done to me unless it was God's will.

I also knew beyond doubt that God is a good God[1] and if, in His sovereign will, He allowed something to happen to me that in my flesh I didn't enjoy. That doesn't mean He allowed it to happen to hurt me. It meant God allowed it to happen for my good. Why? Because God is good and He makes… "All things work together for the good of those who love God, to those who are called according to His purpose[2]".

280) What happened after this meeting with Ms. McGrutter?

My property and mattress were ransacked that afternoon by Officer Colon. The next evening he placed me in handcuffs and took me outside the TCU. While we were outside, he said, "Have you heard about the inmates who were buried on the recreation yard?"

I responded, "I heard the rumor. Is it true?"

He said, "You're going to find out if you keep running your mouth about what you think you saw."

281) What happened about 10 to 12 days later?

I had another interview with Ms. McGrutter. When I sat down in her office she said, "You have nothing wrong with you that you can't handle. You're going to be meeting with the psychologist tomorrow. You may leave."

The next day, I was called to the psychologist's office to meet with her and Ms. McGrutter. When I entered her office, she said, "Mr. Hempstead, Ms. McGrutter said that you don't want to take her advice."

I responded, "Doctor, the only two things she told me to do was to stop talking about the things I witnessed and not to accept reality. I was sent here to talk about what I witnessed, and I'd be crazy if I denied that reality is objective. I was told that I was sent here to talk about the things I saw. That way you all can evaluate whether or not you think I have Post Traumatic Stress Disorder."

She said, "Mr. Hempstead, you're going to be meeting with the treatment team in the next day or two. You may leave."

A day or two later when I met with the treatment team, a psychiatrist I never saw before said, "Mr. Hempstead, we believe you can make it in general population. I'm going to prescribe you some medication. It will help you out. You may leave."

From that day forward, a nurse gave me a pill to take each night. I never took the pill. I always threw it away. A short time later, a nurse and doctor told me that if I had taken that medicine, it would have caused me to have heart problems. The nurse and doctor also said I did not have any symptoms that would have justified being prescribed that medicine. After they told me this, I filed a grievance on the Regional Medical Center TCU Psychiatrist that prescribed me the medicine.

282) What happened upon your discharge from the Regional Medical Center TCU?

I was placed in administrative confinement pending protective management review.

283) Did the security staff do anything to you while you were housed in administrative confinement there?

Yes. Over my first about two weeks, they denied me several trays of food. Additionally, when I was taken out of my cell to go see a medical sick-call nurse, an officer grabbed me by my throat and threatened me with violence if I continued talking about Rainey's death and the events that happened at Dade CI.

284) Why were the staff at Regional Medical Center mistreating you when the accusations you were making didn't concern them?

The majority of the staff in the FDC consider themselves to be like a big family. If you mess with one of them, you mess with them all.

285) Did you file any grievances while in administrative confinement pending protective management review?

Yes. I continued filing grievances and pursuing justice for Darren Rainey and the inmates in the Dade TCU even though medical and security staff threatened and abused me.

Why? It was the right thing to do.

286) Who came to see you about two weeks after you were replaced in administrative confinement?

The person whom I wrote to and called by the pseudonym "Randy Evans" came to visit me. Mr. Evans had the ability to get me back to Dade CI. As I noted, I cannot tell you this person's real name or anything about him; however, I can tell you that he visited with me twice at Regional Medical Center.

287) How could Randy Evans get you back to Dade CI when you had two notations in your files keeping you from returning there?

In my files, it stated that I was deemed a security threat at Dade CI. Additionally, the paperwork that the Everglades CI Mental Health Team placed in my files said I could have Post Traumatic Stress Disorder as a result of the events I witnessed while housed at Dade CI. It was these two issues that prevented me from returning there. However, I knew Mr. Evans had the ability to get me back to Dade CI even though these things were in my files and on the FDC computer. I just had to convince him to do it.

288) What about the grievances in your files that pertained to the events that led to the death of Darren Rainey and the other things you witnessed while housed in the TCU?

They would also be a problem. If I was at Dade CI and the staff there looked in my files and saw those grievances, they would know I was trying to bring them to justice for what they did to Rainey and for what they did to the other mentally disabled inmates in the TCU. I also had to get Mr. Evans to remove the grievances from my files and the references to the grievances from the FDC computer.

He had the ability to make arrangements for the paperwork to be removed from my files and for the notations on the computer to be temporarily removed, and for me to be transferred back to Dade CI.

289) Do your FDC files show any unusual transfers or transfer actions?

Yes. It shows two. One of the times, I was at Zephyrhills CI, and I was supposed to transfer from there to Washington CI. That transfer was stopped, and I was instead transferred to Apalachee CI East Unit. The second time, I was transferred from Wakulla CI Annex to Everglade CI. What distinguishes these transfers from the others in my files was who authorized them.

My transfer from Zephyrhills CI to Apalachee CI East Unit in 2007 was authorized by one of the highest ranking classification officers at the main FDC Office in Tallahassee, Florida. My transfer from Wakulla CI Annex to Everglade CI was authorized by the FDC Inspector General's main office in Tallahassee, Florida. Randy Evans was behind both of those transfers. It should also be noted that after these transfers occurred, investigations were being conducted at Wakulla CI and Apalachee CI East Unit.

290) Did you discuss your reasons for wanting to return to Dade CI with Randy Evans?

The primary reason was to get the evidence I needed to prove what happened to Darren Rainey. But I did not tell Randy Evans this was my reason. I told Mr. Evans about everything I witnessed at Dade CI. However, I told him I wanted to return for a second reason. I withheld the primary reason because I knew if I told him I wanted to get evidence on what happened to Darren Rainey, he wouldn't have helped me.

291) How did your first meeting go with Randy Evans?

It had been years since we last spoke. I had last spoked to Evans in 2009 prior to leaving Everglades CI. After some initial small talk, he asked a lot of questions about my time at Dade CI. I answered his questions, and I told him about the security threat and Post Traumatic Stress Disorder papers in my files, the grievances I filed, and the information on the FDC computer. We spoke for about five hours.

Regional Medical Center's security staff didn't give me any more trouble after this meeting with Randy Evans.

292) What motivated you to want to return to Dade CI?

Since my discharge from the Dade CI TCU, I had spent months praying and crying. During that time, God, by grace, taught me to understand that He didn't raise me to be weak. He showed me that He, by grace, led me down the paths I traveled and gave me the life experiences I had so I could be the person He wanted me to be. I saw that God did not call me to the seminary to teach systematic theology or apologetics or to the pulpit to pastor a church. God had called me to preach the gospel and to demonstrate His love to those who the world had forsaken and to be a voice for the voiceless.

What motivated me to want to return to Dade CI was to get the evidence I would need to aid in proving what happened to

Darren Rainey and to bring to light the torture and abuse of the mentally disabled inmates in the Dade CI TCU.

293) Will you tell me about your second meeting with Randy Evans?

He told me that I would be transferring from the Regional Medical Center in transit to Martin CI. He told me to request protective management as soon as I arrived at Martin CI and that it would be approved. When an inmate requests protection, one of three things happens: 1) his request is denied, 2) his request is approved and he is transferred to another institution, or 3) it is approved and he is placed in a protective management unit.

Also, he said when I was transferred from Martin CI, I would transfer back to Dade CI. Finally, he told me that after I arrived at Martin CI, he and somebody else would be there to see me.

294) So what happened when you were transferred from Regional Medical Center?

I transferred from there to South Florida Reception Center. I spent a few days there, and I was then was transferred to Martin CI. Upon my arrival there, I requested protective management like I was directed to by Mr. Evans. I was then placed in administrative confinement pending protective management review.

About three weeks later, Randy Evans and another man I will call by the pseudonym "Jim Knowels" came to visit me. During that visit, we discussed in detail my return to Dade CI.

I still did not tell them my primary reason for wanting to return to Dade CI. I learned my file and my information on the computer would be amended to no longer include the security threat status, PTSD paperwork, and the grievances I had submitted.

I also, cannot tell you any more about Jim Knowels.

295) Who were the assistant warden and colonel at Martin CI while you were there in 2013?

Royce Marlow was the assistant warden. I knew him when he was the major and colonel at Dade CI. He previously worked in the TCU, and he was the colonel at Dade CI when Darren

Rainey died. Morris was the colonel at Martin CI. I knew him when he was a major at Everglades CI.

296) At that time, were you still in the "Valley of Sorrows"?

It was around that time that God started bringing me out of the Valley of Sorrows. I still had issues with sadness, and I would often times cry. However, it was around that time that I could see the light shining in my life to bring me out of the darkness.

I knew my mission.

297) What happened after your meeting with Randy Evans and Jim Knowels?

A couple of weeks later I was transferred from there to South Florida Reception Center. I spent a few days there, and I was then transferred back to Dade CI. I arrived back at Dade CI on or about June 9, 2013.

Chapter 15: Dade CI (June-December 2013)

298) What happened upon your return to Dade CI?

When I arrived there, I knew several of the security staff from the TCU who were receiving and processing us (inmates) into Dade CI. All of those security staff looked upon me as a good and easy to get along with inmate. Just prior to this receiving and processing ending, Colonel McCarter and Major Urbino came into the visitation park where we were located. McCarter had been promoted to colonel while I was away. I could also tell that he was not happy to see me.

The major gave the Orientation Security Statement. During his presentation, he noted inmates could be denied a food tray if they arrived at the chow hall not properly shaven. As soon as he made this statement, Colonel McCarter interrupted him and said, "Nobody will be denied a meal on this compound. If you're not properly shaven when arrive, we will take your ID and tell you to go and shave and to return for ID and a food tray. If you don't follow the order to shave, you'll be given a disciplinary report. Are there any questions?"

When no questions were asked, Colonel McCarter and Major Urbino walked away and left the visitation park. As they walked past where I was sitting in a group of inmates, I overheard

Colonel McCarter tell Major Urbino, "Why did you tell those inmates they wouldn't be fed? Didn't you see the white inmate in the front row with the black hair? That's Hempstead."

I was assigned to be housed in Foxtrot Dorm (F-Dorm) Wing One. F-Dorm had three wings. Wing One housed general population inmates; Wing Two housed disciplinary confinement inmates; and Wing Three housed administrative confinement inmates.

299) Did you call Windy upon your return to Dade CI?

Yes. She wanted to take immediate action to have me transferred from there. I told her not to, that I was safe, and was back at Dade CI for a reason. After she heard this, I thought she understood I had arranged to return to Dade CI for a covert reason. We both agreed I would make a check-in call to her every other day.

I could not tell Windy how I got back to Dade CI because I was on an FDC phone, and prison staff were possibly monitoring my conversations with her.

300) Were any of the security staff you knew from the TCU working in general population when you returned.

Yes. Besides Colonel McCarter, I also knew: Captains McCrae, Towns, and Donaldson; Sergeants Clarke, Lewis, Collado, and Terry; and Officers Jackson (Fish), Harrison, David, Wood, Sakay, Jenkins (female), Pena, and Ingram. All of these staff considered me a good inmate and someone they could trust. They also informed other security staff who did not know me that I was trustworthy. All of the above staff (except the captains, and Officer Jenkins) were posted to work in the dorm where I lived.

301) Will you tell me about the inmate environment in general population at Dade CI?

General population was infested with tobacco, narcotics, and cell phones. I never saw an institution that had more of these items than Dade CI. Smoke from the inmates' excessive use of tobacco and narcotics filled every wing. The odor of K2 (synthetic marijuana) was always so strong that you were constantly aware of it. Inmates were constantly flipping-out, twacking-out, and passing-out from the K2. Twacking-out is when an inmate falls to the ground and flops around like a fish out of water.

There was an average of 40 to 60 cell phones per wing. Inmates used cell phones to smuggle tobacco, drugs, and cell phones into Dade. They also used cellphones for income tax fraud, credit card fraud, the Chomo scam, and for numerous other reasons.

Many staff were also involved in smuggling and fraud operations, and several female staff engaged in sexual activities with inmates for money. The majority of the security staff didn't care about anything the inmates did. It was very chaotic. Clotheslines were hanging from everywhere; water was leaking from all the pipes; and buildings were infested with rodents and insects.

Staff and inmates commonly referred to Dade CI as "the ghetto."

302) Did you talk with Ms. Harriet Kryscowski within a week of returning to Dade CI?

Yes. Ms. Kryscowski no longer worked in the TCU but was working as a counselor with inmates in general population. When I received a pass informing me to report to her office, I was happy to learn I would be meeting with one of the few good-hearted people who worked in the TCU.

When I arrived at her office, I saw she was pregnant. It was nice to see that a good lady was becoming a mother. While talking with her, I felt comfortable enough to tell her how I felt when I worked as an orderly in the Dade CI TCU. I told her of my deep sorrow over both Rainey's death and the abuse of the mentally disabled inmates in the TCU. As we talked, I couldn't help but cry. As I cried, I thought she was probably shocked to see my tears because, when I was around staff in the TCU, I had suppressed my sadness.

I was able to speak with her from my heart. I no longer needed to hide my compassion and sorrow. I felt a huge burden lifted from my shoulders.

During my first and second conversation with her, she saw I was burdened with guilt for not doing enough to stop the abuse, the torture, and what happened to Darren Rainey. She showed a genuine concern and tried her best to give me guidance.

During our conversations, I told her I was doing what I could to expose and bring to justice those staff who had scalded Darren Rainey to death and abused the mentally disabled. I informed her that, since the middle of 2012, I had been advising agencies and people in society about these events. I said I wouldn't stop seeking justice for Rainey and the other abused inmates until I was successful. I think she knew I was sincere.

I tried to convince Ms. Kryscowski to help expose any conditions and events of which she had personal knowledge. She didn't show me any sign she would do so. Later in 2016, I found out that Ms. Kryscowski did help. She spoke with reporter Eyal Press from the New Yorker Magazine concerning Dade CI TCU.

I was only able to talk with her for about six to eight weeks before she left Dade CI. When she said she was leaving, I felt she was one of the few staff I would ever miss. She demonstrated by her actions and words that she was a good person. She also showed that she was strong enough to not allow herself to become corrupted like so many around her were.

303) Did Harriet Kryscowski leave because she was worried about your efforts to get justice for Darren Rainey and to get help for the mentally disabled inmates?

I don't know.

304) How did Sergeant Clarke respond when he first saw you back at Dade CI?

He didn't show any emotions. He just asked how I was doing and if I was a permanent inmate at Dade CI.

305) How did you start working as an orderly in the confinement unit?

When I returned to Dade CI, security staff in the confinement unit were not using inmates as orderlies? About a month after my return, an inspection was about to happen. The confinement unit was very dirty. Sergeant Clarke went to Captain Green and asked for permission to use me as an orderly to clean the confinement wings. Clarke told the captain that, when I was an orderly on the

Westside TCU, I kept is so clean that it never failed an inspection. The captain said he would talk to the colonel.

I never thought Colonel McCarter would approve, but he did. Several months later, I was advised that the FDC Inspector General's Office told Colonel McCarter to house me in F-Dorm, Wing One, and to give me a job in the confinement unit.

As soon as I was approved to work as an orderly, several inmates asked me to help them get jobs as orderlies in the confinement unit.

306) Why did other inmates want to get jobs as orderlies in confinement?

Confinement orderlies have the best hustling job on any compound in the FDC. The word "hustle" is slang for "something that is done by a prisoner to make money or canteen." Cleaning cells, fixing radios, and selling drugs are some of the hustles in FDC.

The reason why being an orderly for inmates in confinement is the most coveted hustling job is because inmates in confinement are very restricted in the things they can have (e.g. their property, canteen, books, tobacco, narcotics, and cell phones). They also need things they cannot obtain.

Sometimes confinement staff allowed orderlies to bring these things into confinement units. When this happens, the orderly makes quick money from the inmates. If confinement unit staff refuse to allow an orderly to bring the restricted items into the confinement unit, then the orderly will most likely smuggle in the items.

307) How do orderlies get paid for smuggling items to inmates in confinement?

Let's say you're an inmate in confinement and you want five bags of coffee. One cannot legally have any coffee in a Florida prison confinement. Thus, when an inmate sees an orderly on the confinement unit and no staff are around, the inmate will call the orderly to his cell and ask him how much the orderly will charge to bring the inmate five bags of coffee.

The orderly will then ask the inmate how the orderly is to obtain the coffee. If the orderly is to pick the coffee up from another inmate in the general population, the general population inmate would send 10 bags, five for requesting inmate and five for the orderly doing the transport. If the requesting inmate was going to pay for the coffee via his canteen card, he gave the card to the orderly and told him he could also buy coffee or anything else of similar value for himself.

If the confinement inmate wants to pay the orderly money to purchase canteen for him, the confinement inmate will write or call somebody in society and ask them to send money to the orderly's inmate account. Similarly, the confined inmate could have an inmate in general population put money in the orderly's inmate account or give him a Green Dot or Pay Pal. Again, the confinement inmate gives the orderly twice the desired amount, i.e., $100.00 ($50.00 for the confinement inmate and $50.00 for the orderly).

If the inmate in confinement wants tobacco, narcotics, or a cell phone smuggled into the confinement unit, he will ask the orderly how much the orderly will the charge is for bringing in the contraband. The confinement inmate's goal is to find the lowest price for smuggling in the item.

308) Did you ever smuggle any tobacco, narcotics, or cell phones into the confinement unit?

Of course not.

309) Will you tell me about Chaplain Malcom Tomlin?

Chaplain Tomlin taught Bible studies at Everglade CI, South Florida Reception Center, and Dade CI. He was a retired major from the FDC. I first met Chaplain Tomlin in June 2009 at Everglades CI. I attended his weekly Bible study while I was in Everglades. I also attended his Bible studies at Dade CI after I discharged from the TCU in 2011 and at the end of 2012. When I returned to Dade CI in June 2013, I again attended his Bible study.

When I first attended his Bible studies, I didn't understand his style of teaching because it was so different. However, I eventually learned his style.

Chaplain Tomlin was also in charge of a Bible college course at the three institutions where he was a chaplain. Inmates were able to earn an accredited Master of Biblical Studies Degree from the college courses Chaplain Tomlin provided.

In June 2013, I told Chaplain Tomlin about my desire to teach a Bible study on the gospel. Around the middle of July 2013, he told me to prepare the Bible study. I did, and, at the beginning of August 2013, I began teaching the gospel as a part of Chaplain Tomlin's class. Chaplain Tomlin agreed to let me teach every doctrine that involved God, man, and the gospel. The study lasted until sometime in January 2014. After completing that teaching series, he allowed me to continue as his teaching assistant until I was transferred from Dade CI for the final time on May 19, 2014.

Over the time I got to know Chaplain Tomlin, I learned he was very passionate for Christ and the authority of Scripture. He was conservative in his Christianity, and he had a big heart for prisoners and for evangelizing the unsaved. My most enjoyable times and experiences at Dade CI, were when I was sitting next to him as we taught the Bible.

310) Was Inmate Alford L. still at Dade CI?

Yes. It was nice to see my fellow Christian brother Alford L. my first day back there. He was still housed in G-Dorm, Wing 3. Since I was housed in F-Dorm Wing 1, we had to meet each other outside of our dorms to talk. We met to talk on the recreation yard and in the chapel several days a week. At that time, the Northside of the compound didn't have a church in the inmate recreational yard. ` After talking with Alford L. for a couple of weeks, we decided to organize one. Within a few weeks, we had several inmates attending the services and aiding us in evangelism.

This recreational yard church functioned the entire time I was at Dade CI. Alford L. held the title of Senior Elder, and I held the title of Senior Teacher. He handled all the administrative duties, attended to the general care of the inmates involved in the church, and oftentimes preached. My primary duty was teaching the Bible and addressing the doctrinal and religious controversies that are common in prison. I also gave Alford L. advice concerning different issues that arose involving the general care of the inmates in the church.

Alford L. was a good friend and brother in Christ. He was always supportive of me. I believe he knew I was dealing with a lot while I was there in 2013 and 2014. He always did his best to help me in any way he could. I believe God placed him there to help me keep my mind focused on God. When I wasn't teaching the Bible in the chapel or working in confinement, Alford L. kept me constantly involved in matters pertaining to Christianity on the compound. I'm very thankful to Alford L. for being there as a brother in Christ, a partner in ministry, and a friend when I needed one.

311) Will you tell me about the nurse whose name you can't disclose?

I previously mentioned that prior to my transfer from Dade CI in January 2013, a nurse told me that Dr. Santaro said I spoke with him prior my discharge from the TCU and added other false statements to my file. That nurse continued to show me kindness upon my return to Dade CI. I don't want that nurse to get in any trouble or to be subjected to any retaliation for her kindness; therefore, I will not use her real name in this book. From here forth, I'll call her by the pseudonym "Nurse Kind."

Within a short time after my return to Dade CI, Nurse Kind made arrangements for me to speak with her.

She started our first conversation by saying, "Hempstead, now that you're back at Dade CI, I want to let you know that I'm here for you as a friend if you need somebody to talk to. I know about the things you saw. The things that happen in the TCU are really bad. They have been going on for years, and nobody does anything to stop them. Those poor inmates need help. While you're on this compound, I'm here for you."

I responded, "I appreciate your kindness and, I agree with you about those inmates needing help. Several people think that I should take some type of action to bring federal and state officials to investigate the TCU. What do you think?"

She said, "I think you should. Somebody needs to stop them. What happened to Darren Rainey and those other inmates will cause people in society to listen."

I responded, "Are you Christian?"

She said, "Yes. That's why I'm telling you they need help. I know you're strong enough to do it."

I responded, "I don't feel strong. As a matter of fact, any strength I have exhibited regarding the things I've done over this past year, I don't attribute to myself but to God."

She said, "That is what I mean, Hempstead. God's strength in you is what makes you strong."

I responded, "I still cry when I think about the things that happened and what I failed to do."

She said, "Your love and your belief in God, is your strength. Just remember I'm here for you if you need me." I wanted to share this part of our first conversation upon my return there, to show you a little about the type of woman Nurse Kind was.

I had several conversations with Nurse Kind from a short time after my arrival back to Dade CI until I was transferred from there on May 19, 2014. She was always very kind and encouraging. I'm thankful that God arranged for her to be there during a time that I was still experiencing a lot of sadness over my failures to help the weak and defenseless when they most needed it.

312) What did Classification Officer Ms. Koel say to you when she first saw you back at Dade CI?

About two weeks after my return to Dade CI, I saw Ms. Koel on the road between the classification building and the chow hall.

When she saw me, she said, "So you got yourself back to Dade CI. How did you pull that off?"

I responded, "What are you talking about, Ms. Koel?"

She said, "I noticed your grievances, and other documents are missing from your classification files. They were there before you left here in January, and now they're gone. Even your security threat paperwork is missing. Who took them out?"

I responded, "Ms. Koel, you have been working in the TCU too long. The inmates back there are rubbing off on you. I don't know what you're talking about. If paperwork is missing from my files, then that means prison staff must have taken the paperwork out. I obviously didn't take anything out, but I'm glad you informed me that paperwork is missing. I will investigate and find out who is responsible."

She said, "I believe you know who took the papers out. Just so you know, I submitted the paperwork to leave Dade CI. I'm not going to be here to deal with whatever it is you do."

I responded, "Why are you leaving? I heard that you'd been here close to 20 years."

She said, "It's the best thing to do. I hope you leave me out of whatever it is you start."

I responded, "I'm a good inmate who doesn't cause trouble. I'm not going to start anything." We then ended our conversation and walked away from each other.

I knew that paperwork was missing from my classification files. I just didn't know who removed it from my files or who removed the information from the FDC computer for Randy Evans.

A very short time after this conversation, Ms. Koel stopped working at Dade CI. I think she knew someone helped me get back to Dade CI.

313) Upon your return to Dade CI, did you see the officer who you gave the pseudonym "Robert Anderson"?

Yes. Within a week or two of my return, I saw him. He was surprised that I was able to get back to Dade CI. My immediate concern with him was to be able to meet with him on a regular basis. Since he was still working in the TCU, there were only two ways we could talk regularly. One way was to meet him at a shift change; the second was for him to come to the compound and meet me.

The first time I saw Robert Anderson, we talked for about 30 minutes. We briefly discussed things that had occurred over my six month absence from Dade. I told him I had been communicating with people in society concerning the TCU and didn't want him to get in trouble with the law.

He responded, "I hope you didn't mention my name or tell anybody that I called the DOJ for you."

I said, "So far, I have left you out of everything, and I didn't tell anyone that you called the DOJ. I wanted you to decide whether you would help or not. If you don't want to, I understand. However, I want to remind you of your Biblical obligation to help people in need. Also, you're sort of in a messed up situation. Because you have worked in the TCU for several years, you could easily get tied up in all types of federal and state investigations. Why don't you think about helping, and over our next few meetings I'll tell you everything that's going on."

He responded, "I don't want to lose my job or get arrested."

I said, "You won't lose your job or go to prison for helping. Nobody in the prison system will ever know what you're doing."

He responded, "What do you want me to do?"

I said, "I'm not going to tell you now. Think about what I said, and we'll talk more over the next two weeks."

I wanted to place him in a situation where he would be forced to decide between helping me and possibly avoid becoming a target of the government, or not helping me and possibly become a government target.

Over my next few meetings with him, he agreed to help me. It took a few months to get in a position where we could start pursuing what I needed his help with.

314) Why did you put in for a good adjustment transfer upon your return to Dade CI?

I wanted to have my good adjustment transfer in and approved. That way I could hopefully go to the institution of my choice after I had completed what I was trying to do at Dade CI. When an inmate serves a certain amount of time without receiving any disciplinary reports, he can request a good adjustment transfer to an institution he wants to go to.

315) What happened when the Institutional Classification Team convened the meeting on your request for a good adjustment transfer?

Assistant Warden Williams, Major Urbino, and Classification Supervisor Ms. Jackson presided over the hearing. When I entered the conference room where the hearing was being held, Ms. Jackson said, "Hempstead, didn't we just get rid of you?"

I responded, "Yes, and if you approve my good adjustment transfer, you can get rid of me again."

She said, "We have to approve it. You haven't received a disciplinary report in several years."

She then said, "Hempstead, we're going to approve your transfer request to Lake CI. Your name will go on a waiting list. It'll take you two to three years to transfer. All good adjustment transfers to institutions like Lake CI, where everyone wants to go, take years to process. That is all, Mr. Hempstead. You may leave." I then left the hearing.

316) What were the names of the officers who worked for Sergeant Clarke in the confinement unit?

Officers Cennedy, Drinkwater, Jolly, Levi, Corbet, McBean, and a white officer whose name I can't remember.

317) Were B-Shift security staff denying food to inmates in the confinement unit?

Yes, at almost every meal. Mostly they denied food to inmates who were disciplinary problems.

I told several of the inmates who broke sprinklers in their confinement cells and who were sent to Dade County, Florida jails to be prosecuted to tell the police, their attorney, the state attorney, judge, etc. why they broke the sprinklers. I wanted the paper trail concerning the abuse at Dade CI to be as long as possible.

318) Did the FDC Inspector General's Office investigate the denial of food and the mistreatment of inmates in the Dade CI confinement unit?

Yes. Several inmates filed complaints to the inspector general's office concerning not being fed and other types of abuse in the confinement unit. Assistant inspector generals talked with those inmates. When the assistant inspector generals asked the confinement security staff about the issue, staff would say the inmates were refusing their trays.

Security staff switched their tactics. Instead of not giving inmates their trays, staff contaminated the food with cleaning chemicals prior to serving the trays. The staff contaminated the trays outside the confinement wings where the mounted security cameras could not record their actions. The staff would dip the patties, hot dogs, sausages, sandwich meat, etc. in chemicals.

There were two inmates who really upset Sergeant Clarke and Officer McBean. McBean took those inmates' trays to officers' station bathroom. In one of the trays, he put about a teaspoon of feces, and he urinated in the other. He did this on two separate occasions. After he contaminated the trays, he told me to place them on top of the food cart separate from the other trays. This insured they were served to the inmates they were supposed to go to.

With the use of this new tactic, security staff were able to point to the mounted cameras as evidence that they were feeding the inmates. The mounted cameras recorded the staff giving the inmates full trays of food but did not show the prior contamination. Also, with the new tactic, security staff didn't have to shut off the mounted security cameras for any reason related to not feeding an inmate.

319) On what shift was the contamination of food occurring?

Sergeant Clarke's shift, which was B-Shift.

320) What happened with Sergeant Pierri and Officers Collado and Jenkins in August or September 2013?

Sergeant Pierri told me that something happened with an inmate trying to commit suicide, or dying in the TCU which resulted in the three of them being reposted. They were reposted to work in general population.

321) What happened in the TCU around October 2013?

An inmate was found hanging on the Westside. This caused most of the security staff who worked in the TCU to be reposted to work in general population. The following security staff were reposted to work in general population: Sergeants Mizeal, Johnathan, Perez, and Eli; and Officers Weary, Gruben, Cobis, Lemelis, Forbes, Ruiz, Day, Knight, Patterson, Brunson, and Mac.

322) Why did Sergeant Lewis become the confinement sergeant on A-Shift?

Sergeant Brunson was the confinement officer on A-Shift. At the end of 2012, his wife, Officer Brunson, worked as the boot officer on the Westside. However, she was reposted to work in general population. When this happened, Sergeant Brunson had to be reposted to the TCU.

A married couple couldn't work on the same shift in the general population or in the TCU. One had to work in general population while the other worked in the TCU. Thus, when Sergeant Brunson was moved to the TCU, Sergeant Lewis became the confinement officer on A-Shift.

323) What happened when Lewis became the confinement officer on A-Shift?

On his first day as A-Shift confinement sergeant, he asked me to work for him as his orderly. He also arranged for Officers Jackson (Fish) and Gruben to be reposted to work as his officers in the confinement unit.

324) Will you tell me about Officer Jackson who doesn't have the nickname "Fish"?

That Officer Jackson started dating Officer Clarke at the end of 2011 or the beginning of 2012. In March 2013, Officer Jackson and Sergeant Clarke got married.

325) Will you tell me about the attempted mass poisoning of the whole confinement unit in October or November 2013?

Several inmates in confinement were filing grievances on Sergeant Clarke and his officers. This got him angry, so he threw away all of the blank request and grievance forms as a way to stop the inmates from submitting grievances. He also told the law clerks who made rounds in the confinement unit to stop passing-out requests and grievance forms to the inmates. Sergeant Clarke made the law clerks give the forms they had to him. To further punish the inmates, he removed all of the toilet paper, soap, toothpaste, and toothbrushes from the officers' station. This wasn't enough punishment in Sergeant Clarke's eyes, so he brought two big bottles of liquid laxative to work, to try to poison all of the inmates in confinement.

One morning, just prior to lunch, Sergeant Clarke called me up to the officers' station and showed me two big bottles of liquid laxative. Sergeant Clarke said, "Do you know what this is?"

I picked up the bottles, looked at the labels on them and responded, "liquid laxative."

He said, "I want to mix them with the juice and serve it to the inmates at lunch." Instantly, I knew I had to think of a way to stop Clarke from going through with his plan.

Trying to think quickly, I responded, "Why?"

He said, "They don't have any toilet paper. I want to make them crap all over themselves."

I responded, "The whole confinement unit? What did they do?" He said, "They keep filing grievances. They're all in it together. You got me?"

I responded, "Of course I got you. I'm just concerned. We have close to 130 inmates in confinement. What's going to happen if one or more of them are allergic to something in these laxatives? If somebody dies, you'll be under another murder investigation. Additionally, what happens if any of the inmates in confinement tell the colonel, the warden, or the police that the orderlies served the juice? I'm not concerned for myself because I pass-out the trays. The other orderlies serve the juice. The other orderlies could turn against you."

He said, "You're right. I'll have the officers serve the juice. Don't put any spoons on the trays. Tell the other orderlies they're going to pass out the spoons. Let's pour the laxative in these empty milk jugs, along with this juice pack before the food carts come."

Sergeant Clarke had a powdered juice pack from the chow hall. We had five or six empty milk jugs that staff always kept in the officers' station. As he and I started filling the jugs with water, Officer McBean came into the bathroom area to help us.

When the water, powdered juice, and laxative were added to the jugs, we discovered that the laxative wouldn't dissolve but floated on top of the juice. Also, the laxative and juice together caused a very strong odor.

When I saw that the laxative wouldn't dissolve and smelt odor, I said, "There's no way we can serve that. If the inmates look at it or smell it, they're not going to drink it. Plus they're going to write us up."

Sergeant Clarke said, "McBean, go shut off the cameras in Wings 2 and 3."

Officer McBean then left the bathroom and went up into the attic. Sergeant Clarke then said, "Everything will be OK. The officers are going to serve the drinks. When the food carts come in, place these jugs of juice on the food carts. Make sure the other orderlies pass-out the spoons. I'm going to tell Officers Corbet and McBean to serve the juice. Come back up here to the officers' station when the food carts arrive."

I then left the officers station and went down into the sally port to talk with an officer. The other orderly and Juan Carlo went to get the food carts with Officer Drinkwater and another inmate who went by the name "Bobo."

When the food carts came, I went back up into the officers' station to get the juice jugs so I could place them on the food carts. When I entered the officers' station, Sergeant Clarke and the other officers were laughing about the laxative they were about to serve to the inmates. I made one last statement to them before I took the juice jugs to the food carts. I said, "You know they're going to know the juice is spiked as soon as they see it and smell it." Sergeant Clarke and the officers just laughed and joked at what I said and at what was about to happen.

I took the jugs to the food carts and told the other orderlies that they were going to pass out the spoons and that the officers were going to serve the juice.

When we entered the confinement wings, I started passing-out the trays, and the other orderlies passed-out the spoons. As soon as Officers McBean and Corbet started serving the juice, the inmates started yelling through their doors, "Don't drink the juice, there's something in it. Look at it; there's something wrong with it. They poisoned it." As the juice continued to be served, all of the inmates in both wings were kicking their cell doors and yelling about the juice being poisoned.

Sergeant Clarke ordered the same thing to be done again for the dinner meal. During that meal, the inmates again kicked their cell doors and yelled to each other, warning each other not to drink the juice because it was poisoned.

326) Did the staff shut off the mounted security cameras in the confinement unit?

Yes. They also taught me how to do it for them. Let me explain how it was done. In the F-Dorm Officers Station, there was a steel ladder that led to a large room in the attic that had a large water heater in it. While standing in that room, you could walk to sections of the attic that ran over each wing. In the middle of each of these wings was a box containing switches for turning the cameras on and off and for resetting them.

If you went back to the large room where the water heater was, there was also a fuse box room that contained fuses for everything that ran on electricity in F-Dorm. Security staff could also disable the mounted cameras by shutting off the fuses.

327) Which security staff did you witness shut off the mounted security cameras before they or did something to an inmate they weren't supposed to do?

Sergeants Clarke and Lewis, and Officers McBean, Drinkwater, King, and Gruben.

328) Why did security staff shut off the water in inmates cells in the confinement unit as punishment?

When security staff became angry with inmates, the staff would oftentimes shut the water off in the cells of the inmates they were mad at. Each cell housed one or two inmates. If those inmates were not able flush the toilet, the odor in the small cells became sickening. The inmates also had to deal with the punishment of not being able to wash their hands after they used the bathroom.

When security staff turned the water off, it wasn't shut off by the pipe chases in the confinement wings. The water was shut off by valves in the attic. That way, if any staff from outside the confinement unit, or staff on other shifts tried to find out what was wrong with the water in the cells, it was harder for them to do so.

329) On which shifts did this abuse occur?

It only happened on A and B shifts. The sergeants on those shifts were Clarke and Lewis.

330) Why did security staff shut the hot water off in the confinement wings on shower nights?

If there was only cold water, the majority of the confinement inmates would refuse to shower. This would allow security staff to finish the showering of confinement inmates quicker.

331) What did Officer Wood obtain from the computer in the lieutenant's office in F-Dorm?

He used the access codes of other staff to get the names, social security numbers, dates of births, etc. off the FDC computer system so he could use the information in income tax and credit card fraud. I'm not sure what part of the prison computer system he was accessing, but I believe it was the "Offender Base Information System."

332) So, security staff were stealing the personal information of inmates from the FDC computer and using it in fraud?

Yes. Several of them did that while I was there. It should be noted again that I served time in prison at Washington Correction Institution (now called Northwest Florida Reception Center) with Officer Wood's father, Inmate Michael Ferguson.

333) What did you find in the basement under F-Dorm?

Not too long after Sergeant Lewis started working in F-Dorm, he had me hiding chemicals for him in the dorm. Sergeant Lewis knew other shifts were stashing chemicals, inmate property, etc. in the attic, but he didn't know if they were hiding anything in the basement. Sergeant Lewis asked me if any of the other shifts were using the basement as a storage area. I told him that I knew Sergeant Clarke's shift wasn't, but I didn't know about the other shifts. The attic was clean and had lights in it. However, the basement was dirty, had insects in it, and didn't have any light in it.

On the floor of the officers' station, underneath the water fountain was a large steel plate. By lifting the plate, a person could go down into the basement under F-Dorm.

At the end 2013 Sergeant Lewis instructed me to go down in the basement and hide some bleach. After the steel plate was lifted, I looked down in the basement and noticed it was dark. I then said, "Can I get a flashlight?"

Sergeant Lewis responded, "You aren't scared, are you?" A couple of the officers laughed at what he said.

I then said, "No. I'm smart. There could be rats or spiders down there, and I want to look around." I was then given a flashlight.

When I jumped down into the basement I found out I could not standup. There was only about four feet between the floor and the ceiling. The basement consisted of only three rooms. There was a room under the officers' station, a room under the officers' station bathroom, and a room under the small storage room that was next to the officers' station bathroom. The basement was filled with spider webs, mail, and property that belonged to inmates.

From the basement, I shouted a description of the items I saw to the security staff who were in the officers' station.

As I moved from the room under the officers' station through the three other rooms, I saw more inmate property and several stingers. A stinger is a device that inmates build in order to boil water. The next basement room contained a large quantity of inmate mail, two cell phones, a cell phone charger, several more stingers, and a whole bunch of old shaving razors. I yelled up to Sergeant Lewis and told him what items I saw in that room and asked if he wanted me to bring them up. He told me to leave everything as it was and to return to the officers' station. As I was making my way through the basement, I heard Sergeant Lewis and the officers talking. They were saying that the night shifts must have been throwing the mail in the basement and that the property, stingers, cell phones, and chargers must have been taken from inmates.

When I got back up in the officers' station from the basement, Sergeant Lewis said, "Hempstead, you know we didn't put any of that stuff down there. It had to be the night shift staff who put the mail down there. They're the ones responsible for passing it out. The property also had to have been placed down there by other shifts."

I responded, "I know that none of you put that stuff down there. As far as I know, none of you even knew what was down there."

He said, "You're right, we didn't know. Now don't tell anybody, including other staff that we sent you down there. OK?"

I didn't bother asking why. I knew Sergeant Lewis was aware that, if I brought anything up, inmates in the wings could have seen what was going on. Also, the staff would have had to worry about disposing of the items from the basement or they would have had to file an incident report about the mail and other items. Sergeant Lewis didn't want either of these things to happen. Thus he decided it was better to leave everything in the basement where it had been undetected.

I told several inmates I trusted about the mail and the other items in the basement.

I wanted to get the mail out of the basement and delivered to the inmates it belonged to. I thought some of the mail could have been important or could have sentimental value to both the people who sent the mail and the inmates who were to receive it.

I didn't work on a regular basis on any of the night shift. The only chance I had of doing this was on Sergeant Clarke's shift. I also knew Clarke wouldn't take a chance of getting other staff in trouble. I knew the chances of him allowing me to remove the mail from the basement were slim, but I still had to try. It took me about a week to plan out how I was going to approach Sergeant Clarke to get him to allow me remove the mail from the basement. I decided to ask him to allow me to dispose of the mail myself. If he agreed, he would have put me in charge of removing it. Then, I could covertly returned each piece to the proper inmate.

One day, while I was working, I told Sergeant Clarke, "When I was down in the basement about a week ago, I found a lot of mail. I think we should get it out of there and dispose of it. If we don't, somebody else could find it, and it could cause trouble for confinement staff on all of the shifts."

He responded, "The mail's passed out on the night shifts. They had to have put it down there. How could I get in trouble for it?"

I said, "Inspectors could try to say you were aware of the basement being a hiding place for mail and property. If it was just the inmate property, it would only be a prison issue. The mail makes it a federal issue."

He said, "We'll check it out later on."

"OK," I replied.

Later that day when I was up in the officers' station talking with the staff, Sergeant Clarke said, "What were you saying earlier about mail?"

I responded, "There's a bunch of mail and property in the basement. We should get the mail out and dispose of it, so nobody gets in trouble for it." The officers responded by inquiring why mail was in the basement and saying it had to be the night shifts throwing the mail down there. They all expressed curiosity about how much mail, inmate property, and contraband were in the basement.

In the middle of this discussion, Sergeant Clarke said, "Go down there and get all the mail. Let's see what we got."

I then got a flashlight and went down into the basement. As I passed through the room under the bathroom, I picked up an old laundry bag to put the mail in. I filled the laundry bag with mail and replies to inmate request forms and inmate grievances. When I gathered all the mail into the laundry bag, it was about 75% filled. I took the bag to the hole that lead back up into the officers' station. When I threw the laundry bag of mail on to the officers' station floor, the officers were shocked at the quantity. One of them immediately shut off the light in the officers' station to that the inmates in the wings could not see the bag of mail. When Sergeant Clarke saw how large the bag of mail was, he said, "You didn't tell me there was that much mail down there. Empty it out. Let's see what we got."

After I poured all the mail onto the floor, the officers went through it. They opened the envelopes, skim read the letters, and looked at the photographs that were in a lot of the mail. There were a lot of pictures of women and children, that were, more than likely, the girlfriends or wives of the inmates the mail was sent to. There were a few pictures of people who by their age appeared to be parents or grandparents. As they were searching through everything, I was trying to see if I knew the names of any of the inmates to whom the mail was addressed.

Department of Corruption

About 20 minutes into going through the mail, Sergeant Clarke eventually said, "There's no way you or any of us are going to be able to get all that mail out of the station without any inmates seeing it. Also, we can't throw a little in the trash at a time, because inmates throw the trash out. They'll see it in the trash. A lot of this mail has been down there for months, and it hasn't been found. Put it back down there where you found it. We all need to act like we don't know anything about it being down there."

I responded, "I think I can take a little bit out at a time to my cell and destroy it without getting caught."

He said, "We can't take that chance." Officers McBean and Levy then agreed with Sergeant Clarke. I complied with what the sergeant said, and placed the bag of mail back in the basement.

About two weeks later, I was in the officers' station on one of the night shifts talking with a sergeant. I believe his last name was Hines. Sergeant Hines was a really relaxed and nice sergeant. He told me he wanted to work fulltime in the confinement unit on the night shift.

I knew three of the officers currently posted on the confinement night shift that Sergeant Hines wanted to work on. They were Wood, David, and Collado from the TCU. None of the staff or inmates liked the full-time sergeant who was currently posted on that shift. As Sergeant Hines and I were talking, I thought it would probably be impossible for him to let me bring the mail out of the basement and officers' station. If Sergeants Clarke and Lewis, who I knew for years and who didn't worry about me getting them in trouble, wouldn't let me remove the mail, it was highly likely Sergeant Hines also wouldn't.

Then it occurred to me that maybe I could get Hines to report the mail in the basement as a way of raising his chances of being posted to the confinement unit. I thought that if I could convince Hines to do it, I would get the mail reported, and he would possibly get something he wanted. For this reason, I said, "I know something that could possibly help you get posted to work in the confinement unit."

Sergeant Hines responded, "What is it?"

I said, "You have to keep it between you and me. You can't let anybody know I told you."

He responded, "Ok."

I said, "I believe both of the night shift sergeants haven't been giving all the incoming mail to the inmates that the mail is addressed to."

He responded, "Why do you say that?"

I said, "In the basement, there is a whole bunch of mail that belongs to inmates. If you want, I can go down there and get it. If you report the mail in the basement to the colonel or warden, it could get the confinement sergeants on the night shifts reposted. If that happened, you could take over as confinement sergeant on this shift."

He responded, "How much mail's down there?"

I said, "A lot. About 75% of a laundry bag full."

He responded, "I need to think about it."

I said, "OK. I can go down there and get it, whenever you tell me to."

Nothing else happened that night concerning the mail in the basement.

About a week later, I was called up to the officers' station by Officers Wood and Collado. When I got up to the officers' station, Officer Collado said, "Hempstead, is there any mail in the basement?"

I responded, "Yes. Why?"

Officer Wood said, "We need you to go down there and get it for us, so we can report it to the captain."

I responded, "Which captain?" Officer Wood said, "Captain Dixon."

I responded, "Ok, but you can't tell her that I gave it to you, or knew anything about it. If you do, she's going to try and find out how I knew it was down there."

Officer Wood said, "We're not going to mention your name to her." I responded, "OK." I then went down into the basement and got the bag of mail for them. As soon as they saw it, Officer Wood called Captain Dixon on the radio and asked if she would report to the confinement unit. When she heard there was a laundry bag of mail recovered from the F-Dorm basement she said she would report to F-Dorm. As soon as Officer Wood got done talking with Captain Dixon, I heard her on the radio asking the Dade CI Main Control Room to call the colonel at his home. I spoke with Officers Wood and Collado for a minute or two more, prior to leaving the officers' station.

Captain Dixon came and got the bag of mail. I don't know what happened with it after that. The confinement sergeant who was on that shift was reposted, and Sergeant Hines was posted to take over on that shift as the confinement sergeant.

Afterwards, I never heard anything else about the mail.

334) Tell me about Sergeant Lewis' inmate property theft ring.

When inmates went to confinement at Dade CI, the security staff who were working in the dorm the inmates were housed in were supposed to inventory the inmates' property, put the property that was allowed in confinement in one bag, and send the remainder to the property room for the inmate to have when he was released from confinement.

Instead, the security staff on A-Shift were sending all of the inmates' property to confinement un-inventoried. This required Sergeant Lewis and his officers to do extra work and to inventory all the property of all the inmates who went to confinement during A-shift. Sergeant Lewis decided that since the inmates were committing disciplinary infractions and getting placed in confinement, he would "tax" those inmates for going to confinement on his shift.

The tax was always an electrical item, a pair of personal shoes, or some type of clothing. It had to be something of value, which Sergeant Lewis could then have my co-worker inmate, Juan Carlo, sell on the compound to other inmates for canteen items. Then, Sergeant Lewis took half the canteen from the sale of the stolen property and gave the other half to Juan Carlo as his payment for selling it. The majority of the time, Sergeant Lewis wanted sodas and potato chips. Sometimes he had Juan Carlo get him sandwiches and candy bars. Sergeant Lewis' staff liked his property tax-ring because it provided him with extra snacks, food, and sodas.

As the months passed, I tried to get Sergeant Lewis to stop taking the property of inmates as a tax for having to inventory the property when the inmate when to confinement on Sergeant Lewis's shift. I explained that inmates would, eventually, start asking Juan Carlo and me about their missing property. He told me that if any inmates gave me any trouble to let him know, and he would take care of them.

When I saw that my efforts weren't going to work, I explained to Sergeant Lewis that all the inmates would eventually see that only inmates who went to confinement on the days Lewis worked had missing property. This consistent pattern would prove that Sergeant Lewis and his officers were somehow associated with the missing property. Additionally, I told him that the more property Juan Carlo sold, the higher the chance of an inmate finding out that Juan Carlo was selling property stolen from inmates who went to confinement on Sergeant Lewis' shift.

About three months into the theft ring, several inmates started complaining and asking questions about their missing property. The inmates knew something suspicious was going on, but they didn't know who was behind it. After several more weeks, I had another conversation with Sergeant Lewis. I said, "Sergeant, what I told you was going to happen is happening. Every day inmates are asking questions trying to find out what happened to their missing property. The property room staff are telling the inmates you're behind their property being stolen, by saying the property never made it to the property room to be stored. You would have been better charging inmates for cell changes than stealing their property."

Sergeant Lewis responded, "How much can I charge inmates for cell changes?"

I said, "The normal price is $50.00 to $100.00 per cell change."

He responded, "If you find me some inmates who want cell changes, I'll stop taxing them for inventorying their property."

I said, "OK. I'll see what I can do."

I wanted to stop Sergeant Lewis' theft ring. I figured that if the only way I could do it was to find him an inmate who would pay him for a cell change, I would find one. That day, I found two inmates who were willing to pay $100.00 apiece to move from their wings into my wing. Once they both agreed to pay $100.00, I told Sergeant Lewis that I had two inmates wanting to pay him to move.

Sergeant Lewis told me to get a monthly inmate account statement from each of these inmates so he could look it over. The sergeant also told me to tell the two inmates they would be required to each pay $25.00 right away and would be required to give him the remaining money anytime he wanted it. He said if the inmates decided, after they had moved, not to pay the remainder, he would set them up with false disciplinary reports for weapons (shanks) and have them placed on close management.

Sergeant Lewis gave me two lists of canteen items he wanted as the first payment. After the inmates purchased the canteen for him, he had them moved into F-Dorm Wing One. The agreements Sergeant Lewis made went according to plan. After the first two inmates were moved, Sergeant Lewis had Juan Carlo take over finding more inmates who wanted cell changes.

Sergeant Lewis saw he could make a lot of money doing cell changes. Eventually, he only took his payment for cell changes by Green Dot. This allowed him to make real money instead of canteen for the cell changes.

By God's grace, I was successful in stopping the theft ring.

Sergeant Lewis was still receiving money for cell changes when I was transferred from Dade CI on May 19, 2014.

335) What did you find out at the end of 2013 about the narcotic K-2?

For a while, I thought only Dade CI was infested with K-2. I didn't know that the whole prison system was infested with it. By the end of 2013, inmates started telling me the institutions they came from were also infested with K-2. Apparently, within a short period of time, K-2 had become the most desired narcotic by drug abusers in the FDC. In spite of a wide spread belief that

K-2 is safe and natural, the Florida Department of Corrections deemed it illegal after seeing inmates die from using it

336) Will you tell me about the staff smuggling operations at Dade CI?

The wing that I lived in between June 2013 and May 19, 2014, was considered to have the best-connected inmates housed in it at Dade CI. Many of its inmates had job positions in which they did all types of work for staff. One of the inmates who lived in a cell next to me was one of the primary K-2 suppliers at Dade CI. Also, an inmate who slept two cells from me was one of the main cell phone suppliers.

Staff introduced cell phones, narcotics, tobacco, etc. on a regular basis. Inmates who purchased contraband, drugs, and tobacco from staff were safe from staff busting them; inmates who didn't were not safe. The protected inmates had a "Hands Off" placed on them.

An inmate didn't have to be connected to the smuggling operations to have a "Hands Off" placed on them.   I had one on me from around August 2013 through the end of March 2014.

As I noted earlier, the main compound at Dade CI was separated into two sections, called the Southside and the Northside. The Southside had four Open Bay Dorms (A-E dorms), and the Northside had three T-Dorms (F-H dorms).

A-E dorms housed lower custody inmates, many of whom worked outside the perimeter fence of Dade CI. Some of the inmates who worked outside of the perimeter fence smuggled different types of contraband into the prison. These inmate smugglers were the competition for the staff smugglers.

Since the inmate smugglers were "stepping on the toes" of the staff smugglers by competing with them, staff constantly searched dorms A-E. Whenever there was a search at Dade CI, the search teams started their search and focused their search on A-E dorms.

The search teams were not able to stop the inmates from getting the contraband, drugs, and tobacco into the prison because the staff assigned to the work squads and the gates were being paid very well to overlook the inmate smugglers. The staff who smuggled the items charged a lot more for their smuggling because they could lose their jobs and freedom if they got caught. For these reasons, the staff smugglers resented those staff who allowed inmate smuggling.

The majority of the staff smugglers supplied the inmates who were housed on the Northside of Dade CI. The reason for this was that most of the inmates on the Northside had long sentences and, therefore, had less to lose if they were busted. Also, if any of these inmates were busted, they were likely to not inform on the staff smugglers. Thus, inmates housed on the Northside didn't have to worry about searches as much as the inmates housed on the Southside. Also, staff warned Northside inmates in advance of planned searches.

Whenever the Northside was searched as a front to make it look good, the majority of the inmates weren't harassed or subjected to any type of real searching. When staff did a search, they did it to make it look like they were doing their job. The inmates used to say, "they're just making it look good."

337) How is a "Hands Off" placed on an inmate?

First, I would like to say that "Hands Off" did not exist only at Dade CI. Most of the institutions in Florida have staff who place a "Hands Off" on inmates.

Usually, inmates who had a "Hands Off" on them were connected with the right staff, or were known to be liked and friendly with the right staff.

When security staff are friendly with an inmate and want to show kindness to him for any reason, those security staff tell other staff they know that the inmate is "cool" or "straight." That is the staff's way of saying that particular inmate is his friend in some way or another. It's a slang way for staff to say "leave that inmate alone," or "don't harass him," or "keep your hands off him." This is the common unofficial protection language of Florida prison security staff.

338) How did the "Hands Off" label worked for you at Dade CI?

During the time I was in general population at Dade CI, my cell was never searched by security staff until after April 2014 when they found out that I was communicating with the media and others about Dade CI staff. However, prior to April 2014, I did have one situation during which my cell came close to being searched by the FDC Inspector General's Office.

One night, a sergeant who was by the book was working F-Dorm. After passing-out mail, he decided to walk around the wing and do a security check. Three inmates were in a cell so high on K-2, they weren't able to comprehend the other inmates who were yelling "one time," "hot water," and "fire in the hole." Inmates yell messages as a way telling the other inmates that staff have entered the wing. The sergeant walked by the cell that the three high inmates were in and smelt the K-2. After he directed them to exit the cell, he searched and found four cell phones in the light fixture. When an inmate uses his light fixture to charge cell phones, that light fixture is called a "Gas Station."

The next morning, our wing was subjected to Dade CI's version of a surprise FDC Inspector General search. We knew about the search five minutes in advance, so most of the inmates were able to get their contraband into their wall safes.

When the assistant inspector generals, security staff and K-9 dogs came in the wing, the inmates were told to stand in front of their cells. Sergeant Padaroia walked into the middle of the wing, looked directly at me, and said, "You, inmate. Come here. You look fishy." As I walked up to him, he was making a scene by saying real loud and assertive, that I was acting fishy. When I got in front of him, he asked me to give him everything in my pockets. As I was taking my address book, some papers, and a pen out of my pockets, he winked his eye at me and gave me a partial smile. After I gave him everything in my pockets, he patted me down and gave me back the items that were in my pockets.

He then said, "I'm going to search your cell personally. Go wait in the day room." As the assistant inspector generals and security staff searched every cell, Sergeant Padaroia stayed in my cell. After staff had searched every cell and all the inmates were back in their cells, he called me back to my cell. As he was closing my cell door, he said, "Lewis said to look out for you."

Sergeant Lewis was the confinement sergeant that day. About an hour after the search, Sergeant Lewis called me up to the officer station and said, "Did they mess with you?"

I said, "No. Padaroia stayed in my cell the whole search."

Sergeant Lewis said, "I told him to keep the inspectors out of your cell because I didn't know if you were straight."

I told him, "I appreciate that, but I didn't have anything."

Sergeant Lewis said, "You look out for us, so I was looking out for you, just in case."

339) What are bondsmen, and what does posting bond mean?

A bondsman is an inmate who is connected to a lieutenant or higher ranking staff who has the ability to have disciplinary reports disposed of.

Dade CI and a lot of institutions in the FDC have inmates who are bondsmen.

If an inmate is involved with anything that can have him placed in confinement, he will usually try to find out if there's a bondsman on the compound. If he finds one, he will usually befriend him and work out a deal in advance to post bond should he ever be issued a disciplinary report or placed in confinement. When an inmate pays a bondsman to get rid of a disciplinary report, it's called "posting bond."

"Jail" is slang for confinement. If an inmate doesn't "post a bond," he'll go to "jail" on the majority of disciplinary reports. Bonds are be paid by Green Dots, Pay Pals, Western Union, any type of monetary payment, canteen, narcotics, tobacco, and a few other ways. Bonds usually range between $50.00 and $250.00.

340) What is the "Chomo Scam"?

In a Chomo Scam, inmates open an e-mail and social media accounts with fake names. They make the social media sites look as if they belong to a child. They also find pictures on the internet of a young teenage boy or girl and place those pictures on the social media sites. That way the inmate can act like they are the kid in the pictures. After everything is set up, the inmate will post things on the fake social media sites that make him sound like a sexually active kid. The inmate will visit internet locations frequented by both adults and kids.

Most inmates who run a Chomo Scam impersonate two to five boys and/or girls at a time.

When an adult starts communicating through e-mail with the inmate via one of the kids the inmate is impersonating, that inmate will use various tactics to try and get the adult to say something sexual to the kid the inmate is impersonating. The more sexual things statements the adult sends to the inmate, the more evidence the inmate will have to use against the adult.

Once the inmate has enough evidence to extort the adult, he telephones the adult and tells him that he's the parent of the child with whom the adult had been communicating. The inmate will say the adult is a sick pervert and threaten to report the adult's sexual misconduct to the police. After talking for a while, the inmate says he has bills to pay, and, if the adult who sent the sexual material will help him with his bills, he will not report him to the police. The inmate impersonating the parent will tell the adult he has all the e-mails and material the adult sent to his child, and, if the adult doesn't pay, he'll turn everything over to the police and the FBI in the area where the adult predator lives.

The first payment will always be in the hundreds. After the first payment is made, the inmate will continue to extort the adult for as much money as possible. The adult sex offender usually knows they were scammed. The reason why this is called the Chomo scam is because in the Florida prison system a common slang for sexual predators is "Chomo."

341) What is a wall safe?

Inmates make holes in the walls in their cell and elsewhere to hide their cell phones and contraband. They then make a door to cover the hole out of whatever the wall is made out of, or something close to it. After the inmate covers the hole, he uses soap or toothpaste to cover any remaining cracks. Later, he can open the door by using a pry bar to pry it open.

342) Will you tell me about Inmate Michael W.?

I was incarcerated with Michael W. at Everglades CI and during all three times I was housed at Dade CI.

At the end of 2013 beginning of 2014, while I was teaching a Bible study in the chapel on the Sovereignty of God, I brought up the Darren Rainey incident. I brought it up as a way to speak from my heart about the Sovereignty of God. When I was done talking, Michael W. raised his hand and said, "I knew that you were a witness to what happened to Darren Rainey, and to a lot of bad things that happened to other inmates. I've been praying for you, for a long time. I believe God has called you to be their voice. I would like to help you in any way that I can with getting help for the inmates in the TCU who need help."

It meant a lot when Michael W. said this because he was living evidence of the physical abuse an inmate could be subjected to for speaking out against FDC prison staff. Over the decades Michael W. had been incarcerated, security staff had kicked many of his teeth and broken numerous bones in his body. He had been gassed with chemical agents many times and subjected to all types of other evils for speaking out against things he felt were wrong. He was a man with a lot of his own problems, but he was also a man who believed that nobody should pick on the weak.

During my last six months at Dade CI, Michael W. and I talked a lot.

Chapter 16: Dade CI (January 1, 2014 - May 19, 2014)

343) Were you accused of telling inmates at Dade CI to covertly record staff with cell phones?

Yes. In the beginning of 2014, an inmate nicknamed "Frog" told security staff that I told some inmates they should do their best to obtain audio and visual recordings of staff. Frog told staff that I said inmate recordings would be good evidence to have in case staff did something to the inmates they were not supposed to do.

344) Did staff question you about what Frog told them?

Yes. I, of course, said I never told any inmates to do any such thing.

345) Was there a rumor in the beginning of 2014 that there were several recordings of Sergeant Clarke discussing the Darren Rainey murder and calling you "Cody"?

Yes. Around the end of August 2013, when I walked into the officers' station, several staff said, "Cody." Officer Cennedy then said, "Sergeant Clarke was just telling us about the Rainey incident. He told us how you saw everything. You're his Cody. Tell us about it."

I responded, "I would rather not talk about it. Clarke, I also don't think you should be talking about it. It could still be under investigation."

Sergeant Clarke said, "They're straight, Hempstead. It's not under investigation. It's over with."

I responded, "I'll let you guys talk about it for now." I then left the officers' station.

Over the following several months, the officers who worked on Sergeant Clarke's shift constantly wanted to talk about what happened to Darren Rainey and about other things that happened in the TCU.

Around the beginning of 2014, Frog had told security staff that Clarke and his officers were recorded several times discussing the Darren Rainey case and calling me "Cody." "Cody" is common slang for a co-defendant. From around the end of August 2013 until around January 2014, I was referred to a lot by security staff on Sergeant Clarke's shift as "Cody."

I can confirm such recordings were made.

346) Did Frog tell security staff how he knew you recommended inmates should record staff?

Yes. He said he heard me tell several inmates they should do it.

347) Tell me more about the officer you call by the pseudonym Robert Anderson?

He agreed to help me obtain evidence on the Darren Rainey case and the unconstitutional conditions of the TCU.

348) Did any inmates other than yourself have regular access to the officers' station on Sergeant Clarke's shift?

Yes, my two co-orderlies (Juan Carlo and Bobo), and me.

349) What do you know about these recordings of Sergeant Clarke?

They were given to selected people in society for safe-keeping. For confidentiality reasons, I can't presently tell you who received those recordings and who now has them. I can say that I did not hear those recordings while I was incarcerated in Dade CI in 2014. However, I was debriefed on them by somebody in society who listened to all of them, and in 2016, I had a chance to listen to all of them.

These recordings include Sergeant Clarke telling the truth on the history of the *Hot-Water-Shower* treatment and what happened to Darren Rainey. The statements Clarke made are consistent with what I state in this book. He and his staff also mentioned several other things concerning abuse, torture, and criminal activity at Dade CI.

350) Does somebody you know have copies of these recordings?

Yes. Copies of the recordings were made just in case there was an attempt to cover-up what happened to Darren Rainey. I wanted to make sure I had copies of the strongest possible evidence to prove the *Hot-Water-Shower* treatment and what happened to Darren Rainey.

351) Were your relationships with Dade CI staff harmed by the allegations that you instructed inmates to record staff and that you also participated in some way?

Yes. After those allegations were made, security staff started conducting a lot of searches in my wing, trying to find cell phones. This showed that staff to some degree had to believe what Frog told them.

Also, around that time, an inmate sent a picture to the FDC Inspector General's Office of a sergeant we all called Mosquito Man sleeping in an officers' station. He was on duty and was not supposed to be sleeping. There was another incident in which several inmates sent pictures of sewage flooding in a wing to a TV news station. Those incidents gave support to what Frog said, and may have caused the staff to believe what he told them about me was true.

352) In January 2014, why did you consider it bad news when you heard that Sergeant Clarke and Officer Jackson would be getting married in March 2014?

A husband and wife were not allowed to both work on the main compound or in TCU. One spouse had to work on the main compound, and the other had to work in the TCU. The marriage of Sergeant Clarke and Officer Jackson meant Sergeant Clarke would be returning to the TCU. Officer Jackson couldn't return to the TCU because she was recently kicked out of it. This bad news meant Sergeant Clarke would be back around the inmates who had either witnessed or been victims of the *Hot-Water-Shower* treatment and inmates who were in the TCU when Darren Rainey died.

353) Did this news upset staff at Dade CI?

Yes. It upset Robert Anderson because it meant that Sergeant Clarke would be working in the same location as Robert Anderson.

354) How did you decide to contact the media about inmate abuse and Rainey's death?

At the beginning of 2014, I had told Windy that it seemed like the Miami-Dade Police Department and FDC Inspector General's Office were refusing to investigate the Rainey case or any of the abuse in the TCU. I expressed my concerns about the statute of limitations expiring on the cases. I also told her I was concerned about Sergeant Clarke returning to the TCU. After hearing this, Windy said, "We should contact the media."

We discussed her idea. She recommended contacting a newspaper. She also said she would contact them for me if that's what we agreed to do. We both agreed to think about it for a few days.

Around the beginning of February 2014, we contacted the *Miami Herald* newspaper. After they heard what happened to Darren Rainey and about the treatment of the mentally disabled inmates in the TCU, they showed an interest in obtaining more information.

I did not personally talk to the media on the telephone during this time.

Also, because of her concern for my safety, Windy asked me to make a check-in telephone call to her once a day, and I did.

355) How did you feel when the *Miami Herald* showed an interest in the Darren Rainey case and the abuse of the mentally disabled inmates in the TCU?

I felt it was a blessing from God, even though I knew a lot of potential negatives could come to me from FDC staff from talking with the media. However, I was willing to accept the negatives if it meant getting justice for what happened to Rainey and the mentally disabled inmates in the TCU.

356) Were you fearful of being physically harmed?

I wasn't fearful. I knew what I was doing in trying to get justice for Rainey and help for the mentally disabled was God's will. I knew that God is Sovereign and nothing happens that is outside of His decretive will. Even though I knew these things, I was always aware of the potential threats to my safety. But, I always knew the only protection I had was God and that sometimes a person has to be willing to suffer for what is right.

357) Did you tell any inmates at Dade CI that you had contacted the media?

Yes. I told Inmates Alford L. and Michael W. Alford L. and I had several conversations about what I was doing. He always supported the actions I took.

Michael W told me, "I'll be ready for war if staff try to get any inmates to turn against you."

A couple of days after I told him about my contact with the *Miami Herald*, he introduced me to Michael S. who had been in prison for decades. He was a litigator. Michael S. said, "I've known Michael W. for a long time. He's a good man. When he told me what you've been doing, what you're about to do, and that he's backing you, I told him that I would like to help. If you need me to do any research for you in the law library, I will. Also, if staff try to turn any inmates against you, Michael W and I will be ready. We won't have to worry about any old school inmates. It's the new school junkies who will stab their mom for a fifty sack of K-2. They'll be the only ones likely to cause problems."

I responded, "I appreciate your kindness. I've heard a lot about you from others, and I know you're a good man. Let us all pray that nothing crazy happens."

358) In February 2014, did the *Miami Herald* ask to interview you?

Yes, and I agreed to the meeting. About a week later, I learned that the *Miami Herald* representative wanted to come and visit me like a regular visitor would on the weekends. The reason was to take every precaution the representative deemed appropriate for my protection. Since that first meeting, they have always done everything possible to make sure I was never placed in harm's way.

I requested that the *Miami Herald* representative be asked to make an appointment to visit me as a *Miami Herald* representative. I had two reasons for wanting to go this route. First, if the *Miami Herald* representative came in like a normal visitor, he or she wouldn't have been able to take any notes, and I wouldn't have been able to give them any paperwork. If they visited me as a *Miami Herald* representative, these restrictions did not apply. They could take notes, and I could give them paperwork. Second, I didn't think the staff would believe that I was talking with the media about incidents that happened years earlier at Dade CI. I thought that the staff felt that I was OK with the evils they had committed.

The *Miami Herald* representative agreed to visit me as a *Miami Herald* representative.

359) Did you tell Randy Evans or Jim Knowels you were going to meet with a *Miami Herald* representative?

No. They would have both objected to me doing such.

360) Why have you not mentioned Evans and Knowels when describing this incarceration at Dade CI?

I have explained that they got me back to Dade CI, and I mentioned I did not tell them I was going to meet with the media. If I explained anything more about my communications with them, they could be identified.

361) What else happened in March 2014?

Sergeant Clarke and Officer Jackson got married while they were on vacation for the month.

362) Did Sergeant Nickolis and his officers try to intimidate you in March and in the beginning of April 2014?

Yes, Sergeant Nickolis worked as a sergeant on one of the night shifts in the dorm I was housed in. In March 2014, he started harassing me saying he believed I was a bad inmate and he was going to catch me doing something bad.

At the beginning of April 2014, Sergeant Nickolis, Officer Edwards, and another officer searched my cell. During that search, Sergeant Nickolis took a piece of contraband out of his pocket and said, "Look what I found in your cell."

I responded, "You didn't find that in my cell. You just took it out of your pocket. I don't know what type of game you're playing, but I want to talk to the captain."

He said, "Captain Dixon is Security Two. Are you sure you want to talk to her?"

I responded, "Yes. I want to talk to her. Why don't you call her and tell her your lie about finding that in my cell."

He said, "Hempstead, I'll talk with you later on." The sergeant and the two officers then left my cell.

That night I went to bed around 11:00 pm., and around 3:00 am, my cell door opened. When I looked out of my cell door, somebody in the officers' station flashed me with a flashlight directing me to come to the officers' station. After putting on my shoes, I left my cell and went there as I was directed.

When I got there, Sergeant Nickolis directed me to sit on the floor. I sat where he directed me to sit, which was in the middle of him and his two officers. They were in a circle around me. Sergeant Nickolis started the conversation by saying, "Why don't you tell us about your time here at Dade CI?" I followed his direction and started with my first incarceration there, then my second incarceration, and finally my third incarceration. During my brief overview, which lasted about 15 minutes, I didn't mention the *Hot-Water-Shower* treatment, or what happened to Darren Rainey. When I got done with my overview, Sergeant Nickolis asked, "So why are you writing the media?"

In each of the wings at Dade CI, there was a small wooden mailbox on the wall. When inmates had mail to send out, they placed it in the mailbox in their wing. Security staff posted in each dorm on the 7:00 pm to 7:00 am shift picked up the mail from each wing. Inmates had to send their mail out unsealed so security could inspect the mail prior to it leaving the institution. I knew prior to sending my letters to the *Miami Herald* newspaper that security staff would be able to read my letters, but that was OK with me. My letters didn't have any details in them. I responded to Sergeant Nickolis' question by saying, "The media is in the process of coming to visit me."

He responded, "About what?"

I said, "It has nothing to do with you or your officers. However, I can tell the media about this meeting and that you recently lied when you said you found something in my cell."

He responded, "I could stop that meeting."

I said, "Sergeant, you're getting yourself involved with matters that have nothing to do with you. What's going on is bigger than you can imagine. If you were to attempt to stop the media visit, you would be in more legal trouble than you could handle."

He responded, "Why don't you tell us about the inmate who died in the shower?"

I said, "I'm sure a lot of other people told you about it."

He responded, "Is that what you are talking with the *Miami Herald* about?"

I said, "Are you subjecting me to retaliation for asserting my First Amendment right to communicate with the media? I think you are because you're trying to intimidate me to not talk to them. It doesn't matter what you do sergeant, and I'll tell you why, if you physically harm me or lie on me and place me in confinement, I'll tell the media and FBI what you did. Additionally, I will sue. I have filed federal lawsuits against prison officials before, and I have no problem with doing it again."

He responded, "Since you're going to the media to snitch, why you don't tell me where some cell phones and drugs are?"

I said, "One, because I don't know where anything's at, and two, if I knew where anything was, I wouldn't tell you. I'm not stupid, sergeant. I know you're the type to lie and say an inmate is a snitch so other inmates will hurt the inmate you don't like. Don't you remember you just tried to set me up a few hours ago?"

He said, "I could put you in confinement right now for what I showed you in your cell earlier."

I said, "You know as well as I do, Captain Dixon is not going to approve me going to confinement. I was doing my time, not messing with anybody and you guys just started harassing me for no reason. You're just making things worse by subjecting me to this interrogation."

He responded, "Hempstead, you can go back to your cell. I can see you're just going to play hard ball. This was no fun. You may leave."

The next day, I filed approximately 10 grievances on Sergeant Nickolis, Officer Edwards, and the other officer. I explained in detail everything that happened with the search of my cell and Nickolis threatening to set me up with a false disciplinary report. I also explained in detail the three o'clock in the morning interrogation I was subjected to in the officers' station. My grievances were sent to the Tallahassee, Florida main office for the FDC, and the warden and colonel at Dade CI. These grievances were all responded to, so they should be in my prison files.

363) What did you ask Sergeant Lewis and other security staff the day after these incidents with Sergeant Nickolis and his officers?

I told them about the incidents and asked them to get Sergeant Nickolis off my back if they weren't supporting his actions. Sergeant Lewis and the other staff I spoke with said they would look into it.

364) Why did Sergeant Nickolis make you sit down on the ground in the middle of him and his officers?

It was to intimidate me and make me feel vulnerable.

365) Weren't you scared to say some of the things you said to Sergeant Nickolis?

I wasn't scared because I knew God is in sovereign control. Additionally, my past experiences have taught me that staff who are going to be abusive or set an inmate up, don't talk to the inmate like Sergeant Nickolis was talking to me prior to doing anything. Finally, I knew that Sergeant Nickolis was like several of the security staff at Dade CI who only picked on inmates who were fearful. I knew if I didn't show any fear, he would back away and leave me alone.

Sergeant Nickolis was just a bully trying to scare me from talking with the *Miami Herald* newspaper.

366) Did you tell Windy about your problems with Sergeant Nickolis?

Yes. I told her about them, what shift and days he and his officers worked, and who their captain was. Windy said she would draft some e-mails on Sergeant Nickolis and his officers. I agreed with her about preparing the e-mails. I asked her to not send them to anybody until we saw if Sergeant Nickolis and his officers were going to leave me alone.

367) What happened when Sergeant Clarke and Officer Jackson returned to work from their vacation after getting married?

Sergeant Clarke was posted to work in the TCU, and Officer Jackson was posted to work in the general population.

368) What happened with Chaplain Diaz in the weeks prior to your first meeting with the *Miami Herald* representative?

Chaplain Diaz was the Senior Chaplain at Dade CI. She was Catholic, and she knew me very well. I was the only Protestant Christian inmate who taught the Bible in the location that was used for the chapel. She didn't like Chaplain Tomlin allowing me to teach the Bible in his class. By policy, Chaplain Diaz couldn't tell Chaplain Tomlin how to run his class. He was a Protestant Christian, and he could run his class how he wanted to.

In the weeks prior to my first meeting with the *Miami Herald* representative, Chaplain Diaz called me into her office and said, "Hempstead, I was told about some of the things you witnessed in the TCU. I would like to talk to you about them. Is that OK?"

I responded, "It depends what you're talking about. If I may ask, who told you about what I witnessed?"

She said, "Assistant Warden Williams told me. Sometimes when people see things that bother them, they want to talk about what they saw. If they can't talk about what is bothering them, they sometimes go and talk to the wrong people. Were you bothered by the things you saw in the TCU?"

I responded, "Apparently Assistant Warden Williams has been told by the Tallahassee, Florida FDC office that the media wants to talk to me, so he's enlisted your help to try to convince me to not meet with them."

She said, "Our concern is that you just need somebody to talk to, and you're going to the wrong people."

I responded, "With much respect, I've been in prison a long time. I don't need anybody to talk to personally about the things I witnessed. I've talked to God about them for years. I don't know why you or Mr. Williams think I'm going to be talking with the media about anything concerning Dade CI."

She said, "The computer shows you're from Pinellas County, Florida. Have you ever lived in Dade County?"

I responded, "I would rather not answer that question."

She said, "If you talk with the media about anything that happened in the TCU, you will open a Pandora's box. It'll be a box of worms. Do you understand me?"

I responded, "I know I am Presbyterian and you are Catholic, but don't you even believe what the Catholic Church teaches? Don't you believe in a standard of right and wrong? I never said I was going to talk to the media about anything that happened here at Dade CI. However, if I was, why would you try to stop me? You should support me. The Christian thing would be to support anybody who is trying to help others. Chaplain Diaz, Catholics believe in helping the weak."

She said, "I believe in helping the weak. I just don't think your weighing the pros and cons of what your about to do. Think about what I have said. I'm going to call you out to talk with you tomorrow."

I responded, "I deem you telling me about the pros and cons as a threat. Did Assistant Warden Williams tell you to threaten me?"

She said, "No. He did not, and that wasn't a threat. I'm the Senior Chaplain here at Dade CI. It is my job to be concerned for you."

I responded, "I have to go. I'll talk to you tomorrow when you call me out. Thank you, Chaplain."

Chaplain Diaz and I had three or four more conversations prior to my first meeting with the Miami Herald. In all those conversations, she tried to convince me to not meet with the *Miami Herald* representative.

369) Did you lose your job as an orderly in confinement at the end of March 2014?

Yes, I did. The colonel ordered that inmates could no longer work in confinement as orderlies. I believe the colonel gave this order because of my pending meeting with the media.

370) Was the heat being turned up on you at Dade CI?

Yes. Ever since the security staff was informed that I told inmates they should record staff and that I was behind several recordings of Sergeant Clarke and his officers, the heat started rising. Then, when security staff found out I was preparing to talk with the media, the heat rose more with Sergeant Nickolis' retaliatory actions, and also with Chaplain Diaz trying to convince me to not meet with the media.

During this period, I was in constant lengthy prayer, asking God for grace and strength.

371) Did you talk with Nurse Kind in the two week period before your meeting with the Miami Herald?

Yes. Since my return to Dade CI in June 2013, I had several conversations with her. She was always kind and always spoke words of comfort. About two weeks before my first meeting with the *Miami Herald* representative, I had a meeting with Nurse Kind. When I got to the location where we talked, I said, "Thank you again for allowing me to talk to you."

She responded, "Are you OK?"

I said, "I'm stressed, and I just wanted to talk. I'm about to meet with the media about Darren Rainey and the other things I witnessed in the TCU. If everything works out with the media, justice will probably finally come for Rainey and the mentally disabled inmates in the TCU will possibly get the help they need. A lot of good can come from this meeting. Even though I know these things and nothing will stop me from talking to the media, I have concerns, and I'm a little stressed. I'm going to be talking with them about a real murder investigation concerning Darren Rainey, and other criminal offenses. Security staff will not be happy. The staff could easily label me as a snitch with the inmates to try and get me killed, or just pay an inmate to stab me. The staff could also just kill me, or they could poison my food if I end up in confinement. My biggest concern is going to confinement. If I go to confinement, they could put blood pressure or mental health medicine in my food to stop my heart and then tell everybody I overdosed."

She responded, "The things you said could very well happen. Are you willing to take that chance?"

I said, "Yes, because this might be the only way Rainey can get justice, and the inmates in the TCU can get help."

She responded, "I want you to give me a telephone number for your sister and for the reporter who is supposed to meet you. The only way I will call them, is if you are harmed or placed in confinement. Don't tell anybody you gave me these numbers. Will your sister know what to do if I have to call her and tell her you need help?"

I said, "Yes." I handed her a piece of paper and said, "Here are their names and phone numbers."

She responded, "If for any reason staff try to place you in confinement after you speak with media, I want you to fake like you're having problems standing. If staff try to make you walk, walk for five or 10 seconds, then fall. After the second fall, act like you hurt your back. My goal will be to use your medical problems to get you in an infirmary cell in medical. The doctor is a Christian. I'll be able to talk him into putting you in the infirmary and transferring you for medical reasons if we have to. If I have to ask the doctor for help, I will tell him that I directed you to fake your medical problems so we could help protect you and get you off this compound. He's a good man. He will help us. Will you be able to fake the medical problems?"

I said, "Yes."

She responded, "Now that we covered those things, I want to tell you something. God puts His people in strategic positions to use them, how He wants to use them for His glory. I believe God called you and put you in the position that He did because He has ordained that you take a stand for the mentally disabled."

I said, "I know that God wants me to speak out, and I believe what you said. It's just sometimes I feel weak."

She responded, "What did you tell me about courage a few months ago?"

I said, "Courage can only exist in the face of fear."

She responded, "Exactly. You're not a weak person. You're one of the strongest people I've ever met. A weak person doesn't do the things you've done. A weak person doesn't say, I could be killed if I take this action, but I'm still going to take it because it's the right thing to do."

I said, "When I talk about feeling weak, I'm not saying that my feelings of weakness stop me or in any way hinder me. God doesn't want our feelings to control us. My feelings are not the lord of my life. Jesus is my Lord. When I feel weak, I recognize the feeling and what Jesus wants me to learn from it. What Jesus wants me to learn from my weaknesses, is that I'm human and I'm subject to them. Jesus doesn't want me to fall into my weaknesses, but to lean on Him more. What I'm saying is my weaknesses bring me into a closer relationship with my Lord. It's like the Apostle Paul said in 2 Corinthians 12:9, 10.

She responded, "I understand what your saying. The beautiful thing about you, Harold, is your sincerity in your beliefs."

After this conversation, I spoke with Nurse Kind two more times before my meeting with the media.

372) What does 2 Corinthians 12: 9, 10 say?

In those verses, the Apostle Paul said, "And He said to me, My grace is sufficient for you, for My strength is made perfect in weakness. Therefore most gladly I will rather boast in my infirmities, that the power of Christ may rest upon me. Therefore I take pleasure in infirmities, in reproaches, in needs, in prosecutions, in distresses, for Christ sake. For when I am weak, then I am strong."

373) Did you tell the Christian community at Dade CI about your efforts to get justice for Darren Rainey and help for other mentally disabled inmates in the TCU?

I knew that after I met with the media, I could be subject to any type of retaliation and transferred from Dade CI. Over the time I had been at Dade CI, I developed a strong Christian love for those who attended the Bible studies I taught and co-taught. Knowing that I would be transferred from Dade CI fairly soon, I didn't want to leave them without saying good-bye. For months they showed me great kindness and love by allowing me to share the Bible with them.

I told them of my pending transfer at the Wednesday Bible study in the Chapel before Chaplain Tomlin arrived. I started it by saying, "There's something that's been going on for a long time now that I need to talk to you men about. I'm going to be leaving Dade CI soon, and I don't want to leave you without saying good-bye. Over these months, I've grown to have a strong, Christian love for all of you. I know you're probably wondering why I'll be leaving, so let me explain.

"If any of you saw a small child or senior citizen being beaten, would you help them?" When I asked this question all of them raised their hands. I then asked several of them to tell me why they would help the child or senior citizen. They all said they would help because it was the "Christian thing to do," "Biblical thing to do," or "right thing to do."

After telling them they were all right, I said, "There are several scriptures in the Bible that command us to help those who are in need. Additionally, we have numerous examples in the Bible of people helping others in need. In the Bible, the greatest example of somebody helping others was Jesus dying as our substitute for the forgiveness of our sins.

Mankind couldn't do anything to save themselves. We couldn't reconcile ourselves to the Father, redeem ourselves from the bondage of sin, become righteous, self-regenerate, or in any way do anything to get ourselves in right standing with God. Because we sinned against God, He didn't owe us anything but justice which would have sent all of us to hell for eternity. But instead of God giving us justice, He did what needed to be done to reconcile us to Him. We sinned against God, but He provided the Lamb to reconcile because we couldn't reconcile ourselves to Him. That's why the Atonement of Christ was vicarious.

The second person in the Trinitarian God of heaven and earth, incarnated in the Man Christ Jesus, because since Adam's sin, all mankind has been born sinners. A sinner can't atone for his own sins, nor for the sins of others. That is why the good pleasure of God and His love, moved Him to send His Son to incarnate, keep the whole law of God perfectly without sin, and then die for our sins.

The Penal Substitutionary Vicarious Atonement of Christ gave Christ's sheep everything that is required unto salvation. Jesus did it all, and we did nothing. He did it because we couldn't. He helped us, because He loved us and because we could not help ourselves. Our condition without God was total loss and eternity in hell. The essence of the gospel is God helping those who can't help themselves. God knew that we couldn't do anything to save ourselves, so He took action to provide everything that was required for salvation for all those that Jesus died for. When I say God helped us, I am not saying He assisted us in our salvation, I am saying he did everything."

"Brothers and friends, let me tell you the reason why I'm going to be leaving here soon. In 2011 and 2012, I worked as an orderly in the TCU. During that time I witnessed all types of abuse of the mentally disabled inmates housed there, and what I believe was one to three murders by staff. Very soon, I'm going to be talking with the media about the things I witnessed. When I do, I'll more than likely be transferred from here."

In that Bible study I told the class a lot about the Darren Rainey incident and the abuse I witnessed in the TCU. I never mentioned any of those things to Chaplain Tomlin. It was well known that I taught and co-taught the Bible with him. I didn't want to get him in any trouble with staff at Dade CI. As long as he didn't know anything about my efforts to get justice for Darren Rainey and help for the mentally disabled inmates, if he was questioned by anybody, he could sincerely and truthfully say that he didn't know anything.

374) Describe your first meeting with the *Miami Herald* representative.

I was told about a week in advance that the *Miami Herald* representative would be at Dade CI to talk to me on April 14, 2014.

I gathered all the grievances I had filed on what happened to Darren Rainey and on the non-feeding and abuse of inmates in the TCU. I also made notes of what I wanted to address when speaking to the representative.

Around 10:00 am on April 14, 2014, I was told to report to the visitation park. When I arrived there, I met with the *Miami Herald* representative. During our conversation, I explained in as much detail as possible Darren Rainey's death, the *Hot-Water-Shower* treatment of mentally disabled inmates, and the non-feeding and abuse of mentally disabled inmates in the TCU. I gave the representative the grievances I brought with me, so the *Miami Herald* could make copies of them for their records.

During that visit, several staff came into the visitation park and saw me talking with a person from society. At that time, none of them knew that the person I was talking to was from the *Miami Herald* newspaper. A day or two later, the majority of the security staff at Dade CI found out who the person was that I spoke with that day.

375) How was the interview with the *Miami Herald* representative?

The interview took about two hours. The representative asked several questions and took notes. I could tell the representative was very experienced in interviewing because I was not able to analyze where the representative stood as it concerned the things I was saying.

376) Did you think the *Miami Herald* newspaper would publish any article on the Darren Rainey case?

For years, Windy and I worked alone in our attempt to get justice for Darren Rainey and to stop the abuse of the mentally disabled inmates in the TCU. In a way, I didn't have any hope that anybody would ever help us. I'm a Christian convicted of burglaries and serving 165 years in prison; Darren Rainey was a mentally disabled African American Muslim serving time for minor possession of crack cocaine; and the mentally disabled inmates were all convicted felons. I didn't think there was anybody in society who cared enough to help.

Within a short time, I found out that I was wrong. I discovered that God had ordained that the *Miami Herald* representative He sent to talk to me would be a person who had a big heart and wanted help the weak. I also learned that society was full of people with big hearts and a desire to help the week.

377) After meeting with the *Miami Herald* representative, did you file a complaint with the Miami-Dade Police Department Internal Affairs Division?

Yes. Within two or three days, I filed a complaint against Homicide Detective Herbert Sanchez. The complaint was about Detective Sanchez refusing to investigate the Darren Rainey case. I never heard anything about the complaint. I don't know if they threw it away or what happened to it.

378) Did Detective Sanchez come to interview you the week after you met with the Miami Herald?

Yes, the week after I met with the representative from the Herald, I was directed to report to the Dade CI Security Building. There, I met two men who identified themselves as Miami-Dade Police Department Homicide Detectives Wilbert Sanchez and Daniel Aiken. They were the homicide detectives assigned to investigate Darren Rainey's death. We met in Colonel McCarter's office but the colonel was not present.

After they introduced themselves, Detective Sanchez said, "I would like to ask you a few questions, is that OK?"

I responded, "May I ask, why you're finally deciding to talk with me when it's been almost two years since he died?"

He said, "We've been investigating the case, and now it's time to talk to you."

I responded, "How have you been investigating the case, when you haven't spoken with any of the witnesses?"

He said, "How do you know we haven't spoken to any of the witnesses?"

I responded, "Because I know all of them and the suspects, and if you spoke with any of them they would have told me."

Department of Corruption

He said, "Are you talking with staff and inmates on this compound about what happened?"

I said, "Yes, and I'm talking with people in society. Are you here to talk to me, because I spoke with the *Miami Herald* last week about what happened to Darren Rainey, or are you here because I filed a complaint with your Internal Affairs department about your refusal to investigate the Rainey case?"

He said, "I didn't know you filed a complaint with Internal Affairs. If I may ask, what did you tell the Miami Herald?"

I responded, "Please forgive me for being upset and so assertive, but I have been trying to talk to you for two years about what happened. You asked what I told the Miami Herald. I told them everything that I've written in letters to you for almost two years. Did you get my letters?"

He said, "Yes. I got your letters. Let's talk about some of the things you said in your letters. Why don't you tell me what happened to Rainey?"

I responded, "Are you serious? I've written you dozens of pages of letters telling you what happened, and you want me to again tell you verbally everything that I told you in detail in my letters?"

He said, "We're investigating the case so we need your statement. Do you remember what date Rainey died on?"

I responded, "Yes. June 23, 2012. If you're investigating this case, why aren't you recording my statement and how come you're asking me things, I already told you in my letters?"

Detective Aiken said, "He did tell us 'June 23, 2012' in his letters."

Detective Sanchez said, "I'm not using a recorder, but I am taking notes. How did Rainey die?"

I responded, "The answer to that question is also in my letters. My letters tell every single detail about Rainey's death. If you just came to test my memory to see if I'll tell you verbally everything I told you in my letters, then I'll give you what you want." I then retold the detectives everything that I said in my letters to them.

Chapter 16: Dade CI (January 1, 2014 - May 19, 2014)

During my presentation, Detective Sanchez kept asking questions concerning matters I addressed in my letters and in my presentation. Every time he did so, I responded, "I answered that in my letters, but I'll do it again."

Several times throughout that interview when I told Detective Sanchez that I addressed a question he asked in my letters to him, Detective Aiken would say, "Hempstead did address that in his letters."

Towards the end of the interview, Detective Sanchez said, "How do staff treat you here?"

I responded, "By prison standards, I live like a king. I have one of the best jobs on the compound, several days a week staff bring me in food from society, and my relationship with the majority of the security staff on this compound make it where I can't get in any trouble."

He said, "Then why are you doing all this?"

I responded, "Doing all what?"

He said, "Why are you making such a big ordeal out of everything?"

I responded, "Are you serious? Did you just ask me why I'm making a big ordeal out of everything? The staff were steam cooking mentally disabled inmates in a shower to the point where one died. And you are asking me why I'm making a big ordeal out of it.

"I'm making a big ordeal out of it because I had to witness it. I had to hear his last words. I've had to deal with the sadness that I've had and all the things I failed to do. I'm also making a big ordeal out of it because it's the right thing to do."

He said, "How will the staff respond to you, if they find out that you are pushing these matters with the media and law enforcement?"

I responded, "They could kill me, physically abuse me, or transfer me to another prison. They could do anything they want to do, and they would probably get away with it, just like you're allowing them to get away with what they did to Rainey."

He said, "We're not allowing them to get away with anything."

Throughout this meeting, Detective Sanchez told me several times that I shouldn't be talking with the media, or anybody else about what happened to Darren Rainey, or anything I witnessed in the TCU.

That meeting lasted about an hour and a half.

379) Why do you think those detectives came to see you?

Since they came and spoke with me for the first time the week after I spoke with the media, it's obvious that they only spoke with me because they found out I spoke with the media.

Also articles published by *Miami Herald* after May 18, 2014 show that directly after the *Miami Herald* representative spoke with me, the representative started investigating Darren Rainey's death. Also, during that investigations, the representative contacted the Miami-Dade Police Department and Dade County Medical Examiner's office.

380) Why do you think the detectives interviewed you in the colonel's office at Dade CI?

I believe it was a scare tactic to try to intimidate me to stop talking.

381) Do you believe the detectives were really there to investigate the Darren Rainey case?

No. I believe they came to see me to try to convince me that they were investigating the Darren Rainey case, hoping that would stop me from speaking with the media. Additionally, several things Detective Sanchez said during the interview showed he was trying to intimidate me to stop talking with the media and others, about the Darren Rainey case.

382) Did you file any complaints with any agencies after your April 2014 interview with Detective Sanchez?

Yes. I mailed a sworn complaint on Detective Sanchez refusing to investigate the Darren Rainey case to the Washington D.C. office of the U.S. Department of Justice. I also mailed several letters to the Miami-Dade Police Department and to the Dade County, Florida Medical Examiner's office.

383) Did Sergeant Clarke threaten you after your meeting with Detectives Sanchez and Aiken?

Yes. About two weeks after the interview, I was on Dade CI's list of blood spill certified inmates. When inmates cut themselves, an inmate certified in cleaning up blood would be called to the location where the inmate cut himself to clean up the spilled blood. Around the end of 2013, I was mysteriously called to clean up blood from an inmate who cut himself in Wing J-2 of the TCU. I was confused as to why I was called because, most of the time, staff used inmates housed in the TCU to clean up blood from inmates housed there.

When I went to the TCU to clean up the blood, Lieutenant Joiner saw me. I knew her from when she was a sergeant and the major's secretary. She allowed me to clean up the blood from the inmate, but I knew she wasn't happy to see me in the TCU.

A few days after this incident, I was told that a memo was issued stating that I was not allowed to enter the TCU for any reason. That memo kept me out of the TCU for months.

Then mysteriously, at the beginning of May 2014, I was directed to report to Wing J-3 of the TCU to clean up blood again. I immediately knew something was wrong. What added to my concern was that it was on Sergeant Clarke's shift, and it was within an hour of his shift ending. I did not want to go, but for some reason I went, against my better judgment.

When I got to the central section of the TCU, I saw Officer Jolly. When she told me the blood was in the shower next to Cell J-3201, I got a stronger feeling to not go to Wing J-3 and to leave the TCU. Contributing to my feeling that I was in danger was that, as far as I knew, no inmate ever cut himself in the shower next to Cell J-3201. It was also the same shower that Darren Rainey died in.

When I got to Wing J-3 and went up the stairs to the shower, I saw there was no blood in the shower. Within seconds of reaching the shower, I saw Sergeant Clarke standing in the doorway of the office next to the shower. He stared at me for about two seconds, and then, as he started walking quickly toward me, he said, "Come here, snitch boy." I took off running.

I ran down the stairs from the upper tier and fell. When I landed, I felt a sharp pain in my right wrist. I scrambled up and ran toward the front door of Wing J-3. When I got close to the front door, I felt Clarke's hand grab the back of my head and slam it into the wing door. As soon as my face hit the door, blood started coming out of my nose. At the same time Colonel McCarter appeared in front of the officers' station door in the hallway. When Sergeant Clarke saw the colonel, Clarke didn't do anything else to me.

I used my shirt to try to stop the blood coming out of my nose. When the colonel saw Sergeant Clarke and me, he came into Wing J-3 instead of going into the officers' station. When he got inside of the wing, the colonel asked, "Hempstead, what are you doing back here?"

I responded, "I was called back here to clean up blood."

Sergeant Clarke said, "An inmate cut himself. We called medical for an orderly. The orderly came and cleaned it up, and then Hempstead came in afterward. Medical staff must have sent two orderlies by accident."

Colonel McCarter asked, "Hempstead, what's wrong with your nose? Why are you bleeding?"

Before I could answer him, Clarke said, "He slipped and fell."

McCarter said, "I asked him. Hempstead, why are you bleeding?"

I responded, "I fell."

Colonel McCarter said, "Go to medical and get checked out before you go back to your dorm."

I said, "OK." I then left the TCU.

I told Colonel McCarter I fell, because if I told him that Sergeant Clarke just slammed my face into the door, the colonel would have placed me in administrative confinement under investigation. My life would have been in serious danger, if I was placed in confinement. I believed the best chance I had at staying alive was to stay in the general population.

About an hour later, I was finally able to stop the blood from flowing out of my nose.

That night, I noticed that I had a lot of pain in my right wrist. I thought that I may have sprained it, when I fell down the stairs. I didn't think it was broken.

The next morning, I woke up with a minor black eye. Apparently my right eye was damaged when Sergeant Clarke slammed my face into the door. A few days later, my right wrist turned black. I was not able to move like normal, and it hurt a lot. I thought it was broken. I signed up for the medical sick-call, and the sick-call nurse said my wrist was possibly broken. She referred me to the doctor for an x-ray. The doctor agreed with her recommendation and ordered x-rays of my wrist. I never received the results while I was at Dade CI, and, for the rest of the time I was at Dade CI, I had to take pain medicine several times a day.

384) Why you were so concerned about going to confinement?

Over the years that I had worked as a special housing orderly at Dade CI, I saw staff shut off the mounted security cameras in the confinement unit; unlawfully use chemical agents on inmates and physically abuse them while in confinement; not feed inmates; poison inmates' food with medicines, chemicals, feces, urine, etc.; and place inmates they didn't like in the cells with physical and/or sexual predators knowing that the predators would harm the inmates staff doesn't like. I also saw mentally disabled inmates being placed in a *Hot-Water-Shower* as punishment.

As long as I stayed in the general population, I didn't have to worry about any of the above things.

385) After the incident with Sergeant Clarke, did Sergeant Nickolis and Officer Edwards retaliate against you?

Yes. Sergeant Nickolis and Officer Edwards came to my cell and told my cellmate and me to go wait in the day room. Within five minutes, he called us back to the cell. When we returned to the cell, I noticed that my property was thrown all over the cell and my cellmates' property wasn't touched.

While I was organizing my property, an inmate who lived directly across from me came to my cell and said, "Hey, I watched them when they ransacked your stuff. They both lifted up your locker and turned it upside down. When all of your stuff was on the ground, they kicked it everywhere. Then they pulled your mattress off the bunk, and threw it on to the ground. After they did that, they left your cell."

I responded, "Thank you for letting me know that."

386) Did Windy e-mail the Florida Governor in May 2014 about you being subjected to retaliation?

Yes. I called Windy the day after Sergeant Nickolis and Officer Edwards ransacked my cell. I told her what happened and that the retaliation was getting out of hand. She immediately said she wanted to e-mail the Florida Governor. She said, "You should have let me send some e-mails for you when you went back to that compound. I'll get them to stop messing with you. I'm going to e-mail the governor and tell him you're a witness to what happened to Darren Rainey. I'll also tell him the staff are retaliating against you and that your life is in danger. I can send enough -emails to persuade the staff there to leave you alone."

I responded, "Do you have the Governor's e-mail address?"

She said, "No, but I'll get it. I can have it within a few minutes."

I responded, "OK. Please draft that e-mail, and, if you can, will you send copies of it to the FDC Secretary, the warden here, and the *Miami Herald* representative I spoke with?"

She said, "Yes, I have the *Miami Herald* representative's e-mail address. I'll get the other e-mail addresses. I won't send it, until I read it to you, and you approve it. Call me back in an hour."

An hour later, when I called her back, she had the e-mail drafted. She read it to me, and it didn't require any corrections. She knew the Rainey case and everything that had been happening so well, she didn't need my help. After reading me the e-mail, she said, "All you have to do is tell me to send it, and I will."

I responded, "Send it."

She said, "I know you've been doing the check-in calls every day for more than a month now, but I think it's time to go to twice a day."

I responded, "OK, and don't forget that my number one concern is going to confinement here. I already explained why. If I miss a check-in call, that means I'm physically hurt or in confinement. If that happens, please send e-mails to whomever you want, and do whatever needs to be done to get me on the phone."

She said, "OK. As long as you can talk and you're not hurt, I'll get you on the phone." After this conversation, I started doing check-in calls to Windy twice a day.

I knew the day after Windy sent the e-mails, that they got the attention of the FDC. As a result of those e-mails, the rest of the time I was at Dade CI, Sergeant Nickolis and his officers didn't enter the housing wing I lived in unless all the inmates housed in the wing were in their cells with the doors locked.

I found out a short time later that everyone except the Dade CI warden e-mailed her back, acknowledging receipt of her e-mails.

387) What happened on the day before the *Miami Herald* published the article about Darren Rainey's death?

I went to bed around 10:00 pm. I was falling to sleep when my cell door opened and I started hearing inmates yelling "One time, captain upstairs", and "The captain is going upstairs." Within seconds, Captain Towns stopped at my cell door, shined his flashlight in my cell and said, "Hempstead, you need to call your sister. She won't tell me what it is about. I think there's medical problems in your family. Call her now!"

I responded, "OK, Captain."

After he left, I went to the phone and called Windy. When she answered, she said, "Is anybody around you listening?"

I responded, "No. Why?"

She said, "OK, listen. Tomorrow you're going to be on the front page of the *Miami Herald* newspaper. Casey Frank just called me a little while ago and told me how to locate the article on the internet. He wants me to read it to you. That way, you're aware of what it says. I'll read it quickly. Let me know if I need to slow down." After Windy read it to me, she said, "What do you think? Is anything inaccurate?"

I responded, "No. everything is accurate. Julie K. Brown apparently did a thorough investigation because it mentions several things about Dade CI that I didn't tell them. We've got to be on point tomorrow. Anything is subject to happen. I'm going to give you the names of all the captains who'll be working over the next several days. If I'm locked up in confinement, they would have to approve my placement there. If for some reason I'm placed in confinement, put the captain's name who put me in confinement in any e-mails you send the Governor and anybody else. From 7:00 am to 7:00 pm tomorrow Captain Dixon is working; 7:00 pm to 7:00 am is Captain Towns; 7:00 am to 7:00 pm on Monday is Captain Green; and 7:00 pm to 7:00 am is Captain Knight."

She said, "Obviously your stay at Dade CI will be over soon. Starting tomorrow, do a check-in call every hour. Make sure you don't miss any of them. I'll be calling up there if you miss any calls."

I responded, "OK. I'm not going to miss a call, unless there's a problem."

After we ended our call, I told several inmates in the wing who I could trust, that Dade CI would be in the *Miami Herald* newspaper the next day. The inmates I spoke with were those I would need help from, if certain things happened.

388) What happened on May 18, 2014 when the *Miami Herald* article was published?

When the cell doors opened for breakfast, the inmates in my wing started their day like normal. About 10 minutes after the cell doors opened, inmates were in the day room turning through TV news stations. Inmates in most housing wings in the FDC watch the news when they get up in the morning. Within about five minutes of them turning through the channels, someone noticed that one of the news stations was talking about an article published by the *Miami Herald* newspaper about a "brutal and unexplained death" at Dade CI.

Within seconds of the first inmate seeing the TV news broadcast, he and others were yelling to the inmates in the wing that Dade CI was in the news. Within minutes, everyone in the wing who was awake was in the day room watching the news broadcast. Several of them knew that I was behind what was on the news, because it was talking about Darren Rainey dying in the shower.

While the inmates were watching the news, several of them said, "Let's go see if we can find the *Miami Herald* article that the news is talking about." Those inmates then went to their cells to locate the *Miami Herald* newspaper article on their cell phones. Over the next hour, I was asked dozens of questions by inmates about what was going on and about Darren Rainey.

When the inmates went to breakfast, Inmates Michael W. and Michael S. were waiting outside the dorm for me. When Michael W. saw me, he said, "It's on the TV in my wing, and in the other wings in G-Dorm. The news is saying the *Miami Herald* has an article in it today on Rainey. From now on, I'm going to hang with you 24/7. If staff try to get a Git (young inmate) to stab you, I'll take care of it."

I responded, "I'm sure staff will be finding a way to transfer me today or tomorrow. That's how FDC is. I just have to make it, until they get me off the compound."

Michael S. said, "I don't think they're going to transfer you. That's retaliation."

I responded, "They have to transfer me. If something happens to me, FDC staff would be liable." Both Michaels went to breakfast with me. On the way to breakfast, while at breakfast, and on the way back, I heard inmates and staff talking about the *Miami Herald* article and the TV news broadcasts. When both Michaels and I got back to my dorm, they said they would be back at my dorm when work-call was announced. When work-call is announced in the FDC, inmates leave their housing units and report to their jobs.

I went into my wing and heard that numerous inmates found the *Miami Herald* article on their cell phones. When the inmates found out that my name was mentioned in the *Miami Herald* article, they started saying, "Hempstead, staff are going to kill you"

"You're the witness that can put them in prison.", and

"You better hope you get transferred quickly, because staff are probably plotting to kill you."

After count was completed, an inmate came to me and said, "You need to wear a hat and shades if you go outside, so it'll be harder for staff to identify you."

I responded, "I have a hat, but I don't have any shades."

He said, "Here, use mine. They might keep you alive longer."

I thanked him for allowing me to use his shades. I wore them when I left my housing wing that day and the following day.

When work call was announced, I left my housing wing and met Michael W. and Michael S., who were waiting outside my dorm. The three of us went under the hut in front of F-Dorm, and Michael S. said, "Is everything straight?"

I responded, "Yeah, so far staff haven't said anything to me."

Michael W. said, "It's good you're incognito. It'll be harder for staff to recognize you with the hat and shades on."

Michael S. said, "I have to go to the law library. I'm going to leave there in about an hour. I'll meet you both on the recreation yard when I leave the law library."

I responded, "OK. We'll be out there all morning."

We were going to the recreation yard to hang out because a lot of inmates hung out there. The chances of staff harming me were much less with a lot of inmates around. Additionally, I was very friendly with hundreds of inmates who knew me from my Bible studies and from my prior job as a confinement orderly. This meant that I would have a lot of witnesses around me on the yard who would tell the truth if staff tried to do something to me they weren't supposed to do.

After Michael W. and I arrived on the recreation yard, we spoke with several inmates about the Darren Rainey case and what was going on with the media. About an hour later, Michael S. joined us.

The two Michaels and I got in the canteen line. When we were going back to the recreation yard from the canteens window, the officer at the recreation gate said, "Hempstead, is that you? I think I need to pat you down. Pull over so I can search you." I took off my hat and shades so everybody would know it was definitely me.

When all the inmates saw it was me, they started saying real loud, "Are you going to set him up?"

"Are you going to jump on him?"

"If you want trouble officer, we can set it off!"

The officer responded, "It might be better that I don't search you. I could end up in the next newspaper article."

The two Michaels and I then went back on the recreation yard until it closed. When it closed, we waited till everybody was off the yard before we left it. When there's a potential threat to your life in prison, you don't want to walk in a crowd of inmates. It's easy to get stabbed in a crowd. As we walked off the recreation yard, we talked about the three of us going to the chapel that afternoon.

After lunch both the Michaels and I went to Chaplain Tomlin's Sunday service.

I knew I would be leaving Dade CI fairly soon, and I probably would never see Chaplain Tomlin again. I wanted to thank him for all his kindness and say good-bye. When I saw him, I said, "Chap, I don't know if you know already, but my name is in an article in the *Miami Herald* about an inmate who staff killed here. This is probably going to be the last time I see you. I wanted to thank you for all the kindness you have shown me. You're a good man, and I have really enjoyed all the times we spent together in the Bible. I'll keep you in my prayers."

He responded, "I heard about the article. Are you OK? Do you think they're going to transfer you?"

I said, "Yes, I just don't know when."

He responded, "If you leave, take care of yourself. You know Jesus will always be with you. Follow the Shepherd, stay in the Word, and preach the Gospel."

I checked in with Windy every hour like we had arranged. When I called her prior to going to the chapel, I told her I would be about 20 minutes late on my next call because I was going to a chapel service. Throughout that day, Windy stayed in contact with the *Miami Herald* representative. I didn't have any problems with any staff that day.

The primary thing that was spoken about by staff and inmates on May 18, 2014 was the article, "Brutal and Unexplained Death" published by *Miami Herald* Reporter Julie K. Brown.

389) What happened the next day when the *Miami Herald* reporter Julie K. Brown published a second article?

On May 19, 2014, the *Miami Herald* Reporter, Julie K. Brown, published a second article on the brutal death of Darren Raney and on Dade CI. For a second day, staff and inmates talked constantly about the media attention to the Darren Rainey case and Dade CI.

That morning, I called Windy as soon as I awoke to let her know I was OK. I continued to call her until noon when the inmate collect calling telephone stopped working. It was reasonable to say that security staff shut the inmate collect calling phones off to hinder my communications with Windy.

Around 3:00 pm, I was in my cell writing a letter to the FBI about the Darren Rainey case when I heard several inmates yell:

"One time, Sergeant Fanfan in the house!"

"Fanfan's going upstairs!"

"Hot water, upstairs!"

I knew Fanfan was coming to my cell. Fanfan was the sergeant who was working on the night Darren Rainey died.

I had just enough time to cover the letter to the FBI before Sergeant Fanfan appeared at my cell door and said, "Cuff-up."

I responded, "You're going to turn this into something bigger than what it already is."

He said, "Are you going to cuff-up?"

I responded, "Of course I'm going to. I hope you know that I'm a listed witness, and anything you do to me can be used against you in court. You're also opening yourself up to more criminal and civil liability." I then let Fanfan place handcuffs on me.

As he started escorting me, Officer Pena was walking toward my cell. Officer Pena said, "I need his locker combination." Fanfan said, "What's your locker combination?"

I responded, "I'm not going to say my locker combination out loud where other inmates can hear it."

Fanfan said, "Pena, use the locker key in the officers' station." Sergeant Fanfan was holding my arm real tight as he escorted me down the stairs. I told him several times that he was hurting my arm.

When we got outside of my dorm, I started talking real loud. I wanted to make sure inmates in their dorms could hear me. That way they would look out their cell windows and I would have witnesses if the sergeant physically abused me. I told Fanfan real loud, "Whatever you're about to do, I deem it as retaliation. You know you were the sergeant working on the night Rainey was killed, so it'll be real easy to prove any type of retaliation you subject me to."

Sergeant Fanfan didn't respond to anything I said to him.

After we got about a hundred feet from the front of my dorm, a female sergeant saw Sergeant Fanfan escorting me and she heard me talking really loud. The female sergeant came up to us and said, "Fanfan, I'll take him from here."

The female sergeant then took me to the Center Gate so she could switch out her radio battery. When we got there, the Center Gate officer said, "It's about time they got you. I'm surprised it took so long."

I responded, "You're surprised it took them so long to subject me to retaliation?"

The sergeant escorting me then said, "Come on, honey, I need to get you to the captain's office."

When we got to the captain's office, Captain Green said, "Hempstead, come on in here." After I entered the office, the sergeant shut the door behind me, leaving only Captain Green and me in his office. Captain Green then said, "Hempstead, your sister snitched on you. She said you've been calling her all day. How have you been calling her?"

I responded, "Captain, I know you don't know me as well as other staff on the compound, but I'm not stupid. You know Windy didn't snitch on me, and you know I was calling her by using the inmate collect call telephones. You or somebody else shut the phones off in my wing, and that's why she started calling you. As I'm sure the phone recordings show, my sister and I had it set up where I would call her every hour and let her know I'm all right. The recordings also show that she and I agreed that if I missed a call, she would take action to get me on the phone so she knew I was alright. Captain, I don't know why I'm in handcuffs and why your officers are subjecting my cell to a retaliatory search, but I want to let you know what's going to happen if I don't call my sister and let her know I'm OK. The recordings of my conversations with my sister on Saturday night show I gave her the names of the captains who worked on every shift. My sister knows your name, and if I don't call her and let her know I'm OK, she'll be sending an e-mail to the Governor with your name in it. Finally, Warden Cummings will tell you that my sister already e-mailed the Governor about the staff here. I would like to know if I'm going to confinement."

He said, "I never said you were going to confinement and I don't know what the officers are doing in your cell. I never told them to search your cell."

I responded, "If I'm not going to confinement, then why I am in handcuffs? Additionally, if you didn't tell them to subject my cell to a retaliatory search, then will you call them and tell them to stop messing with my property?"

He said, "I never told them to put you in handcuffs. When I'm done talking to you, I'll tell the sergeant to take the handcuffs off you. I'm not going to tell the officers to stop searching your cell. That's their job. When you get back to your dorm, you better call your sister and tell her to stop calling up here. Do you understand me?"

I responded, "I'll call her." He then told the sergeant to come in and take the handcuffs off me. Staff were in the middle of a count, so I couldn't leave the building until count was completed.

About two minutes after going into the lobby to wait, Officer Patterson came into the lobby. When he saw me he said, "Hempstead, Hempstead, Hempstead, what's going on?"

I responded, "I'm sure you already know, so there's no reason to act like you don't."

He said, "Why did you do it?"

I responded, "Because it was the right thing to do."

He said, "I know you remember seeing me the night Rainey died. You know, I wasn't working in the TCU? I was working in the medical department. When I heard the call over the radio, I went to Wing J-3 to see what was going on."

I responded, "I know you weren't posted in the TCU that night."

He said, "Did you say my name to anybody?"

I responded, "You mean about how you used to starve and physically abuse mentally disabled inmates?"

He said, "I didn't do that. What are you trying to get from all this? Are you trying to get help on the case you're in prison for?"

I responded, "I'm not trying to get anything but justice for Rainey and help for the mentally disabled inmates. If you knew the law, you would know I can't get any help on my criminal case for doing what I'm doing. You know, some people really believe there's a right and wrong. For years I worked around you guys, constantly talking with all of you about the Bible, and trying to get you guys to stop doing the things you were doing. You should have known I was opposed to your actions. God obviously blinded you for a reason."

He said, "I didn't do anything. I'm a good guy. If you are going to do anything, you should focus on the Rainey incident."

Right around that time, count was cleared, so I ended the conversation with Officer Patterson and returned to my cell.

When I got to my cell, it was ransacked. My cellmate was trying to put everything in order. Several inmates in the wing said they didn't think I was coming back. I quickly organized my property and put it back in my locker so I could go to dinner. The wing I lived in was about to be called for dinner chow.

I didn't call Windy to let her know I was OK. I knew that Captain Green only allowed me to leave his office and return to my wing because he wanted me to call her and tell her I was alright. He thought if he let me call her, it would keep his name out of an e-mail to the Governor. I wanted Windy to have all the time she could to get me help. I knew the clock was counting down, and I didn't know what was going to happen.

When dinner chow was called, I left with the other inmates in my wing to go to eat. When I got outside my dorm, Inmates

Alford L. and both Michaels were waiting for me. Alford L. said, "We heard Sergeant Fanfan came and got you. Are you OK?"

I responded, "Yeah, they'll probably be coming back to get me before the night's over."

Michael W. said, "That's retaliation. If they do anything other than leave you alone, it's retaliation."

I responded, "They will have criminal and civil liability if anything happens to me."

As we were in the chow hall line getting close to the window to get our trays, I saw Sergeant Padaroia go into the building where the captain's office was located. A minute or two later, he left the captain's office, went into the chow hall, walked up to me and said, "What happened to your wrist?"

My wrist had been in an ace bandage since the nurse and doctor both said they thought it was broken.

I responded, "I fell down some stairs."

He said, "OK." He then left the chow hall. I noticed him stop about 10 feet outside the chow hall exit door and put on his gloves.

I told Alford L. and both Michaels, "Padaroia's waiting there for me. When I leave, he's going to take me in."

Michael S. said, "Here, you can have my dinner. I know you won't be able to eat if they place you in confinement." Alford L. and Michael W. then gave me their food and told me I needed to eat as much as possible. Both Michaels left and Alford L. stayed and talked with me until I was done eating. When I was finished, he said he was going to wait to see if Sergeant Padaroia stopped me when I walked out of the chow hall. As I got up to leave, I told him, "I pray that God takes care of you and the Recreation Yard Church."

Alford L. said, "I pray that God protects you."

As I walked out of the chow hall, Sergeant Padaroia said, "Hempstead. I hate to do this to you, but I have to put you in handcuffs. The captain wants to see you."

I responded, "I just left the captain's office 20 minutes ago. What is going on has nothing to do with you Padaroia."

He said, "The captain wants to see you again. I'm sorry Hempstead. I don't want anything to do with what's going on, but I have to do my job. The captain's my supervisor, and he told me to bring you to him in handcuffs."

I responded, "I understand. Thank you for allowing me to eat my dinner and for not getting me from the chow hall."

He said, "I wanted to make sure you had your dinner. I know your wrist might be broken, so I'll be easy with the handcuffs on that wrist."

I responded, "I appreciate that." After being placed in handcuffs, I was escorted back to the captain's office.

When I entered the captain's office, Captain Green said, "It came down from up top. You're going to confinement."

I responded, "I didn't call my sister because I knew what you were going to do. You do know that in the last e-mail my sister sent the Florida Governor, she told him that staff here were going to place me in confinement as retaliation, so by placing me in confinement you're doing exactly what she told the Governor you were going to do!"

He said, "If you didn't want to go to confinement, you should have kept your mouth shut and not go snitching to the media and police. Confinement is only the beginning of it. If I could have my way, you would be in Alaska where we don't have to worry anymore about you snitching to the media and police in Dade County. Sergeant, get him out of here!"

I was taken to the medical department to receive a pre-confinement evaluation. When the nurse took my vitals, he asked, "Are you OK? Your blood pressure's a little high."

I responded, "If you knew how my last two days have been, and what could happen over the next few hours, you would know why my blood pressure is high."

He said, "Do you know how to go medical emergency and access sick-call?"

I responded, "Yes." We then left the medical department and Sergeant Padaroia escorted me to the confinement unit.

On the way to confinement, I thought about what Nurse Kind had said about falling down and faking like I was having problems walking if I ever got put in a situation where I was being taken to confinement. A lot of me wanted to do what she recommended, but I couldn't. I didn't want to be subjected to any type of physical abuse, but if it was God's will that I suffer to help others, then I had to submit to His will.

I thought about Jesus' prayer in the Garden of Gethsemane. In His human nature, He didn't want to bear the suffering that awaited Him. The suffering that He was to face was so severe that He even said that His soul was, "Exceedingly sorrowful, even to death"[1].

Jesus then said the words that were real personal to me on May 19, 2014. The Bible says, Jesus, "Fell on His face, and prayed saying, "O my Father, if it is possible, let this cup pass from me; nevertheless, not as I will, but as you will."[2]. These words of Jesus were personal to me, because I understood that it was my duty to have faith in God and submit to His will no matter what, even if it meant me suffering.

Sergeant Padaroia escorted me to the F-Dorm Confinement Unit, and I was placed in a shower so that I could be searched.

Since Sergeant Lewis was the confinement sergeant, he came down from the F-Dorm Officers' Station and took custody of me from Sergeant Padaroia. When Padaroia left the wing, I told Sergeant Lewis, "What's going on so far has nothing to do with you. You give every inmate who comes to confinement a booking call. Are you going to treat me like other inmates and give me a booking call, or are you going to retaliate against me and not give me one?"

He said, "I'm going to treat you like the other inmates and give you a booking call. Now you know the captain don't want you on the phone, so you're going to have to be quick. How long are you going to need?"

I responded, "About five or 10 minutes at the most."

He said, "I'm going to handcuff you in front. Come on, you got to use a phone in Wing 2. The phones in this wing are broke." He then took me to Wing 2. I wanted Windy to know I was still alive, and to make sure she knew I was being processed into confinement.

When Windy answered the phone, she said, "Are you OK?"

I responded, "Yes. They're processing me into confinement. Please do what you can to have me out of here as quick as possible."

She said, "I've already sent some e-mails. I'm talking with Casey. I'm going to e-mail the Governor again. I'll have you out of there soon. Hang in there."

After being on the telephone with her for two or three minutes, the booth officer started flashing Sergeant Lewis and me with a flashlight. She then yelled over the intercom, "The captain's at the front door."

Sergeant Lewis then said, "Hempstead you have to hang up. If the captain catches you on the phone, I'm going to lose my job. I'll let you call her back." I told Windy, I had to go because the captain was coming, but that I would call her back. After I got off the phone, Lewis and I rushed back to Wing 3 and I got back into the shower. As soon as I got in the shower, Lewis told the booth officer to let the captain in the front door.

When the captain came in, he gave a camcorder to Officer Pena and told him to turn it on and film him. When the camcorder was on and aimed at him, the captain said, "My name is Captain Green. The date is May 19, 2014." After Officer Pena stated the time, Captain Green came over to the shower I was in, put a shower guard in front of the shower and told me to strip. The shower guard was so the camcorder couldn't see the lower part of my body. After I was strip searched, I was taken out of the shower and escorted with the camcorder recording me to the security building.

When we arrived at the security building, I was placed in a holding cell. Captain Green then told Officer Pena, "The camcorder has to stay on Hempstead. Do not allow the camera to stop filming him for any reason. Tallahassee said keep a camera on him. Additionally, don't say anything to him." For the next three hours, I sat in that holding cell.

Around 8:45 pm, Captain Knight came into the hallway in front of the holding cell and said, "The van's here to get him." I was then taken out of the holding cell and escorted to a van. I was told that all my personal property was on the van. Later on, I found out that my law work that was in the law library was not on the van. It took about two weeks to get it mailed to me.

After being placed in the van, I noticed that the officer with the camcorder got into the van and continued filming until we left Dade CI and drove away.

390) Did you feel that God stopped your placement in confinement on May 19, 2014?

Yes. My years of experience working for staff as their orderly caused me to believe that if I was placed in confinement, there was a high likelihood that I would be subjected to some type of abuse and possibly more. That is why I was so concerned about going to confinement. My wrist was broken. I knew I couldn't do anything to physically defend myself because of my wrist. If there were any attempts to physically harm me, I would have had to focus on protecting my wrist. Accordingly, I had to have faith that God would protect me.

When I was being escorted to confinement, I wanted to fake a fall and the medical problems that Nurse Kind recommended, but I couldn't. I had faith that God was in sovereign control and that whatever happened was His will. I knew I was Biblically commanded to submit to God's decretive will, which I couldn't change no matter what I did. When I ended up not being processed into confinement but instead being emergency transferred, it gave me joy that God gave me the grace to trust Him in that stressful and trying time. I also believed that God gave me the strength and courage I had to be bold in my speech and actions, all the time I was at Dade CI.

391) What were you thinking as you were being driven away from Dade CI?

I thought about the staff and inmates who helped me during that incarceration at Dade CI. I believe God moved them to help me in the ways they did. I am very thankful for all of them. They all helped me so much at a time in my life when not only I needed them, but others needed them as well.

I was happy about leaving there, but I was concerned about where I was going.

I was also concerned about my sister Windy. I thought about how my loving sister was probably very worried about my safety and health. However, when I thought of Windy, my only comfort was knowing that her worry and fear would not demobilize her. Her concern would spur her onward, would cause her to be more proactive.

Chapter 17: Suwanee CI Annex (May, June 2014) and Columbia CI (June 2014-September 2015)

392) Tell me about your arrival at the Suwannee CI Annex.

We arrived at about 5:00 am. A female captain and several officers were there waiting for us in the gate area. One of the officers was holding a camcorder with a light on it, which he had aimed toward the van.

The captain directed one of the transport officers to open the back of the van where I was seated. After the officer opened the door, the captain said, "What is your name, DC number, and county of conviction?" She held my file and a picture of me in front of her. The answers to her questions were in my file. After I answered her initial questions, she asked if I was physically harmed or threatened and if I had any bruises on me.

I answered all of her questions, and the officer shut the door. Then the camera officer asked, "Captain, do I shut off the camera now?"

The captain said, "No, you have to keep the camera pointed at the van. When it gets to the confinement unit, you have to record Hempstead getting out of the van, then everything that happens with him until he's placed in a confinement cell." The captain then told the transport officers, "See that building over there? When this gate opens, I need you to drive as slow as possible to that building. My officer needs to jog next to the van while keeping the camcorder pointed at the van. The camera can't be taken off Hempstead."

The transport officers said, "OK." The gate opened, and the transport officers drove slowly forward. The officer with the camcorder jogged next to the van, all the while, pointing the camcorder at the van.

After arriving at the confinement unit, I was escorted from the van to a holding cell. There I was interviewed by a nurse. I told the nurse that I had had x-rays taken of my right wrist prior to leaving Dade CI because a doctor and a nurse said they thought it was broken. I told her I was never informed about the results of the x-rays. Finally, I told the nurse I was on a Low Residue Diet because of problems I had with digesting of certain foods, that I had a pass for a lower bunk and back brace because I had a reduced lordosis and lower back damage, and that I was prescribed pain medicine for my right wrist and damaged back.

After talking with the nurse, I was placed in a confinement cell without any pain medicine and without my back brace. The camera officer stopped filming me once I was in my cell. Finally, a big sign was placed on my cell door that said, "House Alone."

393) Tell me about the conditions at Suwanee CI Annex.

Around 9:00 am on my first day there, the warden came to my cell and said, "Your sister has been e-mailing me all night. I called her and told her that I would personally check on you and make sure you're OK. I'm going to make sure you don't have any problems while you're here. Have you had any since you arrived here?"

I responded, "No. I need my property, pain medicine, and back brace."

He said, "I'll see what I can do about those things."

While I was incarcerated there, I never received any pain medicine, my Low Residue Diet, or my back brace, but I did eventually receive my property.

Throughout the approximately five weeks I was housed in the confinement unit, I witnessed multiple incidents of security staff physically battering inmates. I also witnessed security staff placing physically aggressive inmates in the same cells with sex offenders. This was done so the aggressive inmates would physically batter the sex offenders, and take their food from their trays.

Most of the time I was there, I studied the Bible, prayed, wrote letters, and slept.

394) Did you speak with Windy while you were at Suwanee?

Yes, within two days of my arrival to Suwanee CI Annex, Windy got the warden to let me talk to her on the phone. When I talked with Windy on the phone, she asked, "Did they hurt you?"

I responded, "No, I'm OK. I'm on house-alone-status, and I haven't had any physical issues since I've been here."

She said, "There's a lot going on out here. The *Miami Herald* has published a lot of articles, and other newspapers have too. Did the warden talk to you? He told me he did."

I responded, "Yes. He came to see me. How is mom doing? Does she know what's going on? Please tell her I'm OK and that I love her, and give her my address."

She said, "I already gave it to her. She knows you're OK, and she knows what's going on. She said she wrote you this morning." After talking for about five minutes, we had to end the call. I was able to speak to Windy again after

About two weeks later, the warden gave me the approval to speak with Windy again.

395) Were you interviewed by a Disability Rights Florida attorney?

Yes. Around the end of May 2014, I received a letter from Disability Rights Florida saying one of their lawyers would be traveling to Suwanee CI Annex to talk with me. At the beginning of June 2014, I was told to get ready to go talk to a visitor. I was handcuffed, and escorted to the visiting area.

About five minutes later, a woman came to me and introduced herself as "Molly Paris," a civil rights attorney with Disability Rights Florida. She said her organization and Florida Legal Services were investigating the Dade CI TCU. She and her co-workers had read the *Miami Herald* articles, and she wanted to know if I would tell her all I knew about what happened to Darren Rainey, the *Hot-Water-Shower* treatment, and the abuse of the mentally disabled inmates at Dade CI TCU. Over the next two hours, I told her everything she wanted to know. I also gave her all the grievances I filed on the matters she asked about. They were the same grievances I gave to the *Miami Herald* representative to review.

Ms. Paris promised to return them once she was done them. She also told me that she and others had already been inside the TCU investigating the conditions. They were attempting to decide if they had enough evidence to file a class action lawsuit challenging the unconstitutional conditions at the TCU. Ms. Paris gave me her business card so I could write to her with more information.

396) Did Miami Dade Police Department detectives interview you a second time?

Yes. After my meeting with Ms. Paris was over, I was escorted back to my confinement cell. After lunch, I was told to get ready again, because I had some more visitors. This time I was taken to the assistant inspector general's office who told me two detectives would soon be there to talk with me. Within minutes, Miami-Dade Police Department Detectives Wilbert Sanchez and Daniel Aiken showed up to talk with me about the Darren Rainey case.

After Detective Sanchez told me they were there investigating the Rainey case, I responded, "You told me that in April 2014." When I saw he planned to record my statement, I asked him if the *Miami Herald* articles got the detectives in trouble and if news articles were why they were finally starting an investigation into Rainey's death. During my recorded statement, Detective Sanchez asked me questions concerning matters I already explained in my prior letters to him and in my interview with him. During the interview, he also tried to limit what I said, just like my last conversation with him.

I do not think Detective Sanchez ever wanted the truth. Both of the times he interviewed me, it seemed he was trying to make sure nobody was prosecuted for what happened to Darren Rainey. This interview lasted about an hour, and I was then escorted back to my confinement cell.

397) Were you also interviewed by the Inspector General's Office?

Yes. While incarcerated at Suwannee Annex, I was also interviewed by an assistant inspector general about the retaliation I was subjected to by Sergeant Nickolis, Officer Edwards, and the other officer at Dade CI.

398) Tell me about being placed on protective management and about your transfer to Columbia CI Protective Management Unit?

Around June 10, 2014, security staff told me my status was switched from "pending investigation" to "pending protective management review." As soon as I heard this, I knew I was going to be recommended for placement in a protective management unit. I immediately submitted some request forms and a grievance stating my desire not to be placed in a protective management unit.

A few days later, an officer came to my cell and told me to get ready to see the Institutional Classification Team. When I went in front of them, the classification supervisor said, "Hempstead, we're going to recommend you be placed in a protective management unit."

I responded, "I've been on protective management status before, I don't want to go back on it."

The warden said, "Hempstead, you need to go on it. It's for your own good."

The classification supervisor said, "If you have any issues, you can take them up with the state classification officer. He'll be around to see you. That is it. You may leave."

The state classification officer never came to see me. I submitted several request forms and grievances on the Institutional Classification Team's recommendation to place me on protective management status. However, on June 20, I was transferred from Suwannee CI Annex to the Columbia CI Protective Management Unit.

399) What is protective management status?

FAC 33-602.221 (1) (J) defines protective management as, "A special management status for the protection of inmates from other inmates in an environment as representative of that of the general population as is safely possible."

FAC 33-602.220 (3) (c) 3 lists seven reasons why an inmate can be placed on protective management status. This rule states in part: "The following elements shall be considered in determining whether protective management is necessary:

- A record of having been assaulted;
- A reputation among the inmate population, attested to in writing by staff, as an informant or trial witness;
- Verified threats, verbal abuse, or harassment;
- A former criminal justice activity resulting in verified threats, verbal abuse, or harassment;
- A conviction of a crime repugnant to the inmate population;
- Reliable confirmed evidence of sexual harassment;
- Other factors such as physical size, build and age producing a risk from the inmate general population."

400) Did the Columbia CI Protective Management Unit house inmates who should not have been there?

Yes. There were two types of inmates housed in the protective management unit. The first group included inmates who met one or more of the above qualifications including former law enforcement officers, ex-government employees, ex-confidential informants, transgender, petite inmates, serial sex offenders, inmates who had a history of being raped in general population, and high profile inmates.

The second group who consisted of inmates who did not qualify for protective management. They were gang members, identified predators, potential predators, high aggressive risk inmates, and moderate aggressive risk inmates. These were the inmates who didn't qualify to be in the protective management unit.

401) Tell me a little about Columbia CI and its Protective Management Unit.

Columbia CI is located in Lake City, Columbia County, Florida. It was a close management/security threat dumping ground just like the Suwanee CI Annex. It was also a Psych.3 institution with a long history of being in the top five most violent institutions in the FDC. I was previously incarcerated there in 2003. While I was there in 2003, I worked as a special housing orderly in their Close Management Unit.

The Columbia CI compound consisted of two sections. Section one contained the security building, visitation park, chapel, library and law library, education department, laundry building, medical and classification building, chow hall, Y-dorm, and a gun tower. Y-dorm was also referred to as the Protective Management Unit.

A center gate separated section one from section two. An officers' shack and gun tower were located at the center gate. Section two consisted of eight housing dorms, four canteen windows, two barber shops, and a recreational yard.

The protective management unit (Y-dorm) was behind the medical and classification building in section one. It had a fence around it. The building was originally constructed to be used as a disciplinary confinement unit. Inside the protective management unit, there were four wings of cells, two small wings with seven cells per wing for a total of 14 cells, and two long wings with 16 cells each, for a total of 32 cells. There were 46 cells altogether, 44 housed two men and two of the cells housed only one man. The single man cells were for inmates in wheelchairs.

There were two showers on the small wings and four on the long wings. The building was not air-conditioned, and none of the cells had windows. There were two fans on each wing for a total of 8 fans. There were two telephones where inmates could make collect calls and one television. The day room held approximately 30 inmates. The officers' station was air-conditioned. A holding cell and a staff bathroom were in front of the officers' station, as was, a kiosk machine for inmates to download songs that they purchased for their MP3s and MP4s.

The recreational yard for the protective management inmates was directly behind it. It was about the size of four basketball courts and had a half-court basketball court, two park benches, one pull-up bar, one set of dip-bars, and a volleyball net. There were no shaded areas on the recreational yard.

402) Will you tell me about your first week in the Columbia CI Protective Management Unit?

Within five minutes of my arrival, I was escorted from the transport van to the medical building. Inmates in the FDC are required to see a nurse upon their arrival to an institution. When I was talking to the nurse, the officer escorting me said my property had to be taken to the property room. I knew what he said was false. He was trying to get my property out of my possession for some reason. I looked at the time on my watch and the name on the officer's shirt. The medical department had mounted security cameras. If anything improper happened, I knew the officer's name, and I had the camera footage as evidence that he was the officer who took my property from me.

When I was finished with medical staff, I was escorted to the protective management unit. As soon as I entered the unit, I was overtaken by the tremendous heat in the building. It was easily 20 degrees hotter in the unit than it was outside.

I was left with Sergeant Harris, the supervisor of the Protective Management Unit for that shift. The first thing Sergeant Harris said was, "Where is your property?"

I responded, "The officer who escorted me to the medical department said my property had to go to the property room."

He said, "Your property was supposed to come here with you, so I can inventory it. I'll get it for you." I told him the name of the officer who took my property. Sergeant Harris said I was assigned to cell Y2-117, the first cell in front of a mounted camera at the end of one of the long wings.

My immediate concern was calling Windy to see how she was doing, catch her up to date with everything that had happened with me, and inquire about what was going on in society with the Darren Rainey case and Dade CI.

I engaged in small talk with several inmates over my first few hours there. I found out the protective management unit was rife with homosexual activity, more so than in the general population. Several inmates told me that, every Friday, the majority of the inmates in the unit celebrated, "Freaky Friday," and, every Saturday, they celebrated, "No Panties Saturday." They said the unit was full of gang members and violent inmates; that many of the inmates in the unit were biased against inmates who filed grievances; and that several inmates in the unit would place contraband in other inmates' cells for security staff. At that time, none of the inmates knew anything about me or my past.

Sergeant Harris got my property for me around 3:00 pm. When he saw all my Christian books, he said, "Are you Christian?"

I responded, "Yes. Are you?"

He said, "Yes, I couldn't be anything but a Christian. Jesus has blessed me tremendously."

I responded, "If it's OK, may I ask what denomination?"

He said, "Pentecostal. I believe in the gifts."

I responded, "I've known a lot of Pentecostals in my life. Several of them have shown me great kindness and love."

He said, "What about you?"

I responded, "I'm Presbyterian in America."

He said, "We're going to have to get together and talk a little bit every now and then."

I responded, "I would love that."

After the next count, we went to dinner. The food in the chow hall there was fairly good.

After dinner, I was finally able to reach Windy on the phone. It was nice to hear her voice and hear that she, my mom, and the family were OK. After Windy told me these things, she said, "So much has been going on. First, Casey wants you to add him to your phone list. He and Julie   want to talk with you more about the Rainey case and Dade CI." After she gave me his phone number, she said, "Now let me tell you everything going on in the media. The *Miami Herald* has published dozens of articles on Rainey, Dade CI, and other deaths and problems at other institutions in Florida. All of the articles that they have published on the Florida prison system have also been republished by numerous other newspapers and TV news stations."

"Additionally, I've been talking with people from other states about the Rainey case and you. Do you know that when the *Miami Herald* published their first article on the Rainey case, people across America started e-mailing the Governor asking him to have you transferred from Dade CI for your protection? The lady who owns Dog Justice for the Mentally Ill posted a notice on her blog asking everybody who read her blog and listened to her radio show to e-mail the Florida Governor and ask him to transfer you from Dade CI and to protect you. Her radio station is also called Dog Justice for the Mentally Ill. I've been talking with her. She's really nice. She wants to do everything she can to help out."

"Oh, Yeah, I almost forgot to tell you. Julie spoke with inmate Mark Joiner. Joiner is there at Columbia CI. Have you seen him?"

I responded, "No. He must be in general population. If he is in population, I probably won't see him. Protective management inmates are not supposed to have contact with general population inmates."

She said, "Julie's about to release an article on her interview with Joiner. I think she's also trying to talk with Daniel Medberry."

"Do you know George Mallinckrodt?"

I responded, "Yes, why?"

She said, "I've talked to him several times. He released a book called, *Getting Away with Murder*. Mallinckrodt said your name's in his book and that the book has to do with the Rainey case and the TCU. I'm going to buy a copy of it for me, and one for you."

I responded, "Mallinckrodt wants to sell us copies of his book?"

She said, "Yes, I already know what you're thinking. If he wants me to pay for the copies, I'll pay for them."

I responded, "How did he write a book on the Rainey case when he wasn't working in the TCU when it happened? How can he write a book on what he doesn't know about?"

She said, "I don't know, but we'll find out soon!"

I responded, "Be careful when you talk to him. Don't volunteer any information to him. I'll tell you more about Mallinckrodt in futures calls. Will you do me a favor and mail me copies of all the *Miami Herald* articles and any other article you want to send?"

She said, "Yes." During that conversation, I told Windy the things I heard about the protective management unit. I also told her about the heat and lack of ventilation.

During that first day, I noticed that most of the time, inmates only wore their boxers or a pair of shorts when they were inside the unit. It was too hot to wear the clothing specified by FDC rules. Several inmates told me that, because of the heat, I would never get to sleep if I slept in my bunk. They said the only way to get to sleep was to lay on the floor, to wear only shorts or boxers, and to put wet washcloths or towels on my chest, neck, and so on. They said the cold, wet towel would aid in keeping me cool and that I could use the washcloth or towel to wipe the sweat off myself throughout the night.

Around 8:00 pm that night, homosexual activities became very prevalent. Numerous inmates were French kissing other inmates, sexually related noises were being made by several inmates on the wing, and inmates who were walking down the wing moved to positions from which they could view the homosexual activities occurring in cells. After those things started, I didn't leave my cell for the rest of the night.

On my first night, I remember thinking, "Where did they send me?" The extreme heat made me think about hell, and the homosexual activity made me think of Sodom and Gomorrah. I laid on the floor that night in just a pair of shorts with two wet washcloths. I tried to sleep. But it was so hot. I literally got no sleep.

When the cell doors were opened for breakfast, I drank two strong cups of coffee to try to fight the tiredness. In certain environments in prison, an inmate needs to be at his sharpest mentally. The Columbia CI Protective Management Unit was that type of environment.

Throughout day two, the inmates started to learn that I was not their type. In conversations with me, they found out that I wasn't gay and didn't do drugs or smoke cigarettes. I had been in other environments during my incarceration where I stood out as different in comparison with the majority of the inmates, so that wasn't my first time. A Christian should not compromise his morals to please the majority. I knew by standing out from the other inmates, I could become a potential target, but I was willing to accept that. A Christian will sometimes have to suffer for what is right.

During my second day, several inmates found out why I was on protective management status. Security staff told some of them what the internet said about me. The information they had was the type one could find on Google. Security staff did not tell the inmates that my protective management paperwork stated, "confirmed risk factor established based on inmate's link to high profile investigation." By my third day, everyone knew why I was on protective management.

On my third night in the protective management unit, my cell was searched by a large Spanish officer. During that search, he took four or five of my Christian books, two autopsy reports, and several face sheets of inmates. About 30 minutes after the search, I was called into the officers' station. The officer who searched my cell said, "I've searched a lot of cells over my time working in FDC, and I've never found face sheets and autopsy reports. Why do you have these things in your cell?"

I responded, "The face sheets are part of the discovery in a federal lawsuit I filed in 2007. A federal judge ordered the Florida Attorney General's office to provide me with them. The autopsy reports are from dead inmates who were housed in Dade CI's TCU. It's my position that those inmates died from starvation. I'm sure you already know I'm on protective management for my communications with the media and law enforcement about matters relating to the Dade CI TCU."

He said, "I'm going to call the captain and see what he says. If he says to give you the papers back, I will. Go wait outside for a minute." I then left the officers' station as he directed. When he called me back into the station, the officer said, "The captain said to give you the papers back. The books I took from your cell, I'm going to send to the property room as confiscated. Your name and DC number are not written on them."

I responded, "Sir, if I may? The property rule says that an inmate is not supposed to alter the condition of the property he buys from the condition it's purchased in. If I put my name on my books, the books would then be altered. You're taking my books from me because I followed the rule and didn't alter them."

He said, "You're going to have to take that up with the property room." When our conversation was over, I took the paperwork he had returned back to my cell.

On my fourth day, someone went into my cell and stole my battery operated shaver, Sony radio and earbuds, two packs of batteries, and a bag of coffee. I had been incarcerated at the worst institution in the FDC; I had been housed at approximately 22 institutions in the Florida prison system, and I never had any of my property stolen prior to that incident.

That night I started thinking about how I had to try to get out of that protective management unit.

The next day, when Sergeant Harris did his morning count, I stopped him and said, "Sergeant Harris, I can't continue to take the heat and other conditions in this place. I need to talk to somebody."

He said, "Let me finish my count, and I'll call you to the officers' station to talk."

When he called me to the officers, station, he said, "What's going on?"

I responded, "For the last several years, I have dealt with very bad conditions at Dade CI. I never thought that I would be sent to a place as bad as this. I did not even think a place like this, with these types of conditions existed. I want to transfer from here."

He said, "I'll call whoever you want me to call on this compound and tell them you want to talk to them. If I can recommend somebody, I recommend Dr. G. who is a Christian. She may be able to help you."

I responded, "Will you call her for me?"

He said, "Yes." He called her and told me she would come to the protective management unit in about 20 minutes to talk with me.

When Dr. G. arrived, I spoke with her in the day room in the protective management unit. We sat down at the table, and she said, "Sergeant Harris said you wanted to talk with me."

I responded, "Yes. Do you know why I'm on protective management status?"

She said, "Yes. You're the inmate who spoke with the *Miami Herald* about the Darren Rainey case and the abuse in the TCU at Dade CI. You did the right thing. When I heard you were here, I hoped I would get a chance to talk to you. How are you doing?"

I responded, "I'm OK, but I have an issue. I was on protective management status years ago, and I had myself removed from it because I did not want to be on it. I did not want to be on it then, and I do not want to be on it now. I believe I was placed on this status as punishment for asserting my First Amendment rights to communicate with the media and law enforcement about the Darren Rainey case, and Dade CI.

"This place is obviously punishment. It's unconstitutionally hot, and it's full of homosexuals, predators, gang members, and thieves. We have barely any privileges, and the list goes on."

She said, "You know this is a bad place. Bad things happen to inmates here. I don't think you should be on this compound."

I responded, "I agree, but how can I get transferred from here?"

She said, "The only two quick ways are by medical and mental health transfers. Do you have any medical problems?"

I responded, "I have a hurt wrist which I've been told is probably broken. I also have a damaged back and problems digesting certain foods."

She said, "Those things would only get you transferred to Regional Medical Center. That's not a good place either.

I don't know if it'll work, but I can try to get you approved for a TCU. They definitely wouldn't send you to the TCU's at Dade CI or South Florida Reception Center, nor would they send you to any that are for close management inmates. If I could get you approved, you would more than likely go to one of the TCU's at Charlotte CI, Lake CI, Zephyrhills CI, or Regional Medical Center."

I responded, "Regional Medical Center wouldn't be good for me. I had some serious issues with their staff when I was incarcerated there in 2013. If you can get me approved for one the other TCUs, I could probably convince their Institutional Classification Teams to release me from this status."

Dr. G. said, "I don't know for sure if I can get the main office to agree to send you to a TCU. After what you did to the Dade CI TCU, the main office will probably not agree to send you to one, thinking that the media will report about you going to a TCU if you are admitted to one. We can try though. "We're going to have to make it look good. How have you been sleeping?"

I responded, "Not good. It's too hot in here."

278

She said, "Would you have an issue with going to the infirmary for a few days? It's air-conditioned, so you'll be able to catch up on your sleep. Additionally, if you're on infirmary status, it'll be easier for me to try and get you into a TCU."

I responded, "I have no issues with going to an air-conditioned location, and then transferring to another air-conditioned location."

She said, "OK, I just want you to know there's one small issue. Inmates that have tried to get into TCUs in the past usually go to confinement to wait, not the infirmary. I don't think you would be safe in confinement, so I'm going to try and get you placed in the infirmary. If I can get you into the infirmary, you can have to go in one of the cells there because of your protective management status. Both of those infirmary cells currently have inmates in them. I'm going to have to get one of those inmates moved out so I can move you into one of those cells. I have to keep you out of confinement. Inmates die in our confinement, and they are constantly being battered by staff and cellmates. You wouldn't be safe there. Would you have a problem with me asking the warden to issue a memo to keep you in the infirmary, so none of his staff try to move you from the infirmary to confinement?"

I responded, "I don't have any issues with you talking to the warden."

She said, "I'm going to go talk to him. If he issues the memo, I'll have you moved to the infirmary, OK?"

I said, "OK."

The warden issued the memo, and I was moved into an air-conditioned cell in the infirmary by myself. The lack of sleep as a result of the extreme heat in the protective management unit made me so tired that I slept all Friday and Saturday, and only woke up for my meals and to shower.

Late Saturday afternoon, an officer tried to move from the infirmary to the confinement unit. It was the same officer who took my property on my first day at Columbia CI. The officer didn't even ask the medical staff for permission to move me. A nurse noticed him at my cell door placing handcuffs on me through the food flap and said, "You can't move him."

The officer responded, "Why?"

Department of Corruption

The nurse said, "There's a memo here from the warden saying he's not to be moved for any reason."

The officer shut my food flap, went to the nurses' station, and talked briefly with the nurse before leaving the medical department without me.

On Monday morning the inmate in the cell next to me started making a big disturbance. Within a short time, the assistant warden, colonel, captain, and several officers, were in front of my neighbor's cell and my cell. When I saw the colonel, I recognized him from somewhere. I wasn't sure where until I saw "Godwin" on his name tag.

I knew Colonel Godwin when he was a captain at Washington CI Main Unit in 2007. In 2007, a sergeant at Washington CI told me I was on Godwin's "Hit List." At that time, I had a hands-off on me by the colonel at Washington CI, and Godwin didn't like that. Godwin didn't know that Colonel McAlpin had been served with a federal civil rights lawsuit that I filed against him and other staff and that I had Washington CI staff under multiple investigations. Colonel McAlpin did not want any additional liability should something happened to me while I was there; so, he directed all of his staff to leave me alone Eventually, Godwin learned of the lawsuit, which caused him to dislike me even more. In the end, he got wrapped up in an investigation. Even though it was seven years later, I knew Godwin recognized me when he saw me in 2014.

Monday morning, Dr. G. told me that if I wanted to go back to the protective management unit, she would continue trying to convince the FDC's main office to send me to a TCU. She also said that she spoke with a staff member who had made arrangements to put me in a cell closer to a door that led to the recreation yard for the protective management unit. This cell was about 10 feet from the officers' station and on a short wing. Being closer to the door meant I would have better ventilation. The proximity to the officers' station meant most inmates would be deterred from doing anything they weren't supposed to do near my cell. The cell being on a short wing meant there were fewer inmates nearby.

I told Dr. G. I would go back to the protective management unit and wait to see what the main office did about the TCU referral. I was returned to the protective management unit and was assigned to Cell Y2-114. Everything Dr. G. said about the cell was true. However, it was still tremendously hot, and I had a cellmate, the first I had since I transferred from Dade CI.

403) Did Dr. G. leave Columbia CI a few weeks after you met her?

Yes. It was rumored that she was forced to quit; however, I don't know for sure what happened. I have always wondered if whatever happened to her, happened because she tried to help me.

Three weeks after I returned to the protective management unit, I told Columbia CI staff who worked with Dr. G. that I no longer wanted to go to a TCU. I decided I didn't want to go to a TCU because I did not qualify to be in one and felt it would have been manipulation if I went to one.

404) Was your first cellmate at Columbia CI battered by gang members in your cell?

Yes. My first cellmate was in his twenties and about to be released to society. He was my cellmate for only a week or so. He told me he was on protective management because he had protection problems with the Latin Kings gang. He was a drug addict who was getting drugs from inmates in the unit and not paying them. Most of the inmates he was getting drugs from were members of the Latin Kings gang.

When Latin Kings found out my cellmate was on protective management from the Latin Kings, four of five of them, one of whom had a shank (prison knife) came to my cell and badly beat him right in front of me. A lot of his blood was on the floor of our cell. Several staff members quickly responded and broke up the beating.

I was supposed to be on protective management status for my protection, and the first cellmate I had was jumped by multiple gang members with a shank in front of me and in the cell I lived in.

After this incident, I started thinking about how absurd it was to house gang members in a protective management unit with ex-law enforcement officers, confidential informants, government officials, and with inmates who were on protective management specifically to protect them from gang violence. I believe the FDC knew they were violating their 8th Amendment Constitutional duty to protect the above classes of inmates from harm by housing them in the same unit with gang members who wanted to harm them. I began to think that I should take some type of legal action to help protect the inmates in the protective management unit from the gang members housed with them.

405) Tell me about the gang activity you witnessed at the Columbia CI Protective Management Unit.

When I arrived, there were approximately two dozen gang members among the roughly 80 inmates housed in that protective management unit. There were inmates actively representing Folk Nation, Latin Kings, Crips, Bloods, as well as, other gangs. They were constantly fighting each other and battering inmates who weren't gang affiliated. On numerous occasions, they were involved with multiple fights in one day. Gang members were most widely known for extorting the physically weak inmates housed there.

What confused me was, why did the FDC have the gang members housed in protective management status when they were, by rule, supposed to be housed in close management status? FAC 33-601.800(1)(D) defines "close management" as "The confinement of an inmate apart from the general population, for reasons of security or the order and effective management of the institution, where the inmate, through his or her behavior, has demonstrated an inability to live in general population without abusing the rights and privileges of others."

In the FDC, gangs are considered, "security threat groups." FAC 33-601.800(1) (S) defines "security threat group" as a "former or ongoing inmate/offender, group, gang, organization, or association consisting of three or more members who have:

- A common name or common identifying signs, colors, or symbols;
- Members or associates who individually or collectively engage in or have engaged in a pattern of gang activity, criminal activity, or department rule violations; or who have the

282

- Potential to act in concert to pose a threat or potential threat to the public, staff, visitors, other inmates or offenders, or the secure and orderly operations of an institution, probation office, other department property, or department activity or function."

FAC 33-601.800(2) (A) 2.N states that inmates who are gang/security threat group leaders are to be placed on close management one. FAC 33-601.800(2) (C) 2.G states that all validated gang members are to be placed on close management three.

The problem with gang members victimizing inmates in protective management unit weighed on my heart. I had to do something to help the victims and potential victims housed in the Protective Management Unit.

406) Please tell me about your second cellmate, Timothy Jones.

My second cellmate, Timothy Jones, was from Tampa, Florida and was in prison for first-degree murder. When he was in society, he would get high on crystal methamphetamine and crack cocaine. When he ran out of drugs, he would go into the crack infested neighborhoods and rob drug dealers. He drove into the bad neighborhoods and acted like he was there to buy crack. If a dealer walked up to Jones' vehicle alone and handed him some crack, Jones would either shoot the dealer or quickly stab a knife into the dealer's stomach or chest. Jones then sped off with the drugs. He did this for a long time before he was finally caught and arrested for first-degree murder. Jones loved to use drugs that made him speed.

Within a day of becoming my cellmate, he was buying mental health medications off several inmates in the protective management unit.

Inmates in the FDC who are prescribed mental health medications receive their meds in "single dose" units, that is, a nurse gives the inmate the dose prescribed for him at the time he is prescribed to take it. Several types of these mental health drugs can cause a person to speed if taken in large doses. For instance, a number of inmates crushed Wellbutrin into powder and snorted it.

They said it gave them a high just like powdered cocaine, and they called it "chain-gang-coke."

Jones loved Zoloft. He said it was like crystal methamphetamine when he consumed it in large quantities. When he first became my cellmate, he couldn't obtain enough Zoloft to get high. For this reason, he just bought whatever mental health medications and street drugs he could obtain.

Over his first several weeks in my cell, I saw him consume 20 to 50 pills at a time. He first consumed large doses of pills that made him speed. When he was done speeding, he would take multiple large doses of pills to make himself hallucinate. Jones usually stayed awake for three to seven days at a time, and then he slept for a day or more straight.

Jones was also a Satanist. All the time we were cellmates and I was sleeping, Jones was awake and either high, speeding, or hallucinating in our cell.

The FDC said they were protecting me, but they had me housed in a cell with a drug-addicted satanic murderer who would stay awake for days speeding and/or hallucinating on medications and other drugs.

Within a few weeks of him being in my cell, he overdosed. Security and medical staff rushed him to the infirmary and then to a hospital to have his stomach pumped. He was then taken back to Columbia CI and placed in mental health observation and then confinement. He became my cellmate for a second time when he was released from confinement.

407) Was Timothy Story your third cellmate in the protective management unit?

Yes, Timothy Story was transferred to Columbia CI from the Martin Correction Institution Protective Management Unit. He said he was surprised he wasn't put in confinement because he had been in confinement at Martin CI for possession of narcotics (K-2). He was a heavy user of K-2, and he owed a lot of money to inmates at the Martin unit. Story didn't have the money to pay them, so he told his classification officer that he had a problem with smoking K-2 and that there was too much of it in the Martin CI Protective Management Unit. His classification officer wrote him a disciplinary report for possession of narcotics for admitting the use of K-2. Since Story admitted smoking K-2, that meant he admitted possessing it. Before he could go to court for the disciplinary report, he was transferred to Columbia CI.

After Story volunteered this information, I asked him what he was in prison for. When he said he was in prison for murder, I thought, "Another drug addicted killer as a cellmate." I also learned that the Columbia CI Classification Officer, Ms. Glass, disposed of Story's narcotics disciplinary report so she could place him in a cell with me.

All the time Story was my cellmate, he spent his time getting high on K-2. I have seen many inmates who are high on K-2 get very violent and have all types of hallucinations.

Story was only my cellmate for about two months. He signed out of protective management because he felt that the inmates he owed money to at Martin CI would transfer to the Columbia CI Protective Management Unit and try to kill him. From my understanding, he owed close to a thousand dollars to inmates at Martin CI for drugs.

408) Did Timothy Jones become your cellmate again?

Yes, Timothy Jones got placed back in my cell when he was released from confinement. He started getting high on pills his first day back in my cell, and I called Windy to tell her about it. I didn't tell her about Jones before because I was trying to deal with it myself and did not want to add more to Windy's plate. At that time, Windy was dealing with multiple problems in the FDC. She was in almost constant communications with media, bloggers and civil rights groups about prison conditions, and she was engaged in numerous other activities in an effort to bring reform to the prison system. On top of all these things, she was taking care of our mom and her own family.

When I called Windy about Timothy Jones, I told her all I knew about him and everything that had happened so far. I then said, "I'm concerned about the guy dying in my cell because he won't stop popping pills. I just want you to be aware of what's going on. I'm going to tell Casey and Julie, so they're aware."

She responded, "If you want, I can e-mail somebody there and ask them to move Jones."

I said, "I'll deal with it for now. If it gets worse, then I'll take you up on that offer. I'm going to keep trying to work with him. I'm trying to get him to come to Christ and give up Satan and the drugs. His dad is a Christian."

Jones stayed as my cellmate for several more weeks until he overdosed again. On the night he overdosed, I was in my cell brushing my teeth, while Jones was talking to another inmate. Suddenly, he passed-out, hit the ground, and started flopping like a fish out of water. I immediately ran to get the dorm sergeant. Within two or three minutes, nurses, and several security staff were at my cell. Jones was placed on a stretcher and escorted to medical. About 20 minutes later, I was told by staff that Jones was going to be taken to the outside hospital.

When Jones came back from the outside hospital after overdosing the second time, he was placed in confinement for a month or two. When he was released from confinement, he was again placed back in the cell with me. He continued to use large quantities of pills and constantly stayed high; however, he remained as my cellmate until I was transferred from the Columbia CI Protective Management Unit

409) Did you receive medical care for your broken wrist and other medical issues upon arriving at Columbia CI?

No. I wasn't given any medical care for any of my medical problems until after I filed dozens of grievances about being denied my 8th Amendment Right to Adequate Medical Attention. Over my first about eight months there, I filed 20 to 80 grievances a month about medical staff denying me adequate medical attention, about my placement on protective management, and about matters relating to Dade CI.

About six weeks after I arrived there, I was finally able to convince the doctor to order an x-ray of my right wrist. The x-ray results confirmed that it was broken. I was told that the x-ray they took of my wrist at Dade CI had disappeared.

About six weeks after I arrived at Columbia CI, the doctor ordered that I be placed back on my Low Residue Diet and that my lower bunk and back brace passes be renewed. He also ordered a wrist support and pain medicine for my broken wrist and damaged back.

410) Did you refuse surgery at the Regional Medical Center because of the protection problems you had with staff there?

Yes. When the Columbia CI doctor saw that the x-ray showed my wrist was broken, he referred me to see an orthopedic surgeon at Regional Medical Center. He did not give me any advance notice he was doing this. If he had, I would have told him I didn't want to go to Regional Medical Center for any reason. I mentioned earlier, the last time I was at the Regional Medical Center, staff had threatened me with violence for speaking out about Rainey's death and prescribed a harmful medication for me.

One morning about two weeks after the doctor looked at the x-ray results, I was told to get ready to go on a medical run to see an orthopedic surgeon. However, I wasn't told where.

I was then escorted to a van and transported to Regional Medical Center. When I got there, an orthopedic surgeon examined the x-ray and my wrist. He said my wrist was broken and I needed to have surgery, including a bone graft and, possibly, a screw in my wrist. I agreed because I didn't think it would take place at Regional Medical Center and that I would be awake for the surgery.

We were at the Regional Medical Center for about two hours. While I was there, I saw some of the staff who had problems with me when I was there in 2013.

A few weeks later, I was again told to get ready for a medical run. After getting ready, I was transported from Columbia CI to Regional Medical Center. I was confused as to why I was there. When a nurse told me I was there for wrist surgery and that the medical staff intended to put me under anesthesia, I refused the surgery. I signed a refusal slip and was transported back to Columbia CI.

About ten days later, I was told a third time to get ready to go on a medical run. This time I told security and medical staff at Columbia CI that I wanted to refuse all trips to Regional Medical Center, but the security staff made me go anyway.

When I got to Regional Medical Center, I again signed a refusal. I was concerned about the anesthesia. Some of my close family members were allergic to anesthesia, and I was concerned about my health. Also, the FDC said I had statewide protection issues with prison staff, and I previously had protection problems with Regional Medical Center staff. I was not liked by many of their staff. And I definitely did not want to be put under anesthesia while there.

We were only there for about two hours before returning to Columbia CI.

After my first transport to the Regional Medical Center, I started filing grievances stating I couldn't go there for any reason because I had protection problems with its staff. I wrote that if I had to have the surgery I needed at Regional Medical Center, then I wanted to refuse the surgery. I noted I did not want to go back there for any reason.

About a month later, I was told I was transferring from Columbia CI. When I got on the bus, one of the security staff told me I was transferring to Regional Medical Center. This caused me stress. I didn't know why I was transferring to Regional Medical Center. Having previously been subjected to retaliation there, it was reasonable to say I would be subjected to retaliation again. Since I was on the bus going to the Regional Medical Center, I couldn't do anything but pray.

I remember saying in my prayer, "God, I know beyond doubt that You are sovereign and that nothing happens unless it's Your will. I also know that You make all things work together for Your glory and my good. However, I must admit that I'm stressed. I don't know why I'm transferring to Regional Medical Center. I'm stressed because I previously had problems with the staff there, and I really don't want to have problems with them again. God, only You know all things and only You know if I'm going to be battered or subjected to any type of retaliation. If it's Your will that I suffer in any way for any reason, then I accept Your will and just ask that You give me the grace to not fall under whatever cross You have for me.

"If it's not Your will that these things happen, then I ask that You please help me. God, will You please help me get out of Regional Medical Center as quickly as possible? Additionally, will You please protect me from harm while I'm there."

This is a shortened version of my prayer that morning. This was another incident that I had to trust in God's sovereign will that He would protect me.

After we arrived at Regional Medical Center, the two transport sergeants took me to the new arrival location. When we got there, they took me into an office where a nurse was processing inmates. I sat down in a chair at the nurse's desk, and the nurse asked me several questions that are asked of all new arrivals to an institution. After I answered her questions, she took my vitals. When she was done taking my vitals, she said, "Why is your blood pressure so high? Are you, OK?"

I responded, "No, I'm not OK. I don't want to be here. I'm on protective management status because the main office says I have statewide protection issues with security staff. In 2013, I had protection issues with the staff here. I don't want to be here."

She said, "Do you know what you're here for?"

I responded, "No."

She said, "Let me check." She then looked on the computer and said, "You're here for surgery on your wrist."

I responded, "I refused that surgery two times here and in multiple grievances at Columbia CI."

She said, "If you don't want the surgery and you already signed a refusal, then you don't have any reason to be here. Let me look for the refusals you signed." After she found them, she said, "The refusals are in your file. I don't know why you're here. Do you want me to see if I can get you out of here?"

I responded, "Yes, please."

The nurse then left the office for about five minutes. When she came back into the office, she had the intake sergeant with her. The intake sergeant said, "You're here for wrist surgery. The nurse said you have refusals in your file saying you don't want the surgery. Do you want the surgery?"

I responded, "No, sir."

The intake sergeant then told the sergeants who transported me there, "We have no reason to have him here since he doesn't want the surgery. You can bring him back to where he came from."

One of the transport sergeants said, "We can't do that. The main office approved his transfer here."

The intake sergeant said, "The main office approved his transfer here for wrist surgery. Since he's not having the surgery, he has no reason to be here. Additionally, we don't have a bed to put him in. We need our beds. I'll call the main office and the warden. We don't want him." The transport sergeants then escorted me out of that building, back to the bus, and I was then transferred back to Columbia CI.

That day and the days that followed, I thought about how I had never seen or heard of an institution sending an inmate back to the prison he came from on the day the inmate arrived at an institution. I knew what happened that day was an act of God. It was another incident to add to a long list of incidents that God had saved me from.

I badly wanted to have surgery on my wrist. I just could not have it at Regional Medical Center. When God did not allow me to be processed into Regional Medical Center, it showed me that it was God's will that I not be housed there because my life would have been in danger if I was.

My broken wrist was never repaired while I was incarcerated in the Columbia CI Protective Management Unit.

411) Did someone put a fraudulent document in your medical file to prevent the release of your records?

Yes. Around August 2014, I signed a release of medical records giving the *Miami Herald* permission to purchase all the documents in my medical files they wanted to obtain.

While they were in the process of obtaining my medical files, a document was produced saying I didn't want the *Miami Herald* to have my medical files. The document was not in my writing and was not signed by me. When Casey Frank of the *Miami Herald* received the document, he saw it was not signed and not in my handwriting. By that time, Casey Frank had read hundreds of prison grievances and letters from me. He knew it was a fraud.

The FDC Inspector General's Office claimed they conducted an investigation into this matter. At their request, I gave them writing samples, and the Florida Department of Law Enforcement conducted a handwriting analysis. The analysis showed I had not written the fraudulent document. Additionally, they appear to have done nothing to try and find out who wrote it.

The assistant inspectors general did not obtain writing samples from Columbia CI medical staff who were the most reasonable suspects. Around that time, I was filing a lot of grievances and paperwork on Columbia CI medical staff. They may have thought the *Miami Herald* wanted my medical files to investigate any claims I was making against the Columbia CI medical staff and may thought the fraudulent document would keep the *Miami Herald* from getting my medical records. The *Miami Herald* didn't want my medical files for anything associated with Columbia CI, and the fraudulent document didn't stop the *Miami Herald* from obtaining my medical files. I also signed another release of medical records.

In January 2015, the *Miami Herald* published an article on this fraudulent document. I also submitted several grievances and mailed a complaint to the Florida Governor's Chief Inspector General Melinda Miguel.

412) Were excessive heat and poor ventilation a problem in the Columbia CI Protective Management Unit?

Yes. During my approximately 19 years of incarceration, 17 of which were in the FDC, I have never been housed in a dorm as hot as the Columbia CI Protective Management Unit. I was told that security staff were supposed to go into the unit and test the temperature on every shift. They didn't do this. The only time I ever saw staff testing the temperature was in the evening hours; usually after 8:00 pm. When they did test the temperature, it was always in the hallways and never in the cells.

The summers were very hot, and the winters were very cold. Every time I saw staff testing the temperature, I asked what the temperature was. Between June and the beginning of October 2014, the temperature was always between 87 and 98 degrees Fahrenheit in the hallways. In the winter months, the temperature was between 40 and 75 degrees Fahrenheit.

There was no cooling system. In summer during the extreme Florida heat, the unit's inside temperature was even hotter than the outside temperature. The air was also very dry. Trying to combat the heat, inmates wore only boxers or shorts and tried to hang out in front of the fans as much as possible. They carried wash clothes or towels that had been dipped in cold water to both wipe off sweat and to try to stay cool. Many inmates suffered from constant heat rashes, and, on a regular basis, some passed-out from heat exhaustion.

Staff did not test the temperature in the cells because it was much hotter than the hallways. It got hotter and hotter with each step you made into the cells. It would be realistic to say, that even with the cell doors opened, the back walls were five to 10 degrees hotter than in the hallways. When the steel cell doors were locked shut in summer, the temperature inside the cells was 15 to 20 degrees hotter than in the hallways. Temperatures always ranged between 100 and 115 degrees Fahrenheit. Due to the extreme heat, inmates barely slept during the summers.

All this was due to no cooling system. There were no fans or ducts blowing air into the cells; the cells had no windows: and the construction of the steel cell doors did not allow for any ventilation. Y-Dorm was an old confinement unit, and the cell doors were constructed to prevent contraband, such as, flattened bags of tobacco, narcotics, coffee, etc., from being slid through the top, sides, or bottom of the door. This was done by the steel plates that were on each edge of the door, making them airtight.

The winter months were welcomed by the inmates in the unit. We could more easily deal with the cold by wearing more clothing.

413) Were there weapons and thieves in the Columbia CI Protective Management Unit?

Yes. During my first several months in the unit, I saw staff find and seize more than 20 shanks. All of them were ice picks. I know other inmates had shanks because inmates who had been robbed by other inmates told me the perpetrators had pulled a shank on them.

There was also a lot of thievery in the Columbia CI Protective Management Unit. Ten or so inmates were thieves who continually stole other inmates' personal property and canteen.

414) Do you know anything about the confinement unit at Columbia CI?

Yes. Dr. G. was the first person to tell me how bad the Columbia confinement unit was. Several inmates also told me about the conditions there. They said that the confinement staff was constantly physically abusing inmates and denying them meals. Also, to retaliate against or punish an inmate who confinement staff did not like, the staff would place a physically or sexually aggressive inmate in the cell with an inmate the staff did not like.

In 2014, the *Miami Herald* published an article about an inmate being killed in the Columbia CI confinement unit. They published a second article on an inmate being beaten almost to death and on the staff's attempt to cover up the beating.

415) Did failure to follow FDC regulations cause problems in the Protective Management Unit?

Yes, for example, the FDC has a classification cell housing system called, the *"Inmate Risk Management System/Sexual Risk Indicator."* Every close custody inmate in the FDC is ranked according to whether or not he either poses a physical threat to other inmates or is likely to be a target of abuse. This is done using a five-point classification system known as the *Inmate Risk Management System*, which has the following rankings:

1) Identified Predator (IPD)
2) Potential Predator (PPD)
3) Identified Neutral (INZ)
4) Potential Prey (PPY)
5) Identified Prey (IPY)

Inmates whom the FDC has designated as an "Identified Predators" are the most physically aggressive inmates in the FDC. Inmates classified as "Identified Preys" have been identified as the type of inmates other inmates will prey upon. The other levels on the "Inmate Risk Management System" appear between these two levels.

Similarly, the *Sexual Risk Indicator* addresses sexual assault. Its five categories are:

1) High Aggressive Risk (HAR)

2) Moderate Aggressive Risk (MAR)
3) Neutral Sexual Risk (NSR)
4) Moderate Victimization Risk (MAR)
5) High Victimization Risk (HAR)

Inmates designated as "High Aggressive Risk" have been identified as the most sexually aggressive inmates in the FDC. Inmates designated as "High Victimization Risk" have been identified by FDC as being at high risk of sexual victimization.

Around August 2014, an inmate brought me a housing roster he got out of the trash can in the officers' station. It showed that the FDC had dozens of inmates designated as "Predators" and "Sexually Aggressive" inmates housed in the protective management unit.

Inmates designated as a predator or as sexually aggressive were housed in the same wings as the inmates who were classified as likely to be prey or victims of sexual assault. The housing roster showed me that the inmates I had witnessed committing acts of physical and sexual violence, extortion, and robbing were known to the FDC and had been designated by the FDC as predators and sexually aggressive inmates on the *Inmate Risk Management System/Sexual Risk Indicator*.

Bewildered, I wondered how the staff could say they were protecting the inmates in the unit when they purposely housed the FDC's worst inmates in the same unit as the inmates who needed the most protection. How was this in anyway "protection?"

When I became aware of this problem, it started weighing on my heart that I had to do something to try and help the victims and potential victims housed in protective management from the "Predators" and "Sexually Aggressive" inmates housed with them.

416) Was the Columbia Protective Management Unit in violation of the Prison Rape Elimination Act?

I previously mentioned that there was a lot of homosexual activity on the protective management unit. Also, the housing roster showed that staff had housed inmates who were likely to be victimized with inmates who were identified as sexually aggressive. The sexually aggressive inmates in the unit used physical intimidation to get unwilling inmates to engage in sexual acts. The predators commonly targeted the young inmates, petite inmates, mentally disabled inmates, homosexual inmates, and some of the former law enforcement officers.

A lot (but not all) of these inmates were scared to tell staff that they were being victimized and request protection from these sexual predators. They knew if they requested protection, they would go to confinement where they could be physically abused by staff and denied their meals. They also knew the majority of the protection requests made by inmates in the Protective Management Unit were denied. When protection requests were denied, the inmates were sent back to the unit to live with the inmates they requested protection from. This placed the inmates who requested protective management in even more danger.

Despite many inmates not requesting protection, many others did request it. FDC records will show that several inmates requested protection from sexually aggressive inmates in the protective management unit during the time I was incarcerated there.

The FDC is one of the many prison systems in our nation who receive money from the Federal Government to comply with the Prison Rape Elimination Act (34 U.S.C. § 30301). One of the reasons the FDC instituted the *Inmate Risk Management System/Sexual Risk Indicator* was to have it as a tool to aid in trying to stop the serious statewide problems of inmate-on-inmate abuse, murders, sexual batteries, and rape. What I was witnessing in that Protective Management Unit was evidence that the FDC wasn't protecting inmates from prison rape, which they were obligated to do by the Eighth Amendment of the U.S. Constitution and federal law.

The FDC, by its own rules, is supposed to house sexually aggressive inmates on close management FAC 33-601.800(1) (D). The following sections of FAC 33-601.800 show that inmates designated as sexually aggressive are supposed to be housed in close management status (not protective management status): FAC 33-601.800(2)(A)2.L; FAC 33-601.800(2)(B)2.B, F, and H; and FAC 33-601.800(2)(C)2.D.

Having to witness the things that the victims went through and their fear burdened my heart with sorrow. I constantly

Department of Corruption

thought about how I had to do something to try to help those who were in need.

417) Let's talk about specific cases of abuse. Tell me about Inmate Larry Allen.

Larry Allen was housed in the Protective Management Unit while I was there. He told several staff, other inmates, and me that he used to be a captain in the FDC.

While in the unit, he filed dozens of grievances. He filed numerous grievances about staff housing gang members in the unit on staff not complying the *Inmate Risk Management System/Sexual Risk Indicator*, and several other problems.

Allen wrote out e-mails and mailed them to his daughter to send to people for him. The e-mails were about things he wanted to fix in the protective management unit. His daughter sent the e-mails to the highest ranking officials in the FDC. He told me he had a history of filing grievances and having his daughter send e-mails prior to his arrival at Columbia CI.

About a month after Allen began filing grievances and sending e-mails, Sergeant Hardwick and Officer McManus started subjecting him to retaliation. They told several inmates in the unit that Allen was a child molester and, if anybody wanted to rob him, staff wouldn't stop them. An inmate named Jason Shira (or Shirah) took the offer. He stole all of Allen's personal property from his locker when Allen was at dinner chow. A few days later, when Allen received his weekly canteen order, Shira stole all of it. Allen reported that his property and canteen had been stolen, but security staff didn't do anything about it.

Sergeant Hardwick and Officer McManus then told Shira and some gang members that Allen had been telling on inmates in the protective management unit. They falsely alleged that Allen was reporting the shanks, drugs, tobacco and tattoo guns that were in the unit. Staff knew this would cause protection problem for Allen. As far as I know, Allen was not reporting on any of the above matters. Staff wanted to punish Allen for filing grievances and having e-mails sent to high ranking officials in the prison system.

Around this time, Sergeant Hardwick and Officer McManus started engaging in the almost constant searching of cells in the

296

protective management unit. They told the inmates the reason why they were searching cells was that the administration told them to look for the items Allen was (allegedly) telling on.

From the time Allen arrived in the protective management unit, I was friendly with him. We used to go to chow together, sit at the same table, and constantly talk about the conditions in the unit and in the FDC. It was my position that Allen wasn't telling where contraband was because he did not know where it was. I asked him if he was reporting contraband, and he told me that all of his grievances were on staff not doing things they were supposed to do and none were about contraband. The staff was creating protection problems for Allen by lying on him to the other inmates.

Threats and harassment from gang members made Allen request protection. When he requested protection, he was placed in confinement where he was in more danger. His daughter made sure that he was transferred from Columbia CI, so I never saw him again after that.

418) Will you tell me about Inmate Everett McNeely?

Everett McNeely showed me his law work. He was in prison for sexual battery on children. He was mentally disabled and never had a girlfriend. He told me he was on protective management status because he got raped several times in general population. The sad thing was that sexually aggressive inmates in the protective management unit were also making him engage in sexual acts.

McNeely also had problems with staff and inmates in the unit because of his sexual battery charges against children. Officer McManus told a day room full of inmates that he would give any inmate who punched McNeely in the face a Subway sandwich. Sergeant Hardwick constantly harassed McNeely, called him names, took his property from him, and even set him up with a major disciplinary report.

419) Will you tell me about Gabriel Garcia and Christopher Whitehead?

Garcia was a 19-year-old petite inmate who said he was from Tampa, Florida. At one point he told me he was in the protective management unit because he was raped in general population.

I noticed him when he first came into the protective management unit. About an hour after Garcia arrived, a sexually aggressive inmate was in his cell talking to him. From that moment, Garcia became the partner of that sexually aggressive inmate.

The sexually aggressive inmate who took Garcia as his partner Garcia's first day in the protective management unit ended up being beaten up by a young inmate who was a gang member. After this, the sexually aggressive inmate was transferred to another unit. However, as soon as this occurred, Garcia ended up becoming the victim of yet another sexually aggressive inmate.

Whitehead was another 19-year-old petite inmate. I was told that he was in the protective management unit because he had several relatives who were correctional officers in the Florida prison system. During the approximately 15 months I was incarcerated in that protective management unit, he was the victim of approximately a dozen sexually aggressive inmates.

In a conversation with Whitehead, I asked him if he was a homosexual in society. He told me he wasn't. When I asked him why he was engaging in homosexuality if he wasn't a homosexual, he said, "What else can I do? I don't want to be hurt."

I told Whitehead numerous ways to address the problems he was having even though I knew he wouldn't take my advice.

420) Tell me about the inmate who you believe was killed in the protective management unit in 2014.

I could be wrong, but I believe his name was Myong. When I saw him entering the protective management unit, I remembered him being housed in the Dade CI TCU in 2010. He was in a wheelchair and assigned to a wheelchair cell on one of the long wings in its protective management unit.

Myong was known to be rich, so members of the Latin King gang started acting like they were his friends and wanted to protect him. They did this as a way to run an extortion on him. The Latin King who was running the majority of the extortions was nicknamed "Jersey" because he was allegedly from New Jersey. His last name was something very close to Tolintino.

When Myong arrived at Columbia CI, he had a digital watch. A short time later, his watch was stolen. I heard that Jersey stole his watch and sold it to another inmate. When Myong found out that Jersey stole his watch and some of his canteen, Myong tried to stop communicating with Jersey and being friendly with him and the other Latin Kings. Myong told the security staff that Jersey had stolen his watch and canteen and that Jersey and the Latin Kings were harassing him and trying to extort him.

Officer McManus supplied Jersey with cigarettes and dip. Jersey and the Latin Kings sold the cigarettes and dip to inmates in the protective management unit. If Jersey was placed in confinement, McManus would have lost money because Jersey wouldn't have been able to continue selling if he was in confinement.

Also around that time, Officer McManus, Jersey, and the Latin Kings started calling Myong a child molester. Myong wasn't in prison for any sexual crimes against children; the false label was placed on him to cause protection issues for him with other inmates in the protective management unit.

After about two weeks of Officer McManus, Jersey, and the Latin Kings harassing Myong and of inmates harassing and falsely accusing him of being a child molester, Myong tried to request protection from Jersey and the Latin Kings. He wanted to go to confinement pending a protection investigation on Jersey and the Latin Kings. Sergeant Hardwick and Officer McManus would not allow him to request protection. When Myong tried requesting protection on one of the night shifts, the sergeant on that shift also did not permit him to make the request.

The next morning, the sergeant who had worked the night before told several inmates Myong had tried to request protection. The sergeant claimed that Myong named several reasons why he wanted protection, one of which was that "inmates kept trying to put razor blades in his food and cell." The razor blades in Myong's cell could result in him receiving a disciplinary report and placed in disciplinary confinement. Razor blades in Myong's food could have killed him. The sergeant said Myong gave him a razor and told him an inmate put it in Myong's cell.

That afternoon when we were going to lunch, Myong started urinating and defecating on himself at the Center Gate. As soon as he did these things, he started complaining about severe stomach pain and not feeling well. Instead of being taken to the medical department like he was supposed to be, he was pushed in his wheelchair back to the protective management unit.

For the next about two days, Myong complained of having stomach pain and not feeling good. He also continued to urinate and defecate on himself. He declared a medical emergency several times, but none of the security staff told medical staff about his medical emergency. Eventually, an inmate was able to convince staff to have a nurse come to the protective management unit to see Myong. The nurse just went to Myong's cell and talked to him.

One morning when all the inmates got up to go to breakfast chow, several inmates said Myong looked like he was about to die in his cell. The inmates on his wing said his cell was full of urine, feces, and vomit. At breakfast, inmate Frederick Hooten told me he was going to go to Myong's cell when we got back to the unit to see how Myong was doing. When we got the unit, Hooten checked on Myong. After checking, Hooten told me he saw vomit and urine in Myong's cell and could smell feces, and it looked as if the vomit and urine had blood in them. When Hooten asked Myong how he was doing, Myong responded that he didn't feel good.

Throughout that day Myong continued having the same medical problems and continued trying to go to medical for help.

That night security staff finally took Myong to the medical department. After a nurse took his vitals, she saw he was in very bad health. The Columbia CI medical doctor directed that Myong be taken to the outside hospital immediately. The next morning, several security staff said Myong died from allegedly overdosing. A lot of the inmates in the protective management unit knew that wasn't true.

It was my position that Myong didn't overdose, so I decided to try to investigate his death as much as I could. As soon as I started covertly questioning inmates about Myong, I found out that dozens of inmates were willing to tell me what they knew about him and his death. My goal was to reconstruct his life since he came to the protective management unit and then investigate anything that stood out.

Frederick Hooten expressed displeasure about Myong's death. Like several other inmates, Hooten thought that Myong was killed, and he wanted to report such to the proper authorities immediately. He asked me who he could write to report Myong's death as a possible murder. I knew Hooten didn't have any solid evidence that Myong was killed, but there was a lot of circumstantial evidence. I gave him three addresses to write. The first address was to the Tallahassee, Florida office of the Florida Department of Law Enforcement, the second address was to the Florida Governor's Chief Inspector General Melinda Miguel, and the third address was to *Miami Herald* Reporter Julie K. Brown. Hooten immediately placed letters in the mail to these three parties. He wrote them concerning his belief that staff aided inmates in killing Myong.

Approximately a week later, Hooten was placed in confinement by the FDC Inspector General's Office. About a month later, he was transferred to the Martin CI Protective Management Unit.

Following Myong's death, Jersey visited the law library for the first time since he arrived at the protective management unit. I was friendly with the law clerk, and I knew if I asked him what Jersey was researching, the clerk wouldn't tell Jersey. When I asked the law clerk, he told me it was murder. When I heard he was researching murder, I knew that I had to find out what Jersey was in prison for. Within a day or two, I found out that he wasn't in prison for murder. This added to my suspicion. The first time he visited the law library, he researched murder, and he wasn't in prison for murder. He did this after the suspicious death of an inmate, and Jersey was the only inmate with a motive to hurt Myong.

During my investigation into Myong's death, I also found out that Jersey bought several razor blades from an inmate with the nickname "E" about two weeks before Myong died. "E" had blond hair and was a houseman who lived on one of the small wings in the protective management unit.

My investigation led me to believe that Jersey placed razor blades and/or medication in Myong's food. I don't believe Jersey did this to kill Myong. I believe Jersey thought doing this would get Myong placed in a self-harm observation status cell and then transferred to a Crisis Stabilization Unit. This would have got Myong out of the protective management unit where Jersey wouldn't have had to worry about Myong informing on him.

It was unreasonable to say that Myong did anything to hurt himself. Dozens of inmates, including myself, heard him requesting protection, complaining to staff and inmates about not feeling good, and declaring several medical emergencies that staff refused to acknowledge. The numerous attempts to request protection showed he was scared of being hurt. Myong was suffering and wanted help. A suicidal person doesn't beg for medical help.

From my knowledge, investigators only spoke with four or five inmates concerning his death. The investigators didn't speak with me despite them knowing I had information concerning Myong's death and that I wanted to speak with them.

Not too long after the Myong's mysterious death, the *Miami Herald* published an article that referenced his death.

421) Were sex offenders in the protective management unit targeted because of their crimes?

Yes. Sergeant Hardwick and Officer McManus had a strong dislike for sex offenders. Especially ones who had sexually abused kids. Sergeant Hardwick and Officer McManus told gang members and sexually aggressive inmates which inmates were imprisoned for sexual abuse of children and revealed any details they could find out about the sex offenders' cases. They also did things to incite the gang members and sexually aggressive inmates against the sex offenders. I remember both of them saying several times, "Inmates who sexually abused kids should be sexually abused in prison. Throughout their sentence, they should have done to them whatever, they did to kids."

The gang members and sexually aggressive inmates knew they could do whatever they wanted to do to the inmates who were in prison for sexual crimes against kids when Sergeant Hardwick and Officer McManus worked. Hardwick and McManus also harassed the sex offenders, ransacked their cells, and set them up with false disciplinary reports.

422) Did the *Miami Herald* publish an article on abuse by Warden Samuel Culpepper?

Yes. The *Miami Herald* was preparing an article on Warden Culpepper, who had a long history of being considered by inmates to be one of the evilest and meanest wardens in the FDC. I was at Apalachee CI East Unit and Washington CI when he was a warden at those two institutions, so I knew how he ran institutions.

The article on Warden Culpepper discussed several of his evil policies. The article noted that Culpepper approved of his staff gassing inmates with a chemical agent. I had explained Warden Culpepper's footprint procedure. He had footprints spray painted on the floors in the confinement cells and ordered that inmates must stand on the footprints during inspections and when specific staff entered the confinement unit. This was enforced even if it was three o'clock in the morning. The inmates who weren't standing on the footprints in their cells were gassed with a chemical agent.

I believe the article also references some inmates who died, possibly as a result of the chemical agent at the institution(s) where Culpepper was the Warden.

Several years ago, Culpepper was promoted to a Regional Director who was in charge of all the institutions in a region. In 2017, I read that he was the director of Region Two.

423) Do FDC staff engage in psychological warfare against inmates?

Yes. The issue with the footprints in the confinement cells is a form of psychological warfare. That unwritten practice makes inmates feel like they are not human. They think, "If staff will gas me with a chemical agent if I do not stand where they order me to stand, then they are treating me worse than animals are treated."

Florida prison staff also have an unwritten policy they refer to as "Reckless Eyeballing." If an inmate is caught looking at staff for about five seconds or longer, the staff will aggressively say to the inmate, "Why are you reckless eyeballing me?" If the inmate doesn't respond the right way and talk himself out of the situation, it could result in the staff physically abusing the inmate, or placing him in confinement.

If an inmate is caught wearing pants that are too loose, security staff will take the inmate to laundry and exchange the inmate's loose pants for really tight pants. It is not good for inmates to wear tight pants that show the shape of their butt and legs because they then have a higher risk of sexual victimization.

Florida prison security staff use many types of psychological warfare tactics, which cause inmates to feel that they are not being treated like humans. Most security staff are very disrespectful, rude, and mean. You can tell by how they talk to us, that they don't think we deserve to be treated like humans.

Correctional studies show that the better the relationship is between staff and inmates, the better the conditions are in the prison system for both of them. In the Florida Department of Corrections, bad relationships between staff and inmates result in bad conditions for both of them.

424) Is the Columbia CI sergeant you nicknamed "Stickman" an example of the poor treatment of inmates?

Yes. There was a sergeant who worked in Columbia CI Protective Management Unit whom many staff and inmates called "Little Hitler" because he looked and acted like Adolf Hitler. When the *Miami Herald* published an article on the suspicious death of Inmate Myong, the *Herald* attributed their report to anonymous sources. Afterward, the sergeant everybody called "Little Hitler." called me into the officers' station and told me that he thought I was one of the anonymous sources. He also said that he wanted me to know that Inmate Myong wasn't killed. I told him I wasn't one of the anonymous sources and everybody was entitled to believe how they wanted to believe.

About three weeks later, I was on an inmate telephone during a thunderstorm and the phone shut off as it often did during thunderstorms. When the phone shut off during a storm, security could turn the phone back on by flipping the phone button to the off position and then back to the on position. When the telephone shut off on me, I motioned with my hands asking "Little Hitler" and his officer to flip the phone switch off and on. The sergeant used his hand and index finger and motioned back to as if to say "one second," or "one minute."

I waited by the phone for about five minutes, and neither of the staff flipped the phone button off and back on. I thought they might have forgotten, so I went to the front of the officers' station to talk to them through the station's flap. I only got a chance to say, "I'm sorry. I don't know if you forgot," before the sergeant interrupted me and said, "Hempstead, you don't run the Protective Management Unit, and you're not my boss. The phone will turn back on when it turns back on."

I responded, "OK, thank you," and walked away. I was confused about why he snapped back at me as he did. I thought he might have just been having a bad day.

About 15 minutes later, we went into a count. During the count, he came onto the wing where I was housed carrying a wooden stick about two feet long and hitting the bars and walls with it. When he got to my cell, he hit my cell door with the stick, stood in the doorway, and talked to me for about a minute. All the time he talked, he hit the stick against the palm of one of his hands. He said I wasn't his boss, that I should stop worrying about Columbia CI, and that I should worry about Dade CI if I wanted to make it to any court hearings concerning Dade CI.

This sergeant had been walking around the Protective Management Unit hitting the stick against bars, walls, and cell doors for several days prior to him bringing the stick to my cell that night. That meant the security cameras had recorded him over a several day period unlawfully bringing a weapon (the stick) into the unit and using it to intimidate protective management inmates.

The day after the sergeant brought the stick to my cell, I organized the filing of approximately 20 grievances on him. That same day, the lieutenant in charge of the protective management unit reviewed the footage from the mounted security cameras. This included the video footage from the mounted security camera pointed directly at my cell door.

While he was watching the footage, he called me into the office and asked me what happened. After I explained, he asked me what I wanted him to do. I responded that I wanted him to take care of it.

I thought that by bringing it to his attention, the lieutenant would have the sergeant reposted outside of the protective management unit because I was a listed federal and state witness against prison staff and was on protective management from staff. The videos clearly showed the sergeant threatening me with the stick. The lieutenant took the stick out of the Protective Management Unit and never reposted the sergeant.

The sergeant then started harassing all the inmates in the protective management unit. He denied the inmates recreational activity when he worked, shut off the fans during counts, and didn't give the inmates enough time to eat. The inmates in the protective management unit knew I had filed paperwork on him. By harassing all the inmates, the sergeant was sending a message to them to take care of his problem, which was me, if they wanted the sergeant to back off them. This is commonly done in the FDC. It is one of many ways that staff create a hostile environment for an inmate they don't like. It oftentimes is successful in causing inmates to physically hurt the inmate targeted by the staff member.

When the sergeant started doing these things, I told Windy what was going on. Windy sent e-mails to the Columbia CI Warden concerning the sergeant who was causing me problems. The warden and other Columbia CI staff tried to cover up for the sergeant.

Because the Columbia CI Warden and other staff did not have the sergeant reposted or take any type of action to stop his retaliation, Windy sent an e-mail to the Federal Bureau of Investigation and the U.S. Department of Justice concerning the retaliation. The e-mail stated everything the sergeant did and how the Columbia CI Warden and staff were trying to cover-up the sergeant's retaliatory actions. Windy sent copies of the e-mail to the Columbia CI Warden. Not too long after she sent the e-mail, the sergeant was reposted to work in the confinement unit. About two months later, the sergeant returned to the protective management unit.

Upon his return, he acted like he wanted to do everything he could to help the gang members in the protective management unit. He told them how he didn't like that inmates kept telling on the gang members and getting them placed in confinement. He showed gang members information on the FDC computer about inmates who informed gang members. After about a week of doing this, the sergeant tried to tell a gang member that I had told on him. The sergeant was not able to show the gang member any documents because there were not any to show. The sergeant was lying to the gang member and trying to get me physically harmed. The gang member and all the inmates in the protective management unit knew that the sergeant didn't like me. They knew that the sergeant was the type to lie on inmates. They also knew he was the type to try and get inmates to hurt other inmates that he didn't like.

Windy sent another e-mail to the Federal Bureau of Investigations about the sergeant and sent a copy of the e-mail to the Columbia CI Warden. I was still dealing with this sergeant I nicknamed, "Stickman," when I transferred from Columbia CI to the Martin CI Protective Management Unit in September 2015.

425) Was the Florida Department of Corrections a focus of media attention from May to December 2014?

Yes. After my placement in the Columbia CI Protective Management Unit in May 2014, Windy began to brief me on a daily basis about the media attention to the prison system. After the *Miami Herald* released their first article on the Darren Rainey case and Dade CI, hundreds of inmates and their families wrote and called *Miami Herald* Reporter Julie K. Brown. Their letters and calls were about murders and other acts of cruel and unusual punishment in institutions throughout the FDC. As the *Miami Herald* was publishing articles on the Darren Rainey case and Dade CI in May and June 2014, they were also investigating other incidents at other institutions. As a result of their investigations, they published dozens of articles on several mysterious deaths of inmates and numerous acts of cruel and unusual punishment in the FDC. Newspapers across the nation republished all or part of these *Miami Herald* articles, and TV news stations also reported on the matters mentioned in the Herald's articles.

Julie Brown's articles captured the depths of evil that the FDC had fallen to. She reported Darren Rainey's death in a shower that was rigged to reach temperatures in excess of 160° Fahrenheit and how the same shower was used to punish mentally disabled inmates. She reported on a Spanish inmate with medical problems who was possibly gassed to death with a chemical agent at Franklin CI; she authored an article on how two mentally disabled inmates at Charlotte CI were possibly beaten to death by security staff; and she reported evidence showing that women prisoners in FDC were possibly being raped and killed by security staff.

The articles that Julie Brown wrote caused the world to see the severity of the staff-on-inmate violence and the deplorable, unconstitutional conditions of the Florida prison system. Julie Brown also reported on the hundreds of inmates who were dying in the Florida prison system each year.

By July 2014, the Tampa Bay Times newspaper, Palm Beach Post, and News Service of Florida joined the *Miami Herald* newspaper in investigating and reporting on the unconstitutional conditions of the FDC. Additionally, within a month or two of the *Miami Herald* publishing their May 18, 2014 article on the Darren Rainey case and Dade CI, the Florida Governor and dozens of Florida political figures made public statements on the Darren Rainey case, and all types of other matters that the *Miami Herald* published articles on concerning incidents in the Florida prison system.

The above is a brief synopsis of the media activity at the end of 2014, and several things that happened as a result of the media attention to the Florida prison system that started with the Darren Rainey case.

426) Tell me about the FDC Assistant Inspector Generals who blew the whistle at the end of 2014.

Inmate Randal Jordan Aparo died at Franklin CI on the night he was gassed with a chemical agent by Franklin CI staff. After the investigation into his death was closed, three FDC assistant inspectors general were ordered to go to Franklin CI to investigate a variety of matters, none of which was Aparo's death. During their investigations, several people kept making statements saying staff killed an inmate at Franklin CI.

One of these inspectors decided to look into the alleged murder that so many people kept mentioning. After he reviewed the video footage from the mounted security cameras on the night Aparo died and all the documentation relating to his death, the inspector came to the conclusion that Aparo was killed by staff. He then had the two other inspectors review the same video footage and documentation, and they reached the same conclusion.

When these inspectors brought their findings to FDC Inspector General Jeffrey Beasley, he directed them to not go forward on their findings and to keep quiet. These three inspectors thought this was wrong and then went to FDC Secretary Michael Crews. They contended that Secretary Crews told them he couldn't help them and directed them to the Governor's Chief Inspector General, Melinda Miguel. When she refused to give the assistant inspectors general whistleblower protection, they filed a lawsuit under the Whistleblower Act. The *Miami Herald* and other media outlets reported extensively on the Randal Jordan Aparo case.

427) Did the Florida Governor's Chief Inspector General Melinda Miguel fail to follow-up on information she received about Darren Rainey?

While the *Miami Herald* was investigating numerous matters in the FDC, they discovered that Melinda Miguel received a letter in 2012 about the Darren Rainey case. The writer of the letter said he was a high ranking official in the FDC. His letter mentioned a cover-up in the Darren Rainey case and the drastically deteriorating Florida prison system. Miguel's office sent the letter to the Tallahassee, Florida main office of the FDC. If I remember correctly, the letter ended up in the file of the FDC Deputy Secretary, Timothy Cannon.

Miguel's office and the FDC never investigated anything in the letter. At the end of 2014, the *Miami Herald* published an article on this letter and on the failure of Miguel and the FDC to conduct any investigations into the contents of the letter.

428) Did Randy Evans or somebody you know write the letter to Melinda Miguel?

I can't answer that question at this time.

429) Did you give a copy of your journal to the Miami-Dade Police Department in November 2014?

Yes. Homicide Detective Wilbert Sanchez and his new partner came to Columbia CI to pick up the journal I kept while housed in the Dade CI TCU. He said his boss needed it, that it would eventually go to the Dade County, Florida State Attorney, and that I would eventually be able to receive it back. Prior to giving him the original, I made a copy of it for my records. I mailed additional copies to Windy, Casey Frank and Julie Brown of the Miami Herald, and, several weeks later, to Reporter Eyal Press of the New Yorker.

430) Why did the Miami-Dade Police Department want your journal?

They said they wanted it for their alleged investigation into the Darren Rainey case. Neither Detective Sanchez nor his partner asked me any questions on the Rainey case in November 2014. They only wanted the journal.

431) Did *Miami Herald* Reporter Julie K. Brown visit you at Columbia CI in December 2014?

Yes. At the beginning of October, Casey Frank told me Julie Brown would be traveling in the Columbia County, Florida area around the beginning of December. He said that, if I wanted to speak with her, I should mail a letter to the *Miami Herald* stating so. I had already been telling the *Miami Herald* about the conditions in the Columbia CI Protective Management Unit. When I learned she was coming, I asked if I could get some inmates together who would be willing to talk about the extremely violent conditions in the unit. The *Miami Herald* agreed to this.

I assembled three inmates whom I thought would be helpful. The three inmates I got were Larry Allen, Edward Mann, and a Haitian. Larry Allen was a former captain in the FDC. Edward Mann was a former detective in the Orange County, Florida Sheriff's Department, or the Orlando, Florida Police Department. The Haitian was a former confidential informant for the Broward County, Florida Sheriff's Department and, I think, also for the Leon County, Florida Sheriff's Department. I'm not providing the Haitian's name because he could be housed in general population in the FDC. All three inmates wrote letters to the *Miami Herald* stating their desire to meet with Julie Brown.

When Julie Brown came to Columbia CI, Larry Allen was in confinement pending a protection investigation, but he was still allowed to meet with her. The interviews went well except for one problem. The major at Columbia CI sat in on all the interviews with a cell phone in her hands. I think, but I don't know for sure, she was recording our conversations with Julie Brown.

Prior to the interview, I told the other three inmates that the Columbia CI administration would probably have staff real close to us during our interviews, so the staff would know if we said anything about Columbia CI. I suggested that the inmates get a folder and put 20 or more sheets of paper in it. Also, I told them to write down everything they wanted to say to Julie Brown and insert the paper with their statements in with the other papers. That way, if security staff were close by and the inmates didn't feel comfortable with talking, they hand their notes to Julie Brown and only tell her verbally what they felt comfortable telling her. I think Edward followed my advice. I don't know if Larry did, because he went to confinement a week or two prior to the interviews, and I never saw him again. The Haitian didn't follow my advice and talked a lot about the unconstitutional conditions in the unit while the major was listening about five feet away from Haitian. A few weeks after the interviews, the Haitian was transferred to another protective management unit.

When I was interviewed, I talked to Julie Brown about the Darren Rainey case and the abuse of the mentally disabled inmates in the Dade CI TCU. Most of what I wanted to say about Columbia CI's Protective Management Unit I had already reported in my telephone calls to the Miami Herald. `

432) Did Julie Brown's reporting get national attention in late 2014 and early 2015?

Yes, her articles caused newspapers in other states to investigate the prison conditions in their states. Additionally, the newspapers in the other states were also publishing articles on the abuse of mentally disabled inmates and the unconstitutional conditions of their prisons.

433) What started being installed in every housing wing in the FDC at the end of 2014?

Mounted security cameras.

434) In August 2014, did you and Windy discuss expanding your efforts to help Florida inmates?

Yes. Windy began to express her feelings that we should do all that we could to try and help as many FDC inmates and their families as possible. She believed God placed us in the position that we were in because He wanted us to help others. She wanted to do this as we also continued to seek justice for Darren Rainey and help for the mentally disabled inmates in the Dade CI TCU.

When I initially spoke out about Rainey and the mentally disabled inmates at Dade CI, I did not imagine that the media would publish dozens of articles on the FDC, that civil rights groups would begin challenging the conditions in the FDC, or that the U.S. Department of Justice and the Federal Bureau of Investigations would initiate investigations into the Florida prison system.

I thought about what Windy was saying. I thought about my sorrow as I watched the physical and sexual abuse in the protective management unit. I realized Windy was right. We had to do what the Bible commanded and help.

435) Please summarize your activism the latter part of 2014 and the first part of 2015 your efforts to get off Protective Management Status.

I started by filing additional grievances related to the Darren Rainey case and the Dade CI TCU. I also filed several grievances on my placement on protective management status, on the conditions there, and on all types of matters in the FDC

When I found out that prison staff had predators and sexually aggressive inmates housed in the Columbia CI Protective Management Unit, I told the *Miami Herald* and the Florida Governor's Chief Inspector General Melinda Miguel.

After I found out that prison staff altered the *Inmate Risk Management System/Sexual Risk Indicator* levels of some inmates to try and cover up the inappropriate mixing of inmates with predator and prey ratings, I told the *Miami Herald* and

Melinda Miguel what FDC staff did. I explained that they could obtain old housing rosters and other prison paperwork and compare it with the new rosters and paperwork to prove prison staff were trying to cover up the inappropriate mixing.

I talked with several inmates trying to obtain as much information as I could about the names of protective management inmates who had been seriously physically abused or raped by other protective management inmates. I provided all of the information I received to the *Miami Herald* newspaper.

In both 2014 and 2015, I wrote the FDC Inspector General's Office and the Florida Governor's Chief Inspector General Melinda Miguel several letters (some of which were anonymous) about the extremely violent conditions in the Columbia CI Protective Management Unit.

In 2014 I filed a Petition for Writ of Habeas Corpus in the Columbia County, Florida Circuit Court. In that Habeas Corpus, I contended that I was placed on protective management as retaliation for asserting my First Amendment rights to Freedom of Speech, and Redress of Grievances. I explained in detail the unconstitutional conditions of the protective management unit and how those conditions amounted to cruel and unusual punishment in violation of the Eighth Amendment of the U.S. Constitution.

I filed two civil rights lawsuits in the Jacksonville, Florida Federal District Court (Case Numbers 3:2015-CV-00130; and 2015-CV-00374). Those lawsuits explained in detail the Darren Rainey case, the non-feeding and physical abuse of mentally disabled inmates in the Dade CI TCU, the unconstitutional conditions in the Columbia CI Protective Management Unit, my retaliatory placement on protective management status and all types of other matters concerning the FDC and myself. Those two lawsuits can be located on the Public Access to Court Electronic Records interne cite.

In 2014, I drafted and mailed sworn affidavits to the U.S. Department of Justice concerning several different violations of the constitutional rights of FDC inmates. In those affidavits, I requested that federal investigations be conducted into the violations mentioned in the affidavits. In 2014, also mailed

copies of these sworn affidavits to the *Miami Herald* newspaper,
Tampa Bay Times newspaper, Palm Beach Post, News Service of
Florida newspaper, Eyal Press of the New Yorker Magazine,
Howard Simon of the Florida ACLU, Steven Wetstein of SPAN,
Molly Paris of Disability Rights Florida, Peter Sleasman of
Florida Legal Services, Randal C. Berg of the Florida Justice
Institute, Lance Weber of the Human Rights Defense Center, the
Commissioner of the Florida Department of Law Enforcement,
the Florida Governor's Chief Inspector General Melinda Miguel,
Florida Senator Greg Evers, Susan Chandler, and Windy.

These are the main people who received my sworn affidavits
at the end of 2014. I continued this activity in 2015 by mailing
sworn affidavits to the U.S. Department of Justice and more than
a dozen law enforcement and government agencies, media, and
civil rights groups.

Topics covered by the sworn affidavits included:

- The Darren Rainey case.
- The non-feeding of mentally disabled inmates in the
  Dade CI TCU.
- Predators and sexually aggressive inmates being
  housed in the Columbia CI Protective Management
  Units.
- The extreme violent conditions in FDC Special
  Housing Units.

All the time I was in the Columbia CI Protective
Management Unit, I continued to talk with the *Miami Herald*
newspaper on the inmate phone several times a week on the
Darren Rainey case, Dade CI, the treatment of mentally disabled
inmates in the Dade CI TCU, and all types of other problems in
the Florida prison system.

436) Why did you mail the Florida Governor's Chief Inspector General Melinda Miguel letters and sworn affidavits?

When Melinda Miguel's office received a letter from a
Florida inmate, her office copied the letter for their records, typed
and mailed a response letter to the inmate, and mailed both the
inmate's letter and a copy Miguel's response letter to the
Tallahassee FDC Inspector General's Office. The response letter

from Miguel's office acknowledged receipt of the inmate's letter, stated that the inmate's letter was mailed to the Inspector General's Office, and that it was assigned a Chief Inspector General case number. Thus, mailing letters to Melinda Miguel's office was both a good way to attempt to get a problem fixed and to leave a paper trail concerning my efforts to have problems fixed in FDC.

437) Was Windy also actively involved in civil rights activities during this period?

Around the end of July 2014, Windy started going on the radio show "Dog Justice for the Mentally Ill." While on the radio show, she spoke extensively on the Darren Rainey case, the mentally disabled inmates in the FDC needing help, and the unconstitutional conditions of the Florida prison system. Windy went on this radio show several times at the end of 2014.

Around August 2014, Windy also became friends with Susan Chandler, who ran the Wobbly Warrior Blog, www.wobblywarrior@wordpress.com. Chandler had devoted her life to helping victims. When she read the *Miami Herald* articles on Darren Rainey's death, she started blogging on the Rainey case. When Windy saw how blogging could be used to help others, she wanted to open a blog. Within a month or two of Chandler and Windy talking, Chandler helped Windy design her own WordPress blog.

Windy's blog was named, helpmybrotherharoldhempstead@wordpress.com. As soon as Windy's blog was opened and made public, she was blogging a lot on the Darren Rainey case, other problems in the Florida prison system, and on me. After she opened her blog, she also placed things on her other social media sites concerning these things. At the end of 2014, Windy became well known in Florida for her involvement in prisoner civil rights activism; she was receiving hundreds of e-mails and requests a month for help on all types of matters concerning the abuse of inmates in the FDC.

438) Did Windy and you seek help from civil rights leaders?

Yes. We petitioned the following people and groups for help with the Darren Rainey case: Reverend Jesse Jackson of the Rainbow Push Coalition; Reverend Al Sharpton of the National

Action Network; and Alicia Garza and Opal Tometi of Black Lives Matter. We started making these contacts in 2014 and continued to contact them in 2015.

439) Did you talk to Randy Evans and Jim Knowels while you were at Columbia CI?

Yes. They came to Columbia CI at the end of 2014 and several times in 2015.

440) Did you receive a visit from two Department of Justice U.S. Assistant Attorney Generals, and a Federal Bureau of Investigation agent at the beginning of 2015?

Yes. The interview was for approximately four hours. It concerned the Darren Rainey case and the Dade CI TCU. I cannot provide any more information concerning these individuals, or the facts concerning what we discussed.

441) Why did several staff and inmates begin calling you Miami Harold at the end of 2014?

One morning, I was in the chow hall waiting for my breakfast tray. Since I was on a special diet, I had to wait for the diet cook to call my name to get my tray. When my tray was ready, he yelled, "Harold Hempstead."

A sergeant in the chow hall, who I didn't know, said, "Did he just yell Harold Hempstead? Is Miami Harold in this chow hall? Where is Miami Harold? Oh, crap, I see you. What's up Miami Harold? You don't know me, but I have listened to about a hundred of your telephone calls. I have no problem with you. Are you hungry? I'll get you an extra tray."

I told the sergeant I appreciated his offer of an extra tray, but I wasn't that hungry. I tried to keep the conversation with him very short because he was very loud and all the inmates in the chow hall could hear him talking. After this situation, the same sergeant made a big scene calling me "Miami Harold" on about five or more occasions in the chow hall.

This sergeant calling me "Miami Harold" led to other staff and inmates calling me the same name. This sergeant's name was "Camacho."

442) Did Florida officials and other agencies respond to the publicity in the *Miami Herald* and other media?

Yes. In 2014, Florida Senator Greg Evers was the Chairman of the Criminal Justice Committee in the Florida Senate. When he became aware of all the acts of murder, violence and other unconstitutional conditions in the FDC, he started holding Senate committee hearings to investigate the conditions in FDC. During the several months of Senate hearings held by Senator Evers, dozens of prison staff and former prison staff testified about the conditions in the Florida prison system.

One of the first people who testified at the hearings was former Dade CI TCU Counselor George Mallinckrodt. During Mallinckrodt's testimony, while showing a picture of me, he told the Senate Criminal Justice Committee that all the media reporting and federal investigations and Senate investigations into the FDC started as a result of me. He also told the committee that everything came as a result of my involvement with the Darren Rainey case and my initial communications with the Miami Herald. Senator Evers also asked my sister Windy to testify in front of his committee.

She expressed a desire to do so, but when it came time for her to make the trip to the Florida capital, she wasn't able to. One of her sons was really sick; she had to take him to the hospital, and she needed to be with him. With his health being fairly bad, she couldn't leave him with somebody else while she went on a trip to the Florida capital. Senator Evers also spoke extensively with the media on his desire to try and reform the FDC. One of the things he was pushing for the most, was to try and pass a law to bring about an independent oversight committee to oversee the FDC.

When the American Civil Liberties Union (ACLU) of Florida and representatives with the other civil rights groups in Florida read Julie Brown's investigative reporting on the Darren Rainey case, Dade CI, and other matters in the FDC, they joined together and sent a letter to the Washington D.C. Office of the Department of Justice. ACLU of Florida Executive Director Howard Simon authored the letter that the other civil rights groups joined in signing. The letter requested that the U.S. Department of Justice investigate the Darren Rainey case, the Dade CI TCU, and the alarming number of inmate deaths in the FDC.

In December 2014, the **Washington D.C. Office of the Department of Justice** ordered a federal investigation into the FDC. Julie Brown reported on this in December 2014. This alerted prison staff across the state that the federal government was investigating the Florida prison system.

One of the Florida civil rights groups, involved with a lot of the activism in 2014 and since then, is "Stop Prison Abuse Now" (SPAN). Stop Prison Abuse Now is a Miami, Florida-based civil rights group which was founded in the wake of the *Miami Herald* reporting on the Darren Rainey case, and the abuse of mentally disabled inmates in the Dade CI TCU. They were very proactive in their activism for prisoner rights from the time they were founded. SPAN spokesman Steven Wetstein placed a petition on Change.org around July or August 2014, requesting 250,000 signatures asking for the Federal Bureau of Investigations to investigate the Darren Rainey case. They received the signatures for this petition within a very short period of time. Wetstein and other SPAN activists also engaged in a protest at the Tallahassee, Florida main office of the FDC. The protest was over Florida inmates dying and the cruel and unusual punishment in the FDC. The protesters held signs saying different things. Some of the signs had my name on them as the inmate who first spoke with the *Miami Herald* newspaper about the Darren Rainey case and the unconstitutional conditions in the FDC. Wetstein and the founders of SPAN became very friendly with Windy from the time SPAN started advocating on the Darren Rainey case, and against the abuse in the FDC.

443) Tell me about the federal lawsuit filed by the Florida Legal Services and Disability Rights Florida concerning the Dade CI TCU.

This lawsuit was filed in the end of 2014. They filed a 42 U.S.C.§ 1983 Civil Rights Complaint Class Action lawsuit in the Miami, Florida Federal District Court (Case Number 1:14-CV-23323). The lawsuit referenced the hot water shower treatment of mentally disabled inmates, the Darren Rainey case, and other matters relating to the abuse of the mentally disabled inmates in the Dade CI TCU.

The lawsuit was to obtain an injunction directing the FDC and Wexford Health Sources, Inc. to correct the unconstitutional conditions in the TCU. The lawsuit can be found on the internet on the "Public Access to Court Electronic Records" site. .

In 2015, the FDC and Wexford Health Sources Inc. settled this lawsuit filed by Florida Legal Services and Disability Rights Florida. The settlement was in favor of the civil rights groups and the inmates. The settlement was designed to correct the constitutional deficiencies in the Dade CI TCU. In the middle of 2015 and afterward, I was told by several inmates who had been housed in the Dade CI TCU that a lot of the things that the settlement said were supposed to be enforced, were not being enforced in the TCU. Mentally disabled inmates were still being physically abused and denied large quantities of food. I was also told that Sergeant Lewis and some of the other evil security staff at Dade CI were back working in the TCU.

The *Miami Herald* published an article on this law suit and the settlement in 2015.

444) In March 2015, did Florida ACLU receive a letter from the D.C. Office of the Department of Justice?

Yes. Executive Director Howard Simon received a letter from the Washington D.C. Office of the Department of Justice. The letter said that a Department of Justice investigation was ordered into the Darren Rainey case and Dade CI TCU and that a preliminary investigation would be done to determine if they had enough cause to conduct a Civil Rights of Institutionalized Persons Act investigation into the treatment of all of the mentally disabled inmates in the FDC.

The *Miami Herald* published an article at the beginning of 2015 on this letter.

445) Were there staffing changes in the FDC as a result of Julie K. Brown's 2014 articles and Senator Evers' hearings?

Yes.

- Warden Jerry Cummings and Assistant Warden Dykes were both forced to resign.

319

- Roland Clarke quit the FDC and went to work for the Miami Gardens, Florida Police Department.
- Cornelius Thompson also quit working in the FDC. He went to work for the Federal Bureau of Prisons at Coleman in Florida.
- FDC Secretary Michael Crews was forced to resign. He did an excellent interview with Julie K. Brown about conditions in the Florida prison system. It can be found on the internet.
- It should also be noted that in the end of 2014, Michael Crews directed that mounted security cameras be installed in every housing wing in the FDC.

446) Did Julie Jones replace Michael Crews as FDC Secretary Michael Crews at the end of 2014?

Yes. Also, Secretary Jones tried to blame the abundance of problems in the FDC on a lack of staff. Additionally, she made numerous statements contending that the problems in the FDC would be fixed under her leadership. It is my position that the problems have only gotten worse under her leadership.

447) Did the Florida Governor issue two Executive Orders on the FDC in 2015?

Yes. In one of the Executive Orders, he tried to make it look like he was ordering changes in the FDC. The reason why I say he "tried" to make it look like he was ordering changes, is because everything listed in his Executive Order was already the law in Florida. I wrote a response to this Executive Order and mailed it to Windy. In my response, I cited everything the Governor said and the already existing rules and laws. I showed that the Governor didn't do anything in his Executive Order except falsely act as if he was ordering something new to be instituted in the FDC. My response to this Executive Order was placed on Windy's blog and Susan Chandler's blog.

The second Executive Order ordered that two private agencies audit the FDC. The problems were obvious in the FDC. In my opinion, the Governor should have focused on fixing the problems he was aware of instead of not fixing those problems and allegedly trying to find more problems that would not be fixed. Those audits were done in 2015 or the beginning of 2016. It's my position that the problems in the Florida prison system that the audits showed existed are still not fixed as of the time that I'm writing this book in 2018. It should also be noted that in 2015, Florida Senator David Richardson started trying to bring reform to the FDC. You'll find his name in several *Miami Herald* articles concerning the FDC

448) Tell me about George Mallinckrodt's 2014 book *Getting Away with Murder*.

The cover of Mallinckrodt's book had the name of the book *Getting Away with Murder* and a picture of Darren Rainey's face on it. The cover would cause you to think that the book was about the Darren Rainey case. However, when you read it, you would find out it wasn't about Darren Rainey.

In 2014, three people who read Mallinckrodt's book said it appeared as if Mallinckrodt was about to release a book about his experiences as a mental health counselor around the time that the *Miami Herald* started publishing articles on the Darren Rainey case. When Mallinckrodt saw the newspaper articles on the Darren Rainey case, he saw that he could sell a lot of copies of his book, if he somehow made his book appear that it had to do with Darren Rainey. In an attempt to make his book appear like it was about the Rainey case, Mallinckrodt put a chapter or two at the beginning of the book and a few chapters at the end of the book that referenced things involving Darren Rainey. Mallinckrodt then put Rainey on the cover and called it, *Getting Away with Murder*.

After he did these things, he advertised his book like it was about the Darren Rainey case when it really wasn't. As I previously said, the book is really about Mallinckrodt's experiences as a counselor. The three people who said these things made a lot of sense.

449) Do you have some criticisms of George Mallinckrodt's book?

Yes. First, he makes statements in his book presenting the mentally disabled inmates in the TCU as animals in a zoo.

Second, George Mallinckrodt didn't mention in his book that he put your name in an incident report on Officer Gruben without your permission. It is my position he left this out because he knew it would make him look bad.

Third, Mallinckrodt didn't mention in his book that I told him that he shouldn't go to the Dade CI warden and tell the warden his security staff were doing wrong. Neither did he explain the reasons why I told him not to go the warden. I think he didn't want to say that an inmate gave him good advice that could have helped him keep his job. It's also my position, that if Mallinckrodt's followed my advice, he wouldn't have lost his job.

450) Did George Mallinckrodt make false statements in his book, to the media, and to Windy concerning you?

Yes. He told Windy I was paranoid, or in other words a very fearful person and that to some degree, I was scared to leave my cell. It's my position that Mallinckrodt didn't know that Windy had documentation from my mental health file that showed I never had any problems with paranoia or fearfulness.

Additionally, my life, prison history, and *Miami Herald* articles showed I wasn't paranoid or a fearful person. A paranoid or fearful person doesn't spend decades placing his life in danger to help others. It should also be noted, that I told Mallinckrodt through others and the mail, that his false statements about me were attacks on the credibility and stability of the primary witness in the Rainey case and several other cases being investigated in the FDC. Additionally that if Mallinckrodt's statements were true (which they're not), they would violate the federal Health Insurance Portability and Accountability Act (HIPAA).

451) Why do you think George Mallinckrodt misled Windy and others about you?

I'm not sure. He might have confused me with somebody else, or he might have thought if he attacked my stability from the beginning, it might weaken any statements that I might make about him.

452) What do you think about George Mallinckrodt's statements that he contacted the *Miami Herald* newspaper

and Federal Bureau of Investigations about Darren Rainey's case prior to you contacting them?

One, it's easy for a person to say he did something that he doesn't have any evidence to prove that he did. Two, if Mallinckrodt contacted the Federal Bureau of Investigation about the Darren Rainey case, they would have a record of it, and that record would be obtainable under the Freedom of Information Act. I'm also positive that the Federal Bureau of Investigations would have conducted some type of inquiry into what Mallinckrodt told them if he called them. Three, I believe if Mallinckrodt contacted a *Miami Herald* reporter about Darren Rainey, the reporter would have more than likely investigated what Mallinckrodt reported and made contact with him.

Additionally, Mallinckrodt presented himself in his book as contacting people in society to try and get justice on the Darren Rainey. He never wrote about trying to get justice of the evils done to many other inmates in the Dade CI TCU. This could be because the media attention was on the Darren Rainey case and that would sell his book.

Another obvious answer is, he never tried to contact authorities to seek justice for mentally disable inmates! Why is this the obvious answer? Because Mallinckrodt himself in his book refers to the mentally disabled inmates in the TCU as animals in a zoo. His own words, in his book, show what he thought of the mentally disabled inmates in the Dade CI TCU.

George Mallinckrodt may have told the Dade CI Warden what security staff were doing to the inmates in the TCU either to get help for the inmates, or because Mallinckrodt didn't like that the security staff were making his job harder. I don't know.

453) What do you think about the things George Mallinckrodt has done since 2014 to help inmates?

I appreciate everything Mallinckrodt has done to help inmates who are in need. It, also, doesn't matter to me what his motives were for his activism.

454) Tell me about your efforts to get off protective management while at the Columbia CI.

As I wrote in the beginning of this chapter, I started objecting to being housed in the Columbia CI Protective Management Unit soon after I arrived. I believe I was placed on protective management as a punishment for asserting my First Amendment rights to communicate with the press. This was particularly true given the conditions in the Columbia Protective Management Unit. I made formal requests and I filed a Petition for Writ of *Habeas Corpus* in 2014 with the Columbia County, Florida Circuit Court. In that petition, I contended that I was placed on protective management as retaliation for asserting my First Amendment rights to Freedom of Speech and Redress of Grievances. I explained in detail the unconstitutional conditions and how those conditions amounted to cruel and unusual punishment in violation of the Eighth Amendment of the U.S. Constitution.

455) Did other inmates tell you on a regular basis that your life was at risk?

Yes. Around July or August 2014, inmates started saying, "I'm surprised you haven't been killed yet." and "You know they're going to kill you?"

The majority of the inmates I met in the years following 2014 were surprised I wasn't killed, and they believed I would eventually be killed. I heard inmates make the above statements two to ten times a week. They believed I was going to be killed for exposing what happened to Darren Rainey and for exposing the unconstitutional conditions of the FDC.

Later, when I was housed at other correctional institutions, inmates continued to remind me that my life was at risk until I was transferred to Tennessee on March 17, 2017.

456) Please describe your protective management status at the end of 2014.

As far as I know, I was the only inmate on protective management status in order to be protected from FDC staff. This showed that the FDC didn't trust their own staff. If they did, they wouldn't have had to protect me from them. I filed several grievances and two Petitions for Writ of *Habeas Corpus* asking to be removed from protective management status.

The protection problems I had were institution specific. I thought I could have lived in the general population in other institutions. This means I needed to be assigned a special review status that prohibited me from being housed in places where I was in danger. In prison-speak, I needed to be "special reviewed" from specific FDC institutions.

457) Did Windy place a petition on Change.org to get you moved from the FDC to the Federal Bureau of Prisons?

Yes. However, she closed the petition down when she realized it could get me moved out of Florida. The petition had over 50,000 signatures when she closed it down. I wanted to remain in Florida to be near my family so they could make visits.

458) Will you tell me about the attempt to involuntarily interstate compact you?

Around the beginning of 2015, I was told that I had to go meet Columbia CI Classification Officer Ms. Glass in her office. When I got to her office, she tried to make me sign papers to be involuntary interstate compacted. I refused to sign the papers. After some minor debating, she agreed to let me go back to the protective management unit without signing the papers. She told me before I left her office, that my refusal to sign the papers wouldn't stop me from being involuntarily interstate compacted to another state.

When I got back to the Protective Management Unit, I called Windy and told her what happened. I explained to Windy that involuntary interstate compact meant that the FDC was trying to send me to the first prison system in another state that was willing to receive me.

I also told Windy everything that Ms. Glass said. Most importantly, I explained to Windy that Ms. Glass told me that the newly appointed Secretary of the FDC, Julie Jones, was the person behind this. Additionally, I explained that it was my position that Secretary Jones was trying to send me out of Florida in retaliation for me asserting my First Amendment rights to

Freedom of Speech, Redress of Grievances, and Access to the Courts on matters concerning FDC.

Finally, Windy and I discussed who she should call and what actions she should take to try and stop the retaliation I was being threatened with. Within hours, she told several individuals in the media and lawyers with different civil rights groups about the threat to involuntary interstate compact me. That day and the next day, the media and civil rights groups inquired with FDC why I was being threatened with an involuntary interstate compact. Florida Legal Service's Lawyer Peter Sleasman agreed to represent me in a court action to challenge it.

In the afternoon, on the day after I was threatened to be involuntarily interstate compacted, FDC Deputy Secretary Timothy Cannon called Windy. During that call, he told her that he had spoken with Secretary Jones, I wasn't going to involuntarily interstate compacted, and there wouldn't be any more attempts to involuntarily interstate compact me.

A few hours later, I was told by the Columbia CI Warden, Assistant Warden, and Major that the main office for the FDC said I wasn't going to be involuntarily interstate compacted and there wouldn't be any more attempts to do such to me.

459) Why are you now in the Tennessee Department of Corrections?

Because I was involuntarily interstate compacted on March 17, 2017.

460) So FDC Secretary Julie Jones didn't keep her word?

Correct.

461) Tell me about other significant contacts you had with the media in 2015.

In August 2015, the *Miami Herald* newspaper published an article about my activities called the *Caged Crusader.* It is the most thorough newspaper article published on me.

Also in that August, I got a letter from *WTVT Fox 13 Tampa Bay, Florida* Reporter Craig Patrick in August 2015. He wanted to know if he could interview me on camera about the Darren Rainey case and the FDC. I mailed him back a letter agreeing to the interview.

Chapter 17: Suwanee CI Annex (May, June 2014) and Columbia CI (June 2014-September 2015)

At the end of 2014, I was contacted by Eyal Press, a reporter for *The New Yorker* magazine. He told me that Harriet Kryscowski (former Dade CI coach and counselor) contacted him about the Darren Rainey case and the abuse of the mentally disabled inmates in the Dade CI TCU. He asked if I would be willing to talk with him for an article he wanted to write. I wrote him saying I would like to talk with him and for him to please make arrangements to visit me. I gave Mr. Press Windy's name and contact information and told Windy and Casey Frank about Eyal Press. I asked Windy to provide him with copies of all the documents he needed and any information she could help him with.

When I read in Mr. Press' letter about Harriet Kryscowski, I again realized what a good woman Ms. Kryscowski was. Even though she no longer lived in Florida and it had been more than a year since she worked at Dade CI, she didn't forget about the Darren Rainey case, the weak, and those in need of help in the Dade CI TCU.

In early 2015, Mr. Press came to Columbia CI to interview me about the facts for the article that he was going to write. We spoke in the same office *Miami Herald* Reporter Julie K. Brown and I had previously spoken. A Columbia CI lieutenant sat in on this interview. While Eyal Press was in Florida, he also interviewed several other people who he thought could be helpful in his investigation.

His articles appeared in *The New Yorker* in 2016, *A Whistle-Blower Behind Bars* on April 27, 2016 and *Madness* featuring Harriet Kryscowski on May 2, 2016.

462) When and why did you leave the Columbia CI Protective Management Unit?

In September 2015, I transferred from the Columbia CI Protective Management Unit to the Martin CI Protective Management Unit. I requested this transfer for reasons I cannot disclose at this time.

Chapter 18: Martin CI (September 2015 - May 24, 2016)

463) Please tell me about Martin CI and its Protective Management Unit.

Martin CI has always been considered one of the most violent institutions in the FDC and either the first or second most violent in South Florida. It is located in Indiantown, Florida and is a Psych.3 institution, which means it houses inmates with psychological problems. It is a dumping ground for gang members and the worst inmates in Florida. It did not have either a TCU or a Crisis Stabilization Unit located at it.

I was housed in the Martin CI Protective Management Unit. I have been incarcerated at Martin CI three times; this was my third.

All of the dorms in Martin CI were Butterfly dorms except Delta dorm, which was a T-Building. The protective management unit was located in Bravo Dorm (B-Dorm) Wings one and two. Wings three and four were used for administrative and disciplinary confinement. In the middle of the four wings, was a sally port and an officers' station.

Martin CI was full of predators, sexually aggressive inmates, and gang members who are victimizing the inmates who actually qualified to be in a protective management unit by federal 1 law and prison rules. Martin CI's protective management unit had more street narcotics than the Columbia CI protective management unit. There was a constant strong odor of K-2 in the unit all the time I was there.

464) Who were the warden, assistant warden, colonel, and classification officer there?

When I first arrived there, the warden was Robert Hendry. He was an assistant warden at Columbia CI in 2014 when I was housed there. He was a good man.

The assistant warden was Royce Marlow. I knew him and worked for him as an orderly when he was the major in the Dade CI TCU. I also knew him when he was a colonel at Dade CI. He was the colonel there when the *Hot-Water-Shower* was being used to punish mentally disabled inmates and when Darren Rainey died in the *Hot-Water-Shower*.

Mr. Colon was the colonel. He was also a good man.

My classification officer was Joann Posten. She was my classification officer for my two prior incarcerations there, and she was involved in both of my prior transfers from Martin CI.

465) Were there staff changes during your third stay and Martin CI?

Yes. Warden Hendry was promoted to Bureau Chief of Security at the Tallahassee, Florida main office of the FDC, Assistant Warden Marlow was forced to resign, and Colonel Colon was promoted to an assistant warden and transferred to Central Florida Reception Center.

After Assistant Warden Marlow was forced to resign, several staff and inmates at Martin CI contended that I was behind his forced resignation. This rumor created issues for me with the staff. Also, the new Warden, Elizabeth Mallard, Assistant Warden, Mr. Swineberg, and Colonel who took over at Martin CI were very retaliatory and nothing like Warden Hendry and Colonel Colon.

466) Let's focus problems in the Martin CI, protective management unit. Were there problems with mail delivery?

Yes. Several inmates told me that staff were throwing away mail at Martin CI. In my first two months there, I did not receive several letters people in society had mailed me. I first talked to the staff about the mail problem, and, when they didn't take any action to fix the problem, I began to file grievances trying to get it fixed.

Staff responded blaming the post office for not delivering the mail on time. I knew this was not true. I also knew that if I told the local postal inspector that Martin CI staff said post office employees were not delivering the mail on time, the postal inspector would investigate the matter, establish that the post office employees were timely, and would come down on Martin CI staff for not delivering the U.S. Mail to inmates.

I filed a grievance stating I was going to advise the postal inspector of staff's contention that the local post office employees were not getting the mail to Martin CI on time. In my grievance, I noted that the postal inspector would, more than likely, come down on Martin CI staff after he established that the post office employees were doing their jobs. Also, I wrote a letter advising the Governor's Chief General Inspector Melinda Miguel that Martin CI staff were not processing and delivering U.S. Mail to the inmates at Martin CI. Finally, Windy reported the problem to the area's postal inspector and told him Martin CI staff were blaming the post office for delivery problems.

Within two weeks, I was told that Martin CI Colonel Colon had ordered a search and investigation of the Martin CI mailroom. This resulted in the discovery of boxes of old mail that hadn't been given out to the inmates. During the next several weeks, security staff passed-out large stacks of old, undelivered mail to inmates. Some of it had been received several months earlier.

The mail problem was fixed, and the mail was arrived on time for several months. The problem began again when a new administration took over at Martin CI around March 2016.

467) Tell me about recreation, homosexuality, narcotics, and drug abuse problems in the Martin protective management unit.

The protective management inmates had almost no access to the recreation yard. We were only allowed to go to the recreation yard one to five times a month for about an hour per visit.

As in Columbia CI protective management unit, homosexual activity was very prevalent in the Martin CI protective management unit. As I detailed in an affidavit I wrote in March 2016, much of this was predatory and arose due to the housing of at risk inmates with inmates who were classified as either known predators or potential predators. See below for the affidavit.

The Martin CI protective management unit was flooded with K-2. There was a constant odor of K-2 being smoked in both protective management wings. Inmates were constantly flipping-out, passing-out and twacking-out. The meaning of these terms is as follows:

- Flipping-out: Inmates start acting like different types of animals. The most common animals I saw them act like were dogs, horses, and rabbits. I also saw inmates flip-out, start hallucinating, and get violent. The term flipping-out is used to denote anytime an inmate on K-2 hallucinates, hears voices, or gets violent.

- The term passing-out denotes when an inmate on K-2 passes-out and doesn't move
- Twack is another name for K-2. Twacking-out is when an inmate high on K-2 falls to the ground, and starts flopping like a fish out of water, and usually vomiting at the same time.

468) Were protective management unit inmates at Martin CI directed to walk in the same area as the general population?

Yes. We walked in the same area on an almost daily basis. Inmates on protective management status are supposed to be the most protected inmates in the FDC. By rule, general population inmates were not supposed to have any physical contact with protective management inmates. However, at Martin CI, the staff allowed all of the general population inmates to have physical contact with the protective management inmates.

This was a serious problem because the protective management unit inmates at Martin CI had some of the most serious protection problems in Florida. Three of them were on the Federal Witness Protection program, and the Federal Bureau of Prisons was hiding them in protective management status in the Florida prison system. Approximately 20 of the inmates in the Martin CI protective management unit were former law enforcement officer. Some of these former officers were involved in the arrests of inmates housed in Martin CI's general population. Other inmates in the protective management unit had gang contracts on them, and there were hundreds of gang members in the general population. The Martin CI staff were placing these inmates and the other protective management inmates in danger by allowing general population inmates to have physical contact with them.

469) Tell me about your first two cellmates in the Martin CI Protective Management Unit.

I don't remember their names. The first was a K-2 abuser who was constantly high from the time he woke up till the time he went to bed. Within a week of me being there, he asked me for

331

help in getting from the dayroom to our cell. He was so high on K-2 that he didn't think he could navigate the 20 feet from the dayroom to our cell. He was my cellmate for about four to six weeks.

All the inmates referred to my second cellmate as Classification Officer Ms. Posten's boyfriend. In prison lingo, this meant the inmate was very friendly with Ms. Posten. I was his cellmate for two or three weeks.

470) At the end of 2015, did you learn that Timothy Jones, your cellmate at Columbia CI, stabbed someone?

Yes. Not too long after I transferred from Columbia CI, Timothy Jones attempted to kill his cellmate James Nash. I was told that Jones used a pencil to stab Nash in his eye, face, and neck. I was also informed that Nash was blinded in that eye and had to be hospitalized after it happened. A criminal investigation was conducted and Jones was placed on close-management-one and transferred to Florida State Prison.

Nash was sleeping when Jones stabbed him. Every night that I was housed with Jones, he was awake and high on drugs. He flipped-out while he was high and stabbed Nash. I was blessed that God made sure that Jones didn't cause me any physical harm while I was sleeping or awake.

I learned about what Jones did to Nash while I was gathering information on prison staff not complying with federal law and the *Inmate Risk Management System/Sexual Risk Indicator* in any of the four protective management unit within the FDC. As noted above, I started this project while I was in the Columbia CI protective management unit.

FDC staff had been telling me since June 2014 that there was a statewide confirmed risk to my safety. While staff were telling me this, they were housing me with drug-addicted convicted killers and dangerous inmates. I knew from my approximately 15 years of incarceration that FDC had a long history of housing inmates they disliked with physically and sexually violent inmates. They did this to increase the chances that someone would harm the inmate they did not like.

I had been on protective management status since June 2014. Before the Jones incident, I had not complained about my cellmates. However, what Jones did to Nash caused me to realize that I had to protect myself and take a stand to stop prison staff from continuing to house me with inmates I wasn't supposed to be housed with. If I continued to allow prison staff to house me with dangerous inmates, they could blame any cellmate who harmed or killed me.

I told Windy, the media, people I knew who were in civil rights groups, the Federal Bureau of Investigations, Chief Inspector General Melinda Miguel and several others about the problems I was having with prison staff placing me with dangerous inmates. When I told Warden Hendry about these matters, he said, "I want to make sure nothing happens to you. I'm going to have you housed in a cell by yourself in the Protective Management Unit."

That same day, I was directed to move to cell B2-102, which was a single man cell.

Later on, I found out that Assistant Warden Marlow and Colonel Colon agreed with Warden Hendry's order to house me alone. The cell I was moved to was directly in front of a mounted security camera.

471) Were there any good staff at Martin CI?

Yes. I knew several good officers there and one nice classification officer. I'm also sure there were other good staff there that I didn't know.

472) While you were on protective management status in Columbia CI and Martin CI, did any inmate threaten or harm you?

No.

473) Was the abbreviation for Florida Department of Corrections changed in late 2015 or early 2016?

Yes. For decades the Florida Department of Corrections used the abbreviation, "FDOC" on all their signs, logos, etc. to denote the Florida Department of Corrections. At the end of 2015 or beginning of 2016, Florida Department of Corrections Secretary, Julie Jones, ordered that "FDOC" be switched on all their signs, logos, etc. to "FDC." She claimed to have believed an abbreviation change would somehow contribute to changing the conditions in the Florida prison system. At the end of 2014, Windy started calling the Florida Department of Corrections, the "Florida Department of Corruption." Windy was well known for doing this, and some people thought Julie Jones switched it from FDOC to FDC in response to Windy calling it the "Florida Department of Corruption."

474) Did a new FDC Inspector General take over at the beginning of 2016?

Yes. His name was Lester Fernandez.

475) What were you told about the Dade County, Florida State Attorney Katherine Fernandez Rundle?

There were a lot of inmates incarcerated at Martin CI who were convicted out of Dade County, Florida. Some were previously employed for the court and law enforcement in Dade County. For instance, a former Dade County judge with the last name Davis was incarcerated in Martin CI.

Several of the inmates had been in the Dade County State Attorney's Office interacting with the office in its official capacities. Two of these former government officials said that Dade County, Florida State Attorney Katherine Rundle was well known for making racist statements about black people and for sharing songs by David Allen Coe, who is considered by many to sing some of the most extreme racist music. They said Rundle found humor in Coe's songs.

I don't know if these allegations about Katherine Rundle are true. Both of these inmates were convicted by her, and they both knew I was involved with trying to get justice for Darren Rainey who was black and was killed in the jurisdiction of the Dade County State Attorney's Office.

476) Tell me about your medical issues while you were in Martin CI.

I did not receive any medical care upon my arrival at Martin CI. After filing about two dozen grievances, I started receiving medical care for my stomach, back, and eyes, but not on my broken wrist. It took a while before I started receiving medical care for my wrist.

A few days after I arrived, I passed-out and hit the ground. Stress, not eating properly, and not doing any exercise were causing me health problems that would eventually get worse.

477) Were you referred to see an orthopedic surgeon for your broken wrist at the end of 2015?

The doctor at Martin CI ordered more x-rays of my right wrist. These showed my wrist was still broken, and I was again referred to an orthopedic surgeon. Eventually, I was taken to see Dr. Check Kam, an orthopedic surgeon. Dr. Kam confirmed that the x-ray showed my wrist was still broken and ordered an MRI to see if the bone was dead, which it might have been because of the long time I had gone without surgery. He also said I needed a screw placed in my wrist and a bone graft. I think he also said that, if the bone in my wrist was dead, I would need a cell transplant to bring the bone back to life before the bone graft. He said the bone graft wouldn't work if the bone was dead. He also said I would eventually get severe arthritis and have other medical problems with my wrist if I didn't have the surgery.

478) What did the MRI show, and what did the orthopedic surgeon say should be done?

Dr. Kam said the MRI showed that the bone in my wrist was still alive and asked if I wanted to have surgery. I said I did. After he explained the procedure, I asked him if I could receive a local anesthetic instead of general anesthesia. I told him I was starting to have heart and breathing problems and that close relatives of mine were allergic to anesthetics.

He said I would be OK and to speak with the doctor at Martin CI. Dr. Kam said he was an orthopedic surgeon and the Martin CI doctor would handle the other matters with my health and advise him (Dr. Kam) if I was healthy enough for the surgery. I then asked him if that meant I could have the local during the surgery. This time he responded, "No, all prisoners are put to sleep during surgery."

I did not receive surgery on my broken wrist during nine months I was housed at Martin CI, and I lived with the pain in my wrist all the time I was housed there.

479) Were you having problems with your heart and you breathing?

Yes. I had problems with an irregular heartbeat and breathing. They got worse as the months passed. Also, I had issues with my heart rate and blood pressure being real low and then high.

480) Did your medical care deteriorate in the spring of 2016?

Yes. In retaliation for arranging for several inmates in protective management to be interviewed by Julie K. Brown of the *Miami Herald* in April 2016 and for my own participation in an interview with her, Martin CI staff restricted my access to medical care, discontinued my special diet, and withdrew my medications. I detailed this retaliation in an affidavit I sent in May 2016. Below is an excerpt:

Excerpt from SWORN AFFIDAVIT

"To: Ms. Vanita Gupta, Assistant U.S. Attorney General., U.S. Department of Justice, Civil Rights Division. Florida Senator Greg Evers, Wexford Health Sources Inc., American Civil Liberties Union, Attn.: Howard Simon. Stop Prison Abuse Now, Attn.: Steven Wetstein

"ARNP Chatalier discontinued Affiant's Low Residue Diet which he started receiving about six years ago for his stomach condition which causes him to defecate up to seven times a day and gives him severe stomach pain. Since Affiant's diet was discontinued on April 7, 2016, he's had severe stomach pain and has been using the bathroom several times a day.

"Affiant has sinus rhythm with sinus arrhythmia. On May 2, 2016, Affiant passed-out in his cell. He reported this to Classification Officer Ms. Posten, and Correctional Officers Johnson and Pellirenne. Affiant wasn't permitted to see medical staff. He also told Martin CI staff for several weeks that he had been having chest pain, and that over those weeks, he was not allowed to see medical staff.

"On April 7, 2016, ARNP Chatalier also tampered with Affiant's pain medicine and discontinued his allergy medicine. Now Affiant has no pain medicine for his broken right wrist, sciatic nerve damage, and hurt back. Affiant has been living in pain with these medical problems.

"Affiant has two or more cysts in his right wrist. Medical staff are refusing to prescribe him an antibiotic to prevent infection from entering his body.

"Affiant was approved to see an orthopedic surgeon for wrist surgery before this retaliation starts. Health Service Administrator Ms. Rebele told Affiant that he would be taken out of his cell and placed in another cell the night before his surgery. The conditions in the other cell would violate Affiant's 8th Amendment Right to Protection from Cruel and Unusual Punishment. Ms. Rebele also told the Affiant that, if he didn't want to go to the other cell the night before his wrist surgery, that he would be denied wrist surgery on his broken wrist."

481) Did you receive the Maurice Rosen Act of Courage Award from the Florida ACLU in 2015?

Yes. Before I left Columbia CI, Casey Frank of the *Miami Herald* told me the Florida ACLU of Florida was giving awards to reporter Julie K. Brown and to me. Julie Brown's award was for reporting on the conditions in the FDC. I don't know the name of the award she received.

When I heard I was to receive the Maurice Rosen Act of Courage Award, I didn't know what to think. I felt I did not do anything to get an award. I just did what God wanted me to do. I didn't think that I was worthy of any type of award, but I do feel blessed and honored that the ACLU of Florida wanted to show me kindness by giving me one.

The award ceremony was in Miami, Florida in October 2015. I was in the Martin CI protective management unit when it took place, and my sister Windy and her son Patrick travelled to Miami to receive the award for me. Windy met with Florida ACLU Executive Director Howard Simon and several other representatives of the ACLU; Steven Wetstein and other representatives of Stop Prison Abuse Now; Randal Berg of the Florida Justice Institute; George Mallinckrodt, as well as, several other individuals involved with the protection of civil rights.

A day or two later, the ACLU. Stop Prison Abuse Now, Windy, and others met together for a press release concerning the FDC. This press release discussed a letter signed by more than a dozen Florida civil rights groups. The letter was directed to the United States Department of Justice, Civil Rights Division in Washington D.C. and requested a Civil Rights of Institutionalized Persons Act investigation into different matters in the FDC.

Windy and Patrick then returned to their home in central Florida when they were done in Miami.

482) Did you file a federal lawsuit against FDC staff at the end of 2015?

Yes, I filed a 42 U.S.C. § 1983 Civil Rights Complaint lawsuit in the Dade County, Florida Federal District Court (Case Number: 1:15-CV-23367). The lawsuit was against several prison staff and can be located on the "Public Access to Court Electronic Records" internet site.

483) What was in the affidavit on PMUs you mailed to several individuals on March 15, 2016?

The sworn affidavit stated the following:

Sworn Affidavit

"To: Vanita Gupta, Assistant U.S. Attorney General, U.S. Department of Justice, Civil Rights Division, American Civil Liberties Union of Florida, Attn: Howard Simon

"Stop Prison Abuse Now, Attn: Steven Wetstein

"Protective management status in the Florida Department of Corrections (FDC) is a classification status FDC uses in an attempt to comply with their 8th Amendment Constitution duty to protect prisoners from harm by other prisoners and the U.S. Supreme Court's decision in Farmer v. Brennan, 511 U.S. 825, 164 S. Ct. 1970 (1994).

"The following types of inmates are legally housed in Protective Management Unit status: Prior law-enforcement officials, ex-government, high profile inmates, transgender, petite or young inmates whose size or characteristics show they would have protection problems in general population, and inmates FDC has verified have been subjected to sexual battery (FAC 33-602.220(3)(c)3).

"FDC has been housing gang members in Protective Management Units for approximately 10 years. These gang members are reigning terror in Protective Management Units by committing severe acts of violence against the inmates, FDC is supposed to be providing with the most protection. Out of the approximate 400 protective management inmates in FDC, dozens of them are registered gang members with FDC and the Florida Department of Law Enforcement (Fla. Stat.§ 874.09).

"FDC uses the words security threat group to identify gangs and gang members. The following rules say that FDC staff are supposed to house gang members in close management: FAC 33-601.800 (2)(A) 2.N, (2)(C) 2.6. Instead of placing gang members on close management which they qualify for by FDC's own rules, FDC staff have been placing them in protective management status which they do not qualify for by FDC rule: FAC 33-602.220 (3)(c)3.

"FDC has a classification system called the Inmate Risk Management System/ Sexual Risk Indicator (IRMS/SRI). The two highest rankings on the IRMS system are Identified Predator and Potential Predator. FDC staff consider these inmates to be the most physically aggressive inmates in FDC. Prison staff have been placing inmates in Protective Management Units that FDC deem predators or who qualify to be ranked as predators by their own IRMS classification system. These predators do not qualify for protective management by FDC rule FAC 33-602.220 (3) (c) 3. However, these predators do qualify for Close Management by FDC rules: FAC 33-601.800 (2) (B) 2.B., F., H., 33-601.800 (2)(C)2.D. These predators are committing severe acts of physical violence in protective management units to inmates

Department of Corruption

FDC staff are supposed to be providing with the most protection.

On the SRI classification system, High Aggressive Risk and Moderate Aggressive Risk inmates are considered the most sexually aggressive inmates in FDC. Prison staff have been placing inmates who have these rankings, or who qualify to be ranked as such in protective management units. These aggressive risk inmates have been raping and sexually battering the inmates in protective management units that FDC is supposed to be providing with the most protection. By FDC's own rules, these sexual predators qualify for close management (FAC 33-601.800 (2) (A) 2.L, 33-601.800 (2) (B) 2.H), and do not qualify for protective management status (FAC 33-602.220 (3) (C) 3.). This also a violation of the Prison Rape Elimination Act (34 USC § 30301).

"FDC staff have not only permitted these gang members, predators, and sexually aggressive inmates to be housed in protective management units in violation of FDC's own rules, but they have also allowed these inmates to reign physical and sexual terror on inmates who qualify for protective management, and that FDC is supposed to be providing with the most. In other words, FDC staff are placing gang members, predators, and sexually aggressive inmates in the same housing wings with ex-law enforcement and government inmates, high profile inmates, transgenders, petite inmates, and inmates FDC has recognized on their own IRMS classification system as Identified Prey and Potential Prey inmates. This is in violation of federal law. Marsh v. Butler County, Ala., 268 F. 3d 1014 (11th Cir. 2001); Brown v. Budz, 398 F 3d 904 (7th Cir. 2005).

"Additionally, staff at the institutions where protective management units are located refuse to adequately discipline the inmates when they commit their extreme acts of physical and sexual violence. Since Affiant's June 20, 2014 placement on protective management, he has witnessed inmates spend an average of 30 days or less in confinement

340

for stabbing and sexually battering protective management inmates, hitting them in the head with broomsticks, hitting them in the face and head with steel locks, and physically battering them. After spending 30 days or less in confinement, the gang members, predators, and sexually aggressive inmates are placed back in a protective management unit where they resume their reign of terror. The failure of FDC staff to take corrective action in response to high rates of assault or to particular patterns of assault violates the 8th Amendment of the U.S. Constitution (LaMarca v. Turner, 662 F. Supp. 647 (M.D. FLA. 1987); Abrams v. Hunter, 910 F. Supp. 620 (M.D. FLA. 1995). This failure to take corrective action also violates FDC's following rules: FAC 33-600.800 (2) (A) 2.B, L, (2) (B) 2.C, F, H.

"The following FDC documents will prove the matters stated herein (1) The housing rosters on all four protective management units. (2) The classification files of all the inmates on protective management status. (3) The disciplinary records and protective management records of all the inmates on protective management in FDC. (4) The incident reports for the last five years of all the incidents in the four protective management units.

"Affiant previously filed 42 USC § 1983 Civil Rights Complaint lawsuits in the Jacksonville, Florida Federal District Court (Case No.: 3:2015-CV-00130, and 3:2015-CV-00374), and the Miami, Florida Federal District Court (Case No.: 1:15-CV-23367) that can be located on the Public Access to Court Electronic Records internet site. These lawsuits mention in some detail the violations of federal law mentioned herein.

"Copies of prior sworn affidavits that the Affiant filed on the unconstitutional conditions of FDC Protective Management Units can be reviewed at http://www.helpmybrotherharoldhempstesd@wordpress.com; http://www.wobblywarrior@wordpress.com; and SPAN (Stop Prison Abuse Now) at nationsinside.com

Department of Corruption

"FDC has a long documented history of setting up inmates with frivolous disciplinary reports and subjecting them to retaliatory transfers when they assert their rights under the 1st Amendment of the U.S. Constitution. Affiant is concerned that FDC staff might attempt to censor his assertion of his 1st Amendment rights by subjecting him to retaliatory disciplinary action via a frivolous disciplinary report, or to a retaliatory transfer. Affiant was not told this would happen as of the date on this affidavit, but he does know that FDC staff do not like that he is trying to obtain help for the victims in protective management units.

"Around the beginning of April 2014, Affiant's wrist was broken prior to him transferring from Dade CI. Affiant was called to the Transitional Care Unit at Dade CI to clean up a blood spill on the upper tier in Wing J-3. The events that happened after he arrived there caused him to get nervous and take flight running down the stairs from the upper tier to the lower tier in Wing J3. Affiant fell while doing this and broke his right wrist. Since this happened, staff have refused to arrange surgery for Affiant's broken wrist at a safe location. Affiant believes staff might attempt to transfer him to a location where he cannot have the wrist surgery at the doctor's office he has been approved to have surgery at. Affiant believes FDC staff will do this as a form of punishment for his attempts to help the victims in protective management units.

"FDC staff are clearly subjecting the inmates who qualify for protective management to violations of their 8th Amendment Right to Protection from Cruel and Unusual Punishment by failing to protect them from prison rape in violation of the Prison Rape Elimination Act (34 USC § 30301).

"Relief sought: Affiant is requesting that the U.S. Department of Justice conduct an investigation into the unconstitutional conditions in FDC Protective Management Units to protect the civil rights of those incarcerated in them in accordance with Civil Rights of Institutionalized Persons Act (42 USC§ 1997). Affiant will assist in any way he can with said investigation."

Unnotarized Oath

'Under penalty of perjury, I swear that everything stated herein is true and correct.

Executed on this 15th day of March 2016.

Affiant: {Signature of Harold Hempstead appears here on original document}

Harold Hempstead, D.C. #268866

Martin C.I.

1150 Southwest Allapattah Road

Indiantown, Florida 34956

c.c.: Florida Senator Greg Evers, Chief Inspector General Melinda Miguel, FDLE Commissioner, Florida Justice Institute (Randall Berg), Florida Legal Services, Disability Rights Florida (Molly Paris), Forgotten Majority Inc., Human Rights Defense Center (Lance T. Weber), *Miami Herald* newspaper (Julie K. Brown), CBS4 Miami, Florida (Michelle Gillen), WTVT Fox 13 Tampa, Florida (Craig Patrick), New Yorker magazine (Eyal Press), Windy Hempstead, Susan Chandler, George Mallinckrodt.

484) Did prison staff question you about this affidavit?

Yes. Martin CI Captain Knight questioned me. He didn't tell me who asked him to question me. He asked several questions about the predators, sexually aggressive inmates and gang members in the protective management unit. He also asked me what could be done to fix the problems listed in my affidavit. I explained the only way the problems could be fixed was if the predators, sexually aggressive inmates, and gang members were placed on close management, released into the general population, or housed separately from the other inmates housed on protective management status. I explained that housing physically and sexually violent inmates and gang members with non-violent inmates was a clear violation of federal case law concerning the 8th Amendment of the U.S. Constitution and FDC rules.

485) Were ex-law enforcement officers also concerned about being in the Martin CI, Protective Management Unit?

Yes. During the almost two years I was housed in the Martin CI, protective management unit, several ex-law enforcement officers requested to sign-out of protective management and to go to the general population. They did this because they said they felt they would be safer in general population. They felt that, overall, the conditions in general population could not be as bad as they were in the protective management unit.

I was able to obtain a list of about 15 ex-law enforcement officers and one former Dade County, Florida Circuit Court Judge who signed out of Martin CI protective management status and went back to general population. I was also told all wanted to go back to the general population because of the violence and very bad conditions inside the Martin CI Protective Management Units.

486) In April or May 2016, did you mail letters to the Chief Inspector General Melinda Miguel about Martin CI's retaliating against you?

Yes.

487) Did you meet with Randy Evans and Jim Knowels while you were housed at Martin CI?

Yes. Several times, but I can't tell you what we discussed at this time.

488) Tell me about your meetings with three different reporters at Martin CI in the end of 2015.

Between October and December 2015, I met with *Miami Herald* Reporter Julie K. Brown, *WTVT Fox 13* Tampa, Florida Reporter Craig Patrick, and CBS 4 Miami, Florida Reporter Michelle Gillen. The interview with Julie Brown was specifically on the Darren Rainey case. The interviews with Craig Patrick and Michelle Gillen were in reference to the Darren Rainey case and other matters in the FDC.

344

I was not subjected to any type of retaliation by prison staff for these interviews.

489) Did Reporters Craig Patrick and Michelle Gillen air reports on their interviews with you?

Yes. They both aired two or more television news reports on their interviews with me. I believe their reports were aired between December 2015 and May 2016.

490) Around March 2016, did the *Miami Herald* begin investigating Florida's four FDC protective management units?

Yes. When the *Miami Herald* told me about the investigation, I told them I would like to see if I could get some protective management inmates to talk with *Miami Herald* Julie Brown about the violence and unconstitutional conditions in the protective management units. The Herald told me if I could, to let them know.

Eight protective management inmates other than myself agreed to speak with Julie Brown. One had been housed in the Columbia CI protective management unit when I was housed there. He wrote letters to the Governor's Chief Inspector General Melinda Miguel, the Florida Department of Law Enforcement Commissioner, and *Miami Herald* saying he thought that inmate Myong was killed. The second inmate said he had been on protective management for decades. The only thing that I could verify about him was that he used to be a confidential informant. The third inmate said he had been in protective management for decades. He was a Caucasian, and he was in prison for murdering a black man. His case received a lot of media attention because he was a known racist associated with the Church of the Creator. The fourth inmate was a Tennessee inmate serving time in the FDC on interstate corrections compact. Tennessee newspaper articles showed he was a high ranking Vice Lord gang member. If I remember correctly, he was the head of one of the Vice Lord gangs in Tennessee.

The fifth inmate was a former law enforcement officer in Broward County, Florida. He had been housed in the Martin CI Protective Management Unit for several years. The sixth inmate, who went by the nickname "Face," was with one of the Aryan

Department of Corruption

Nation gangs in the Florida prison system. The seventh inmate
was a Spanish inmate who was a confidential informant for
several different law enforcement agencies. Finally, the eighth
inmate was an inmate who professed to be a member of the
Nation of Islam.

**491) At the end of 2015, did you challenge your protective
management status by filing a petition for Writ of *Habeas
Corpus*?**

As previously mentioned, I filed a Petition for Writ of
Habeas Corpus in the Columbia County, Florida Circuit Court
challenging my June 2014 placement on protective management
status. When I was transferred to Martin CI, I had that petition
transferred to the Martin County, Florida Circuit Court, and I then
amended that petition. In addition to challenging my placement, I
sought as a relief to be released to the general population. The
amended petition explained the extremely violent and
unconstitutional conditions in all four FDC Protective
Management Units.

**492) What is a "special review" and did you seek one while
you were on protective management status?**

Special review is a classification designation that prohibits
an inmate from being housed at an institution where he is likely to
have protection problems or because he would be a threat to the
institution. It's like a "keep separate."

All of the time I was housed on protective management, I
was trying to be special reviewed from Dade CI, Regional
Medical Center, South Florida Reception Center, and Everglades
CI.

I did not want to go to the Regional Medical Center because
of my 2013 protection problems with Regional Medical Center
staff. I wanted to be special reviewed from South Florida
Reception Center and Everglade CI because there were staff at
those institutions who had known me at Dade CI. Some of those
staff were being investigated by the federal government. Also, I
was very well known to all the prison staff who worked at
institutions in Dade County, Florida because of the extensive
media coverage citing me as the inmate who blew the whistle on
the Darren Rainey case, Dade CI, and the FDC. I was eventually

346

special reviewed from Dade CI, and I more than qualified to also be special reviewed from South Florida Reception Center and Everglade CI.

493) What happened with Sergeant Wilcox concerning meals for protective management inmates?

The protective management unit inmates who were on a diet had to give their identification cards to general population inmates in the chow hall to receive their diet trays. Inmate I.D. cards were also used by inmates to purchase canteen, and the canteen windows were operated by inmates. It is a violation of prison rules for an inmate to give his I.D. card to another inmate for any reason.

I disagreed with the requirement to give a general population inmate my I.D. card in order to get my diet tray in the chow hall. However, I still did it. Over the time I was housed there, I saw general population inmates who worked in the chow hall steal I.D. cards from protective management unit inmates. Staff did nothing about this, and I began objecting to protective management unit inmates surrendering their I.D. cards in order to receive their diets. For a short time, several staff who worked in the chow hall stopped making protective management inmates do this.

One day at lunch, a staff member told the protective management unit inmates if we wanted our diet trays, we had to give our I.D. cards inmate workers. We all did. However, when another inmate and I received our diet trays without our I.D. cards on them, I told the officer at the tray window, and he did not do anything to help get our I.D. cards back. When this officer said it was time to leave and return to the unit, I said I wanted to talk to a captain. In the process of trying to get the officer to ask the captain to come to the chow hall, Sergeant Wilcox came up to the officer, the other inmate (Michael) and me and said, "What's going on?"

I responded, "We told the officer that we didn't get our I.D. cards back, and he acted like he didn't care. An inmate in the back is trying to steal our cards, and we don't know who it is. I need my card back. I have money on my card, and I don't want to have it stolen." Sergeant Wilcox then went into the section of the chow hall where the general population inmates were.

When he came back, he had our I.D. cards. As he was walking towards Michael and me, Sergeant Wilcox said, "Michael, I got yours and Big Deal's cards. Big Deal, you're a Bitch. Here's your card. Get out my face."

As the other inmate and I walked out to return to the unit, Sergeant Wilcox walked out with us. When we got outside, he looked up at the sky and yelled at the birds, "Get out of here. Make way. Big Deal is coming. Make way for Big Deal." He then spoke to us saying, "Alright, Michael and Big Deal, you have a nice walk back to the check-in unit."

When we got back to the protective management unit, I continued with my day as normal. An hour or two later, I was on the phone with Windy when Sergeant Wilcox and two officers came in and began harassing other protective management inmates. Because Wilcox had never before been in my wing and because of him just starting an issue with me in the chow hall, I took what he and the two other officers were doing as retaliation. As I watched them go cell to cell harassing inmates, I told Windy what was going on. Because Wilcox was known for physically battering inmates and setting them up with false disciplinary reports, I felt it was in my best interest to tell Martin CI Warden Hendry about my recent issues with Sergeant Wilcox.

While on the phone, I asked Windy to send an e-mail to Warden Hendry advising him of the issue in the chow hall. I wanted to put a stop to protective management inmates having to give their I.D. cards to general population inmates who worked in the chow hall. Windy told me to call her back later on that night, and she would read me the e-mail before she sent it to Warden Hendry.

When the protective management inmates exited the dorm to go to dinner chow, Sergeant Wilcox and the same two officers were outside the dorm waiting for us. As soon as Wilcox saw me, he yelled, "There goes Big Deal. What's up, Big Deal? Everybody, that's Big Deal." He then started yelling at the birds, "Get out of here, Big Deal is coming. Go, get out of here." Sergeant Wilcox's actions that day, and his history caused me to know that I had to take the threat that he posed seriously.

When I called Windy back that night, I told her everything that happened at dinner with Sergeant Wilcox. She added that information to her e-mail and sent it while I was on the phone with her. Warden Hendry e-mailed a response saying that he was on vacation but that he would forward her e-mail to Assistant Warden Marlow and direct him to take care of the problems.

I knew Assistant Warden Marlow from when he was the major in the Dade CI TCU in 2010. He did not have a history of being fair, by the book, or helping protect inmates. He had a history of covering up staff abuse and mistreatment of inmates. Since Warden Hendry was on vacation, he was not available to oversee Marlow's actions. Marlow also knew that he was a subject in the federal investigations of matters at Dade CI. Finally, he knew I was the inmate who helped launch the federal and state investigations of him and his old co-workers at Dade CI. It's more than likely that Marlow thought Sergeant Wilcox was doing a lot of people a favor in harassing me and would do more people a favor if he set me up or caused me harm.

When Marlow didn't take any action to get Sergeant Wilcox to leave me alone, I asked Windy to send additional e-mails concerning Sergeant Wilcox to Warden Hendry, other prison officials, the Federal Bureau of Investigations, the media, and several people with different civil rights groups in Florida. Eventually, Sergeant Wilcox was reposted to a location where he didn't have any contact with me.

494) Did Julie K. Brown interview you and other inmates in April 2016?

Yes. In early April 2016, *Miami Herald* Reporter Julie K. Brown came to Martin CI to conduct her interviews with the other protective management inmates and me. While she was at the front gate, there was a violent incident involving less than a dozen inmates. None of them were killed, and the problem was quickly and easily contained. However, Warden Mallard used the incident to cancel Julie Brown's interviews. She did this by placing the compound on lockdown.

The warden had her staff tell Julie Brown she could not conduct the interviews because inmates could not leave their cells during a lockdown. What Mallard and the staff didn't know was

Martin CI being on lockdown was news. Julie Brown posted the news that Martin CI went on lockdown on Twitter as soon as she left the Martin CI parking lot. Warden Mallard's attempt to keep Martin CI out of the news got Martin CI placed in the news. That day, we were only on lockdown for about an hour.

The *Miami Herald* reset the appointments, and, about two weeks later, Julie Brown came back to Martin CI to interview the other inmates and me. The interviews happened over a two day period around April 21, 2016.

During those interviews, we discussed murders, and physical and sexual abuse, and staff-on-inmate abuse inside the protective management units. We also described the staff retaliation against protective management inmates for filing grievances, everything I have listed in this chapter about the conditions in protective management units, as well as, a lot of other smaller matters.

495) Did Martin CI staff retaliate against any of the inmates before these media interviews?

Yes. In the period before the interview, I wasn't subjected to any threats or abuse, and I didn't witness any of the other inmates get threatened or abused on those days. However, one of the other inmates alleged that he was threatened and physically abused by staff on the day that he was interviewed. Since I didn't witness the abuse, I can only state what that inmate said.

496) Was there retaliation after the interviews?

Yes. Warden Mallard, Assistant Warden Swineberg, and Classification Supervisor Mr. Parrish had me moved from house alone status into a cell with a physically and sexually violent inmate. His name was Ronald Davis. He smoked K-2 and did other drugs which caused him to hallucinate. By the grace of God, I didn't have any physical or sexual problems with him while I was housed with him.

The staff at Martin CI were punishing me for speaking out against the conditions inside the protective management unit. They wanted me to sign-out of the protective management unit so that it would be harder for me to gather information on incidents in protective management units. Also, if I was no longer in the unit, I could not get any more protective management inmates to talk with the Miami Herald.

Chapter 18: Martin CI (September 2015 - May 24, 2016)

This was a very difficult time for me. I was trying to deal with the retaliation. I had been under stress or years, was not working out, and not eating healthy. I began to have heart and breathing issues. I was denied medical care for these problems, which concerned me. I thought I was on the verge of having a heart attack.

I told Windy, the media, and friends about my health issues. Windy sent e-mails explaining that I was being denied health care for my heart and other medical problems to the Federal Bureau of Investigation, the FDC Inspector General, several individuals in the media, and several lawyers and high ranking people in civil rights groups. This led to dozens of e-mails and phone calls being made by the media, civil rights groups, etc. to the Tallahassee, Florida main office of the FDC, and Wexford Health Sources, Inc. The e-mails and phone calls caused Warden Mallard and the medical staff at Martin CI to stop the retaliation as it concerned my health care and to reinstate my medical treatment.

God helped me to learn that I could not spend all of my time helping others and that I had to also be concerned for my health. I began to exercise in May 2015, and now I'm in a lot better health and shape.

In May 2016, I mailed a sworn affidavit to the U.S. Department of Justice and more than a dozen other individuals concerning the retaliation I was receiving. The sworn affidavit stated:

SWORN AFFIDAVIT

To: Ms. Vanita Gupta, Assistant U.S. Attorney General., U.S. Department of Justice, Civil Rights Division. Florida Senator Greg Evers, Wexford Health Sources Inc., American Civil Liberties Union, Attn.: Howard Simon. Stop Prison Abuse Now, Attn.: Steven Wetstein

"In March and April 2016, Affiant mailed two sworn affidavits about the unconstitutional conditions of the Florida Department of Corrections (FDC) Protective Management Units to the Department of Justice, and almost two dozen representatives of the State of Florida, human rights leaders, news reporters, and bloggers. Copies of those sworn

affidavits can be read at:
'http://www.helpmybrotherharoldhempstead@wordpress.c
om; http://www.wobblywarrior@wordpress.com;
www.savetheholyhead@blogspot.com; stop prison
abusenowatnationsinside.com

"About the second week of March 2016, a reporter with the
Miami Herald Newspaper started making arrangements to
interview several inmates at Martin CI about among other
things the unconstitutional conditions in FDC Protective
Management Units. Affiant was one of those inmates.

"Immediately following the reporter disclosing the names of
the inmates she wanted to speak with to FDC staff several of
the inmates started reporting being subjected to different
types of reprisal by Martin CI staff.

"From the time arrangements started being made for Inmate
L.S. to speak with the reporter, he was mysteriously moved
from the cell he had been in for over a year into a different
cell and then given three gang members as cellmates over
the next about 30 days.

"Inmate J.C. was placed in confinement about 10 days prior
to speaking with the reporter. He reported that he went to
confinement for possession of ink. Ink pens are sold in the
inmate canteen.

"Inmate F.H. reported that he was threatened by a
correctional officer on the way to the interview with the
reporter, and punched in his face by a correctional officer on
the way back to his housing dorm from the reporter
interview.

Affiant has been subjected to the following forms of
retaliation since around the middle of March 2016:

"Mailroom Supervisor, Ms. Walker started withholding his
incoming and outgoing mail. Ms. Walker withheld mail
Affiant mailed to: (A) The *Miami Herald* newspaper. (B)
Florida ACLU Director Howard Simon. (C) Several personal

letters Affiant mailed family and friends. Ms. Walker also withheld incoming mail to the Affiant from the ***Miami Herald*** newspaper, Ministry of Reconciliation Outreach, civil rights leaders, and possibly other individuals.

"ARNP Chatalier discontinued Affiant's Low Residue Diet which he started receiving about six years ago for his stomach condition which causes him to defecate up to seven times a day and gives him severe stomach pain. Since Affiant's diet was discontinued on April 7, 2016, he has had severe stomach pain and has been using the bathroom several times a day.

"Affiant has sinus rhythm with sinus arrhythmia. On May 2, 2016, Affiant passed-out in his cell. He reported this to Classification Officer Ms. Posten, and Correctional Officers Johnson and Pellirenne. Affiant wasn't permitted to see medical staff. He also told Martin CI staff for several weeks that he had been having chest pain. Over those weeks, he was not been allowed to see medical staff.

"On April 7, 2016, ARNP Chatalier also tampered with Affiant's pain medicine and discontinued his allergy medicine. Now Affiant has no pain medicine for his broken right wrist, sciatic nerve damage, and hurt back. Affiant has been living in pain with these medical problems.

"Affiant has two or more cysts in his right wrist. Medical staff are refusing to prescribe him an antibiotic to prevent infection from entering his body.

"Affiant was approved to see an orthopedic surgeon for wrist surgery prior to this retaliation starting. Health Service Administrator Ms. Rebele told Affiant that he would be taken out of his cell and placed in another cell the night prior to his surgery. The conditions in the other cell would violate Affiant's 8th Amendment Right to Protection from Cruel and Unusual Punishment. Ms. Rebele also told the Affiant that, if he didn't want to go to the other cell the night prior to his wrist surgery, that he would be denied wrist surgery on his broken wrist.

"Since around April 10, 2016, Affiant stopped receiving his FDC grievances back that he filed on the issues mentioned herein.

"Around January 2016 Bureau Chief of Security Robert Hendry, Martin CI Assistant Warden Royce Marlow, and Martin CI Colonel Colon placed Affiant on house alone status in Cell B2-102 Single, because his prior cellmate (Timothy Jones) attempted to kill the cellmate (James Nash) he received after the Affiant. Timothy Jones and the Affiant were not compatible as cellmates. They should have never been housed in the same cell. On May 6, 2016, Affiant was moved from Cell B2-102 Single to B1-108 Lower by Martin CI Warden Elizabeth Mallard, Assistant Warden Mr. Swineberg, and Classification Supervisor Mr. Parrish. The mounted security camera tapes for Bravo Dorm Wing 2 on May 6, 2016, between 11:30am and 12:00 pm, will show these three staff in the Affiant's cell (B2-102 Single) taking a picture and talking to the Affiant. This was prior to these staff directing that the Affiant be moved to Cell B1-108 Lower. These staff moved Affiant into Cell B2-108 Lower with Inmate Ronald Davis whose criminal history proves he has a long history of physical and sexual violence. FDC records will prove that Ronald Davis shouldn't be housed with the Affiant by the Inmate Risk Management System/Sexual Risk Indicator (IRMS/SRI). Affiant is listed as Identified Prey on the IRMS/SRI system. Housing violent offenders with non-violent offenders violates state law.

"After Affiant's May 6, 2016, retaliatory cell change, Martin CI staff have alleged that they moved Inmate Y. Nunez into Affiant's prior cell (B-102 Single) because he qualified to be housed in said cell. The grievances and request forms in Inmate Y. Nunez's classification files show that he has been told for over four months that he didn't qualify to be housed alone for any reason. Additionally, in January and March

354

2016, the ADA Team at Martin CI told inmate Y. Nunez that he didn't qualify to be housed alone. Finally, FDC staff Robert Hendry, Royce Marlow, and Colonel Colon have held that Inmate Y. Nunez didn't qualify to be housed alone. Accordingly, there's substantial evidence that proves that Martin CI staff didn't move Inmate Y. Nunez into B2-102 Single because he qualified to be housed in said cell, but because said staff wanted Affiant to be housed in the cell where Inmate Y. Nunez was housed (B2-108 Lower) with a physically and sexually violent offender.

"In March 2016, Warden Mallard told Affiant that he had to place all of his active legal materials in the law library where he couldn't access them six days a week to obtain access to the courts on his legal matters. This is in violation of FAC 33-501.301(4)(c) which says inmates will be afforded access to their legal materials. The law library storage records will prove that thousands of pages of Affiant's law work is in the law library storage closet where Affiant can't access his law work six days a week. This is in violation of his First Amendment right to Access to the Courts.

"On May 6, 2016, Affiant was threatened by staff between 11:30 am and 12:00 pm with frivolous disciplinary reports, to be placed in confinement, and to have his personal property taken from him.

"Affiant has filed several complaints with Chief Inspector General Melinda Miguel concerning the retaliation he received from Martin CI staff and the unconstitutional conditions in FDC Protective Management Units. The following is a list of the dates on the letters Affiant received from Miguel's office and the case numbers her office assigned to Affiant's complaints: (1) November 12, 2015 (Case No.: 201511120007). (2) December 15, 2015 (Case No.: 201512140002). (3) December 15, 2015 (Case No.: 201412110006). (4) February 16, 2016 (Case No.: 201512140002). (5) Two letters on February 23, 2016 (Case No.: 201512140002 and 201511120004). (6) March 7, 2016

Department of Corruption

(Case No.: 201512140002). (7) March 30, 2016 (Case No.: 201512140002). (8) April 29, 2016 (Case No.: 201512140002). Other than these, Affiant has recently filed additional complaints with Miguel's office.

"On May 8 and 13, 2016, the Affiant made a total of nine TIP calls on the matters herein. He gave his name and D.C. Number on each call. The following numbers were assigned to these prison TIP Calls: (1) 971527, (2) 127485, (3) 316384, (4) 812239, (5) 188725, (6) 168806, (7) 593692, (8) 829299, and (9) 144286.

"On May 8, 2016 Affiant's sister (Windy Hempstead) sent an e-mail to several FDC staff, and others about the retaliation Affiant was receiving.

"On May 13, 2016, Steven Wetstein of Stop Prison Abuse Now sent an e-mail to McKinley Lewis and Timothy Reid about the retaliation mentioned herein.

"Affiant is requesting that FDC please preserve the following recordings which are needed for criminal and civil reasons and for the DOJ: The Martin CI, Bravo Dorm, Wing 2 mounted security cameras tapes for May 2, 2016 between 8:00 am and 8:30 am; May 6, 2016 between 11:30 am and 12:00 pm; and May 9, 2016 between 8:00 am and 9:00 am. Additionally, the May 13, 2016 audio recording between an FDC Inspector (who Affiant knew at Dade C.I.) and the Affiant. This recording will show Affiant requested to see a doctor and went into some detail concerning the retaliation he was receiving relating to his health care, and his May 6, 2016 cell change.

"FDC inmates need and want to help the media and civil rights leaders with trying to make FDC a safer place. FDC inmates have a 1st Amendment Constitutional Right to Freedom of Speech to speak with the media and civil rights leaders about the unconstitutional conditions in FDC. When FDC staff take reprisal against inmates for doing the above-listed things, FDC staff are not only violating the federal rights of prisoners, but they are also violating the rights of the media and civil rights leaders. Because this pattern and practice of FDC staff taking reprisal against inmates who speak-out against the conditions in FDC is statewide and systematic, and has led to inmates being severely harmed and killed, Affiant is requesting that the U.S. Department of Justice conduct an investigation into these matters pursuant to the Civil Rights of Institutionalized Persons Act (42 USC:1997).

UNNOTARIZED OATH

Under penalty of perjury, I swear that all the facts stated herein are true and correct.

Executed on this____day of May 2016.

Affiant (Signature of Harold Hempstead appears here on original, handwritten document)

Harold Hempstead, D.C. #268866, Martin CI, 1150 Southwest Allapattah Road, Indiantown, Florida 34964.

CC: Florida Justice Institute (Randall C. Berg), Disability Rights Florida (Molly Paris), Forgotten Majority, *Miami Herald* (Julie K. Brown), CBS4 Miami (Michelle Gillen), WTVT Fox 13 Tampa (Craig Patrick), Florida Department of Law Enforcement (Commissioner), Chief Inspector General for the Florida, Governor (Melinda Miguel), FDC Inspector General (Kenneth Sumpter), Florida Department of Health Medical Quality Assurance, American Correctional Association Standards and Accreditation Department, Windy Hempstead, Susan Chandler, Jeremy Schanche, George Mallinckrodt.

497) In spite of this retaliation, you seem committed to reform. True?

Absolutely? The inmates in protective management status needed my help. If I had to go through suffering to help them, I was willing to. Sometimes people have to be willing to suffer for what is right.

498) Will you tell me about Windy's communications with FDC Region Four Director Thomas Reid?

Thomas Reid had been employed in the FDC for around 20 years. He was known by inmates as being evil and very much against the civil rights of inmates.

The *Miami Herald* published some articles about inmates dying at Charlotte Correctional Institution when Thomas Reid was the warden there.

I believe he was promoted to FDC Region Four Director in the end of 2015, or beginning of 2016.

While I was housed at Martin CI, trying to bring reform to protective management units, Thomas Reid contacted Windy. His purpose was to convince her that he was going to help her and me with the problems I was having with Martin CI staff retaliating against me. This was his way of trying to get Windy to stop e-mailing and calling people about those problems. When Windy first told me about Reid, I told her to not trust him because he was known for being very evil and manipulative. Windy had enough experience and knowledge of his past to know that he would do everything he could, to cover up everything his staff did that he could get away with covering up.

Windy didn't allow him to manipulate her. She continued to do what needed to be done to aid in my protection, and help me try to bring reform to the protective management units.

499) What led to you to being forced out of protective management status in May 2016?

All of the challenges that I made to bring reform to the protective management units since June 2014 led to me finally being forced out of protective management in May 2016.

Martin CI Classification Officer Ms. Posten asked me in May 2016, if I wanted to sign-out of protective management status and return to general population. I told her that I would sign-out if I was going to be treated like the other inmates who signed-out and were transferred to one of the three institutions they requested. These other inmates were allowed to name three institutions they wanted to go to and were sent to one of the institutions they chose.

She said I wouldn't be allowed to choose three institutions to be transferred to if I signed out of protective management status. I told her that I felt like I was being subjected to retaliation in violation of my 14th Amendment right to Equal Protection by not being treated like the other inmates. I also told her that I didn't think I should return to general population without being special reviewed from Regional Medical Center, South Florida Reception Center, and Everglades CI because I would have serious protection issues with staff at each of those institutions.

Not too long after my conversation with her, I was taken in front of the Martin CI Institutional Classification Team for a hearing on my protective management status. While at the hearing, Classification Supervisor Mr. Parrish, said, "Do you want to sign-out?"

After I answered no, he told me to step out of the office.

When he called me back into the office, he said, "We're going to recommend you return to general population. If the state classification officer agrees with our recommendation, you'll have 30 days to appeal. You may leave."

When I got back in my housing wing, I called Windy and told her what happened.

She e-mailed the state classification officer and told him that Martin CI staff had been subjecting me to retaliation for trying to bring reform to the protective management units, and now they were recommending I be released to general population as a form of retaliation. Windy also sent two e-mails to the Federal Bureau of Investigations and about a dozen civil rights lawyers, reporters, and federal and state officials concerning the retaliation I was being subjected to.

I knew that staff probably wanted to release me to general population at Martin CI because it was one of the most violent institutions in Florida. If that happened, there would have been a serious threat to my safety. For this reason, I called the prison TIP line and told the Inspector General's Office that there would be a serious threat to my safety if I was released to population at Martin CI. I knew that I had upset a lot of staff at Martin CI, and, if I was released to population, they could have arranged for an inmate to hurt or kill me.

Department of Corruption

Since staff had begun retaliating against me, I had been making check-in calls to Windy twice a day. Just like at Dade CI, Windy knew what to do if I missed a phone call.

On May 23, 2016, when the protective management inmates were leaving the chow hall at lunch, almost all of the highest ranking staff at Martin CI were waiting outside the chow hall. When I saw them, I knew something was about to happen with me. One of the lieutenants told all of the inmates to get in a line. When we were all in a line, a lieutenant yelled, "Harold Hempstead, step outside the line."

When I stepped outside the line, Captain Scarpati said, "Hempstead, come with me."

When we got to his office, Captain Scarpati gave me a request for protective management form and said, "Who do you have problems with on this compound?"

I responded, "I don't have problems with anybody, but you know who has problems with me."

He responded, "Why don't you tell me who has problems with you."

I responded, "The people behind this charade that is going on are the staff who have problems with me. What am I supposed to do with this request for protection from?"

He responded, "I need you to write the names of the people who you have a problem with on that form."

I responded, "I don't have any problems with anybody. Why don't you tell me who I'm supposed to have problems with so I know?"

He said, "Somebody called the warden and main office and said staff and inmates here are conspiring to kill you."

I responded, "I know you all really want me off this compound, but I highly recommend you think of some other reason to get me out of here. You know as well as I do, that story is fake. If you stay with that story, it'll cause several investigations."

He said, "It's not fake."

I responded, "So you have the name and phone number of this alleged caller?"

He said, "The calls were anonymous. They blocked their phone number."

I responded, "Of course. So the only evidence that these calls happened are prison staff who don't want me at Martin CI. I'm not going to put anything on this form, because I don't believe the story."

He said, "I don't need to lie to you. If I had a problem with you, I could lie and say you hit me or spit on me, or anything I want to say, and then have you placed on close management. I'm doing what I was told to do. If you don't want to make a statement, that's fine. I have to place you in administrative confinement pending a protection investigation. This officer is going to take you to medical, so the nurse can check you out before you go to confinement."

While I was being escorted to the medical department and then to the confinement unit, I noticed that all of the inmates in both protective management wings were on the protective management unit recreational yard.

After being placed in confinement, I wasn't given any of my property, or any toilet paper, soap, and so on. I asked every staff who walked past my cell for these items, and they didn't give me any of them.

While the protective management inmates were on the recreation yard, several security staff were searching both wings in the protective management unit. When the search was done, all of the inmates were escorted from the recreational yard, back to the protective management unit and locked in their cells.

In the morning hours, on May 24, 2016, Captain Knight came to my confinement cell and placed a heightened security status sign on my cell door. Heightened security status meant that I couldn't leave my confinement cell without a lieutenant or higher ranking staff present and a camcorder recording everything I did. I knew I was placed on that status because Windy was sending e-mails and making phone calls to high ranking prison staff and people in society expressing concerns about my safety. I had missed three check-in calls to her, and I was sure that she was worried.

Department of Corruption

On May 24, 2016, a search team conducted another search of the protective management unit. Several protective management inmates went to confinement that day.

In the afternoon hours, Captain Knight came to my cell and said, "Do you want to call your sister and let her know you're OK."

I responded, "Is the call to talk to my sister or just to let her know I'm OK?"

He said, "The call is to let her know you're OK."

I responded, "That would be a lie. I'm not going to call her and lie to her. You have me in confinement for no reason. I don't have my property, or any toilet paper, or soap. I'm not receiving my diet tray, and the trays I am receiving are missing food."

He said, "So you don't want to call her?"

I responded, "I'm not going to call her and lie to her. You're trying to make me lie to her."

He said, "OK." He then walked away from my cell and exited the confinement wing.

I wasn't going to call Windy and say I was OK because she would have backed off her phone calls and emails, which would have placed me in a position where Martin CI staff could have done worse to me, than the things they had already done. I also knew the steps she would take as the hours passed to make sure I was OK. Inevitably, she would be successful in either getting me on the phone where I could tell her the truth, or she would end up getting me transferred from Martin CI.

About 10 minutes after Captain Knight left my cell door, he returned with a sergeant and two officers. One of the officers had a camcorder recording the captain as he walked up to my cell. When the captain got to my cell door, he looked at the camcorder and said, "I'm at Harold Hempstead's confinement cell door. His D.C. number is 268866. I'm going to ask him if he would like to call his sister and let her know he can't receive any visits." Captain Knight then turned and looked at me in my cell and said, "Hempstead, would you like to call your sister and let her know you can't receive any visits?"

I responded, "Is that the only thing I can say to her, that I can't receive visits?"

He said, "Yes. That is it. You can't receive visits."

I responded, "Yes. I would like to call her and tell her I can't get any visits. I'm not going to do like you told me to do the last time, which is lie to her and tell her I'm OK. However, I will call her and tell her I can't receive any visits."

I was then handcuffed and escorted to the telephone to call Windy. When Windy answered the phone, she said, "Are you OK?"

I responded, "The captain told me I can only tell you that I can't receive visits."

She said, "What? That makes no sense. Thomas Reid said I would get to talk to you."

I responded, "They're right here. I can only say I can't receive visits. Other than that, I have to go. I'm sorry."

Windy knew I was in confinement because I had missed my check-in calls and because staff told her. Additionally, she wasn't planning to come and visit me, and she already knew that I couldn't receive visits while in confinement. I agreed to call Windy and tell her I couldn't receive visits because that would be a clear statement to her that something was wrong.

A few hours later I found out that Windy got the message that something was wrong. I found that out when I was emergency transferred around 6:30 pm on May 24, 2016. She had apparently made her point that I was in danger at Martin CI, and she wanted me off that compound.

500) Did the FDC Inspector General's Office ever contact about your TIP calls from Martin CI?

No.

501) What was your transfer from Martin CI to Okeechobee Correctional Institution like?

Around 6:30 pm on May 24, 2016, Captain Knight came into my cell with two officers I never saw before and another officer with a camcorder. I was then handcuffed, searched, and escorted to the front of Martin CI. The property sergeant brought me my law work and other property. That's when I found-out that the transport officers were from Okeechobee CI.

Department of Corruption

When I got in the van, the male officer seat belted me in.
Every other time I had ever been transported in a van, I took the
seat belt off. However, this time, God gave me a strong feeling to
stay belted in. As we left Martin CI, I watched the officer with the
camcorder record us as we drove away. After being on the road
for about an hour, I heard a big boom' and the van went off the
road. The van didn't flip. The officer was able to keep control of
the vehicle.

The first thing the officer said when the van stopped was,
"We hit a miniature horse."

The female officer said, "A miniature horse, are you sure?"

The male officer said, "Yes. I saw it, but I didn't have
enough time to stop. Hempstead, are you OK?"

I responded, "Yes, I'm OK. I've always taken my seat belt
off in transport vans. Thank God, this time, He gave me a strong
feeling to remain belted in."

The male officer said, "I'm glad you didn't take it off." He
then told the female officer that he had to call the captain who, in
turn, said he had to call his colonel.

While the officers made phone calls and talked, I thought
about what had just happened and what might happen in the next
hour or two. The male officer said the van was too damaged to
continue driving even if they brought a new tire to change the
blown tire on the van. That meant I was going to be moved from
the van I was in to another van on a dark country road late at
night. Based on my past history with the FDC and knowing that I
wasn't too favored by many FDC staff, I didn't really like that
idea. However, I obtained comfort in knowing God is sovereign,
and, He who had protected me throughout my life and through so
much, would continue to protect me until it was my time to die
and be with Him in heaven.

Eventually, the Okeechobee CI colonel and major showed up
with another officer and van. The colonel told the transport
officers they had to wait until an Okeechobee County sheriff's
deputy arrived before they moved me. I did not know the colonel
arranged for a deputy to be present, but, in my eyes, the non-
biased deputy would protect me from possible foul play by the six

prison staff. When the deputy came, I was moved into the other van with no issues.

Less than an hour later, we arrived at Okeechobee CI.

Chapter 19: Okeechobee CI (May – December 2016)

502) Will you give me some general information about Okeechobee CI?

Okeechobee CI is located in Okeechobee County, Florida. It was a Psych-1 and 2 institution, which meant it didn't house Psych-3 inmates. Also, it was not a dumping ground for inmates on close management or gangs. However, it did have many inmates who were gang members and who were previously housed on close management. Two of the wings in Delta Dorm housed inmates who were in the faith-based program.

Okeechobee CI had a lot of violence, but it wasn't anywhere close to as violent as were the previous three institutions where I was housed. Also, in contrast to my prior three housing situations, I was going to general population at Okeechobee CI.

503) Tell me about your arrival to Okeechobee Correctional Institution.

Upon my arrival to Okeechobee CI, there was a captain and officer with a camcorder waiting for me. The officer recorded the van entering the Okeechobee CI gate and me getting out of the van. After I got off the van, the officer continued to record me as I was escorted to the medical department, checked out by a nurse, and then taken to the administrative confinement unit. The officers gave me everything I was supposed to receive in confinement. The confinement staff was fair, and the confinement unit was clean.

I stayed in administration confinement for approximately two months.

504) What did you think about your transfer to Okeechobee CI?

My transfer to Okeechobee CI meant I was no longer on protective management status. For almost two years, FDC staff from the Tallahassee main office and from the institutions where I was incarcerated said that I couldn't be released from protective management status. They said there was a severe threat to my safety, and I would probably be killed at any correctional institution in Florida. Then, out of retaliation for trying to bring reform to the protective management units, FDC staff released me from protective management status against my request and sent me to an institution I didn't want to go to and that wasn't in my best interest to be incarcerated at.

Also, Martin CI Captain Scarpati told me that he was placing me in administrative confinement pending a protection investigation because it was thought that staff and inmates at Martin CI had been plotting to kill me. Thus, I was released from protective management status to the general population while there was an investigation pending into a plot to kill me.

505) Was your protective management status reviewed when you were in the confinement unit?

Yes, when I arrived there, I was still on administrative confinement status pending a protective management investigation.

I filed five to 10 grievances while I was in confinement there about my retaliatory release from protective management status and about the events that happened at Martin CI on May 23 and 24, 2016. Also, I started mailing letters to Windy, the *Miami Herald* newspaper, and several other people my first day there about everything that happened at Martin CI on May 23 and 24, 2016, and since my arrival to Okeechobee CI.

Finally, upon my arrival there, I started asking the inmates in the cells next to me and in other confinement cells about Okeechobee CI. I had never been there before, so I wanted to learn as much about that institution as possible.

During my questioning of other inmates, I found out that Lars Severson was the warden. I knew him when he was employed at Dade CI in 2010 and 2011. I also found out that there were two officers and a mental health counselor there whom I knew from Dade CI, and Royce Marlow's wife was also there. I knew Royce Marlow when he worked at Dade CI and Martin CI. I was special reviewed from Dade CI because the FDC held that I had protection problems with Dade CI staff. These protection issues with Dade CI staff were one of the several reasons I was on protective management status for two years. It made no sense for prison officials who said I had protection issues with Dade CI staff to then house me at Okeechobee CI where several former Dade CI staff who knew me were employed.

Additionally, I found out that several of the high ranking staff employed at Okeechobee CI were formerly employed at Charlotte CI. I was told they were transferred to Okeechobee CI following with a serious investigation at Charlotte CI involving the death of an inmate. Some of the *Miami Herald* articles written by Reporter Julie K. Brown about the deaths of inmates at Charlotte CI referenced several staff members from Charlotte CI and who were now working at Okeechobee CI.

Within days of my arrival, a sergeant came to talk to me. She asked me why I was placed under a protection investigation at Martin CI and if I had any protection issues with inmates at Okeechobee CI. A few days later, the Institutional Classification Team held a hearing on my protective management investigation. At that hearing, I explained the reasons why I was on protective management for two years, that I had been brought from Martin CI to Okeechobee CI the day after being told there was a plot to kill me, and that I was a witness in several state and federal investigations of Florida prison staff.

The Institutional Classification Team said there was no way they could put me in general population because the threats to my safety were so severe that they would lose their jobs if anything happened to me. The Classification Supervisor, Ms. Garret, said Windy had been calling and e-mailing her and other FDC staff. She asked if I would write Windy and let her know I was OK. I told Ms. Garret that I had already written my sister and told her I was O.K., but that she would not stop calling and e-mailing until she heard my voice.

When I showed surprised that Windy had not already e-mailed the FDC Secretary and Florida Governor, the Institutional Classification Team made arrangements for me to call her while I was there with them. I couldn't say a lot to Windy because three of the highest ranking Okeechobee CI officials could hear everything I said. I told Windy that I hadn't been physically harmed, I was on house-alone status, and to please follow my requests in the letters I mailed her.

Department of Corruption

A few days after I met with the Institutional Classification Team, FDC Region Four Director Thomas Reid came to Okeechobee CI. While he was there, he had me escorted from my administrative confinement cell to an office to talk to him. After he identified himself, he told me he was behind everything that happened with me at Martin CI, that he told the Martin CI Institutional Classification Team and the state classification officer to release me from protective management back to general population, that he had me transferred to Okeechobee CI, and that he believed I could make it in general population. He also said that he had been talking to Windy and he was going to do what he could to keep me in his region so that he could oversee my status. He didn't ask me any questions. He was trying to let me know that if I continued to try to expose and bring reform to protective management units or other prison-related matters, I would have to deal with him. Our conversation lasted for about 10 minutes.

Because regional directors don't normally talk with inmates privately in offices, Thomas Reid's conversation with me got the attention of confinement staff. As I walked away from the office, I heard Sergeant Sanders ask Reid about me. Reid told him, "That's the inmate associated with the Feds and media who blew the whistle on the stuff down there at Dade CI and across Florida."

About a week or so after I met with the Institutional Classification Team, Classification Supervisor, Ms. Garret, told me that the state classification officer denied my protection investigation. She said that Thomas Reid directed the state classification officer to deny it. She also said that Thomas Reid told the State classification officer and Warden Severson that I would be safe at Okeechobee CI. She asked me if I wanted to file a grievance on the denial of my protection investigation. I told her that I did.

In the several grievances I filed on my protection related matters, I explained:

(1) How for almost two years, I was told that I had statewide protection issues with FDC staff and I couldn't be released to general population. However, I was released to general population in retaliation for trying to expose and bring reform to protective management units.

(2) I was special reviewed from Dade CI, but they had me housed at Okeechobee CI where several former Dade CI staff were employed.

(3) I was released from protective management status to general population status while under a protection investigation into an alleged plot to kill me.

I also raised other issues in my grievance. I filed these grievances to make sure there was a paper trail showing I contested my retaliatory release from protective management to Okeechobee CI. I knew none of my grievances would be granted and that I would not be placed back in a protective management unit because I was being sent to the general population because of my attempts to expose the unconstitutional conditions at FDC protective management units.

506) What else did you learn about Okeechobee CI while on the confinement unit?

About two weeks after my arrival, confinement orderlies began to bring me letters from inmates in population. Several were from an inmate nicknamed Birdman whom I was housed at Dade CI. He was called Birdman because he was known for feeding birds. Birdman told me that when my name appeared on the call-out list as a new arrival, inmates and staff all over Okeechobee CI started talking about me. He said there were a lot of inmates from Dade CI, and the majority of them had read newspaper articles with my name in them concerning the FDC. He also said all the inmates spoke favorably of me, but several of the staff were trying to place labels on me that could get me hurt and possibly killed in population. Finally, he said that there were a lot of inmates on the compound who filed grievances and lawsuits trying to change the conditions in the FDC.

While I was in confinement, I also heard there were a lot gang members at Okeechobee CI and that inmates were taking contracts to cut and stab inmates for money. I learned inmates were getting Buck-Fifties on a regular basis. A Buck-Fifty is when an inmate cuts another inmate on his cheek from his mouth to his ear.

Additionally, when I was in the confinement unit, I discovered that FDC officials had installed audio recording equipment in all the confinement units in the Florida prison system.

While I was in confinement, I didn't receive any medical attention for any of my medical problems until I started filing grievances on being denied adequate medical attention.

All the grievances I filed on my protection matters were denied. I was taken off administrative confinement pending protective management review status and placed on regular administrative confinement status.

I did not have any cellmates when I was in the confinement unit.

507)   Will you tell me about your release to general population at Okeechobee CI?

Upon my release from confinement, I was assigned to live in Echo Dorm (E-Dorm) Wing 2. My cellmate's name was Jenouch Pasco. He was an African American inmate in prison for the first-degree murder of an elderly white woman. In society, he smoked crack cocaine, and, in prison, he smoked K-2. In less than two years, he was my fourth cellmate who was a drug addicted killer. Federal law and the *Inmate Risk Management System/Sexual Risk Indicator* prohibited this type of housing. Apparently, Regional Director Thomas Reid or some other staff thought that by housing me in the same cell with Pasco, he would eventually try to harm me physically. Whoever placed me in the cell with him didn't know that the sovereign God of all things would protect me while I was housed in the same cell with Pasco, just like He had protected me through everything over the years.

God had arranged for Birdman, whom I knew from Dade CI and several other inmates who I knew from other institutions to be housed in the same wing with me. I asked them to tell other inmates about my past, so the inmate population would know that staff had a reason to falsely label me or try to get inmates to not like me. During the first few hours, I was in Wing E-2, the inmates who knew about my past told dozens of other inmates in my wing, and in other wings about my past communications with the media, civil rights groups, and so on.

I also learned efforts to falsely label me had begun before my release to the general population. The confinement sergeant had falsely labeled me while I was still in confinement.

508) What did you find out concerning Windy after your release from confinement?

Prison officials retaliated against Windy in prison paperwork and lied on her. The statements they made were farfetched; there was an abundance of evidence that proved their statements about her were lies; and they switched their statements several times concerning their lies about Windy. The lies were an attempt to get Windy to back out of prison reform.

509) How did Windy respond to the retaliation she was subjected to?

She knew that prison officials had a long history of retaliating against inmates and staff who tried to bring reform to the FDC. However, she had never been subjected to any retaliation. It was upsetting to her. She didn't like that she was lied on. Windy eventually found out that the family members of other inmates who were at Martin CI were also subjected to the same type of retaliation and lies as she was.

510) Did you receive adequate medical care at Okeechobee CI?

No. They didn't start providing me with adequate medical attention until I filed medical complaints with the Florida Department of Health Medical Quality Assurance Commission. I filed complaints on the doctor and two of the senior nurses at Okeechobee CI.

With regards to my wrist, the medical staff tried to make me have the surgery when I was having problems with my heart. They also made false statements and stopped me from having surgery on my wrist. I did not receive surgery on my wrist while at Okeechobee CI.

Also, a medical doctor at Okeechobee CI prescribed Propanol for me. The medicine is for reducing blood pressure and pulse rate and could have killed me. I never took the medicine.

I probably filed between 100 and 200 grievances against the medical staff at Okeechobee CI.

511) Tell me about the cell phone scramblers that were installed at Okeechobee CI.

While I was in confinement, I watched people from society with carts of wire and electronic equipment constantly going to the dorms on the compound. When they came to the confinement unit, they installed electronic equipment in every pipe chase. When I got to general population, I found out that the electrical workers were installing the wiring and equipment in every pipe chase on the compound. The electrical workers told the inmates that prison officials told them not to tell any inmates what the equipment was for, that they were installing.

Several inmates decided to investigate the electrical workers. All of the electrical workers wore shirts with the name of a Jacksonville Florida electronics company on them. The inmates used their cell phones to Google the name of the electronics company and learned that the company installed, among other things, cell phone scramblers in prisons. After the inmates learned this, dozens of them conspired to find ways to beat the scramblers. Within a short time, they found-out 1) the scramblers only worked inside the cells and in the wings, 2) there would be locations in the wings where the cell phones would still work, 3) they could obtain signal booster apps off the internet to boost the signals on their cell phones, and 4) the scramblers might not scramble the frequencies for both of the cell phone carriers in the area.

After the scramblers were activated, the inmates discovered 1) the scramblers did not work on one of the cell phone carriers; 2) they could open both the storage lockers in a cell, place them on top of each other on their sides, and stand behind them to use their cell phones; 3) the scramblers didn't scramble in certain shower stalls, the day rooms, and one or two cells in each wing; and 4) signal booster apps were not needed because there were several ways the scramblers could be beaten.

This caused a lot of joy in the inmate population. How they saw it was that the FDC had spent possibly hundreds of thousands of dollars of taxpayers money on the contract to install the scramblers, and, before the scramblers were even turned on, the inmates had several ways of beating them.

A lot of inmates at Okeechobee CI talked to inmates on their cell phones at Martin CI and discovered scramblers were also installed there. The Martin CI inmates said they had also beaten the scramblers.

512) Are cell phones used to put contracts on inmates and staff at other institutions?

Yes. A lot of inmates who owe money to drug dealers and who don't have the money to pay them, request to be placed on protective management. If they are experienced at their manipulation games, they can get transferred to another institution. A lot of inmates will use the protective management process or go-psych to manipulate transfers, so they don't have to pay their drug debts. I explained how inmates go-psych in the beginning of this book.

Inmates will tell the inspector general's office or security staff about criminal activity on the compound to obtain protective management transfers. Often, the inmates to whom money was owed to or who were told on will use the internet on their cell phones to find out where the debtor or theminformer was transferred. If they have the phone numbers of gang brothers or friends at that institution, they will call them and place a contract on that inmate. The contract will then be carried out against the inmate. He will be beaten, stabbed, or killed.

Sometimes, inmates will also place contracts on staff. The druggies are the main inmates who will take contracts against staff. The most common contracts placed on staff are to have them physically battered.

513) Are prison staff extorted?

Yes. Numerous inmates extort staff.

When inmates find staff who they think would be a good target, they try to learn the staff members full name. Having the initial of the first name and the whole last name is good enough and, most of the time, only the last name is needed. The inmate will Google the staff person's name and the county of the institution to gather as much information as possible. Then the inmate will search Facebook, Twitter, and other social media sites to get information on the staff. The inmate will also use online investigation companies that usually charge a fee of $50.00 or less to provide information on a person. After the inmate has obtained the staff's address, and if possible some names of the staff's family members and pictures of them, he will have enough to run his extortion.

The inmates use the information and pictures to extort the staff demanding that they bring them cell phones, drugs, or tobacco. They will also use the information they have gathered to get the staff person not to be so harsh or to throw-out disciplinary reports or to get the staff to quit their jobs at the prison. This is usually done to new staff in the FDC.

514) Were tax fraud, credit card fraud, and the chomo scam active at Okeechobee CI like they were at Dade CI?

Yes. Those are the most common scams done by inmates at every close custody institution in Florida.

515) Do inmates use cell phones to contact law enforcement agencies in society to place prison staff under investigations?

Yes. Inmates call sheriff departments, the Florida Department of Law Enforcement, and other agencies about prison staff who harass them or cause them trouble. The inmates usually impersonate correctional officers or people in society and say the targeted staff member is bringing drugs or cell phones into the prison system.

I'll tell you an incident with a female officer at Okeechobee CI who was targeted this way. The inmates had nicknamed this female officer Justin Beaver. When she had an inmate drug dealer placed in confinement, an inmate friend of his arranged to have a call made to the Okeechobee County, Florida Sheriff's Department on the female officer.

The inmate who made the phone call told me how the conversation with the sheriff's department took place. He said he called the main phone number for the Okeechobee County, Florida Sheriff's Department. When a deputy answered, she said, "Okeechobee County, Florida Sheriff's Department. How may I help you?'

The inmate responded, "Yes, I have a problem, and I'm hoping you can help. I'm engaged to an officer who works at Okeechobee Correctional Institution. When I went to pick her up

Chapter 19: Okeechobee CI (May – December 2016)

from work yesterday, she asked if I could take one of her co-workers home. Her coworker, who's also an officer, was having car problems. Of course, I told my fiancé that we could. While we were driving, the other officer told my fiancé that she should smuggle something called K-2 into the prison to supplement her income. The other officer said she was making $500.00 extra a week bringing K-2 into the prison for an inmate. I didn't know what K-2 was until I asked my fiancé.

"I don't like that my tax money is being used to pay the checks of officers who are smuggling drugs into the prison system. I also don't like that a drug-dealing officer is trying to convince my fiancé to bring drugs into the prison system. I don't want my fiancé to lose her job or go to prison. Deputy, can you please help me?"

The deputy said, "Yes, we can help you, sir. I just need the name of the officer, her physical description, and whatever else you can tell me about her."

The inmate responded, "If I help you, I don't want my name involved, and I don't want my fiancé to find out. It might cause her to leave me."

The deputy said, "Sir, you can remain anonymous, and there are ways we can investigate what you told me without your fiancé finding-out."

The inmate responded, "OK, I don't know that much. I never met the officer prior to yesterday. The officer was about 5'7, with very short brown hair, like a man, and on her identification card was _____."

The inmate then gave the deputy the real last name of the officer everybody called Justin Beaver.

The inmate told me he used this story when talking with the Okeechobee County, Florida Sheriff's Department because it gave him a good excuse for not knowing the female officer's first name. He knew the officer's last name because it was on her identification card.

About two weeks after this phone call was made, the female officer stopped working at Okeechobee CI.

Inmates also made calls like this on Sergeants Sanders and Hunter at Okeechobee CI.

516) Was there any narcotics at Okeechobee CI?

Yes. It was flooded with K-2 and Molly. A joint of K-2 was commonly sold as cheap as a 90 cents. Just like at every other institution I had been housed at, inmates were passing-out, flipping-out, and twacking-out at Okeechobee CI from smoking K-2. The inmates who didn't smoke it talked constantly how it they could always smell K-2 on the wings.

I was told Molly was a form of speed. The inmates who did Molly always had problems with sleeping.

517) Were there a lot of gang members at Okeechobee CI?

Yes. There were hundreds of gang members there, probably around 400. They were constantly fighting and stabbing each other; selling cell phones, drugs, and tobacco; robbing; and extorting other inmates.

518) What are Buck-Fifties?

Approximately a decade ago, prison officials stopped allowing inmates at psych-3 institutions to receive shaving razors. They did this because inmates at the psych-3 institutions removed the razor blades from their plastic housing and used them to cut other inmates and to cut themselves.

About eight or nine years ago, gang members in the Florida prison system started using razor blades to cut the cheeks of informants. A cut on one cheek of an inmate between his ear and his mouth is called a Buck-Fifty. Over the years, inmates other than gang members began giving inmates other than informants Buck-Fifties. Eventually, Buck-Fifties were being given for all types of reasons, by all types of inmates.

The Buck-Fifty became a prevalent form of violence in Florida prisons because it is hard to get caught for giving an inmate one. When an inmate wanted to cut another inmate, he kept a razor blade on him and watched his victim until he caught him walking in a line or a crowd. The perpetrator then crept up behind his victim, quickly cut one of the victim's cheeks, drop the razor, and try to blend in with the other inmates. If the perpetrator cut the cheek quickly, barely any blood would get on his hand. If any blood got on his hand, he would usually wipe it off with a piece of toilet paper that he had in his other hand.

Chapter 19: Okeechobee CI (May – December 2016)

If a person does a Buck-Fifty like it's supposed to be done, the victim would be cut from his mouth to his ear. Apparently, it is called a Buck-Fifty because it requires 150 stitches to sew shut a cut that extends from the mouth to the ear.

Whenever there was a Buck-Fifty at Okeechobee CI, security staff usually stopped all inmate movement on the compound and tried to catch the perpetrator. One to three Buck-Fifties happened every week that I was at Okeechobee CI. Four or five of them happened to inmates who were in the same lines with me walking to and from the chow hall.

All of the inmates in the FDC worried about getting a Buck-Fifty because it left a permanent scar on their face. Even the inmates who never had problems with other inmates or staff worried about receiving them. Because the perpetrator gives the Buck-Fifty while standing behind his victim, inmates worried about being mistaken for an inmate who was supposed to be the targeted victim.

Because of the high frequency of Buck-Fifties, sometime between August and October 2016, the FDC passed a rule mandating that shaving razors could no longer be distributed in any institution in the FDC. Okeechobee CI staff didn't comply with this rule. They continued to pass-out shaving razors to inmates, and inmates continued to use them to cut other inmates.

It hurt my heart to continue to see and hear about inmates getting their faces cut. I had to do something to try and stop the cuttings, so I started filing grievances and talking with the media and others in society about Okeechobee CI staff arming inmates with razors to cut inmates. The staff knew the inmates were giving Buck-Fifties to other inmates with the razor blades from the shaving razors and the staff knew they weren't supposed to be giving razors to inmates.

By God's grace, I was eventually able to get them to stop passing-out the shaving razors. However, the Buck-Fifties continued. They only continued because the security staff didn't collect all the razor blades that the inmates saved. Prison officials should have ordered a mass search of all the institutions to collect the razor blades that were in the possession of inmates after the razor blades became no longer legal in the Florida prison system.

Since FDC staff didn't do this, Buck-Fifties continued to happen throughout the FDC.

519) Were there any violations of the Prison Rape Elimination Act at Okeechobee CI?

The primary type of rape that was happening there was sexually aggressive inmates forcing passive inmates into having sexual relations with them. That is also the most common type of rape in the FDC. That type of rape was happening several times a day at Okeechobee CI.

520) Were there any violations of the *Inmate Risk Management System/Sexual Risk Indicator* at Okeechobee CI?

Yes. Predators and sexually aggressive inmates were housed in the same wings and cells with inmates designated as neutrals, preys, and inmates at risk of sexual victimization.

521) Were prison staff allowing convicted sex offenders and predators to go to FDC Visitation Parks where children congregate?

Yes. Prison staff have been allowing that to happen for a long time. Even though I was aware that prison officials subjected every inmate who attempted to challenge this problem to retaliation, I felt that I had to do something to try and protect the children who were going to the visitation parks. For this reason, on November 4, 2016, I mailed a sworn affidavit to almost two dozen individuals trying to get help for the children who go to FDC Visitation Parks.

The sworn affidavit stated:

Sworn Affidavit

To: U.S. Department of Justice, Attn: Vanita Gupta, Assistant U.S. Attorney General. Department of Children and Families, Attn: Mike Carroll, Secretary. Florida Department of Law Enforcement, Attn: Richard Swearingen, Commissioner.

Florida Department of Corrections (FDC) staff have been permitting sex offenders and predators to congregate with children at FDC visitation parks on a weekly basis at every close custody institution in Florida where sex offenders and predators are incarcerated. These sex offenders and predators are committing lewd and lascivious acts and sexual battery on children and adults at the visitation parks that FDC staff are allowing them to visit. FDC staff are aware of these things, and they haven't done anything to stop them.

Florida Statute: 775.21 is the Florida Sexual Predators Act. Florida Statute: 775.21 (3) (A) and (B) reads:

(A) Repeat sexual offenders who use physical violence, and sexual offenders who prey on children are sexual predators who present an extreme threat to public safety. Sexual offenders are extremely likely to use physical violence and to repeat their offenses, and most sexual offenders commit many offenses, have many more victims than are ever reported, and are prosecuted for only a fraction of their crimes. This makes the cost of sexual offender victimization to society at large, while incalculable, clearly exorbitant.

(B) The high level of threat that a sexual predator presents to the public safety, and the long-term effects suffered by victims of sex offenses, provide the state with sufficient justification to implement a strategy...

Florida Statute 775.21 (4) list the criteria that sex offenders must meet in order to be deemed a sexual predator.

Florida Statute 775.21 (10)(B) explains how a sexual predator commits a felony if he visits a business, school, child care facility, park, playground or any place where children regularly congregate even if their job requires them to do such.

The legislature deems protecting adults and children from sex offenders and predators so serious that they passed Florida Statute 775.215 (Residency Restriction For Persons Convicted Of Sex Offenses) making it a crime as high as a first degree felony for sex offenders to even have a residence within 1,000 feet of a school, child care facility, park, or playground.

"If a judge issues an order preventing a sex offender or predator from having visitation with children while in FDC, FDC has a rule that says they will honor that court order (FAC 33-601.720)."

However, if a court doesn't issue an order preventing a sex offender or predator from visiting with children, FDC staff won't comply with the Florida Statutes mentioned herein and other Florida Statutes and limit the sex offenders and predators from visiting with children in FDC.

FDC staff are also allowing sex offenders and predators to receive visits from adults in the visitation parks in FDC on the same days, and at the same time, that inmates who aren't sex offenders are receiving visits from children.

In other words, FDC staff have been allowing convicted sex offenders and predators to attend the visitation park every Saturday and Sunday where the children of non-sex offenders are. FDC has been allowing sex offenders and predators who the court issued orders restricting their visitation with their kids and other kids, to attend the visitation park every weekend where kids are visiting with inmates who are not convicted of sex offenses. The FDC's reasoning behind this is that according to their paperwork, the children are visiting with non-sex offenders.

Additionally, FDC staff are aware of all the laws mentioned herein and that they are not supposed to allow sex offenders or predators to attend visitation parks when children are congregating at them. To permit such is to permit sex offenders and predators to violate the Florida Statutes mentioned herein.

Additionally, sex offenders and predators are committing lewd and lascivious acts and sexual batteries on children in the visitation parks, FDC staff are permitting them to visit.

Sex offenders and predators are known for looking at children very lustfully in visitation parks. They are also known for looking up the dresses of ladies and juvenile girls and up the shorts of ladies and children.

Sex offenders and predators are known for showing the shape of their private area with their hands through their pants to ladies and children in visitation parks.

Sex offenders and predators place their children, and children they know on other inmates visitation lists so the sex offenders and predators can visit with their children and other children (i.e., their children, grandchildren, nephews, nieces, and the children of friends) in FDC Visitation Parks.

Sex offenders and predators touch the children of other visitors improperly in FDC Visitation Parks. They hug children, tap kids on their buttocks, touch and grab their legs, and touch the private areas of children.

Sex offenders and predators use their fingers to penetrate the rectums and vaginas of juvenile females and the rectums of juvenile boys in FDC Visitation Parks.

FDC records show that FDC Visitation Parks are insecure. Records show cell phones, narcotics, and tobacco are smuggled into FDC Visitation Parks on a weekly basis, and that inmates are having sexual relations in them with other adults. These facts prove the insecure status of FDC visitation parks.

FDC is aware that the violations of the Florida Statutes mentioned herein have been happening for a long time. They have elected to not do anything about them, because of the inconvenience it would cause them and because of how much it would cost FDC to fix these problems.

During Affiant's close to 17 years of incarceration, he's witnessed the matters herein, has been told by other inmates who witnessed them, and has spoken with sex offenders who have done these things.

Florida Statute: 20.315 reads in part: ... 'The secretary is responsible for planning, coordinating, and managing the corrections system of the state. The secretary shall ensure that the programs and services of the department are administered in accordance with state and federal laws, rules, and regulations, with established program standards and consistent with legislative intent.' The secretary has failed to comply with this statute as it concerns the violations mentioned herein.

"Florida Statute: 944.31 reads in part: ... 'The office of the inspector general shall see that all the rules and regulations issued by the department are strictly observed and followed by all persons connected with the correctional systems of the state'... and ... 'the inspector general and inspectors shall be responsible for criminal and administrative investigation of matters relating to the Department of Corrections'.... The FDC Inspector General's Office has failed to comply with this statute as it concerns the violations mentioned herein.

"Florida Statute: 944.14 reads: 'Subject to the orders, policies, and regulations established by the department, it shall be the duties of the wardens to supervise the government, discipline, and policy of the state correctional institutions, and to enforce all orders, rules, and regulations.' The wardens at each institution have failed to comply with this statute as it concerns the violations mentioned herein.

"Over the close to 17 years that Affiant has been incarcerated in the FDC, other inmates have attempted to get FDC to correct the matters herein. All of these inmates have been subjected to some type of retaliation. History shows FDC staff would rather subject inmates to retaliation for trying to have these serious matters corrected and stop sex offenders and predators from committing the violations of state law mentioned herein.

"It is reasonable to say that thousands (if not tens of thousands) of sex offenders and predators in FDC are allowed to visit FDC Visitation Parks (FAC 33-601.721) where children congregate on a weekly basis. Additionally, it's fair to say that hundreds if not thousands of adults and children are being victimized on a weekly basis by the sex offenders and predators who are allowed to be in the visitation parks with them.

"Affiant respectfully requests that the U.S. Department of Justice, Florida Department of Children and Families, and the Florida Department of Law Enforcement investigate the matters stated herein, and that the Florida Department of Children and Families issue protective orders protecting the children of visitors who go to FDC Visitation Parks from any further victimization by sexual offenders and predators."

UNNOTARIZED OATH

Under penalty of perjury, I swear that everything stated herein is true and correct.

Date 11-4-16 Affiant: (signature appears here on original handwritten document)

Harold Hempstead, D.C. #268866, Okeechobee Correctional Institution, 3420 Northeast 168th Street, Okeechobee, Florida 34972.

C.C.: Julie K. Brown (Miami Herald newspaper), Michele Gillen (CBS 4 Miami, Florida), Eyal Press (New Yorker magazine), Craig Patrick (WTVT Fox 13 Tampa, Florida), Clair McNeill (Tampa Bay Times), Pat Beall (Palm Beach Post), Howard Simon (ACLU of Florida), Steven Wetstein (Stop Prison Abuse Now), Randall Berg (Florida Legal Service), Lance T. Weber (Human Rights Defense Center), Greg Evers (Florida Senator), Melinda Miguel (Chief Inspector General for the Florida Governor), Windy Hempstead, Susan Chandler, George Mallinckrodt, Jeremy Schanche, Second Chance Effort Project, Forgotten Majority.

522) How could prison officials have corrected the problems cited in this affidavit?

This could have been easily corrected by allowing sex offenders and predators to visit with their families and friends on a day or at times when children are not in the visitation parks.

523) Were the wheelchair impaired inmates having problems at Okeechobee CI?

Yes. The best way to explain the problems they were having is to state what was documented in my December 2, 2016, sworn affidavit I mailed to almost two dozen individuals. My Sworn Affidavit stated:

Sworn Affidavit

To: U.S. Department of Justice, Disability Rights Section.
Florida Governor Rick Scott. Florida Department of Corrections, Attn: A.D.A. Coordinator.

The Federal A.D.A. Act (42 U.S.C. § 12101) and section 504 of the Rehabilitation Act (29 U.S.C. § 79) apply to prisoners. Pennsylvania Department of Corrections v. Yeskey, 524 U.S. 206, 118 S.CT. 192 (1998); Harris v. Thigpen, 941 F.3D 1495 (11th Cir. 1991).

MOBILITY IMPAIRED INMATES

"The wheelchair impaired inmates are housed in eight housing dorms at Okeechobee CI. In order for them to leave their housing dorms and go to the chow hall three times a day to eat their meals; to go to medical, dental and mental health, chapel, law library, library, education and classification call-outs; to go to the canteen to purchase food items, stationery, and hygiene items; and to go to the visitation park for visitation, they have to use the large quantity of interconnecting sidewalks. The sidewalks have dozens of large cracks and minor potholes in them. Oftentimes wheelchair impaired inmates are ejected from their wheelchairs when going over the cracks, and by accident, they fall into the potholes. 28 CFR 361; Ganstine v. Buss, 211 U.S. Dist. Lexis 148497. This violation is causing A.D.A. inmates to be physically hurt.

"The dirt and grass on both sides of the sidewalks, etc. are parallel or lesser in elevation than the sidewalks. Oftentimes wheelchair impaired inmates roll off the sidewalks or are intentionally pushed off the sidewalks by other inmates.

When this happens, the wheelchair impaired inmate is ejected from his wheelchair when the wheels of the wheelchair hit the dirt or grass. 28 CFR 36. This violation is causing A.D.A. inmates to be physically hurt. If the dirt and grass were elevated above the sidewalks, it would prevent that.

"28 Code of Federal Regulations 36 is the A.D.A. Accessibility Guide.

"The entrances to the eight housing dorms and several of the other entrances at Okeechobee CI are unsafe for wheelchair impaired inmates to pass through. The elevated steel that the wheelchair impaired inmates have to cross over in the entranceways, oftentimes causes them to be ejected from their wheelchairs. 28 CFR 36. This violation is causing A.D.A inmates to be physically hurt.

"Several of the restrooms at Okeechobee CI don't provide accessible door hardware that can be opened with a closed fist as required by 28 CFR 36, Section 4.23.9.

"Securely attached mats are not provided at the entrance of each building and into each wheelchair impaired shower in violation of 28 CFR 36, Section 4.5.3.

"The counter in the law library that law clerks and orderlies stand behind to help the inmate population with their law work is more than 34 inches high from the floor in violation of 28 CFR 36 Section 5.2.

"The restrooms don't have paper towel dispensers at an accessible height in violation of 28 CFR 36 Section 4.22.7.

"Okeechobee CI doesn't provide adequate direction and accurate information signage for A.D.A. inmates in violation of 28 CFR 36 Section 4.1.3 (16).

"Okeechobee CI has 36 wheelchair accessible cells. Six of those cells are in confinement wings. Okeechobee CI doesn't have a sufficient amount of wheelchair accessible cells to house wheelchair impaired inmates in violation of 28 CFR 36;

and Florida Statute 553.503. This is causing wheelchair impaired inmates to be housed in cells and living quarters that are not in compliance with the A.D.A.

"The wheelchair impaired inmate showers have showerheads stuck to the walls like the regular showers. Those types of showerheads make it where wheelchair impaired inmates can't properly wash the whole backside of their bodies that are in the wheelchairs. The failure of Okeechobee C.I.'s staff to provide handheld showerheads so wheelchair impaired inmates can properly shower themselves is causing them to be denied proper hygiene and is in violation of 28 CFR 36.

"Okeechobee CI has two inmate recreation yards. One of the recreation yards doesn't have any cement, sidewalks. Wheelchair impaired inmates cannot access it. As it concerns the second recreation yard, wheelchair impaired inmates have sidewalks that go to the front and side of the recreation building, basketball court, small pavilion, and toilets. On this recreation yard, wheelchair impaired inmates don't have access to the two large pavilions, two water kegs, the football and soccer fields; and because the basketball court doesn't have any cement areas around it, the wheelchair impaired inmates cannot watch any basketball games. These violations prohibit wheelchair impaired inmates from being able to watch sporting events like the rest of the general population. Approximately 90 percent of this recreation yard, cannot be accessed by wheelchair impaired inmates. None of the three pavilions have tables under them that can be used by wheelchair impaired inmates. None of the recreation yards have a cement sidewalk that goes all around them for wheelchair impaired inmates. These violations make it where wheelchair impaired inmates don't go to the recreation yards to sit in the sun, get fresh air, or watch sporting events. 28 CFR 36: Florida Accessibility Code (Florida Statute 553.503); Ganstine v. Buss, 2011 U.S. Dist. Lexis 148497 (2011).

"Wheelchair impaired inmates cannot have access to the inmate canteens; medical, mental health, dental and classification departments, or pill line to receive medication; and library, law library, and education departments without traveling up and down inclined cement sidewalks. Additionally, to exit the north and south chow halls wheelchair impaired inmates have to travel down inclined cement sidewalks. The health of a lot of the wheelchair impaired inmates prohibits them from being able to push themselves up the inclined cement sidewalks. If staff or inmates don't help them up the inclined sidewalks, they'll have to wait at the bottom of them until somebody agrees to help them. A lot of the wheelchair impaired inmates cannot safely control their wheelchairs when having to travel down the inclined cement sidewalks. This oftentimes scares them to not attempt it. Some of the wheelchair impaired inmates who attempt to travel down the inclined sidewalks without help, end up hitting inmates and fences at the bottom of them, and sometimes they go into the dirt and grass which are about 12 feet from the bottom of the inclined sidewalks. Finally, these inclined cement sidewalks don't have any handrails, 28 CFR 36.

"Inmates who are impaired assistants are extorting, physically and (possibly sexually) battering wheelchair impaired inmates 28 CFR 36.

"The law library at Okeechobee CI doesn't have a primary research book for A.D.A. inmates to research A.D.A. violations. This makes it where A.D.A. inmates can't properly defend themselves against A.D.A. violations in violation of the A.D.A and 28 CFR 36."

RELIEF SOUGHT

For the U.S. Department of Justice Disability Rights Section, Florida Governor, and FDC to take immediate action to correct the A.D.A. violations mentioned herein that are at Okeechobee CI.

Executed this 2 day of December 2016.

UNNOTARIZED OATH

Under penalty of perjury, I swear that everything stated herein is true and correct.

Affiant: (Signature of Harold Hempstead appears here on original handwritten document)

Harold Hempstead, D.C. #268866, Okeechobee Correctional Institution, 3420 North East 168th Street, Okeechobee, Florida 34972

C.C. ACLU of Florida (Howard Simon), Stop Prison Abuse Now (Steven Wetstein), Disability Rights Florida (Molly Paris), Florida Legal Service (Peter Sleasman), Florida Justice Institute (Randall Berg), Forgotten Majority, Human Rights Defense Center (Lance T. Weber), Miami Herald newspaper (Julie K. Brown), WTVT Fox 13 Tampa, Florida (Craig Patrick), CBS 4 Miami, Florida (Michele Gillen), New Yorker magazine (Eyal Press), Tampa Bay Times, Palm Beach Post (Pat Beall), Windy Hempstead, Susan Chandler, George Mallinckrodt, Jeremy Schanche.

524) Did the Department of Justice acknowledge receipt of these sworn affidavits?

Yes. They acknowledged receipt of all of the sworn affidavits I mailed them.

525) Did you continue with your justice seeking activities while at Okeechobee CI?

Yes. I continued to work on the reform of Protective Management Units by corresponding with the *Miami Herald* newspaper and others in society about the extreme violent conditions in the Protective Management Units.

In 2016, Windy and I continued our efforts to get Al Sharpton, Jesse Jackson, Alicia Garza, and Opal Tometi to aid us in obtaining justice for Darren Rainey.

Also, Randy Evans and Jim Knowels came to Okeechobee CI several times and talked with me, but I cannot tell you what we discussed at this time.

526) How did you react to the sit-down that was planned for all the close custody institution in the FDC?

A lot of the inmates in Florida had been upset for years about the conditions in the Florida prison system, the food they were fed in the chow hall, and not being paid to work. Some inmates saw on the internet that people in society were calling for all the prisoners in the nation to sit down and refuse to work on certain days as part of the 45th anniversary of the infamous Attica riot in New York. Some Florida inmates told all of the inmates they knew at Okeechobee CI and at other institutions about the sit-down. When the inmate gang leaders became aware of the sit-down, they issued orders for their gang brothers to get as many inmates as they could to participate in it. In the months prior to the sit-down, inmates were calling other inmates at other prisons across Florida trying to encourage everybody in FDC to sit-down.

When I heard about the sit-down, I was concerned. If it actually happened, it was likely that staff and inmates would get hurt. Many of the inmates were labeling the proposed sit-down as a civil rights movement. A non-violent sit-down in society to try and correct civil rights problems would be deemed a civil rights action. However, in the FDC, any type of mass sit-down is deemed a riot. Since I didn't want any staff or inmates to get hurt, I took action to try and stop the sit-down.

I told the inmates who I knew that it was not the proper way to challenge the conditions in the prison system. I explained that Florida prison staff deemed any type of mass sit-down as a riot. I further explained that on the days the sit-down was supposed to happen, prison officials would have a lot of extra staff on the compound to discipline those involved. Finally, I explained that the inmates involved with the sit-down would, more than likely, be physically battered by staff, issued a disciplinary report, placed on close management, and have a lot of their property disposed of. I also told the *Miami Herald* newspaper and others in society of the planned sit-down.

After about a week of telling the inmates this, I was told that several gang leaders wanted to talk with me. I met with inmates who represented five different gangs. When asked why I was saying inmates in the compound should not participate in the sit-down, I gave them the same reasons I stated above. When they said they were the ones pushing for the sit-down, I told them that dozens of inmates on the compound would more than likely tell on them as the organizers, and, in the end, they and their gang brothers would be the primary people punished. I also explained that engaging in a mass sit-down was not likely to achieve their goals. After about two hours of talking with them, I was able to convince them that it would be in their best interest to call off the sit-down. They agreed and said they would call their gang brothers at other prisons and tell them what I said.

Florida prison officials were told about the sit-down in advance. They arranged for some better quality and larger quantity meals to be served in the chow hall on the main day of the sit-down. Prison staff did this as a way to get the inmates to not sit-down and to go to the chow hall to eat that day. Also, the staff provided better food to make it appear they were responding to inmate demands for better food. After the planned sit-down day, all the chow hall meals went back to the same quality and quantity they were prior to that day. All across Florida, prison officials brought in extra staff to address any problems that might occur the day of the sit-down.

The gang leaders I spoke with were able to convince the majority of their fellow gang members at the majority of the institutions in Florida to not sit-down. However, they weren't able to convince everybody. The *Miami Herald* published articles about inmates at about 10 of the approximately 60 close custody institutions in Florida engaging in violence and riotous activities on the main day of the sit-down. When the gang leaders saw that the talk of the sit-down caused prison officials to give inmates more and better quality food on the planned sit-down day, they decided they would plan for a larger sit-down in 2017.

The gang leaders thought that they could convince prison officials to submit to their demands to correct prison conditions by using violence. This also inspired the gang leaders to focus on getting more organized so they could obtain their goals. At the end of 2016, I told the *Miami Herald* of what the gang leaders were doing. I also wrote anonymous letters to the Governor's Chief Inspector General Melinda Miguel, and the FDC Inspector General's Office advising them of these things. I wanted to do what I could to stop staff and inmates from being hurt.

Prison officials didn't take any action, and the inmates in Florida had another statewide sit-down in August 2017.

527) Will you tell me about the problem you had with a sergeant at Okeechobee CI?

I forgot the Sergeant's name, so I'll just refer to him as the sergeant. He was posted to work in the dorm I lived in on the 6:00 pm to 6:00 am shift. On the nights he worked, he always passed-out the incoming mail. After he saw that I received completed grievances back in the mail on a regular basis, he began shaking his head in disapproval every time he gave me grievances. His head shaking was his way of saying no, no, no, as he gave me responses to the grievances I had submitted.

I took the sergeant's actions as expressing anger about my filing of grievances. Thus, once when he was shaking his head to express his disapproval as the handed me some responses to grievances I filed, I said, "Sergeant, are you mad that I'm filing grievances?"

He responded, "No."

I said, "Then, if I may ask, why do you shake your head in a no manner every time you give me grievances while passing-out incoming mail? I feel like you're saying no, as in I shouldn't be filing grievances."

He responded, "You can file grievances." This conversation happened while he had two or three officers in training with him.

A few days after this conversation, when I was returning from the law library, several inmates told me that the sergeant and some officers were searching my cell. As I walked to my cell, I noticed two officers in training were searching my cell, and the sergeant, along with one or two officers in training, were searching my neighbor's cell. The two officers searching my cell said I couldn't watch the search from outside my cell. I went to the cell next door and asked the sergeant if it could watch the search of my cell. He also said that I couldn't watch my cell being searched. When they were done searching both cells, they left the wing with some items from each cell. My cellmate and I did not receive a property slip for any of the things they took from our cells.

Department of Corruption

My years of experience taught me that the sergeant was subjecting me to retaliation. I didn't want the retaliation to get worse, so I decided to take action to stop it. I filed several grievances on the sergeant. I reported the retaliation to the FDC Inspector General's Office via two or three calls on the prison tip-line, and I mailed a letter to the Florida Governor's Chief Inspector General Melinda Miguel on the sergeant's retaliatory actions.

A few nights afterward, the sergeant came to my cell during Master Roster Count and told me to get ready to go see the captain. The sergeant and I then left my cell and wing. When we were in the sally port of my dorm, he told me he had to put handcuffs on me to take me to the captain's office because it was dark outside. That was false. Every morning, hundreds of inmates walked from their dorms to the chow halls and back to their dorms, in the dark without handcuffs. I had no choice. I had to have the handcuffs placed on me even though I knew, by rule, I didn't have to be put in them.

When we got to the captain's office, the captain and another officer were there. The captain questioned me about why I filed grievances on one of his sergeants. The sergeant and officer said disrespectful things to me and tried to intimidate me. The captain then joined in with the disrespectful comments. I knew from experience that they were being disrespectful and trying to intimidate me because they, more than likely, didn't know my past. The majority of Florida prison staff who are bullies only pick on inmates who they believe won't stand-up for themselves. For this reason, I said, "Captain, does this have anything to do with my association with the Feds, media, and civil rights groups?"

As soon as I said this, the office got quiet. After a few seconds of silence, the captain said, "How are you associated with the Feds and media?

I said, "If you look at the computer, you'll see that you were the captain who was working on the night I transferred here from the Martin CI Protective Management Unit. I was on protective management status for almost two years. The main office said I had statewide protection problems with staff. Right after the *Miami Herald* started writing on the Darren Rainey case and the prison system, I was forced into protection. Two years later, your Regional Director, Thomas Reid, directed I be released from protective management and transferred here. He told me I wouldn't have any problems with the staff here."

As I was talking, I noticed the Captain Googled my name. When he saw the Google hit list, he said, "I remember you. We don't have a problem with you. I knew there had to be a misunderstanding with the sergeant. Sarge, officer, come here and look at this screen." He then showed the sergeant and officer the computer screen with the Google information on me on the screen.

The sergeant then said, "Hempstead, you misunderstood us. We weren't trying to intimidate you or retaliate against you."

The officer said, "We were just joking with you. Don't you have a sense of humor?"

I said, "I didn't know you were joking." From then on, the three security staff acted as if it was just a misunderstanding with the sergeant, and that they were just joking when they were being disrespectful and trying to intimidate me.

Everything ended that night with no problems. Additionally, from that night on, I didn't have any more problems with that sergeant, captain, or officer.

528) At Okeechobee CI, were you told the Traditionalist American Knights of the Ku Klux Klan was conspiring to kill you?

Yes. Warden Severson alleged that he was told that Crime Stopper TIP calls were made by somebody in society to a TIP line. The caller alleged that he was at a Ku Klux Klan (KKK) gathering when his fellow Klansmen were talking about killing a n*gger activist who had caused a lot of legal and media trouble for the prison system. The caller alleged that he and the Klansmen he was talking to both worked at Okeechobee CI. The caller also alleged that his fellow clansmen eventually said my name as the activist that they were talking about.

I also had a conversation about the alleged KKK plot to kill me with two men who identified themselves as agents with the Florida Department of Law Enforcement. They made the same allegations that Warden Severson made about the alleged conspiracy. They also alleged the tip line caller said the FDC Inspector General's Office was destroying and altering paperwork concerning me.

I told Warden Severson and the two alleged agents that even if calls were made to Crime Stopper TIP lines in society that it didn't mean somebody in society made the calls, or that the things the caller said were true. I explained that the caller could have been an inmate on a cell phone who was trying to create tension between the staff and me that could result in Okeechobee CI being placed in the spotlight and staff being placed under investigation. I also told the warden and the two alleged agents that inmates had a history of calling Crime Stopper TIP lines and other agencies in society and reporting fake stories about inmates and staff. I also said Okeechobee CI staff could have made up the KKK plot and made the TIP calls. The staff obviously knew that the TIP calls could get me transferred. Also, I told them that I was sure that Okeechobee CI staff didn't want me on their compound.

I was very surprised when I wasn't placed in administrative confinement pending a protective management investigation. I never heard anything else about the Crime Stopper TIP calls after my conversations with Warden Severson and the two alleged agents. Finally, I was told that the crime stoppers case numbers for the tip calls were 104-65509 and 104-65662.

The alleged agents from the Florida Department of Law Enforcement did not show me their badges. As far as I know, they could have been Okeechobee CI staff aiding Warden Severson in an attempt to get me to take action to get transferred from Okeechobee CI.

Just in case there was trouble later, I told Windy and the *Miami Herald* newspaper about the alleged Crime Stopper TIP calls concerning the KKK. After I transferred from Okeechobee CI, I told several other people.

One of the alleged Florida Department of Law Enforcement agents thought that I might have been called a n*gger activist because I was most known for standing up for justice for Darren Rainey who was black.

529) Did you make any attempts to receive special reviews while at Okeechobee CI?

Yes, I made several attempts to be special reviewed from Regional Medical Center, South Florida Reception Center, and Everglades CI?

530) Were there any good staff at Okeechobee CI?

Yes, I knew several of them.

531) Why were you transferred from Okeechobee CI in December 2016?

During a conversation with Warden Severson in December 2016, he expressed anger over the number of grievances and paperwork with people in society I had filed about staff and problems at Okeechobee CI. During that conversation, he said, "Didn't you put in for a good adjustment transfer?"

I responded, "Yes."

He said, "I'm going to see what I can do to speed that up." Approximately three weeks later, I was transferred to Hardee CI. Based on how everything transpired, I believe the number of grievances and amount of paperwork I filed on problems and staff at Okeechobee CI were what caused me to be transferred.

532) Will you tell me about your transfer from Okeechobee CI?

Prison staff told me I was being transferred the day prior to transferring The next day a bus was scheduled to drop off and pick up inmates from Okeechobee CI and return to South Florida Reception. Center. That night I called Windy and the *Miami Herald* newspaper and told them that I was supposed to transfer the next day to South Florida Reception Center. Windy called Civil Rights Attorney James Cook and told him. He had started helping me around August 2016.

The next morning, I was told to pack my property because I was transferring. I packed my property and took it to the security building. In route to the security building, I saw the major. I told him I was transferring to South Florida Reception Center, and that I had protection issues with the staff there. He said I wasn't going to be transferred to where I wasn't supposed to be housed. I didn't feel comfortable with what he said. I felt like he told me what he did just to get me to go on my way and leave him alone.

The major knew my past and that if I was transferred to South Florida Reception Center, there was a very good chance their staff would attempt to harm me. Several of the staff at South Florida Reception Center were former Dade CI staff whom I had placed under federal investigations, and South Florida Reception Center was in the heart of Miami. Miami was the Florida city where I was most known because of all the all the newspaper articles and TV news broadcasts in Dade County, Florida that mentioned my name.

After being transferred to South Florida Reception Center, I saw two staff in the Transferring and Receiving staring at me. They were formerly employed at Dade CI.

After I was done with processing and receiving, I went to my assigned dorm and cell. A short time later, we had an institutional count. Prior to the count ending, an officer told me to go to the medical department after I was done eating my dinner.

While I was in the chow hall, a black officer and a Spanish officer showed up at the chow hall and called my name. After I went to them, the black officer said, "Come with us." We then left the chow hall and walked toward the medical department. When we got in front of the medical department, we stopped. The black officer then said, "What can we do to you, and get away with?"

I responded, "Why are you messing with me when I don't know either of you?"

The Spanish officer said, "Tell us some things we can do to you, and get away with."

I responded, "You can do just about anything you want, and the only thing I'll have on my side, is I can pass a polygraph or voice stress test about what happened."

The Spanish officer said, "If you don't shut your mouth about Dade CI and the prison system, you're going to have some real problems the next time you come through here. Do you understand me? "

I responded, "Yes."

Chapter 20: Hardee CI (December 2016 – May 17, 2017)

The Spanish officer said, "Inmates die every day in prison by accident, so don't forget that. Now get out of here." I then left and went back to my dorm and cell.

The next morning I was transferred from South Florida Reception Center to Central Florida Reception Center. I stayed at Central Florida Reception Center until a few days after Christmas when I was transferred to Hardee Correctional Institution.

All the time I was in transit traveling from Okeechobee CI to Hardee CI, I was forced by staff to carry all my law work and personal property which probably weighed close to 200 pounds. Security staff forced me to carry all my property even though my files showed I had a broken wrist and damage to my back. Additionally, my files showed I had an active no heavy lifting pass and passes to wear a back brace and wrist support, both of which I was wearing.

Chapter 20: Hardee CI (December 2016 – May 17, 2017)

533) **Please give some general information about Hardee Correctional Institution.**

Hardee CI is located in Central Florida in Hardee County, which borders Hillsborough County. The compound was, for the most part, designed like Martin CI except for some minor exceptions. Hardee CI had two recreational yards, a lot more fences, and it only had Butterfly dorms on the compound. It wasn't a close management security threat group or gang dumping ground, and it was considered by Florida inmates to be one of the top 10 best institutions in Florida.

534) **Will you tell me about your arrival to Hardee CI?**

When the bus arrived, security staff ordered the inmates to line up after we got off the bus. As we stood in line having our shackles removed, I watched the housing sergeant tell two officers, "That's him, with all the property." She then identified me to two officers. We were then escorted to the property room and processed into Hardee CI.

After processing was completed, the other inmates and I were given the locations of our cell assignments. I told the housing

397

sergeant that I had a no-heavy-lifting pass because I had a broken wrist and injured back and asked her if I could use a cart to push my property to my dorm. She said I couldn't and, if I couldn't carry my property to my dorm, I would have to dispose of it.

Prison staff commonly allow inmates to use carts to push their property to different locations, especially those with documented medical problems. Since she said I couldn't use a cart, I did like I had been doing until then. I used my left arm and carried my property in small trips, one bag at a time, 10 to 15 feet at a time. About a minute into doing this, an inmate volunteered to help carry my property to my dorm.

When I got to my dorm, I found out I had been assigned a cell by myself. My cell had a mounted security camera pointed at it, and the inside of my cell could be viewed by the officers in the officers' station.

535) Were there a lot of cell phones, drugs, and tobacco at Hardee CI?

Yes. There was an abundance of all three. Also, while at Okeechobee CI, I heard about an inmate who was having K-2 flown in on a drone. At Hardee CI, I actually knew an inmate who had K-2 and cell phones flown in on a drone. Inmates at Hardee CI also had drugs mailed into them by people they met on the Dark Web.

Hardee CI didn't just have tobacco, K-2, marijuana, and Molly, like most of the other institutions in the FDC. The inmates at Hardee CI also had acid, cocaine, crack cocaine, crank, ice, and different types of pills from society. They were constantly high.

The only institution I had been at that had more cell phones than Hardee CI, was Dade CI. The inmates at Hardee CI used their cell phones for the same scams and reasons inmates used them at the other institutions I had been incarcerated at.

536) Were predators and sexually aggressive inmates incarcerated at Hardee CI?

Yes, a good many. However, there were fewer there than at the other institutions I had been incarcerated at since I transferred from Dade CI.

537) Did you file informal grievances concerning your housing problems in other locations?

Within a few days of my arrival to Hardee CI, I filed several grievances on the four drug-addicted convicted killers I was housed with before transferring to Hardee CI. I also filed grievances concerning other issues relating to the *Inmate Risk Management System/Sexual Risk Indicator*. In these grievances, I stated that none concerned my housing at Hardee CI.

Two or three days after I filed the grievances, the housing sergeant moved a drug-addicted convicted killer in my cell named Thomas Pack. He was very paranoid and was constantly high on K-2 and on any type of drug he could get his hands on. The housing sergeant told Pack that she specifically chose him to be housed with me.

It was obvious to me that the housing sergeant was subjecting me to retaliation. This led to me filing several grievances on the housing sergeant for her retaliatory actions. I also mailed a complaint to the Florida Governor's Chief Inspector General Melinda Miguel concerning the retaliatory actions of the housing sergeant.

538) Did staff at Hardee CI try to intimidate you to stop filing grievances?

Yes. The officer who held the title of Grievance Coordinator threatened me with a disciplinary report and a transfer if I didn't stop filing grievances.

539) Please tell me about your trip to a Miami hospital.

Orthopedic Surgeon Doctor Check Kam ordered that I receive another MRI of my right wrist, because of how long it had been since I received the MRI while I was housed at Martin CI. The purpose of the MRI was to determine again if the bone in my wrist was dead.

One morning while I was at Hardee CI, I was told to get ready to go on a medical trip. After getting ready, I was transported on a van to a hospital in Miami, Florida to get the second MRI on my wrist. The hospital had a floor specifically for FDC inmates. Prison staff from Dade County, Florida (who knew me) worked as correctional officers on the floor where prison inmates were treated and housed.

Department of Corruption

After I received the MRI, I was transported back to Hardee CI. That was the second time I was taken into Miami in less than two months when I should never have been taken into that city for any reason. Prison officials knew they were taking chances with my safety by taking me into locations where Dade County, Florida correctional staff were.

540) How was your medical care while you were housed at Hardee CI?

For the most part, I received good medical care while I was housed there.

As it concerns my wrist, they followed Doctor Kam's recommendation and made arrangements for me to receive the second MRI that I discussed above.

I went back to see Dr. Kam to talk with him about the results. He said the MRI showed that the bone in my wrist was still alive, and he asked if I wanted surgery. When I asked him if I could receive a local instead of being put to sleep with anesthesia, he said I couldn't. When I told him that my sister was allergic to anesthesia and that I wanted to be tested to make sure I wasn't, he said they didn't have a test for that and that I would be OK. I asked him if people in society had the option of having the surgery with a local. He said they did, but he didn't give inmates that option.

When I got back to Hardee CI after talking with him, I asked a nurse and talked to Windy about my chances of being allergic to anesthesia because of the family history. They both said there was a good chance that I would be allergic to it also.

I did not understand why Dr. Kam wouldn't give me a local for the surgery even though he allowed people in society to receive a local for the same surgery. Also, it didn't make sense to me that he was planning on giving me anesthesia when I had been having issues with my heart for more than a year. Dr. Kam seemed to be ignoring my family history of allergies to anesthesia, as well as, the fact that I was also allergic to several antibiotics. The antibiotic allergy was documented in my medical files.

I told the doctor and medical staff at Hardee CI about the problems I was having with Dr. Kam and that I didn't feel

400

medically safe being put under anesthesia for the surgery. They agreed with me that Dr. Kam's actions didn't make sense. They were in the process of working on getting me approved to get the wrist surgery with another surgeon my last few weeks I was incarcerated at Hardee CI.

541) Were there any good staff at Hardee CI?

Yes. There was a lot of them there.

542) Who is Jeremy Schanche?

Jeremy is an activist from Cornwall, Great Britain. At the end of 2015, he contacted Windy and me about helping us to get justice for Darren Rainey and to bring reform to the unconstitutional conditions of the FDC. Jeremy, among other things, uses his blog (savetheholyheadland@.blogspot.com) in his activism. At the beginning of 2017, he agreed to open and manage the blog for me. The address of the blog is: haroldhempsteadcagedcrusader@wordpress.com.

Jeremy has been a good friend and fellow activist since the end of 2015.

543) In early 2017, did Jeremy help distribute your affidavit on children and sexual predators?

Yes. I mailed it again to the same people I previously mailed it to. After a few weeks, during which I received no response, I asked Jeremy to send an e-mail to these same prison officials asking them about allowing sexual predators and children to congregate in the same visitation parks.

544) What other activism did you undertake while in Hardee CI?

I worked with Jeremy to prepare an email on problems associated with prison staff allowing inmates with communicable diseases to work in FDC chow halls. Jeremy sent this email to FDC Secretary Julie Jones.

I met with Randy Evans and Jim Knowels while I was incarcerated at Hardee CI. I cannot reveal what we discussed.

545) With Jeremy's assistance, did you place a petition placed Change.org about Darren Raney?

Yes. It was named, "The Life of Black Mentally Disabled Muslim Prisoner Darren Rainey does Matter." The petition is now closed; however, you can still find it on the internet.

546) Please tell me about the petition posted on Change.org concerning the danger you were in.

Sometime around February 2017 Windy and Jeremy posted a petition on Change.org about me continuing to be housed with drug addicted killers. Thomas Pack was the fifth drug-addicted killer I had been housed with since the end of 2014. It was stressful to continue to be housed in the same cell with dangerous inmates. The staff were intentionally placing incompatible inmates in my cell as a form of retaliation.

After telling Windy and Jeremy about this, we decided to post a petition on Change.org about these dangerous placements. The petition was named, "Florida: Stop Endangering the Witness to your Crimes." The petition stated:

Florida: Stop Endangering the Witness to your Crimes

"It is reasonable to say that the Florida Department of Corrections (FDC) doesn't like that my brother Harold Hempstead won't stop pursuing justice for the brutal murder of mentally disabled inmate Darren Rainey by Dade Correctional Institution staff. It is also reasonable to say that FDC's dislike for that and other matters that my brother is trying to bring change to in FDC, is what has caused FDC staff to continue to house my brother with convicted, drug using killers.

"Since June 2015, FDC has given my brother five convicted killers as cellmates. His first cellmate, Timothy Jones, was a methamphetamine and crack cocaine abuser in society who after being awake for days at a time would stab and shoot people from hallucinations. Eventually, he killed a man and was sentenced to life in prison. He was also a Satanist. While housed with my brother he abused several drugs that made him stay awake for days and to hallucinate. Medical and

402

security staff had to remove him from my brother's cell two times because he overdosed. Timothy Jones stabbed his cellmate (that he had after my cellmate) in the eye, etc., with a pen and almost killed him!

"The second convicted killer, Timothy Story, my brother received as a cellmate, was addicted to K-2 (Spice), which made him hallucinate and become violent. FDC staff dismissed a disciplinary report Timothy Story had received for K-2 (Spice), so they could place him in a cell with my brother.

"After Martin CI staff found out that my brother had been communicating with the media, civil rights groups, etc. about the unconstitutional conditions of FDC Protective Management Units, they took my brother out of the cell he was housed alone in, and placed him in a cell with a convicted killer who was in prison for sexual battery (Ronald Davis), and who was addicted to K-2 (Spice) and pills. This was my brother's third drug abusing, killer cellmate.

"My brother's fourth convicted killer cellmate, (Jenouch Pasco), was a crack cocaine abuser in society who killed an elderly white lady and burned her house down.

"When my brother filed a grievance about constantly receiving convicted killers as cellmates, FDC staff gave him a fifth convicted killer (Thomas Pack), as a cellmate, who is a K-2 (Spice) abuser.

"My brother has mailed several sworn affidavits and letters to the Governor's Chief Inspector General Melinda Miguel and numerous others about this problem.

"My brother is not compatible to be housed with these convicted killers. Harold is in prison for burglaries and dealing in stolen property. None of the alleged victims were in their homes during the commission of the alleged burglaries. His criminal case record shows that he's convicted under a ringleader theory, and the legislative history of the dealing in stolen property charge that he's convicted under (Florida

Department of Corruption

Statute: 812.019 (2)) shows he's convicted as a white-collar criminal. The FDC Inmate Risk Management System/ Sexual Risk Indicator (IRMS/SRI) ranks Harold as Identified Prey. This means FDC has identified him as the type of inmate other inmates will try to prey upon. Finally, Harold has eight years with no disciplinary reports, and it is well documented that he is anti to violence, drug use, and crime.

"Florida Statute: 944.012 (6)(B), and FDC's IRMS/SRI system prohibits the housing of violent inmates with non-violent inmates identified as prey.

"FDC records and Miami Herald newspaper articles will show FDC has a problem with inmates killing and seriously harming their cellmates for many years now.

Why does FDC staff continue to house my brother with convicted, drug using killers? I believe the answer is obvious:

"(1) He's the eyewitness who first exposed the Darren Rainey murder and torturing of mentally disabled inmates at Dade CI, and he's a listed federal and state witness to these matters.

"(2) He's been working on exposing the unconstitutional conditions of FDC protective management unit where inmates are being physically hurt and killed on a regular basis.

"(3) He's been working on exposing that FDC is allowing convicted sexual predators to go to FDC Visitation Parks every Saturday and Sunday where children congregate, in violation of the Florida Sexual Predator Act (Florida Statute: 775.21(10)(B)).

"(4) He's been trying to expose that FDC is allowing inmates with communicable diseases, etc. to work in FDC chow halls in violation of federal and state laws.

"(5) He's been trying to expose that FDC staff are arming inmates with razors at non-psych. institutions and that FDC staff know that inmates are using the razors to cut and hurt inmates and staff. Every week inmates at non-psych institutions are given a shaving razor. The blades are being removed from the shavers and being used as weapons.

"Harold has First Amendment Constitutional rights to Freedom of Speech, and Redress of Grievances. He shouldn't be subjected to retaliation for asserting these rights. *Miami Herald* newspaper articles will show that FDC staff engage in a pattern and practice of subjecting staff and inmates to retaliation when they speak out about the unconstitutional conditions of FDC.

"I'm asking for one hundred thousand signatures to present this petition (with more detailed facts) to the Florida Department of Law Enforcement, and the Department of Justice asking them to investigate the issues stated herein. I'll also be asking the DOJ to conduct a 'Civil Rights of Institutionalized Persons Act' investigation into the FDC's pattern and practice of retaliation against staff and inmates who try and expose the unconstitutional conditions of FDC.

Around the end of February, beginning of March 2017, Jeremy sent FDC Secretary Julie Jones an email advising her of the petition and asking her to direct her staff to stop housing me with inmates I wasn't supposed to be housed with.

547) What were you told about the Darren Rainey case on March 15, 2017?

I was told that the Dade County, Florida State Attorney Katherine Rundle was going to issue a memo closing the case with no arrest on March 17, 2017. I was supposed to contact the *Miami Herald* newspaper on March 17, 2017 and make a statement concerning the state attorney's memo on the Darren Rainey case.

Department of Corruption

Chapter 21: Tennessee Department of Corrections
(March 17, 2018)

548)   Tell me what happened on March 17, 2017.

I woke around 3:30 am when Hardee CI Captain Schrank, Sergeant Hamilton, and Officer Cabrara entered my cell. I was strip searched and told to put deodorant in my pillowcase. I did and was then handcuffed and escorted to the front of Hardee CI. All of my law work, Christian books, and property were left in my cell.

When we got to the front of Hardee CI, Captain Schrank told Sergeant Hamilton, "Sergeant, it's on you." Hamilton then slapped me with so much force that fell to the ground.

Officer Cabrara pulled me up saying, "Get up, Hempstead," and held me from behind by both my arms.

Sergeant Hamilton grabbed my throat and squeezed it saying, "You could have had a serious accident, but instead you're being spared. Don't forget that. You hear me?"

When the sergeant let go of my throat, Schrank said, "You really pissed off the wrong person. Think about what he said."

Officer Cabrara then let go of my arms and punched me in my lower back.

I was then put in a van with none of my property and transferred several hours away to Regional Medical Center. While in the van, I was threatened with physical violence because I told the sergeant and officer that I had to urinate really badly.

At the Regional Medical Center, I spent about an hour in a holding cage. I was then put in another van with two sergeants, and we drove away. Two hours later, I began to see signs with the names of cities in Georgia on them. Then I knew. I was being taken out of Florida. I asked where I was going. The sergeants refused to tell me.

As I sat on the van not knowing where I was going or what would happen to me when I got there, I thought about all that I had been through over the years. I had devoted nearly five years of my life trying to get justice for Darren Rainey, help for mentally disabled inmates, and to bring reform to the FDC.

406

Chapter 21: Tennessee Department of Corrections (March 17, 2018)

I was being transferred out of Florida as a form of retaliation for asserting my First Amendment rights to Freedom of Speech, Redress of Grievances, and Access to the Courts. I knew that Secretary Julie Jones and others who worked with her in the main office of the FDC resented my quest for justice for Darren Rainey and my constant efforts to bring reform to the FDC. I also felt that the information I was given on March 15, 2017 was correct and that the Dade County, Florida State Attorney had issued a memo closing the Darren Rainey case with no arrests. If so, it meant I was also being transferred out of Florida to prevent me from answering the media's questions on the Rainey case and from responding to address memo closing the case.

Around 6:30 pm we arrived at a Tennessee prison, Bledsoe County Correctional Complex, located the mountains of Tennessee. Bledsoe County Correctional Complex handled all the new arrivals into the Tennessee Department of Corrections. In Tennessee, they call it a classification prison; in Florida, we would call it a reception center.

Within a few days of your my arrival at the Tennessee Department of Corrections, I found out that, on March 17, 2017, the Dade County, Florida State Attorney, Katherine Rundle issued a memo closing the Darren Rainey case with no arrest.

549) What was the legal basis of your transfer to Tennessee and why were you moved?

The legal name of the type of transfer I was subjected to is Involuntary Interstate Corrections Compact. It was involuntary because I didn't request it. Florida Statute § 941.56 (Corrections), and FAC 33-601.401 governs interstate corrections compact.

I believe there were three main reasons why I was involuntary interstate compacted.

- First, FDC staff and the Dade County State Attorney's office didn't want me in Florida on March 17, 2017 when the state attorney issued her memo closing the Darren Rainey case with no arrests. They knew I was in regular contact with the *Miami Herald* newspaper, and if I was in Florida, I would have been able to respond to the state attorney's memo when it was released. The memo was full of false statements that were easily refutable.

407

- Second, my quest for justice for Darren Rainey and my quest to get help for the mentally disabled inmates in the Dade CI TCU exposed problems in the FDC.
- Third, I raised an issue and tried to put a stop to the FDC practice of allowing convicted sexual predators to go to FDC Visitation Parks where children congregate.

Essentially, they wanted me out of Florida because of my non-stop activism trying to bring reform to the FDC, and I believe this is in retaliation for asserting my First Amendment rights to Freedom of Speech, Redress of Grievances, and Access to the Courts.

Other reasons have been suggested. The FDC claimed that my "spokesperson" requested the transfer. They knew that my only spokesperson was Windy. Windy told me she never said anything to the Florida Department of Corrections that could be construed as her wanting me to be interstate compacted out of Florida. Some have raised the possibility that I was involuntarily moved because threats by the Ku Klux Klan and Florida prison staff to kill me. If this is the reason, I would like to see some evidence proving it. Others suggest I was involuntary interstate compacted because FDC Secretary Julie Jones found out that I was continually housed with drug-addicted killers. I doubt that. She could have ordered her staff only to house me with compatible inmates or to house me alone.

550) Did your transfer violate any of your rights?

Yes, my rights under were violated. FAC 33-601.401(3) (B) states:

> "(3) When Florida is the sending state.

> "(B) Any inmate whose transfer has been requested, but who does not consent to the transfer, shall be given a hearing before the ICT. The inmate shall be given at least 48 hours written notice of such hearing. "

I wasn't given any notice that I was to be interstate compacted, and I wasn't given a hearing before the Institutional Classification Team (ICT). I also didn't sign a Waiver of Extradition like FAC 33-601.401(3) (F) said I was supposed to sign, nor was I allowed to bring my property with me as mandated by FAC 33-601.401(3)(G).

551) What about your property that you were forced to leave at Hardee CI?

Windy, Pastor Myles, and Pastor Dorothy went to Hardee CI and picked-up my property. Pastors Myles and Dorothy have made several attempts to mail me my law work and Christian books; however, the Tennessee prison has not permitted me to receive all of my property.

552) Did you think about all the things you had lost while you were on the van transferring out of Florida?

I thought about them, but I didn't dwell on them. I try to focus on the good things that come to others because of my losses. A lot of good changes have occurred since everything started several years ago. However, there's a lot more work to do.

553) How soon were you able to contact Windy and the Miami Herald?

When I didn't make any of my normal phone calls on March 17, 2017, Windy began inquiring into my status. Florida prison officials gave her the runaround until March 21, 2017 when she found out I was in Bledsoe County Correctional Complex. She started calling Tennessee prison officials that same day, and she had me out of segregation and my Inmate Telephone PIN number activated by March 22, 2017, and I immediately began talking with her and the Miami Herald. Apparently, the people in Florida who wanted to hinder my ability to respond to the state attorney's memo didn't research how the Tennessee DOC telephone system worked.

As soon as I made contact with Windy and the Miami Herald, they briefed me on the state attorney's memo. I responded to the things they told me while we were on the phone. About a week later, I received a copy of the state attorney's memo. After reading the memo, I talked with the *Miami Herald* and Windy about the things that were false in the memo, mailed the Herald long letters responding to the memo, wrote dozens of blogs, and mailed them to Jeremy Schanche.

Schanche posted them the blog he set up for me. The address is: https://haroldhempsteadcagedcrusader.wordpress.com/2017/10/03 /false-statements-made-in-the-dade-county-florida-state-attorneys-31717-written-decision-to-not-prosecute-darren-raineys-killers.

Chapter 22: Response to Dade County State Attorney's Memo on Darren Rainey Case

The Dade County state attorney's closeout memo on the Darren Rainey case can be found at http://www.miamisao.com/pdfs/DarrenRaineyincustodydeathclos eoutmemo.pdf

It was prepared under the direction of Miami-Dade State Attorney Katherine Fernandez Rundle. Ms. Fernandez Rundle has been harshly criticized for her failure to bring any charges against Dade CI staff, and numerous articles in newspapers and other media have questioned her findings. Below is my response to certain allegations and findings in the closeout memo.

554) Law enforcement had no interest in investigating Darren Rainey's death.

A review of the state attorney's memo shows that the Miami-Dade Police Department did not have any interest in investigating the Rainey case from the beginning. The police and fire department responded to the 911 call did not question any of the inmates who witnessed what happened to Rainey. They did not review any of the footage from the security cameras mounted in the Dade CI TCU. They did not test the water temperature in the shower where Rainey died.

I believe if the police had any interest in investigating the Rainey case, they would've done these things when they responded to the 911 call the night Rainey died or very soon thereafter. They did not do any investigation in the last six months of 2012, all of 2013, and the first about five months of 2014. They only began to investigate after the *Miami Herald* newspaper began publishing articles on May 17, 2014. The Herald articles noted that the Miami-Dade Police Department had not done any investigation at that point.

This delay in beginning an alleged investigation almost 2 years shows the police didn't want to investigate the Rainey case. I use the word *alleged* because the investigation they did was not a good one.

555) There are problems with the inmate witness statements in the closeout memo.

When the Miami-Dade Police Department started their investigation into the Darren Rainey case in 2014, they discovered that 12 of the inmate witnesses were still housed in the Dade CI TCU. Based on letters I sent in 2012 and 2014, statements from former Dade CI TCU staff member George Mallinckrodt, and information in the *Miami Herald* articles, the police knew that Dade CI staff were violent toward the mentally disabled inmates housed in the TCU. Instead of arranging to have the 12 inmate witnesses transferred to a safe location prior to speaking with them, the police department detectives interviewed the inmate witnesses in the Dade CI TCU.

Two of the 12 inmate witnesses refused to talk with the detectives. It's reasonable to say that a review of the statements of the other 10 inmate witnesses will show they were scared to say anything bad to the detectives about the Dade CI security staff because the inmates feared retaliation after the police left Dade CI.

Seven of the inmates interviewed by the detectives were severely mentally disabled. Anybody who knew those inmates would doubt they could give accurate answers.

Seven of the other inmates the detectives interviewed gave statements that showed Officer Clarke was using the *Hot-Water-Shower* to punish mentally disabled inmates and that Darren Rainey died in the *Hot-Water-Shower* that Officer Clarke placed him in.

It is well known that eye-witnesses to a crime may not agree as to the details but are certain of the most important facts. In her closeout memo, state attorney Kathleen Hoague said it was the differences in the inmates' statements which caused her to not believe the inmate witnesses.

If you disregard the minor differences in the inmate statements on non-relevant matters, but, instead focused on the relevant facts, you will see several inmate witnesses agreed on the most important facts. Specifically, their statements show that:

- Several mentally disabled inmates were placed in the *Hot-Water-Shower* as punishment;
- Officer Clarke/security staff placed Darren Rainey in the shower;
- Rainey yelled while in the shower that it was hot, and that he was sorry and wouldn't do it again;
- Rainey died in the shower;
- When he was taken out of the shower, his skin looked burned/damaged.

Considering that the inmate witnesses gave their statements to the police two years after Rainey's death, the minor differences were trivial and of no significance. Accordingly, the statements of the inmate witnesses were credible.

The Dade County State Attorney alleged that I told inmates housed in the TCU that staff killed Rainey. Her memo also alleged that I tried to recruit inmates to speak with the media, and others, about what happened to Rainey. I did have a few short conversations with inmates Daniel Medberry and Gregory Shevlin about Darren Rainey; however, any idea that I was discussing the death with several inmates and trying to recruit them to talk with the media and others is outrageous and makes no sense.

First, I was very sad and struggling emotionally over my failure to do enough to help Rainey and the mentally disabled inmates. I had no energy to recruit others to a cause. I was fighting to make it, one day at a time. Two, since I was an orderly, policy mandated that I always had to be in visual and hearing supervision of staff. Only in very limited circumstances was that policy not complied with, so, if I was talking with other inmates, guards would have known and taken action against me. Three, it's only common sense that the more inmates I told about my desire to bring the staff to justice, the more it would increase my odds of the security staff finding-out I was trying to bring them to justice!

Also, the Miami-Dade Police Department recorded the majority of their interviews with the inmate witnesses. When the close-out memo was released on March 17, 2017, these recordings became public record. They were obtained by someone I know. After he and another person listened to them, they told me that the recordings show that the detectives conducting the interviews were not seeking the truth; rather, they were leading the inmate witnesses. Additionally, I was told that the recordings revealed that the state attorney Kathrine Rundle did not include in her memo statements by inmates that were favorable to the prosecution of Officer Clarke and other correctional staff.

556) Problems with statements made by Dade CI staff about Darren Rainey's death.

The state attorney's memo did not state that all the staff interviewed by the police could have been charged with violating federal and state laws if they admitted anything to the detectives. The memo also presented Officer Clarke and other officers involved as the type of people who would admit to committing murder, aiding and abetting in the commission of murder, or being an accessory after the fact to murder.

My review of the statements in the memo made by Officer Clark and other correctional staff who were working the night Darren Rainey died reveals some interesting facts.

Fact 1: The FDC has a "Forced Hygiene Compliance" procedure that is to be followed by all correctional staff when inmates refuse to maintain proper hygiene/wash-up. First, the staff is supposed to get approval from the duty warden to institute the Forced Hygiene Compliance procedure. If the warden approves a Forced Hygiene Compliance shower, five officers and either a lieutenant, shift supervisor, or duty warden are to go to the place where the inmate who is refusing to main proper hygiene is housed. Prior to going there, the staff review the inmate's medical files to find out if he has any medical problems they need to be aware of before entering his cell. The staff are then to report to the inmate's cell. One officer has a camcorder, and he uses it to record all the actions staff take to get inmate out of his cell. Next, the security staff secure the inmate in handcuffs. The inmate is then taken to a shower where the officers bathe the inmate with a suitable sponge or bathing brush. Once this is done, the inmate is given clean clothes to wear. Finally, a nurse then checks the inmate's vital before he is placed back in a cell.

Neither Officer Clarke nor any of the staff who were working on the night Rainey died ever attempted to comply with this procedure.

Let's discuss some of the more obvious reasons why they didn't comply with this procedure.

The first reason is that Rainey wasn't non-compliant on the night he died. As the state attorney said, Rainey complied with Officer Clarke's command to submit to handcuffing. A mounted security camera shows Rainey did not resist being escorted to the shower. Other than the statements by staff who could have been charged with the murder of a mentally disabled inmate, there wasn't any evidence that Rainey would not have complied and showered if he was placed in a regular shower stall. Officer Clarke and the correctional staff who were working with him knew the duty warden wouldn't institute the Forced Hygiene Compliance procedure with an inmate who appeared to be compliant.

The second reason is that, even if Rainey was non-compliant (which he wasn't), the lieutenant, shift supervisor, and duty warden would not have allowed the shower Rainey died in to be used in a Forced Hygiene Compliance shower on Rainey or any other inmate. An examination of the Environmental Health and Safety Manual shows that the rigged shower equipment used in the *Hot-Water-Shower* stall was illegal and the high temperature of the hot water also violated the policy in the manual. Finally, the shower stall was at the end of a hallway in a blind spot outside of the view of all of the mounted security cameras in the TCU.

The third reason Officer Clarke and the other correctional staff did not attempt to get approval for a Forced Hygiene Shower was that they had no intention of complying with prison procedures or the law in helping Rainey get a shower. Their plan was to treat Darren Rainey however they wished, to punish and torture him.

Neither the Miami-Dade Police Department nor its State Attorney Office made any attempts to obtain copies of the Florida Department of Corrections Forced Hygiene Compliance

Procedure or the Environmental Health and Safety Manual. In my letters, I advised them of the importance of obtaining these items. These manuals contain the information that proves Officer Clarke and the other correctional staff who were working with him did not comply with the law or FDC procedures when placing Darren Rainey in the shower where he died.

Fact 2: Sergeant Fanfan alleged that Rainey was taken to the shower in Wing J-3 because Rainey said he didn't want to come out of his cell or go to the shower and because he and Officer Clarke knew, based on previous experience, that Rainey wouldn't willingly turn on a shower and clean himself. In contrast to this statement, the footage from the mounted security cameras shows Rainey willingly and without struggle leaving his cell and walking to the shower.

If Rainey had a history of being non-compliant and objecting to showering, then he would have done the same thing on the night he died, if he didn't want to shower. Since Rainey willingly and without struggle left his cell and walked to the shower, it is reasonable to assume he also would have showered if he was placed in a regular shower with normal water temperature.

Sergeant Fanfan's allegation that Rainey was taken to the Wing J-3 shower because staff could turn the water in that shower is unreasonable. Out of the 11 operable showers located on the Westside, the shower they put Rainey in was the only shower large enough for him to avoid the water if he did not want to shower. If Sergeant Fanfan and Officer Clarke wanted to get Rainey clean, why did they put him in a shower where he could avoid the water? The obvious answer is, Rainey was put in that shower stall as punishment.

I was housed on the Westside all of the time Rainey was housed there, and he did not have a history of refusing to shower or playing with his feces. The booth officer for each shift on the Westside had to complete a "Housing Unit Log" documenting all the activity on the shift.

Exhibit 1 in the closeout memo is a copy of the Housing Unit Log for the night that Rainey died. The log states that Rainey was taken out of his cell to a shower in Wing J-3. If Rainey ever had smeared feces on himself in the past or was ever placed in a shower other than at regular shower times, it would have been documented in a housing unit log. Neither the police nor the state attorney's office looked at these logs to verify the officers' claim that Rainey had a history of placing feces on himself or refusing to shower. Rather, they would have shown he did not.

Finally, if Rainey ever played with his feces or refused to shower, correctional staff would have had to complete an "Incident Report" documenting his refusal. FDC procedures mandated this. If the police and state attorney's office had asked FDC to give them an incident report, they would have found that none existed, proving the claim of by the officers was false. I believe the police and state attorney didn't want any evidence to prove that Sergeant Fanfan and Officer Clarke's statements were false.

Fact 3: Sergeant Fanfan said he did not hear Rainey scream, cry, complain, or kick the shower door. He also said if this had happened, he and other officers would have heard it. Finally, Sergeant Fanfan falsely alleged there were microphones located outside and inside the inmates' cells, which were monitored at the security control desk in the officers' station.

Would Sergeant Fanfan, or any of the staff who were working on the night Rainey died, admit that they heard him yelling, complaining, and kicking the door, and they did not do anything to help him, that they just allowed him to die? Of course not. If they admitted to such, they would've lost their jobs, and they could've been arrested.

I previously mentioned in 2014, Florida Legal Services and Disability Rights Florida filed a 42 U.S.C. § 1983 class action Civil Rights Complaint lawsuit in the Miami, Florida Federal District Court which was settled in 2015 in favor of the inmates. A review of the settlement which can be located on the "Public Access to Court Electronic Records" internet site, will show that the settlement got audio and better video monitoring abilities installed in the Westside TCU.

Yes, the TCU had audio monitoring when the state attorney issued the closeout memo on March 17, 2017 because the settlement in the lawsuit in 2015 resulted in audio monitoring equipment being installed in the TCU. However, there was no audio monitoring in June 2012, when Daren Rainey died. And there was none in June or July 2014, when Sergeant Fanfan, Officer Clarke and the correctional staff who aided and abetted Officer Clarke were interviewed. The state attorney even said several times in her closeout memo that there were not any audio abilities in the TCU on the night Rainey died, and these facts refute the Dade CI staffs' statements that there were.

Fact 4: Officer Clarke alleged that Rainey was wearing a "green shroud" (Ferguson Garment), which the FDC issues to inmates who have tried to hurt themselves. Additionally, Officer Clarke alleged that Rainey had previously smeared feces on himself, had tried to eat his feces, and had gone on hunger strikes.

If the detectives and state attorney's office had investigated these claims, they would have found evidence that refuted them. An investigation would've revealed Rainey was wearing the Ferguson garment because he previously angered staff, so they refused to give him the regular clothing. That is why there was no paperwork showing that a mental health treatment team approved Rainey wearing the Ferguson garment.

Additionally, if Rainey made any statements saying he was going to hurt himself or made any attempts to hurt himself, he would have been housed in a Self-Harm Observation Status cell in Wing J-2. The mere fact that Rainey was housed in Wing J-1 shows he never made any threats or attempts to hurt himself in the weeks prior to his death.

Additionally, if Rainey ever threatened to hurt himself, smeared feces on himself, tried to eat his feces, or went on a hunger strike, a number of documents required by the DOC (incident reports, housing logs, segregation log) would have been generated. The police and state attorney did not try to obtain these documents. If they had, they would have shown that these allegations by Officer Clarke were false.

Fact 5: There's no evidence to support Officer Clarke's allegation that before placing Rainey in the shower, he checked to make sure the water was not too hot or cold

Fact 6: In reference to Rainey allegedly having feces on his body, the footage from the mounted security cameras do not show any feces on Rainey's body.

Fact 7: Officer Hood's statement in the closeout memo does not mention that he did a security check. Footnote 13 and Exhibit 1 in the state attorney's memo showed that at either 8:30 or 8:25, respectively, Offer Hood did a security check. Officer Hood also did not admit he was the officer who the mounted security cameras showed was in Wing J-3 with Sergeant Fanfan at 8:13.17pm.

Some of the security staff made statements similar to those above, and I have not discussed them separately. My discussion only focus on the first person to make the statement in the closeout memo.

557) The police and state attorney's office failed to interview key witnesses.

Gregory Shevlin and the inmate who went by the nickname, "Redneck" should have been interviewed because they were working as orderlies on the night Rainey died. When Rainey defecated on the floor in his cell, Shevlin refused to clean up the feces. Sergeant Fanfan fired Shevlin from working as an orderly, locked him in his cell, and submitted a disciplinary report on him refusing the order to clean up the feces in Rainey's cell. Sergeant Fanfan also locked Redneck in his cell after Shevlin refused to clean up the feces. Sergeant Fanfan let two other inmates out of their cells to clean up the feces and to complete the other work that was required of the orderlies. The video footage from the mounted security cameras for Wing J-3 on the night Rainey died show two inmate orderlies outside of their cells in Wing J-3 with two officers.

Security staff said there was feces in Rainey's cell and on his body. These four inmate orderlies would have provided testimony to refute the allegation there was feces on Rainey's body and would have testified that it was only on the floor in the middle of his cell.

The inmates who slept in the cells in Wing J-1 near Rainey's cell were not interviewed. These inmates could have testified about the threats security staff made to Rainey prior to removing him from his cell.

The inmates who had seen people other than Rainey placed in the *Hot-Water-Shower* for punishment could have also been interviewed. Their testimony would have shown that Officer Clarke made it his practice to punish mentally disabled inmates by using the *Hot-Water-Shower* as a torturing device.

There were other staff who were not interviewed including:

- The security staff who worked on the Westside TCU on the night Rainey died, and the medical staff who were working in the medical department Rainey was taken after he died.
- Security and medical staff who were working on the Westside TCU on other nights that Officer Clarke punished other mentally disabled inmates by using the *Hot-Water-Shower* as a torturing device to punish mentally disabled inmates.

558) Staff who worked with Officer Clarke in 2013 and 2014 were not interviewed.

The police department and the state attorney's office did not interview security staff who worked with Clarke after Rainey was killed. Officer Clarke spoke extensively with Officers Corbet, Drinkwater, Jolly, Cennedy, McBean and other security staff in 2013 and 2014 about the Rainey case and the *Hot-Water-Shower* treatment of mentally disabled inmates. It is my position that the police and state attorney's office knew these witnesses should have been interviewed and did not do so because they were not serious about investigating the Rainey case and the abuse of other mentally disabled inmates at Dade CI.

559) The shower Rainey died in was unlawfully constructed.

The ***Environmental Health and Safety Manual*** that governed the Florida Department of Corrections in 2012 clearly shows that the shower Rainey died in was not constructed according to regulations. It was unlawful because the water temperature exceeded 120 degrees Fahrenheit. The water temperature in the shower Rainey died in exceeded 160 degrees Fahrenheit.

Starting on page six of her memo, the Dade CI state Attorney, Kathrine Rundle stated:

> "Unlike other showers located in the Dade CI facility, this shower's on/off hand fixture located

inside the shower room was inoperable. However, a floor sink is located in the adjacent janitor's closet. It has normal hot and cold water taps that control the flow and temperature of the water coming out of the faucet. A hose is attached to that faucet, and the hose was inserted into a hole drilled through the shared wall. Below is a photograph of the janitor's closet depicting the faucet-hose-PVC pipe connection that enters through the wall of the janitor's closet.

"The water supply was set up in that manner so that even if a corrections officer had an inmate who was refusing to shower, the corrections officer did not have to depend on the recalcitrant inmate to turn on the water. The problem with this arrangement is that due to the size, layout, and dimensions of this particular shower room, if an inmate did not want to take a shower, after the water was turned on, all he had to do was move to one of the back corners or front corners of the shower room and he would be completely outside the direct flow of water coming into the room from the water hose."

This is incorrect for several reasons. First, the on/off hand fixture located inside the shower Rainey died in was operable. Second, the rigged shower equipment that was used water from the sink in the closet to the shower violated the 2012 FDC *Environmental Health and Safety Manual*. Third, the shower Rainey died in was the only rigged shower in TCU, the only shower in a blind spot outside of the view of the mounted security cameras, and the only shower that reached temperatures in excess of 120 degrees Fahrenheit.

It's outrageous that the state attorney attempted in her closeout memo to convince people the rigged equipment was legal. Also, security staff who truly wanted to make sure an inmate cleaned himself would not put the inmate in the only shower stall that was large enough stand outside of the stream of running water. It would not serve any legitimate purpose, and it was in a blind spot outside of the view of all of the mounted security cameras.

560) Officer Clarke put Darren Rainey in the *Hot-Water-Shower* to punish him.

If Officer Clarke wanted Rainey to shower, he would have placed Rainey in a regular shower stall. A regular shower stall would have had water that was tolerable, and, in any of the regular showers, Rainey would not have been able to avoid the water that came out of the showerhead. Officer Clarke placed Rainey in the only shower he could avoid the water in because he wanted to use the extreme heat and steam from the hot water in that shower stall as a torturing device.

561) The footage the state attorney released of the night Darren Rainey died is from another location and is doctored.

The state attorney, in her memo, said the footage from the mounted security cameras on the night Rainey died shows the times I provided concerning when specific things happened were inaccurate. The state attorney didn't disclose, that the time stamps on the recordings that her office released were not from the mounted security cameras that recorded the events that happened with Darren Rainey on the night he died. Rainey was housed in the Westside TCU, the cell he lived in was located in Wing J-1, and he died in Wing J-3. The time stamp location on both of the videos the state attorney released show an "E." Additionally, the time stamps located on the three-minute video states "J-4", and the time stamp located on the 117-minute video states "J-5".

This shows us that the time stamps on both videos came from mounted security cameras on the Eastside in wings J-4 and J-5. The Eastside TCU is about a city block from the Westside TCU where Rainey died. Furthermore, none of the events that happened with Rainey on the night he died happened in Wings J-4 or J-5. It's outrageous that the state attorney tried to manipulate people into believing the time stamps on the videos her office released were the time stamps from the mounted security cameras that monitored everything that happened to Rainey on the night he died when the time stamps on the videos prove that they weren't. The mounted security cameras on the Westside TCU in Wings J-1 and J-3 monitored everything that happened with Rainey on the night he died. If the state attorney had the real-time stamps on the videos that were from the mounted security cameras that monitored everything that happened to Rainey, they would've supported my timeline of events on the night Rainey died.

Additionally, it's my position that there's evidence that shows the videos that the state attorney released were altered. For instance, Exhibit A of the state attorney's closeout memo is the **Housing Unit Log** from the night Rainey died. Officer Edwina Williams, who was working in the officers' station the night Rainey died made all the entries on the log. By policy, the entries in the log were supposed to be made in real time. This log shows that Rainey was taken out of his cell at 7:55 pm and placed in the shower at 8:00 pm. The two videos that the state attorney released show Rainey being removed from his cell at 7:35:08 pm and placed in the *Hot-Water-Shower* at 7:39 pm. By comparing the Housing Unit Log with the false times on the videos, the Housing Unit Log shows Rainey was removed from his cell 20 minutes later, and placed in the *Hot-Water-Shower* 21 minutes later than what the false times show on the two videos the state attorney released.

The housing log lists Officer Hood as conducting a security check of the Westside TCU at 8:25 pm. The footage from the mounted security cameras don't show any officer activity between 8:17:36 pm and 8:56 pm. The fact that Officer Edwina Williams documented in the "Housing Unit Log" that Officer Hood conducted a security check at 8:25 pm and the footage from the mounted security cameras does not show Officer Hood doing that security check, supports that the security check that Officer Hood conducted at 8:25 pm was recorded over. Why would anybody record over the security check Officer Hood conducted? Because the only way time could be added to the video was to slice the footage and add additional fake footage to the real footage. It's my position that the slicing and additional footage was added to the real footage between the time period of 8:17:36 pm and 8:56 pm on the 117 minute video that the state attorney released with her memo, and that is why Officer Hood's 8:25 pm security check isn't revealed on the video footage.

Finally, State Attorney Rundle failed to disclose in her memo that the media have reported since 2014 that FDC officials said the mounted security camera(s) in the Westside TCU malfunctioned on the night Rainey died, and this caused the footage from the cameras to be ruined.

I believe that the state attorney knew the video footage from the mounted security cameras had been altered. The FDC Inspector General's Office had the original video for two years following Rainey's death. FDC corrections staff have a history of altering video footage, and the FDC officials had the most to lose if the video footage remained in its original condition

The white linen sheet I hung in my cell that night did not block my view. The state attorney's allegation that I could not see what I saw the night Rainey died because of a white linen sheet I hung over my cell door at different times is wrong. It is like saying people in a car cannot see through tinted windows because people on the outside cannot see in.

During the day, one can see through a thin sheet covering from inside a house because of the differential in the intensity of the light. The white linen sheets we had were old and had been frequently washed. They were very thin. Try hanging an old thin sheet over one of the windows of your house during the day. Then walk up close to the window. You will notice that when you are in your house, you can see outside, whereas, if you are outside, you cannot see in. How far one can see and how clearly depends on the conditions inside and outside. This will always work as long as it's darker in your house than it is outside the house.

This same principle applies to an inmate in a cell and persons outside the cell as long as it is darker in the cell.

When my deposition was taken for the federal lawsuit that Darren Rainey's family filed concerning Rainey's death, I was shown photographs taken from the video footage of the night Rainey died. In those photographs, I was able to see the outline of my body behind the white linen sheet that covered my cell door window for a short time on that night. The photographs proved that during the time I had the sheet in my cell door window, I was standing very close to it watching what was transpiring outside of my cell.

Additionally, it should be noted that everything I said in my statement was corroborated by other witnesses and evidence.

562) Investigations by news organizations cast support that the suspects in the Darren Rainey case should have been prosecuted.

Several news organizations published articles concerning Miami-Dade state attorney Katherine Fernandez Rundle's failure to prosecute any of the suspects in the Darren Rainey case. I summarize some of these below. I also recommend reading: Articles by Julie K. Brown which have appeared in the *Miami Herald*, such as, *Packed Crowd Slams Fernandez Rundle for Handling of Rainey Case,* May 30, 2017; *Miami-Dade County Fernandez Rundle may face rebuke over decision not to file charges in Rainey case,* May 30, 2017. *Fact checking Fernandez Rundle*, June 12, 2017.

From the *Miami New Times* I also recommend an April 26, 2017 article by reporter Jerry Iannelli, *Miami-Dade Democrats Debate Asking State Attorney to Resign Following Darren Rainey Verdict.*

563) Dade County Medical Examiner's autopsy findings were inconsistent with the facts.

Darren Rainey's autopsy was conducted by Dr. Emma Lew of the Dade County, Florida Medical Examiner's Office. The State Attorney's closeout memo states "Dr. Lew found that the following factors contributed to the cause of death of inmate Rainey: Schizophrenia, undiagnosed Atherosclerotic Heart Disease, and confinement inside the shower room with heat and humidity."

Even though Dr. Lew concluded that the heat and humidity contributed to Rainey's death, she contradicted herself in other parts of her report by saying there was no evidence to show the water in shower was hot, that the skin slippage on Rainey's body was not caused by hot water, and that Rainey did not have any burns on his body. This contradicts what Dade CI staff and inmates said about the hot water and steam in the shower, the burns on his body, and the condition of his skin.

An April 18, 2017 *Miami Herald* newspaper article by Julie Brown, entitled, *Review of key Rainey evidence blocked* had this to say about the skin slippage, "Dr. Michael Baden, a forensic pathologist who was on New York State's Prison Medical Review Board for 40 years, said skin slippage is 'hot water trauma' that can only be caused by prolonged exposure to elevated water temperature."

Citing another forensic pathologist, Dr. John Marraccini, the article says, "Dr. Marraccini reviewed the written autopsy report at the request of the Herald and had concerns."

"Marraccini reviewed the police photographs taken of the shower the night Rainey died. One of them shows what he said appears to be pieces of skin rolled up on the floor of the shower. He questioned how there would be skin in the shower if, as Lew concluded, the skin peeled off after Rainey was pulled out of the stall and carried down to the ground floor of the prison wing, where the guards began resuscitation efforts."

According to this article, Dr. Michael Baden also said, "From all I've seen and all I've read, this was due to scalding hot water. You don't get skin slippage in a few hours."

The next article, *Graphic photos stir doubts about prison death,* was published May 7, 2017. This article states, "The photographs of Darren Rainey's body are difficult to look at. Skin was curling from nearly every part of his body, from the top of his nose to his ankles. Large swaths of exposed body tissue, some of it blood red, and other portions straw yellow. Skin blistering on portions of his face, his ears, and his neck. Deep red tissue exposed on his chest, his back, a thigh, and an arm. Yellow tissue exposed on his buttocks and left leg."

"About the only portion of his body not affected are his feet."

"Paramedic Alexander Lopez saw the injuries firsthand that evening after Rainey collapsed and died in a shower in the mental health unit at Dade Correctional Institution on June 23, 2012."

'"[Patient] was found with second- and third-degree burns on 30 percent of his body,' Lopez wrote, adding that prison staff told him that 'inmate was found on shower floor with hot water running over his body".'

"The autopsy report, which inexplicably took three years to be completed and another year to be released, was puzzling to Rainey's relatives, who said they were pressured by prison officials to immediately have him cremated."

Citing Doctors Michael Baden and John Marraccini, the article states, "The Herald examination of Fernandez Rundle's 101-page report, which summarized a two-year investigation, identified numerous contradictions and omissions regarding both the autopsy findings and other evidence and statements used as the basis to clear the corrections officers."

"… Marraccini and Baden both told the Herald the photos indicate burns over a significant portion of Rainey's body."

In reference Doctor Lew only taking one skin tissue sample from Rainey's dead body, this article states: "Marraccini, former medical examiner in Palm Beach County, Florida faulted the Miami-Dade Medical Examiner for not taking additional skin tissue samples, since it is important to look at skin tissue from the area that suffered the most damage…Baden, who was on New York State prison medical review board for 40 years, said skin slippage is 'hot water trauma' that can only be caused by prolonged exposure to elevated water temperature…I think he suffered thermal burns on his skin. They are not postmortem decomposition. These were heat effects. You don't decompose in a facility right away. The decomposition takes time.' Baden said."

"Marraccini said while it could be true that some of the sloughing happened after Rainey's death, the deep red tissue signifies thermal injuries."

"Explained Baden: 'The reddish area happens while the blood is coursing and the heart is beating. Once the heart stops, that doesn't make the heat effect go away. So there was skin damage while he was alive and further skin damage after he was dead.'"

"Marraccini also noted that one of the photographs appear to show bruising on Rainey's right hand consistent with him banging on the door as some inmates have claimed in their interviews with detectives and the Herald…"

Chapter 22: Response to Dade County State Attorney's Memo on Darren Rainey Case

"The Rainey family, which has brought a civil suit against the Florida Department of Corrections, believes that the police and medical examiner conspired with prison officials to cover up what happened."

"The state attorney also failed to mention that Brittany McLaurin, an investigator with the medical examiner's office, wrote in a report the day after Rainey's death: 'Visible trauma was noticed throughout the decedent's body.'"

"Why in the official report does Dr. Lew discuss the temperature as being 120 degrees?' Marraccini said, 'It doesn't make any sense when you had a health and safety inspector say it was 160 degrees and he lost so much skin. That skin didn't come off from black magic.'"

As a witness, I know beyond all doubt that Officer Thompson shut the hot water off when he went to the shower and found Rainey dead on the shower floor. According to the state attorney's timeline, Exhibit 7 of their memo, that happened at 9:13:05.

According to the first two nurses (Patino and Robinson), who responded to the shower stall, the shower stall was still steamy when they responded to it at 9:29:11 pm. The fact that the shower was still steamy more than 15 minutes after the hot water had been shut off, with the shower door open for approximately three of those minutes, and with the TCU being air conditioned, shows how hot the water was in the shower Rainey died in. Additionally, Nurse Patino said Rainey's "body felt hot" when he was taken out of the shower, which was more than 16 minutes after the shower was shut off.

Nurse Peters took Rainey's body temperature approximately 25 minutes after the shower water was shut off and approximately 10 minutes after his body was taken out of the shower. She said his body temperature was 102° Fahrenheit.

The State Attorney's closeout memo, says, "Nurse Wilson observed that Rainey's skin appeared red and wrinkled and that she told the 911 operator that his body appeared to be 'burned'".

Finally, Lieutenant Alexander Lopez of the Miami-Dade fire and rescue responded to Dade CI on the night Rainey died. Lieutenant Lopez said there appeared to be burns and/or skin slippage on certain parts of Rainey's body. The lieutenant also said, "He was told that Rainey was found unresponsive in a shower, lying on the floor with hot water running over his body". Lieutenant Lopez only spoke with prison staff. This is strong evidence that Dade CI staff knew the hot water was what caused Rainey's death. That is why they told Lieutenant Lopez that "Rainey was found unresponsive in a shower, lying on the floor with hot water running over his body".

564) The *Huffington Post* published a highly critical article on March 28, 2017.

The *Huffington Post* article, *Officials Ruled Inmates 'Boiling' Death An Accident. But Documents Show They Omitted Key Details* was written by reporter Matt Ferner.

The article reports on the results of Captain Dixon's, who was the Environmental Health and Safety Officer at Dade CI, test of the water temperature in the shower Rainey died in. It states: "Dixon told investigators about her first attempt to test the water in the shower room. After the prison officer who accompanied her turned on the hot water from inside the janitorial closet, the water hit the wall of the shower and splashed 'on her hand, and was hurting her because it was too hot', according to an interview report reviewed by *Huffington Post*. Steam 'appeared in the shower within a few minutes of turning on the hot water', Dixon said, according to the report of her interview with Miami-Dade Police Det. Wilbert Sanchez, the lead investigator."

This article also states: "An emergency room record from the Florida Department of Corrections dated the night of Rainey's death also notes substantial burns on Rainey's body. Britney Wilson, who worked at Dade Correctional Institution as a licensed practical nurse, writes in her report, which indicates she examined Rainey's body 10 minutes after it was discovered, that he was found with '1st degree burns to 90% of his body' and that his skin was 'hot/warm to the touch.'"

"She also notes that she took his tympanic body temperature (via his ear), and it was 104.9 degrees (a body temperature above 103 is considered dangerous, according to the Mayo Clinic). These details are largely omitted from the prosecutor's memo, which indicates only that Wilson observed that Rainey's skin 'appeared red and wrinkled', that she told a 911 operator that 'Rainey's body appeared to be burned', and that she 'noticed some skin slippage.' The most notable inconsistency is that the memo says Wilson tried 'unsuccessfully' to take Rainey's temperature."

In reference the pictures of Rainey's body taken about 12 hours after he was discovered dead, this Huffington Post article states the following: "One image shows a rectal thermometer reading of about 94 degrees- the temperature of his body believed to have been taken the morning after his death."

"The photos and the temperature reading were described to Dr. Michael Baden, a nationally recognized forensic pathologist known for his work on many high profile deaths, including the private autopsy conducted on Michael Brown, the unarmed black teenager killed by a police officer in Ferguson, Missouri, and for his work on HBO's 'Autopsy' series".

"Baden explained that the 94-degree temperature may be unusual. 'This temperature would indicate, if the photos were taken about 10 or 12 hours after he died, that his body temperature was much higher than normal when he died', Baden said."

"He explained that when a person dies, body temperature drops about 1.5 degrees every hour, on average, depending on the temperature of the environment the body is kept in. If a person dies in a 70-degree room, 10 hours later, pathologists would expect the body temperature to have dropped about 15 degrees. And that would speed up if the body was placed in a cold environment or slow down in a warm one. Although it's not clear if Rainey's body was put into refrigeration in the medical examiner's office before these photos were taken, that would be a standard procedure, Baden said. That means that if Rainey's body temperature was still 94 degrees the morning after he died, his body temperature may have been as high as 109 degrees when he died."

As it concerns the Dade County, Florida Medical Examiner's findings concerning the cause of Rainey's death, this article states:

Dr. Baden said the autopsy report "raises problems".

"'Number one, schizophrenia is a disease; it isn't a cause of death. Schizophrenia is not a cause of sudden death.' Baden said. Secondly, Baden explained, according to the autopsy report, Rainey's heart disease is 'minimal' and his 'heart is not remarkable for a 50-year-old person'. Lastly, Baden said, the indication that confinement in the shower also contributed to his death does not make sense."

"'That wouldn't cause death itself,' Baden said. 'People don't die in confined spaces unless there's something else happening. The only way you die in a confined space is if you use up all the oxygen.'"

"Baden also questions the notion that the death was accidental."

"'What is being described is a natural death', Baden said. 'Even if it were schizophrenia and it was heart disease, why then is it an accident? Because of the confined space? No. The cause of death as indicated does not appear to me to be consistent with the autopsy findings.'"

Milton Grimes, the attorney for the Rainey family, made the following comment in this Huffington Post article on the state attorney 's memo: "'I can say that a lot of statements in the report are inaccurate based on the discovery we have received. I am confused and troubled by what I've seen', Grimes said and added that there are 'important pertinent and relevant facts that were left out of the prosecutor's memo.'"

565) *Miami New Times* declared State Attorney Fernandez Rundle a disgrace.

On March 20, 2017, the *Miami New Times* published an article entitled *Katherine Fernandez Rundle, Miami's Top Prosecutor, Is a Disgrace*. The article was written by Jerry Iannelli. This *Miami New Times* article not only addresses the Rainey case, but several other matters concerning State Attorney Rundle.

The article notes that between 1993 and March 20, 2017 state attorney Rundle "Has not once charged a police officer for an on-duty killing, or any prison guards involved in any prison guard cases."

Chapter 22: Response to Dade County State Attorney's Memo on Darren Rainey Case

It goes on to state the following concerning State Attorney Rundle's history of being a police brutality enabler and apologist:

"Here is a brief, and by no means comprehensive, list of recent cases in which Rundle has let police officers off easy.

"In 2014, City of Miami Police Officer Reynaldo Goyos shot and killed an unarmed man at a traffic stop. Miami PD's then Chief called the shooting 'unjustified', and a federal review of the department, based in part on Goyos' case, noted a 'pattern of excessive force' at the department.

"In 2015, a Miami cop shot a homeless man in front of 50 children. The man was later identified as 'non-violent'.

"Miami Police Union President Javier Ortiz doxxed and harassed a woman because she videotaped and stopped a Miami-Dade cop who was speeding in his patrol car.

"Officer John Hinson was repeatedly accused of beating up handcuffed subjects, including one incident that was caught on video.

"South Miami Cop Aryo Rezale shot an unarmed former college football player, Michael Gavins, in the back. Gavins said he was simply standing next to the hood of a police cruiser.

"Miami Beach cops shot a man to death on Alton Road during Art Basel after they appeared to have confused the sound of taser fire with gunfire.

"Miami Beach Det. Philippe Archer beat up a woman on camera and also a good Samaritan who tried to stop the beating.

"Miami Beach Police tasered 18-year-old skater Israel 'Reefa' Hernandez to death because he had tagged a building with graffiti.

431

Department of Corruption

In 2015, officers from Miami Beach, Miami Dade County, and Hialeah fired 100 bullets into a moving car, killing an innocent man.

And, most astounding, Rundle refused to charge the cops involved in the so-called Redland shootings, in which a group of Miami-Dade cops carried out a military-inspired ambush-style attack on an alleged armed mob, shot men on video, made conflicting statements to Rundle's office, and possibly tampered with evidence. The cops in that case were sued for what lawyers said was a pattern of luring suspects to staged crimes and deliberately executing them.

566) The People's Progressive Caucus of Miami-Dade and the Brevard County, Florida Democratic Executive Committee issued formal criticisms of Fernandez Rundle's closeout memo.

These documents are quoted below:

"People's Progressive Caucus Condemns State Attorney Katherine Fernandez Rundle over the killing of Darren Rainey.

"The Miami-Dade Democratic Progressive Caucus vehemently condemns the failure of Miami-Dade County state attorney Katherine Fernandez Rundle to press charges for the brutal murder of Darren Rainey.

"Refusing to charge the four prison guards who are responsible for throwing a black, schizophrenic inmate into a scalding hot shower for two hours, resulting in his death, is unacceptable and cannot be overlooked.

'Rundle has declined to bring charges due to an autopsy report that has been heavily criticized by the American Civil Liberties Union, claiming that Rainey suffered from no burns on his body.

"However, the details in this case are gruesome and have shocked our humanity, as testimony from inmates, nurses and medics claim that Rainey suffered burns across his body and his skin was peeling off when found dead in that shower.

There is a pattern of behavior by Katherine "Fernandez Rundle. Whether it was the killing of teenager Israel Hernandez via a taser for tagging a building with graffiti; the shooting of unarmed autistic caregiver Charles Kinsey; or the Redlands shootings, in which Miami-Dade Police Officers ambushed an allegedly armed mob and shot them; the state attorney's office seems to always find excuses to overlook and excuse instances of police brutality.

"Katherine Fernandez Rundle has largely remained unscathed by her awful record. She has been in office since 1993 and usually runs unopposed for reelection. As members of the Miami-Dade Democratic Party, and by extension the Florida Democratic Party, the Progressive Caucus is disturbed to have in our ranks a police brutality enabler and apologist. If the Democratic Party seeks to truly be an inclusive and transformational force in our community, they will hold state attorney Rundle accountable for her record of failure in standing up "for Miami-Dade residents who are victims of State-Induced violence.

"Executive Board of the People's Progressives Caucus of Miami-Dade.

The resolution from the Brevard County, Florida Democratic Executive Committee states:

"WHEREAS the Brevard DEC strongly condemns the state attorney Office's decision not to bring charges against the officers that locked Mr. Rainey in a hot shower for two hours resulting in his death, and the jail's supervisors who failed to report the crime.

"WHEREAS this incident follows a pattern over Rundle's 24-year tenure as Miami-Dade's elected state attorney, in which she has repeatedly refused to hold law enforcement officials accountable for on-duty killings.

"WHEREAS in 2012, Darren Rainey, an African American prisoner with a long history of serious mental illness, was housed in the inpatient unit at Dade Correctional Institution in order to be treated for his mental illness. On the evening of June 23, 2012, correctional officers in the inpatient unit removed Mr. Rainey from his cell, placed him in physical restraints, and escorted him to a locked shower stall.

WHEREAS when the officers finally returned to check on Mr. Rainey, he was found lying in the shower submerged in water, with his skin peeling from his person and per the Miami-Dade Medical Examiner's preliminary report 'visible trauma... throughout [his] body.' He was declared dead by first responders soon after. The hot water temperature of the shower registered 160 degrees Fahrenheit two days after Mr. Rainey's death.

WHEREAS Miami-Dade State Attorney Katherine Fernandez Rundle nonetheless found that 'the evidence does not show that Rainey's well-being was grossly disregarded by the correctional staff.'

WHEREAS Mr. Rainey's death shocked the conscience of Miami-Dade County and the entire country. Katherine Fernandez Rundle's inaction does not represent the values of the Democratic Party. The Democratic Party supports the dignity of all people, including prisoners in the state's care. Her failure to hold anyone accountable for Mr. Rainey's death places the most vulnerable prisoners at risk for more abuse.

THEREFORE BE IT RESOLVED:

The Brevard Democratic Executive Committee (DEC) strongly condemns the state attorney 's Office stalled and incomplete investigation of Darren Rainey's death, and therefore urges Miami-Dade State Attorney Katherine

Fernandez Rundle to resign from office if she cannot pursue justice for all victims of crime, including the most vulnerable.

As Dr. Martin Luther King, Jr. said 'Injustice anywhere is a threat to justice everywhere'. In alignment with the core values of the Democratic Party, we stand with fellow Democrats in Miami-Dade who are urging Rundle's resignation.

APPROVED THIS 17TH DAY OF MAY BY VOTE OF THE BREVARD COUNTY DEMOCRATIC EXECUTIVE COMMITTEE.

567) Settlement of a class action suit and four million dollar settlement for Rainey's death proves his death was unlawful.

The settlement in the class action civil right lawsuit filed in 2014 by Florida Legal Services and Disability Rights Florida that concerned the Dade CI TCU prove the *Hot-Water-Shower* was used to torture mentally disabled inmates (Case number: # 1:14-CV-23323 and 1:15-CV-23367). The complaints in these cases indicate that the primary form of unconstitutional treatment mentioned is the *Hot-Water-Shower* treatment as punishment of mentally disabled inmates. It's my position that all the parties in that lawsuit only agreed to that settlement because they agreed that the *Hot-Water-Shower* treatment of mentally disabled inmates was being committed in the Dade CI TCU.

Additionally, the four million five hundred thousand dollar settlement in the lawsuit filed by Rainey's family proves his death was unlawful. Why else would the defendants in the lawsuit filed by Rainey's family agree to a four million five hundred thousand dollar settlement if Rainey's death was not unlawful?

568) Florida Senator Juan Cuba strongly disagreed with the findings.

Senator Rundle made several public statements strongly disagreeing with State Attorney Fernandez Rundle and her involvement with the Darren Rainey case. He disagreed with her decision not to prosecute and indicated he wanted justice for

Darren Rainey. His statements can be found in 2017 newspaper articles and on his podcast.

569) Additional points concerning information in Kathrine Fernandez Rundle's closeout memo.

Prior to Rainey dying, the night was just like any of the other nights when mentally disabled inmates were placed in the *Hot-Water-Shower* as punishment. When the inmates in Wing J-3 found out that Rainey was dead is when the night changed.

We know putting Rainey in the *Hot-Water-Shower* was a punishment because, out of the 11 operable showers in the TCU, Darren Rainey was placed in the only shower that staff could control the water temperature in, the only shower that reached temperatures in excess of 160° Fahrenheit, and the only operable shower in a blind spot that was outside of the view of all the mounted security cameras in the TCU.

The regular showerhead in the shower stall Darren Rainey died in was not operable despite what the State Attorney's memo stated. Correctional staff cannot control the temperature of the water that comes from the ordinary showerhead.

I was told the bar of soap I gave Officer Clarke was never found in the shower. More than likely Officer Clarke did not give Rainey the bar of soap. Why? Because Officer Clarke didn't place Rainey in that shower stall for Rainey to shower.

The State Attorney claimed it was my position that Officer Roland Clarke purposely scalded Darren Rainey with excessively hot water. The State Attorney knew that I never said any such thing. From the beginning, I said that Sergeant Clarke put Rainey and other inmates in that shower to subject them to the punishment of the heat and steam from the hot water—an unlawful, reckless, and sadistic act that ended in Darren Rainey's death.

570) Correctional staff planned a cover-up from the very beginning.

Officer Thompson, who initially found Darren Rainey dead on the shower stall floor went back to the officers' station instead of reporting his death. I think he did this so he could tell his co-workers that Rainey was dead before calling it in officially. This gave the security staff time to think of a way to cover up his death.

Darren Rainey was left dead on the shower stall floor for eight to 13 minutes before the next security check was completed by Officer Clarke. I explained this to the State Attorney prior to her March 17, 2017 release of the closeout memo.

Officers Clarke and Thompson asked me to lie about Darren Rainey's death. As I detailed in the chapter on Darren Rainey, Officers Thompson and Clarke both told me to lie and say that Officer Clarke was the first officer to find Rainey dead on the shower stall floor. They wanted me to say this to aid them in covering-up that Officer Thompson left Rainey dead on the shower stall floor for about eight minutes while he went to the officers' station and, more than likely, conspired with his co-workers on how to cover-up Rainey's death.

Chapter 23: Miscellaneous Questions Tennessee DOC (March 17, 2017-March 2018)

571) Were you deposed in connection with the Rainey case?

Yes. Milton Grimes, the attorney representing Darren Rainey's family in their lawsuit over Darren Rainey's death, came to Tennessee to take my deposition for the lawsuit. The attorneys representing Roland Clarke and Cornelius Thompson, the old Dade CI Warden Jerry Cummings, the Florida Department of Corrections, and Corizon Health Services were also present for the deposition.

During the more than approximately seven-hour-long deposition, I was asked questions by all five attorneys about the Darren Rainey case.

572) What was the result of the lawsuit brought by Darren Rainey's family?

The defendants agreed to a settlement of $4.5 million and the Rainey family accepted. On January 26, 2018, the *Miami Herald* newspaper published an article written by Julie K. Brown on the settlement. The name of the article is *Florida OK's $4.5 million payout for brutal prison shower death of Darren Rainey*.

Department of Corruption

573) Did you submit Sworn Affidavit in June 2017 to the US Department of Justice?

Yes. I sent the affidavit to the Department of Justice and a dozen reporters, civil rights attorneys, and other people about the unconstitutional mental health care inmates receive in the Florida Department of Corrections. It reads as follows,

"Sworn Affidavit Requesting a Civil Rights of Institutionalized Persons Act Investigation.
To: United States Department of Justice. Civil Rights Section 950 Pennsylvania Avenue Northwest, Washington, DC. 20530

"Affiant was incarcerated in the Florida Department of Corrections (FDC) from June 1, 2000 till March 17, 2017. On March 17, 2017, Affiant was Interstate Compacted from FDC to the Tennessee Department of Corrections.

"FDC has four reception centers that receive all of the inmates entering FDC from county jails in Florida. Staff at reception centers evaluate inmates for mental health, medical, and dental issues. They also have various other things they do relating to the receiving and classification of inmates into FDC.

"Every inmate who enters FDC is assigned a mental health grade. There are five mental health grades in FDC. Inmates who are classified as Psych. 1 or Psych. 2 don't require any mental health medicine or counseling. However, Psych. 2 inmates are seen every 60 days by a counselor to make sure they aren't having any mental health problems. When an inmate receives a Psych-3 level that means mental health staff deems that the inmate needs mental counseling every 28 days and mental health medicine. Psych. 3 inmates can only be housed at Psych. 3 institutions. They cannot be housed at Psych. 1/Psych. 2 institutions. Psych. 4 inmates must be housed in a Transitional Care Unit (TCU). Inmates on TCU status are said to have mental health problems that prohibit them from living in any status other than inpatient mental health treatment. Psych. 5 inmates must be housed in a Crisis Stabilization Unit (CSU). Inmates on CSU status are said to be suicidal and/or homicidal. If an inmate in FDC is involuntarily committed by court order (Baker Act), he is placed in Corrections Mental Health Infirmary (CMHI) Unit status at Lake Correctional Institution.

"Mental health staff employed at reception centers evaluate all inmates entering FDC for mental health problems. However, reception centers have insufficient mental health staff to evaluate all the inmates entering FDC effectively. As a result of the insufficient staffing, inmates with mental health issues are processed into FDC with lesser mental health grades than what they should receive. This causes inmates who need a higher level of mental health observation and care to be placed in general population where they don't receive such, and where they're denied their Eighth Amendment Right to Adequate Mental Health Attention.

"When FDC inmates with serious mental health issues who weren't effectively evaluated at reception centers, transfer from reception centers to close custody institutions, staff at those institutions think said inmates are trying to manipulate staff into believing they have mental health issues when they don't.

"The reason for this is because it's very common for stable inmates to try and manipulate FDC mental health staff into believing they have mental health problems so they can obtain transfers and/or mental health medicines that cause them to get high. With so many inmates trying to manipulate FDC mental health staff into believing they have mental health problems, mental health staff oftentimes incorrectly treat inmates with serious mental health problems like they don't have them.

"Between the years of 2011 and March 17, 2017, Affiant knew dozens of inmates with serious mental health problems housed in general population status at several institutions who should have been receiving a higher level of mental health observation and care than what they were receiving.

"Between the years of 2011 and March 17, 2017, Affiant witnessed mentally disabled inmates being raped, and manipulated, and forced into engaging in sexual acts with other inmates. Affiant witnessed mentally disabled inmates get physically battered by staff and stable inmates because their mental health disabilities caused them to do things that caused staff and inmates to get mad. Affiant witnessed stable inmates manipulating mentally disabled inmates into giving the stable inmates food off their trays from the chow hall, and canteen that the mentally disabled inmates purchased with money given to them by their family and friends. Affiant witnessed FDC staff issue mentally disabled inmates disciplinary reports for disciplinary infractions that the mentally disabled inmates did not commit. FDC staff do this to get the mentally disabled inmates placed in confinement where staff don't have to deal with them. Affiant witnessed large quantities of stable inmates over the years harassing/picking on mentally disabled inmates for humor. Mentally stable inmates manipulate mentally disabled inmates into drinking urine, wiping feces on themselves, and to run around prison wings naked for humor. FDC records show that a large quantity of mentally disabled inmates have been committing suicide on a regular basis in FDC. These things are happening as a result of the inadequate screening, observation, and care of mentally disabled inmates in FDC.

"This information can be verified by (1) Obtaining information from FDC concerning how many inmates committed suicide on a monthly basis from 2011 till March 17, 2017. (2) Investigating the mental stability of inmates in confinement and close management units in FDC. (3) Reviewing any and all information that can be obtained concerning how many mentally disabled inmates are incarcerated in FDC.

"FDC has Transitional Care Units and Crisis Stabilization Units located at Santa Rosa CI Main Unit, Suwanee CI Main Unit, Regional Medical Center, Lake CI, Zephyrhills CI, Charlotte CI, South Florida Reception Center, and Dade CI. All of these institutions combined house approximately 2,000 to 2,500 inmates on these statuses.

"Affiant respectfully requests that the Department of Justice conduct a Civil Rights of Institutionalized Persons Act investigation into the contents of this affidavit.

UNNOTARIZED OATH:

Under penalty of perjury, I swear that everything stated herein is true and correct. Executed on this   18th   day of June   2017.

Affiant: _____

Harold Hempstead, I.M. #577366

1045 Horsehead Road

Pikeville, Tennessee 37367

C.C.: ACLU of Florida (Dr. Howard Simon), Stop Prison Abuse Now (Steven Wetstein), Florida Justice Institute (Randall Berg), Julie K. Brown (Miami Herald newspaper), Craig Patrick (WTVT Fox 13 Tampa, Florida), Michele Gillian, Eyal Press (New Yorker magazine), Windy Hempstead, Jeremy Schanche, Susan Chandler, Melinda Miguel (Chief Inspector General for the Florida Governor), James Cook (Attorney at Law)

574) What else have you done to publicize the problems in the Florida DOC?

After I was moved to the Tennessee Department of Correction, I had the journal I kept in 2011 and 2012 copyrighted. My reason for copyrighting it, is I'm going to release it to society for their review. I believe it'll be helpful in proving what happened to Darren Rainey and the *Hot-Water-Shower* treatment of mentally disabled inmates in the Dade CI Transitional Care Unit.

441

Also, I have written and copyrighted a book named *Constructed Solutions.* The purpose of this book is to bring attention to 20 issues in the Florid Department of Corrections that violate the U.S. Constitution and state laws, and that affects all of the inmates and staff in the Florida Department of Corrections. I am currently (December 2018) exploring options for publication of *Constructed Solutions.*

575) Has the Florida DOC improved since the end of 2014?

No. They have become worse. I believe the reason why it became worse is that the Florida prison system has spent taxpayers' money on painting buildings in the Florida DOC, buying new uniforms for the security staff, purchasing buses to transport inmates, and installing cellular phone scramblers that don't work. Over the years that the Florida DOC has focused these things, the following things have drastically risen:

- Inmate deaths and murders.
- Inmate gang membership and violence.
- Cellular phones, narcotics, and tobacco smuggling.
- Staff-on-inmate violence.
- Riots

Moreover, since the end of 2014, the Florida Department of Corrections has continued to suffer statewide from severe staff shortages that have made the conditions in the Florida Department of Corrections much worse and much more violent.

The inability of all the FDC Secretaries since 2010 to effectively hire staff and correct the conditions in the Florida DOC and the drastic deterioration and severely unsafe conditions in the Florida prison system, shows that Florida Department of Corrections is in serious need of federal intervention and/or independent oversight.

576) Do you have anything else you would like to say about the Darren Rainey case?

Yes.

Roland Clarke, do you remember everything you told your officers about all the inmates you placed in the *Hot-Water-Shower*? Do you remember everything you told your officers about what happened with Darren Rainey? Do you remember the humor and jokes that were made about you beating an "M-1" (murder one), and me being your "Cody" (short for codefendant)? I know you remember these conversations, but if you don't remember them in detail, don't worry. They were all recorded, and you'll get to listen to them fairly soon.

Officers Cennedy, Drinkwater, Corbet, Jolly, and the Caucasian officer who worked for Roland Clarke in 2013 and 2014, I hope you didn't lie to federal agents or prosecutors about the things Roland Clarke told you about the *Hot-Water-Shower* treatment of mentally disabled inmates and Darren Rainey's death. Lying to a federal agent or prosecutor during a federal investigation is a federal crime. If you lied to a federal agent or prosecutor about what Roland Clarke told you in 2013 and 2014, the recordings of your conversations with Roland Clarke which were covertly obtained in 2013 and 2014 will prove that you committed a federal crime when you lied and tried to cover-up federal crimes.

Sergeant Fanfan, and Officers Thompson, Hood, and Gibson, you might not want to thank Roland Clarke, but I do. As a result of his bragging to his officers in 2013 and 2014, he kindly provided evidence against himself and each of you. The evidence he provided is on the recordings.

Sergeant Johnathan, I know you weren't working on the night Rainey died, but Roland Clarke, while being recorded, was kind enough to mention your knowledge of the *Hot-Water-Shower* treatment of the inmates before Rainey. You were his regular sergeant, and you should've never allowed him to start using the *Hot-Water-Shower* as punishment.

Dade County, Florida State Attorney Katherine Fernandez Rundle, I wrote you and told you there were recordings obtained of Roland Clarke in 2013 and 2014 admitting to using the *Hot-Water-Shower* to punish mentally disabled inmates, talking about what happened to Darren Rainey, and calling me "Cody." You should've contacted me. Because you didn't, those recordings can now be used to show the people of Florida who you really are.

Dade County, Florida Medical Examiner, Dr. Emma Lew, I don't know how you are going to explain your findings that the water wasn't excessively hot in the shower Rainey died in when

Department of Corruption

Roland Clarke spoke extensively on recordings about how hot the shower water was.

Finally, I know that some people might doubt the existence of the recordings I've mentioned. To them, I'd like to say two things

- Investigate the events and circumstances I've written about; and
- Only time will tell

End Notes: Biblical References

Chapter 1
1. Romans 3:20
2. 1 John 3:4
3. Galatians 3:24
4. Psalm 111:10
5. Matthew 10:28
6. Luke 11:13
7. Matthew 13:14; Mark 4:12
8. John 3:6
9. 1 Corinthians 2:14
10. Romans 6:1-4
11. 2 Corinthians 7:10
12. Ephesians 2:8
13. 1 Corinthians 12:12-31
14. John 3:3
15. Ephesians 2:10

Chapter 5
1. 1 Corinthians 12:12-31
2. John 15:5; 1 Corinthians 6:15-20; Ephesians 1:22-23; 4:15, 16; 5:29,30
3. Romans 8:10; 1 Corinthians 13:5; Galatians 4:19,20
4. 1 Corinthians 6:17; 12:13; 2 Corinthians 3:17,18; Galatians 3:2,3
5. John 14:23, 15:4,5; Galatians 2:20; Ephesians 3:17
6. John14:20; 2 Corinthians 15:17; Galatians 2:20; Ephesians 3:17,18
7. Matthew 16:24; Romans 6:5; Galatians2:20; Colossians 1:24; 2:12; 3:1; 1 Peter 4:13
8. 1 Corinthians 2:2
9. 1 Thessalonians 5:17
10. 2 Corinthians 13:15;1 Corinthians 10:12; 11:28; Galatians 6:4
11. Matthew 7:21-23
12. Psalm 23:1; 80;1; Isaiah 40:11; Ezekiel 34:11-31, John 10:1-30; Hebrews 13:20, 1 Peter 2:25; 5:4

Chapter 6
1. Hebrews 12:3-11
2. Proverbs 3:11,12; John 15:2; 1 Corinthians 11:32; Revelations 3:19
3. Galatians 3:26

Chapter 7
1. John 14:15, 21-24; 15:14; James1:25; 2:10; 1 John 2:3-6
2. Proverbs 3:7; Matthew 10:28; 2 Corinthians 7:1; 1 Peter 2:17
3. Isaiah 48:22; 57:21
4. Romans 1:24, 26, 28
5. 2 Corinthians 7:9,10
6. 1 Corinthians 15:1-8

Chapter 9
1. Proverbs 3:5,6

Chapter 13
1. Romans 8:28

Chapter 14
1. Psalm 25:8; 33:5; 34:8. Nahum 1:7; Romans 2:4; 11:22
2. Romans 8:28

Chapter 16
1. Matthew 26:38
2. Matthew 26:39

451

457

Department of Corruption

Department of Corruption

Made in the USA
Middletown, DE
20 February 2020